Corruption, Inequality, and the Rule of Law

Corruption flouts rules of fairness and gives some people advantages that others don't have. Corruption is persistent; there is little evidence that countries can escape the curse of corruption easily – or at all. Instead of focusing on institutional reform, Eric M. Uslaner suggests that the roots of corruption lie in economic and legal inequality, low levels of generalized trust (which are not readily changed), and poor policy choices (which may be more likely to change). Economic inequality provides a fertile breeding ground for corruption, which, in turn, leads to further inequalities.

Just as corruption is persistent, inequality and trust do not change much over time, according to Uslaner's cross-national aggregate analyses. He argues that high inequality leads to low trust and high corruption, and then to more inequality – an inequality trap – and identifies direct linkages between inequality and trust in surveys of the mass public and elites in transition countries.

Eric M. Uslaner is Professor of Government and Politics at the University of Maryland–College Park, where he has taught since 1975. He has written seven books including *The Moral Foundations of Trust* (Cambridge University Press, 2002) and *The Decline of Comity in Congress* (1993). In 1981–2 he was Fulbright Professor of American Studies and Political Science at the Hebrew University, Jerusalem, Israel, and in 2005 he was a Fulbright Senior Specialist Lecturer at Novosibirsk State Technical University, Novosibirsk, Siberia, Russia. In 2006 he was appointed the first Senior Research Fellow at the Center for American Law and Political Science at the Southwestern University of Political Science and Law, Chongqing, China.

Corruption, Inequality, and the Rule of Law

The Bulging Pocket Makes the Easy Life

ERIC M. USLANER

University of Maryland–College Park
Southwestern University of Political Science and Law,
Chongqing, China

CAMBRIDGE
UNIVERSITY PRESS

CAMBRIDGE UNIVERSITY PRESS
Cambridge, New York, Melbourne, Madrid, Cape Town, Singapore, São Paulo, Delhi

Cambridge University Press
32 Avenue of the Americas, New York, NY 10013-2473, USA

www.cambridge.org
Information on this title: www.cambridge.org/9780521874892

First published 2008

Printed in the United States of America

A catalog record for this publication is available from the British Library.

Library of Congress Cataloging in Publication Data

Uslaner, Eric M.
Corruption, inequality, and the rule of law : the bulging pocket makes the easy life /
Eric M. Uslaner.
    p.   cm.
Includes bibliographical references and index.
ISBN 978-0-521-87489-2 (hardback)
1. Corruption.   2. Equality.   3. Rule of law.   I. Title.
JF1525.C66U75   2008
364.1′323–dc22   2007052896

ISBN   978-0-521-87489-2 hardback

To Avery,
whose keen insights have always combated
any temptations to assume that corruption can be conquered easily

Contents

Preface

Somehow I think that I was always destined to write about corruption (see Chapter 1). This has been an unintended project starting with some brief discussions of corruption in my 2002 book, *The Moral Foundations of Trust*, and in a few papers that stemmed from it. An invitation to a conference on corruption in 2002 at the University of Göttingen – sponsored by Transparency International – led me to think more seriously about writing about corruption. Over the next five years, this project took many unexpected turns, even as I thought I had completed the research.

One thing that hasn't changed is my overall framework, despite many challenges to my argument and the challenge of applying the framework to cases that I had not considered when I started. Some of these detours (especially Hong Kong and Singapore) came about because wise people challenged me; others came about as I read popular accounts of corruption (Africa) and saw my framework reflected in these stories. Along the way, I have had the good fortune to have friends and colleagues who posed tough questions to me, often as the "price" for inviting me to many interesting places throughout the world – where people were always more than willing to share their stories of corruption with me (some of which I have retold here).

I have accumulated a lot of intellectual debts along the way. Bo Rothstein has been a consistent source of strong argumentation and good friendship throughout the journey to completing this manuscript. He, Mark Warren, and Jong-sung You read the entire manuscript for me and caught numerous problems. Jenny Hunt and Ming Sing read substantial portions of the manuscript and also gave very helpful comments. Gabriel Badescu, Ronald King, and Paul Sum taught me most of what I know about Romania – and then some. Gabriel Badescu and I have worked together on many of these issues, and part of Chapter 5 is a revised version of our joint work. I am also grateful to others who have commented on different parts of the manuscript, listed here alphabetically: Claudio Weber Abramo, Kems Adu-Gyan, Michael Bratton, Nick Duncan, John

Helliwell, Mark Morjé Howard, Karen Kaufmann, Lawrence Khoo, Mark Lichbach, Anton Oleynik, Marion Orr, Martin Paldam, Jon (Siew Tiem) Quah, Leonard Sebastian, and Gert Tinggaard Svendsen. Mitchell Brown provided invaluable research assistance.

My debts on data are enormous. Some of the data I use here are public and were obtained from the Inter-University Consortium for Political and Social Research (ICPSR), which is not responsible for any interpretations, as well as from the aggregate data available on the web sites of the World Bank and of Rafael LaPorta and Alberto Alesina (who are very generous with their data sources and have been particularly helpful). Much of the data I use is proprietary, and I am greatly indebted to the people – and their institutions – who have shared the data with me. Gabriel Badescu shared with me (and translated) his Romanian survey in 2003 (see Chapter 5). Michael Bratton and Tetsuya Fujiwara provided me with an early release of Round 3 Afrobarometer data for Nigeria. Kai-Ping Huang provided the data for the Hong Kong Asian Barometer. James Anderson of the World Bank and Marilynn Schmidt and Mark Phillips of the United States Agency for International Development and the Focus Center for Social and Market Analysis, Bratislava, Slovakia, helped with the Corruption Diagnostic Surveys (Chapter 6). Margit Tavits of the University of Missouri was instrumental in obtaining the Estonian surveys (Chapter 6) from the government of Estonia with the kind permission of the Ministry of Justice, government of Estonia, particularly Mari-Liis Liiv. Vello Pettai of the University of Tallinn helped with translation. Robin Hodess and Marie Wolkers of Transparency International provided the 2004 Global Corruption Barometer Survey; Meril James of Gallup International, the 2000 Gallup International Millennium Survey; and Utku Teksoz of the International Bank for Reconstruction and Development, the 2005 Business Environment and Enterprise Performance Survey (BEEPS); Emma Loades of the World Economic Forum, Elizabeth Anderson of the Economist Intelligence Unit, Oguzhan Dincer, Johannes Fedderke, Jonathan Fox, Rafael LaPorta, Anirudh Ruhil, Friedrich Schneider, Kim Sonderskov, Daniel Treisman, Bryce Ward, Richard Winters, and Jong-sung You also provided key data.

I have been fortunate enough to present my work at a range of forums, both academic and in the "real world." I list these presentations on the following page and I am grateful to the wonderful audiences I had at each venue for asking demanding questions that often made me rethink my arguments. Speaking to people across continents has given me a fresh perspective on the issues of corruption, inequality, and trust in so many different contexts. I am grateful to the many people who arranged these invitations, especially the Southwest University of Political Science and Law, Chongqing, China (especially Fu Zitang and Larry Li), which appointed me its first Senior Research Fellow, as well as Li Bennich-Björkman, Yoji Inaba, Johann Graf Lambsdorff, Fred Lazin, Robert Leonardi, Joseph Lewandowski, Ferdinand Müller-Rommel, Emerson Niou, Susan Rose-Ackerman, Bo Rothstein, Kim Sonderskov, Fengshi Wu, and Milan Znoj.

I am grateful to the following forums for an opportunity to present my work and to benefit from the comments of so many people:

In 2001: At the conference on "Political Scandals: Past and Present" at the University of Salford (United Kingdom), and the conference, "Toward a New Paradigm: Social Capital and Poverty Reduction in Latin America and the Caribbean," sponsored by the World Bank, the United Nations, and the Social Capital Initiative of Michigan State University, Santiago, Chile.

In 2002: At the conference on "Corrupt Transactions Exploring the Analytical Capacity of Institutional Economics," University of Göttingen, Göttingen, Germany; the International Institute in Institutional Analysis of the University of Tubingen (Germany), Sofia, Bulgaria; and the Collegium Budapest Project on Honesty and Trust Conference, Workshop on Formal and Informal Cooperation, Budapest, Hungary.

In 2004: At the Conference on the Caux Initiatives for Business Conference for Business and Industry, Caux, Switzerland.

In 2005: At the University of Uppsala, Uppsala, Sweden; the Conference on the Quality of Government, Goteborg University (Sweden); the WIDER Jubilee Conference, Helsinki, Finland; the Society for the Advancement of Socio-Economics, Budapest, July, 2005; and as a Fulbright Senior Specialist Lecturer at Novosobirsk State University, Russia.

In 2006: At the Southwest University of Law and Political Science, Chongqing, China, as my inaugural lecture as the Senior Research Fellow at the University's Center for American Political Science and Law; the symposium on "Democracy and Social Capital: A Czech-American Dialogue," at the Woodrow Wilson Center, United States Embassy, Prague, Czech Republic, sponsored by the Czech Fulbright Commission, the United States Embassy (Prague), and the Institute of Political Science, Charles University (Prague); the Chinese University of Hong Kong, April 4, 2006; the City University of Hong Kong; the Czech Academy of Sciences, Institute of Sociology, Prague, Czech Republic; the Japan Productivity Center for Socio-Economic Development (Tokyo), at Osaka University (Japan); the conference on "Achieving Global Equity: The Challenges Facing Universities, Governments and Business," University of Plymouth (United Kingdom); the conference on "Social Capital, Sustainability and Socio-Economic Cohesion Within the EU MLG Structure in Development Policy," London School of Economics, London, England; the workshop on "Research on Corruption and Its Control: The State of the Art," The Wharton School, University of Pennsylvania; the seminar on "Public Policy and Ethics in the U.S.A.," Program for Chinese Visitors, Center for Intercultural Education and Development and the International Program in Governance and Policy, Department of Government, Georgetown University; the Conference on "Comparative Reflections on Developing Democracies and the Case of Turkey," sponsored by the Center for International and Comparative

Studies at Northwestern University and the Institute of Turkish Studies, Northwestern University; as a lecturer at the ECPR/DAAD Ph.D. Summer School 2006 on Democracy and Governance in Central Eastern Europe, Center for the Study of Democracy (Zentrum für Demokratieforschung), University of Lüneburg (Germany); and the Economic and Social Policy Institute Summer School in Economic Policy, Belgrade, Serbia.

In 2007: At the Joe and Paulette Rose Annual Lecture in Politics, Ben Gurion University of the Negev, Israel; the Hebrew University of Jerusalem, Israel; the University of Haifa, Israel; the conference on "Social Capital: Building Bridges Between the Social Sciences," University of Aarhus (Denmark); the Workshop on Social Capital and Transition to Democracy in Eastern Europe and the Balkans at the University of Macedonia, Thessaloniki, Greece; the Southwest University of Political Science and Law, Chongqing, China; the National Defense College, the Civil Service College, Khan University/Millennium Foundation, the Conference on "Democratic Accountability and Ways to Fight Corruption" sponsored by the Bangladesh Institute of Peace and Security Studies, and as the keynote address to the conference on "Curbing Corruption in South Asia: A Workshop for Parliamentarians" sponsored by GOPAC (the Global Organization of Parliamentarians Against Corruption) and the National Democratic Institute, all in Dhaka, Bangladesh, under the sponsorship of the United States Department of State; and the International Social Capital and Networks of Trust Congress, University of Jyväskylä, Finland.

Earlier versions of some chapters have been published elsewhere: Preliminary formulations of some of the ideas and data in Chapters 2 and 3 appeared in "Trust and Corruption: Their Effects on Poverty," in Raul Atria and Marcelo Siles, eds., *Capital Social y Reducción de la Pobreza en América Latina y el Caribe: En Busca de un Nuevo Paradigma* (Santiago: Comision Economica para America Latina y el Caribe, United Nations, 2003, translated into Spanish); in "Trust and Corruption," in Johann Graf Lambsdorff, Markus Taube, and Matthias Schramm, eds., *Corruption and the New Institutional Economics* (London: Routledge, 2004); in "Trust and Corruption," in *Global Corruption Report* (Berlin: Transparency International, 2005); and in "Inequality and Corruption," in George Mavrotas and Anthony Shorrocks, eds., *Advancing Development: Core Themes in Global Economics* (London: Palgrave, 2007). An earlier version of part of Chapter 8 appeared as "The Civil State: Trust, Polarization, and the Quality of State Government," in Jeffrey E. Cohen, ed., *Public Opinion in State Politics* (Stanford: Stanford University Press, 2006).

As the project has progressed, I have been fortunate to have support from the Russell Sage Foundation and the Carnegie Corporation for a grant on a related project that is encompassed in my work on the United States (Chapter 8) on "Inequality, Trust, and Civic Engagement," from 2001 to 2004. I am also indebted to the General Research Board of the University of Maryland–College Park for a Faculty Research Award in the spring 2006 semester that provided released time to work on the book, and to my colleagues and especially my department chair, Mark Lichbach, for their advice and support. I also am grateful to Eric Crahan at Cambridge University Press for helping to guide the project to completion and to the reviewers for the press for making this a better book.

I have tremendous debts to my late parents, Abe and Irene Uslaner. My father taught me about corruption in Paterson, though he might shudder that anything so covert, requiring inside knowledge, could be measured. My mother was ever the optimist – except as she introduced me to *The Threepenny Opera*. Of course, my biggest debts are to my wife, Debbie, and our son, Avery, who tolerated all of the various interruptions that a book demands. Avery, as many teenagers, readily accepted an argument that is largely pessimistic when I explained my thesis to him. He even sees me as a hopeless optimist, so it is right that I dedicate this book to him.

Corruption

The Basic Story

> They tell you that the best in life is mental –
> Just to starve yourself and do a lot of reading
> Up in some garret where the rats are breeding.
> Should you survive it's purely accidental.
> If that's your pleasure, go on live that way.
> But since I've had it up to here I'm through.
> There's not a dog from here to Timbuktu
> Would care to live that life a single day....
> Now once I used to think it would be worthy
> To be a brave and sacrificing person.
> I soon found out it wasn't reimbursin'
> Decided to continue being earthy....
> Where's the percentage? asks Mack the Knife.
> The bulging pocket makes the easy life.
> > From "The Ballad of the Easy Life,"
> > Berthold Brecht and Kurt Weill,
> > *The Threepenny Opera*

When I was 13 years old, I delivered a plain white envelope containing a $50 bill to the chief of police of Paterson, New Jersey.

The chief wasn't available to accept the "gift" himself. I gave the unmarked envelope to a sergeant and told him it was from my father. He smiled and said thank you and waved me on my way.

A couple of hours later, a police officer called our stationery store with a very large order for office supplies. The department bought about 50 staplers, which more than sufficed for the 20 or so people who worked at police headquarters (so we knew what some of their children got for Christmas). And it was a gift that kept on giving.

The money wasn't a "bribe." It was a "Christmas gift" (which under city law was also illegal). It wasn't a large offering. Most public officials liked my father. They realized that he could not afford to give as much in "gifts" as our major competitor, who owned a much larger store and was wealthier than my father. A sign of good faith, a little spending money, was all he needed to get far more city business than the competition. Yet he knew that if he forgot the holiday, business would not flow our way.

I learned about corruption – and experienced it – when I was young. Paterson and its surrounding county for many years was dominated by a corrupt Democratic machine, as in many other large- and medium-sized cities (Paterson had a population of about 150,000). Reformers in New Jersey sought to "cleanse" Paterson's political system early in the twentieth century (Norwood, 1974, 52–3):

> ...when the working class did start to build a power base, it was unceremoniously cut off. By 1907 the longtime practice of city aldermen's selling jobs on the municipal payroll was so blatant that the New Jersey Legislature established a special form of government solely for the city of Paterson. It revoked the aldermen's power and left them with only such insignificant duties as licensing dogs, peddlers, and junkyards. The mayor became the single elected official with authority.

By the middle of the century, Republicans alternated with the Democrats in power. Both the city and the county governments have been restructured with a change from a Board of Aldermen to a City Council with greater oversight powers.[1] Theoretically, this weakened the power base of key officeholders and changing the electoral systems was supposed to cleanse the body politic. Yet many government or party officeholders and more than a handful of police officers have since been convicted of or faced indictment for receiving or demanding kickbacks (*The Record*, 2001). In 1988, the state of New Jersey took control of the Paterson school system, charging rampant corruption (Lindsay, 1998).

Corruption persisted as power passed from the Irish and Italians who dominated local politics. In 2003, Mayor Marty Barnes, an African-American, was sentenced to 37 months in jail for extorting bribes from a contractor who received $16 million in city business. The prosecution presented pictures of the mayor "frolicking with prostitutes at a Brazil resort and a paper trail showing kickbacks, clothes, trips, furniture, even a new pool and a waterfall," but the leader of New Jersey's third largest city shrugged off the charges, telling the presiding judge that he became "bogged down" in trying to run the city and "I probably didn't pay as much attention to other things that I should have" (Martin, 2003). Two years later, four administrators in the city's school system were found guilty of extorting cash and goods from city contractors – and the former head of facilities for the school district was indicted on similar charges (*New York Times*, 2005).

Paterson sets the theme for the story I tell in this book. Corruption isn't easily eradicated. Efforts to curb it by putting dishonest leaders in jail or changing

[1] See http://www.reference.com/browse/wiki/Paterson%2C_New_Jersey, accessed November 4, 2006.

institutional structures may have limited success. The most powerful of the corrupt leaders in Paterson never went to jail – a few were indicted from time to time but never served time (Norwood, 1974, 86–90). As some ethnic groups moved out to the suburbs, they were replaced in power by the previously disenfranchised – who continued the city's longstanding tradition of enriching the powerful. No structural or electoral change could eliminate the close ties between officeholders and contractors for city business.

There was little hope that a vigilant media would lead the charge to a public revulsion over corruption. Most people who knew anything about local government understood that the leading paper in town, the Paterson *Evening News*, controlled the local Mafia, which in turn ran the police department.[2] "People in public life in Paterson had learned to fear the *News'* power" because the editors kept files on the private lives of public figures and the publisher, Harry B. Haines, "retaliated against those who thwarted him as he supported those he supported" (Norwood, 1974, 92). The other newspaper in town, the *Morning Call*, had little circulation and even less influence. When new owners tried to take on the *Evening News* and fight for clean government, the dominant paper started a morning edition and within a short time the *Call* fell silent as advertisers deserted it.

Dishonesty in government thrives in places where there is a great gap between the rich and the poor and where there is little trust. The city was marked by a long history of violent labor strikes in the mid-nineteenth through the mid-twentieth century and anti-immigrant violence by the racist Ku Klux Klan and its allies (Norwood, 1974, 56–60). Paterson has never been a wealthy city, but the East Side long was home to the middle and upper-middle classes, with the rest of the city far less prosperous. The city was also ringed by far more affluent suburbs. Crime was a perpetual problem (I was mugged twice outside my secondary school) and there was little social interaction between people of different backgrounds, a legacy of long periods of ethnic conflict, and residential segregation.

Corruption and its persistence has long held a fascination for me, at least since I had to make my first (and only) "payoff." Paterson always seemed to be a city on the verge of collapse, as one major business after another either

---

[2] The police correspondent for the *Evening News* was a confidant of the owner of the paper and he rarely wrote any stories except for an anonymous column, "So They Say," every Monday where he would lavish praise on officeholders and city bureaucrats in what my father called "the kiss of death." Such "praise" was a clear sign that these officials were out of favor and would soon leave public life. The correspondent rarely visited police headquarters, but mostly held court with a large group of men in black suits in a hidden room in the basement at a popular Italian restaurant across the street from the newspaper. I saw the correspondent, Art Guillerman, in his element while working for the newspaper as a summer job when I was in college: The city editor gave me (another) unmarked envelope – an urgent message from the owner of the paper – to deliver to the "reporter" at the restaurant – my second (and last) direct experience in corruption. Norwood (1974, 92) argued that publisher Harry B. Haines "was closely associated with [Paterson's] tight ruling circle." She apparently did not understand how close the ties were.

failed or left the inner city for the fancier suburbs. The one elegant hotel in town, named after the first Secretary of State of the United States who founded the city, had become a haven for prostitutes and crack addicts by the 1980s. Downtown Paterson, which "has everything" in the local lingo of my youth, had been reduced to a cluster of dollar stores when I showed my wife my hometown some years later. It was a town where extortion seemed to be the only way to get rich.

The desire to understand my roots became more intense when I moved, many years later, to my current home in Montgomery County, Maryland, an upper-middle-class community with the second highest college graduation rate of any county in the United States,[3] a strong commitment to tolerance and social interaction among different ethnic and religious groups, and a local government cleaner than most dental offices. The most common route to high-level office does not start with working for the local party organization but rather as a parent activist in your child's school followed by election to the Board of Education. The chief county official is more likely to be an educator, even a professor, than a party activist, and one former County Executive retired to seek a new career, not as a lobbyist but as an Episcopalian priest.

What makes some societies corrupt and others honest? Hoping that the press would stir the public into revulsion against the evildoers or reliance on putting the bad guys in jail will end corruption (see Chapter 2) is wishful thinking. My life experience – and the argument and data I shall present in this book – strongly suggest that it is not the structure of government, but the underlying social and economic conditions.

I begin with a brief summary of the roots of corruption and outline the rest of the book. Then I move to a discussion of what corruption means, its different forms, and how to measure it. The definition of corruption and especially its measurement are controversial. Sorting out what corruption means is particularly difficult and I make no claim to resolving the debate. The measurement issues may be just as tendentious. Since my work relies heavily, though not exclusively, upon the most widely used quantitative indicator of corruption, I need to consider the objections to it.

The Roots of Corruption

The roots of corruption, as I formulate my story in the pages to come, rest upon economic inequality and low trust in people who are different from yourself. Corruption, in turn, leads to less trust in other people and to more inequality. This is the essence of the *inequality trap* I outline in Chapter 2. This trap is the reason why corruption persists in societies (including the city of Paterson) over long periods of time and why it is so difficult to eradicate. You can find

---

[3] See http://www.census.gov/acs/www/Products/Ranking/2002/R02T050.htm, accessed November 4, 2006: 56.3 percent of county residents have at least a Bachelor's degree, only marginally lower than 58.2 percent, in nearby Howard County, Maryland.

corrupt governments in all sorts of political systems, so that changing the form of government in Paterson – or even moving from Communism to democracy in transition countries (see Chapters 4, 5, and 6) – has not been a "cure-all," or even a major factor, in reducing corruption.

The roots of corruption reflect underlying social tensions that rest upon high inequality and low trust in people who may be different from yourself. The link from inequality to corruption is weak in my aggregate analysis, though the survey data from both transition countries and African nations show a more direct connection. The inequality trap starts with high inequality and works through low generalized trust (and high in-group trust) that lead to high levels of corruption – and back to more inequality. I show that high inequality, low trust, and high corruption persist over time. They do not change radically, and countries find it hard to escape the inequality trap (if they are at the bottom). Nor are they likely to fall from grace, if they are at the top. And even countries in the middle don't move up or down. Changes in institutional structure – most specifically democratization – don't lead to less corruption. The two key counterexamples to the inequality trap (Hong Kong and Singapore; see Chapter 7), the two countries that have cast corruption aside, are *not* democracies.

I first lay out the theoretical claims for my argument and then conduct many statistical tests of my claims. I use both aggregate analyses using the most widely used cross-national measure of corruption, the Transparency International Corruption Perception Index. I discuss this measure – often controversial – below. But I do not rely upon aggregate analyses alone to make my case. Much of my argument is based upon *perceptions*. And much of my evidence is based upon how people see corruption. I use a wide range of surveys of both the public and the elite (entrepreneurs and government officials). Some are cross-national: Gallup International (2000), Transparency International's Global Corruption Survey 2004, the World Values Survey (1995–7), the European Bank for Reconstruction and Development/World Bank BEEPS survey of businesspeople (2005), and the Afrobarometer (2002). Others are single-nation surveys, including a 2003 survey conducted in Romania by a Romanian colleague; surveys of masses and elites in Estonia (conducted for the Government of Estonia in 2003), Slovakia and Romania (World Bank Diagnostic Surveys in 1999 and 2000, respectively); special Afrobarometers in Mali (2002) and Nigeria (2005); the 2004 Asian Barometer in Hong Kong; the General Social Survey in the United States (1987); and the American National Election Study (2004).

I thus rely upon diverse data sets. Some are less well suited to test my inequality trap argument than others, but overall, there is considerable support for my argument using a wide range of evidence. The key result from a wide range of survey data is that people throughout the transition nations and in most of Africa see strong connections between inequality and corruption, and in Estonia and Romania there are strong links to trust as well. Where corruption is less widespread – notably in Botswana, the Nordic countries, and (nationally) in the United States – there is no strong link to inequality.

The story for the United States supports the cross-national findings: Corruption is sticky. A proxy measure for corruption in the 1920s – the state-level Presidential vote for a reform (Progressive) candidate for President in 1924 – has a moderately strong relationship with state legislative reporters' perceptions of corruption in 1999. And we can trace this 1924 measure – and the 1999 indicator – back to Nordic heritage. States with high shares of Nordic ancestors in the 1880 Census had higher support for reform candidates in 1924 *and* lower corruption 75 years later.

Honesty is not only sticky, but it seems to be inherited, at least culturally. The writer Andre Codrescu, who emigrated to the United States from Romania and settled in New Orleans, told an interviewer: "New Orleans reminds me of Romania, because New Orleans is very corrupt politically" (Solomon, 2005, 19). So it may be natural that a native of Paterson, New Jersey, develops not only an interest in corruption, but an interest in Romania.

What Is Corruption?

Corruption is an elusive concept. Every definition has problems, some more so than others. Rose-Ackerman (2004, 1) gives the most common definition of corruption, while recognizing the difficulties in this enterprise:

"Corruption" is a term whose meaning shifts with the speaker. . . . I use the common definition of corruption as the "misuse of public power for private or political gain," recognizing that "misuse" must be defined in terms of some standard. Many corrupt activities under this definition are illegal in most countries – for example, paying and receiving bribes, fraud, embezzlement, selfdealing, conflicts of interest, and providing a quid pro quo in return for campaign gifts. However, part of the policy debate turns on where to draw the legal line and how to control borderline phenomena, such as conflicts of interest, which many political systems fail to regulate.

Does corruption depend upon the standards of a given society – or a group of citizens? What you may think of as corrupt, I may consider acceptable. The controversy goes further, as some societies are described as having a culture in which corruption is acceptable. This is dangerous thinking because it encourages stereotypes – and because it fails to recognize that there is an economic and social foundation underlying corruption. "Cultural" arguments see little opportunity to make a corrupt society honest. Yet so does my argument about the inequality trap.

Societies develop "cultures of corruption" because they are trapped in a vicious cycle of high inequality, low out-group trust, and high corruption. People don't become enmeshed in corrupt relationships because they see little moral harm in paying off their patrons or because they admire their leaders who enrich themselves. In these "cultures of corruption," people make payments because there is no way out. They are caught in this inequality trap and they are hardly happy about it. Where high-level corruption is rampant, the very people who are supposed to be "tolerant" of malfeasance resent the illicit tactics that the powerful use to enrich themselves.

There is less disagreement on what people think is corrupt than one might expect. Relying on statutes to determine what is corrupt misses the mark for two reasons. First, statutes vary from one place to another and this doesn't always tell us much about enforcement of the law. Where corruption runs rampant, the rich and powerful are rarely charged with crimes and even more rarely convicted (see Chapter 2). Second, statutes may make fine distinctions that ordinary citizens find puzzling. Members of the United States Congress may not raise campaign funds on the grounds of the Capitol, but they may take a few steps outside on a sunny day and make their solicitation calls perfectly legally. Interest groups in the United States may make "independent expenditures" in federal elections but may neither coordinate their messages with any candidate nor may their advertisements urge people to vote for or against candidate X. The groups' ads may perfectly legally claim that "X is a dedicated public servant who is a credit to our state" or that "X is beholden to special interests and works against the interests of the people of this state."

Another approach is to define corruption normatively. You (2006) sees *fair* institutions as the foundation of good (honest) government, while Rothstein and Teorell (2005) and Kurer (2003) argue that *partiality* lies at the heart of corruption. The equation of honesty and government quality is problematic for five reasons. First, linking fairness with honest government makes corruption all about formal institutions. Yet, politicians don't bribe themselves. They get bribes from private officials, usually businesspeople. This definition of corruption effectively "exonerates" the people who offer the bribes (although I am sure that this is not what Rothstein, Teorell, or Kurer meant to do). Second, defining corruption as unfair politics opens up all sorts of possibilities for what is corrupt. John F. Kennedy, who hardly was at the bottom of the inequality ladder, said: "Life is unfair."[4] Lots of things in life, and especially in politics, are unfair – or seem inequitable. They are not all instances of corruption. To argue, as You (2006, 9) does, that politicians must "follow the principle of fairness" misses the point that politics is about winning and losing, not about fairness. The losers in political battles are less likely than winners to have confidence in incumbent politicians – if not to see them as outright unfair (Anderson et al., 2005).

Third, equating corruption with unfairness, even just the unfairness of the legal system (You, 2006, 5–6), conflates cause and effect. I argue that an unfair legal system is one of the key determinants of corruption (see especially Chapters 2 and 3). *Legal fairness is not the same thing as corruption*, even though they are strongly related. Corruption may be less common in countries with fair legal systems such as the United States or the United Kingdom (see Chapter 3). Yet political events of 2006 – with major scandals facing leading members of Congress and accusations that British Prime Minister Tony Blair "traded"

---

[4] The full quotation is, "There is always inequity in life. Some men are killed in war and some men are wounded, and some men are stationed in the Antarctic and some are stationed in San Francisco. It's very hard in military or personal life to assure complete equality. Life is unfair," cited at http://www.brainyquote.com/quotes/quotes/j/johnfkenn162485.html.

peerages for campaign contributions – suggests that the rule of law does not preclude breaking the law.

Fourth, Kurer (2003) and Rothstein and Teorell (2005) are correct in linking honest government to impartial treatment by bureaucrats – and, as with You (2006) and my own argument in this book, by the legal system. Kurer and Rothstein and Teorell recognize that elected leaders are usually *not* impartial, but we expect the people who implement policy to treat all equally.[5] This concept of corruption focuses too heavily on bureaucrats and not enough on candidates for office – who are at least as likely to be offered bribes.

Fifth, just as there are many ways in which life can be unfair, there are also many motivations for partial treatment by bureaucrats. Soss (2000, 75, 99) details how welfare recipients in the United States see their treatment by bureaucrats as "degrading" and one welfare recipient described her experience at a welfare office: "It's like a cattle prod.... I felt like I was in a prison system." Yet there is no evidence that welfare workers are corrupt. More likely, they are simply prejudiced; Gilens (1999) shows that Americans don't like welfare because most recipients of this means-tested program are African-Americans, whom most Americans – including bureaucrats – see as unworthy of benefits. Prejudice rather than corruption can explain many instances of partial treatment by public servants.

Corruption is shaped by more than fairness – but Rothstein and Teorell (2005), Kurer (2003), and You (2006) are correct in moving beyond legal proscriptions. Their definitions are both too wide (with respect to fairness) and too narrow (each focuses only on *governmental* corruption). Corruption applies to the private sector as well as to public life, as recent examples of high-level corporate misdeeds (especially the Enron and Tyco cases in the United States) show.

The linkage between corruption and inequality – either in income or before the law – points to a weakness in traditional arguments about corruption. Corruption reflects more than legal proscriptions. While hardly free of difficulties, the conception of corruption that I find most compelling is malfeasance (which I use interchangeably with "corruption") as the absence of *transparency*. The leading international anti-corruption agency is Transparency International. Corrupt acts are almost always hidden. If you are behaving honestly in either the public or the private sector, you will rarely have a need to hide your actions. When you flout the law or norms of acceptable behavior, in almost all cases you don't want others to know. Rarely, a corrupt leader will boast of his misdeeds, but such *braggadocio* might lead to legal trouble – or perhaps just envy from those who have not prospered. Even if people know that certain leaders are corrupt, they can rarely point to specific misdeeds – and when they can, they learn about it from some exposé rather than from the guilty parties.

Transparency, according to the *Oxford English Dictionary*, is the shedding of light to make things visible. Corrupt acts thrive on the lack of transparency,

---

[5] Bo Rothstein emphasized this in a private communication (April 1, 2007).

or openness. We hide our corrupt acts from others because we are trying to keep them from realizing that they are excluded from my transactions. Warren (2006, 804) argues that "political corruption attacks democracy by excluding people from decisions that affect them." The excluded party is almost always the loser in the corrupt transaction. Excluding people with legitimate rights to participate amounts to duplicitous actions. We primarily hide actions when we fear others will disapprove of their consequences.

I differentiate between actually perceiving misdeeds and having strong institutions that make "transparency" more likely. Bellver and Kaufmann (2005) create a measure of transparency for 194 nations that focuses on institutions that give people greater access to information about their government and its workings, including statutes that provide for public disclosure, e-government, a free press, an open budgetary process, and disclosure of contributions to political campaigns. Strong transparency institutions *do* lead to less corruption, they report. However, transparency "structures" do not guarantee that people actually know about malfeasance. Institutions that make discovering corruption more likely, as in the Bellver and Kaufmann analysis, are not the same thing as "perceiving" transparency.

Of course, transparency is not a fail-safe indicator of honesty. I am reluctant to share all sorts of personal information with others and I do not share letters of recommendation with their beneficiaries. As with fairness, there are plenty of exceptions to treating corruption as violations of transparency. However, it seems that there are probably fewer exceptions to this notion of corruption than for fairness. The key actor in anti-corruption initiatives seems to agree.

It is unlikely that anyone can find a definition of corruption that will satisfy anyone in either public, private, or academic life. Ironically, we have far less difficulty in agreeing on what behavior is corrupt than in drawing firm lines on what corruption "means."

Part of the difficulty stems from the wide range of activities that fall under the rubric "corruption" (Johnston, 2005, 42): kickbacks, bribes, extortion, providing people with no-show jobs, creating jobs for people who are politically loyal, unreported (or for some people, even reported) contributions to political campaigns, paying a parking or speeding ticket directly to the police officer rather than to the court, paying to advance in the queue at the doctor's office, and even paying university professors for higher grades(!!!).

Heidenheimer (2002, 150–2) distinguished among three types of corruption: petty, routine, and aggravated. Petty and routine corruption are common in less wealthy societies, especially when ordinary people (clients) are beholden to patrons. Petty corruption involves small amounts of money: fixing parking tickets (or paying directly to the police officer), rewarding the doctor for letting you jump ahead of other patients, getting favorable treatment from bureaucrats that others cannot receive – either for small "favors" or "gifts" or by personal connections. Routine corruption involves granting friends contracts for public services or giving "gifts" to patrons, as we often see in traditional societies (where people are expected to reward their leaders who in turn spread largesse to them) and in more contemporary urban political machines (where ordinary people trade their political support in return for jobs, other material benefits, and special treatment in the courts). Aggravated corruption involves big money, often giving kickbacks to political leaders who award lucrative government contracts to their friends, or even bribes.

This is not simply an academic distinction. The boss of New York City's Tammany Hall Democratic party machine in the nineteenth century, George Washington Plunkitt, distinguished between "honest" and "dishonest" graft. "Honest graft" includes providing jobs for political supporters and even using "inside" information available to political leaders to make profitable investments, which is "just like lookin' ahead in Wall Street or in the coffee or cotton market" (Riordan, 1948, 3–4). Plunkitt adds: "I'm lookin' for it every day of the year. I will tell you frankly that I've got a lot of it, too.... I seen my opportunity and I took it" (Riordan, 1948, 4–5). The political boss is clearly making his actions transparent and he does not consider them to be violations of any public trust. He also brags (Riordan, 1948, 6–7) about how his political machine provides patronage (what the British would call "jobs for the boys"):

...the Tammany heads of departments looked after their friends, within the law, and gave them opportunities to make honest graft.... Tammany has raised a good many salaries. There was an awful howl by the reformers, but don't you know that Tammany gains ten votes for everyone it lost by salary raisin'? The Wall Street banker thinks it shameful to raise a department clerk's salary... but every man who draws a salary... feels very much like votin' the Tammany ticket on election day, just out of sympathy.

"Dishonest graft" – "blackmailin' gamblers, saloon-keepers, disorderly people," selling nominations for public office to the highest bidder, eating the "poison" of violating "the Penal Code Tree" (Riordan, 1948, 3–4, 98–9, 41) – is simply wrong. A leader who partakes of "dishonest graft" is a "looter [who] goes in for himself alone without considerin' his organization or his city" (Riordan, 1948, 39–40).

Plunkitt's distinction preceded Heidenheimer's. Most contemporary discussions of malfeasance in public life meld the two conceptions into *petty* and *grand* corruption. Petty corruption also includes some of what Heidenheimer (2002) categorizes as routine corruption – most notably gifts – and most of Plunkitt's "honest graft." Grand corruption is Heidenheimer's "aggravated" corruption and Plunkitt's "dishonest graft."

The key distinction I make between petty and grand corruption is *not* the one either Heidenheimer or Plunkitt have offered. Both consider the key fault line to be moral acceptability. Heidenheimer (2002, 152) argues that petty corruption is likely to be "white corruption," at least tolerable if not deserving of approbation. Plunkitt actually revels in his "honest graft" as contributing to a larger public good: "I made my pile in politics, but at the same time I... got more big improvements for New York City than any other livin' man" (Riordan, 1948, 40). Instead, I focus on how "profitable" corruption is. Petty corruption – small pay-offs, patronage, and gifts to patrons – are often recognized as wrong by ordinary people, *even when the payments help people get by in a corrupt world.* Petty corruption is less "tolerable" than inescapable. People accept petty corruption because they see no way around it. The political and legal systems don't function fairly and may rarely function without an extra "push" (or "gift").

While petty corruption helps a large number of people cope with broken public and private sectors, where routine services are rarely provided routinely, grand corruption enriches a few people. The leaders of public (or private) life make themselves wealthy – Plunkitt calls them "looters" (Riordan, 1948, 40). Despite Plunkitt's protestations that he "took his opportunities" through "honest graft," the "pile" that he made for himself would certainly qualify as grand corruption.

The distinction between petty and grand corruption is critical in my account of corruption. While people don't see petty corruption as moral, they "adapt" to it because they see no way out. Because it involves relatively small sums of money, petty corruption does not engender jealousy and mistrust. People do not associate petty corruption with inequality. They *do* make a clear connection between inequity and grand corruption, as survey data I examine in Romania (Chapters 5 and 6), Estonia (Chapter 6), Slovakia (Chapter 6), and Africa (Chapter 7) make clear. Plunkitt, even as he justified making his "pile," recognized that ordinary people might find his gains ill-gotten and become envious (Riordan, 1948, 69):

A day before the election [for his seat in the New York state senate] my enemies circulated a report that I had ordered a $10,000 automobile and a $125 dress-suit. I sent out contradictions as fast as I could.... The people wouldn't have minded much if I had been accused of robbin' the city treasury, for they're used to slanders of that kind in campaigns, but the automobile and the dress-suit were too much for them.

This distinction is central to the inequality trap. Grand corruption troubles people far more than petty misdeeds – and not just because grand corruption involves breaking the law. In most cases, petty malfeasance also violates legal strictures. Yet, in a wide range of statistical estimations, I show a direct connection between grand corruption *and perceptions of inequality.*

Measuring Corruption

Measuring corruption is even more controversial than its definition. If corruption is not transparent, then it cannot be observed. If you can't see it, you can't measure it. Any attempt to quantify corruption is thus fraught with danger and will engender much criticism.

There are two major approaches to measuring corruption and I shall use them both. Neither attempts to do the impossible: calculate the value of hidden deals. These indicators are *perceptions* of corruption. The most widely used measure is the Transparency International (TI) Corruption Perceptions Index, computed annually since 1995. This index is based upon elite perceptions of corruption in a wide range of countries (now 160 nations), employing a wide range of sources. Since the sources for the TI index vary from year to year, the TI index is an average of estimates over a three-year period (Lambsdorff, 2005b). More recently the World Bank Governance project has developed an even more comprehensive measure of the "control of corruption" (Kaufmann, Kraay, and Mastruzzi, 2005). I use the TI measures in my cross-national aggregate analysis in Chapters 3 and 9, and the World Bank measures when they cover more countries, as in the transition nations in Chapter 4. The two measures are largely interchangeable. The World Bank measure for 2004 is correlated at .984 for the 2004 TI index and .983 for the 2005 TI scale, which I use in most of the book.

The second approach is based upon surveys of elites and especially of the mass public. Most of the rest of my analyses are based upon surveys of Romania, Estonia, Slovakia, Africa, Hong Kong, the Nordic countries, and the United States. I use surveys from a wide variety of sources, with varying question wordings (not always so desirable). Multiple methods and the use of a wide variety of evidence helps to overcome any problems with specific measures. Overall, this mixture of methods adds to the texture of my story: My argument on the inequality trap receives support from both aggregate and survey-based models. The availability of elite surveys (in Estonia, Romania, and Slovakia) provides a more nuanced view of how different people see corruption: Inequality, not surprisingly, bothers ordinary people more than it troubles elites.

I will not detail the methodology of any of these indices here. Yet it is important to consider some of the objections and to respond to them. Aside from arguing that corruption simply cannot be measured, the main critiques focus on weaknesses of the construction of the TI index.

The most damning criticisms of the TI index – and thus also the World Bank measure – are:

- The measures are imprecise and unreliable. They are based upon small numbers of indicators, perhaps as few as three for a particular country. Evaluations of corruption for many countries are based upon outside observers or expatriates and they are particularly inaccurate for the less wealthy countries (Kaufmann, Kraay, and Mastruzzi, 2007a, 13–15; Galtung, 2005).
- Country rankings sometimes vary widely from one year to the next, even though the TI index is a rolling average. These rankings make the index unsuitable for tracking changes and even worse if they are used to punish nations by withholding foreign assistance if their relative score has fallen (Claudio Weber Abramo, personal communication, October 31, 2006; Galtung, 2005).
- The aggregate measures display weak relationships with people's actual perceptions of corruption, so these indices may be fatally flawed (Abramo, 2005).

The best defenses of the indices come from their developers. Lambsdorff (2005b, 8–9) describes and justifies the TI measure and argues that it is strongly correlated over time – with its own previous values – and that the underlying component measures are strongly correlated with each other. The 1996 index has a strong correlation (r =.952, N = 54) with the 2005 scores. Kaufmann, Kraay, and Mastruzzi (2007a, 10–13) make a similar (and powerful) defense of the World Bank measure. Kaufmann and Kraay (2007, 1–3) hold that measurement error is unavoidable but that the aggregate measures are no worse than other indicators of governance and investment. They also admit (2007, 4–6) that these indices *are* perceptions rather than "reality." Yet insisting on "the best" may be the enemy of the good, that subjective and objective indicators of corruption "are complementary rather than alternative approaches," and that "perceptions matter in their own right, since . . . firms and individuals take actions based on their perceptions."

There is certainly variation – perhaps too much – in the rankings of countries on the aggregate indices. Even in the very short time frame of 2003 to 2005 – and recognizing that each year's score is based upon a three-year average – 113 of the 133 nations in the TI Corruption Perceptions Index sample changed their rankings by 10 or more places and 76 changed by 20 or more places. Abramo (personal communication, October 31, 2006) argues that the TI measures are biased since the big movements in rankings occur among the *most* corrupt countries and also those with lower gross domestic products per capita. The TI index thus seems least reliable for poor countries that have higher levels of corruption.

Yet, the evidence is weak for the claim that changes in ranks are greater for countries with higher levels of corruption – and even weaker for the claim that this matters. The TI scores range from 1 to 10, with higher values indicating less corruption. The absolute values of changes in ranking are *positively* related to the 2005 Corruption Perceptions Index, either in "raw" scores or in perceptions (r^2 =.291 and .240, N = 133). There is more variation over time in the absolute value of rankings among the "less corrupt" countries. The standard deviation of absolute changes in corruption rank orders is 19.13 for the 111 countries with TI scores below 7.0 in 2003 and 26.52 for the "more honest" countries. More critically, the fuss about rank orders is much ado about very little. The simple correlations between the 2003 and 2005 indices is .986; the correlation for the rank orders is equally strong at .969. Each year's scores are strongly related to their rank orderings: .907 for 2005 and .938 for 2003.

The wide variations in the absolute values of changes in rankings can be readily explained. First, most countries (141 of 160 in 2005) "share" their raw scores with other nations, so even a minuscule change in a year's score can have a big effect on its relative ranking. Second, most of the variation comes for the "most corrupt" countries because relatively few nations fare well on the Corruption Perceptions Index: 138 of 160 nations have raw scores below 7.0, 121 below 5.0, and 76 countries (48 percent of the sample) below 3.0. Even a very modest increase in honesty can lead to a big change in absolute ranks. Honduras, Ukraine, and Zimbabwe all "improved" their scores from 2.3 to 2.6 – rather modest increases – but each "jumped" 23.5 rankings. Moldova's score improved from 2.4 to 2.9, rising 37.5 ranks, the second biggest rank-order gain but barely noticeable as a raw score. Rankings are a very crude indicator of corruption.

Abramo (2005) charges that the TI index does not tap peoples' actual experience with corruption. The 2004 Global Corruption Barometer, a citizens' survey conducted across 60 countries by Transparency International, includes a question about personal experience with bribery. Abramo (2005, 34) shows that the TI index has modest correlations with this measure of experience and that these relationships are especially weak in poor countries. The correlation of bribery and perceptions that petty corruption is a problem – the proper comparison since most ordinary people have little opportunity to engage in grand corruption – is significant in only 15 of 60 countries he examined and is significant but wrongly signed in five other nations. The pattern of correlations for grand corruption is similar (Abramo, 2005, 19).

In Table A1-1 in the appendix (all tables and figures that begin with "A" are in the appendix), I examine the correlations between the TI Corruption Perceptions Index in 2005 and two questions from the 2004 Global Corruption Barometer with a range of specific questions from that 2004 survey: the bribery (experience) question Abramo discusses and a query as to whether people believe that corruption affects their own lives. The correlations in this table support Abramo's argument that the bribery question is weakly correlated with people's perceptions of both grand and petty corruption. Of the 19 measures in the table, 15 have correlations of .5 or less with bribery. On the other hand, only three of the other measures, almost all more specific, have correlations of less than .5 for the TI index and just two have such low correlations for whether people perceive that corruption affects their own lives. Nine of the 19 indicators have correlations of .75 or greater with the TI index and four of the correlations with whether corruption affects one's own life meet this threshold. The TI measure performs very well as an aggregate indicator *for the specific areas queried*. Only perceptions of the corruption of religion and the media – and to a lesser extent non-governmental organizations – do not correlate strongly with the TI index and at least moderately strongly with the "corruption affects one's own life."

The problem seems to be twofold. First, people may well be bothered by corruption even if they do not encounter it in their daily lives. Across the 63 nations in the sample, only 12.5 percent (2.5 percent in the West) reported any direct experience with corruption. In only seven nations (Albania, Cameroon, Lithuania, Moldova, Nicaragua, Pakistan, and Romania) did 25 percent or more of the population admit to paying a bribe, and in just one other country (Cameroon) did more than 60 percent say yes. On the other hand, 79 percent (including 60 percent in the West) said that petty corruption is a problem. Having to pay a bribe may not be so common: You don't have to pay the police if you don't get a ticket (if you don't have a car); you don't pay the doctor if you don't need to see her – or can't afford to see her; and you don't pay the teacher if you don't have children in school. Furthermore, small gifts may not seem quite so problematic as corruption, even petty corruption, in general (see Chapter 5). So Abramo's attack on the TI index by relating it to "experience" seems misplaced.

Even so, at least one "bribery" question – in the 1992–2000 International Crime Victimization Surveys (ICVS) aggregated to the country level (see Chapter 9 for details) – is related to the TI measure. The ICVS perceptions of bribery question has a more powerful correlation with the TI index ($r^2 = .547, N = 35$, $r^2 = .683$ with a quadratic term added to account for the non-linear relationship), as the lowess plot in Figure A1-1 shows. Lowess is an iterative technique, which fits a spline-like curve, a "locally weighted" regression, smoothed to produce a plot that clarifies the relationship between two variables.[6] In Figure A1-2, I show the same pattern for the perception of grand corruption in the TI Global Corruption Barometer for 2005 and perceptions of grand corruption ($r^2 = .655$, $N = 55$). The most corrupt countries are all clustered at the lower left-hand portion of the graph, where there is less consistency between public perceptions and the TI index because of random fluctuations for the small differences in each measure.[7]

For a smaller set of countries, there is an even more powerful correlation between the 1996 TI Corruption Perceptions Index and public perceptions of corruption in the 1995–7 wave of the World Values Survey ($r^2 = .835, N = 24$) and a robust relationship ($r^2 = .630, N = 42, r^2 = .693$ excluding the outliers of Bangladesh and Spain) for the 2003 TI Corruption Perceptions Index. The Gallup Millennium Survey in 2000 asked whether people would call their government corrupt and the responses across 45 countries to this question correlate moderately strongly with the 2001 TI index ($r^2 = .454, N = 45$) but removing three strong outliers (Australia and Iceland, where people see way "too much" corruption, and Nigeria, where they see too little) raises the r^2 to .680.

The aggregate measures of corruption, including the TI Corruption Perceptions Index, are thus not perfect. But, as Kaufmann and Kraay (2007) argue, they are the best we have and they perform rather well for something that is so difficult to measure.

One should not become too overconfident in using these aggregate measures. There is a lot more to corruption than such indices can tell us, since corruption takes different forms in different places (Johnston, 2005, 49–59). In the economically more developed – and more equal – nations, predominantly in the West, we see grand corruption almost exclusively. In the poorer countries, black markets are common and so is high-level corruption, but both vary according to the success of market reforms (see also Chapter 4 on transition countries). The

---

[6] Lowess is a visual aid to interpreting the relationship between variables. Since it is a "locally weighted" regression with slopes dependent upon the specific bandwidth chosen, there is no regression coefficient. Since lowess uses just the information at hand, there are no significance tests, and since the line connecting the points is a function of the bandwidth chosen, there is no measure of goodness of fit.

[7] For this estimation, the r^2 increases only to .679 with the addition of a quadratic term (which is significant).

patron-client model of corruption, where the petty corruption is prevalent, is most prominent in his "oligarchs and clans" and "official moguls" syndromes, where economic institutions and state capacity are weak. Where economic institutions and state capacity are strong, petty corruption is uncommon.[8]

Where grand corruption is most prevalent, so is petty corruption. Corruption perceptions are divided into two principal groupings: In some countries, almost exclusively developed Western nations, people say that they see primarily grand corruption and not petty malfeasance. In seven nations, more than 20 percent of people say that grand corruption is a problem but petty corruption is not: Germany, Iceland, Ireland, Israel, Switzerland, the United States, and Estonia (the only transition country in this group). In most countries, people see both grand and petty corruption. However, in the West, only slightly more than half of respondents to the Global Corruption Barometer said that both forms of corruption were problems, compared to over 80 percent elsewhere. The aggregate correlation between the shares of respondents seeing only grand corruption and those troubled by both types is −.657.

Where you find lots of people bothered by grand corruption, you also see much concern for petty malfeasance ($r^2 = .917, N = 61$), but where people are less bothered by grand corruption, they are far less likely to see petty corruption. Countries ranked as less corrupt are more likely to have people seeing only grand corruption ($r^2 = .424$). The aggregate correlation between the shares of respondents seeing only grand corruption and those troubled by both types is −.657. Grand corruption may enrich the powerful, but it doesn't touch ordinary people as directly. Higher levels of corruption mean the prevalence of both grand and petty corruption.

Using the Global Corruption Barometer, I created indices for grand and petty corruption through a factor analysis of the specific corruption measures. The grand corruption factor includes questions on whether corruption affects politics and corruption affects business, and how corrupt parties and parliament are. The petty corruption factor includes the measures of offering bribes; whether corruption affects your own life; and the extent of corruption in customs, education, the police, registry offices, utilities, tax collectors, the medical system, the judicial system, and (again) business. People in the West are less likely to have low scores on the grand corruption factor (a mean score of −.248 compared to .444 for transition countries and −.075 for other nations), but this difference is not significant. Petty corruption is almost unknown in the

---

[8] Johnston's (2005, 221–4) categorization of countries by syndromes is largely, though not completely, a linear representation of the Transparency International Corruption Perceptions Index. Using Johnston's data set, I obtained a correlation of −.711 between the 2003 TI index and an index of Johnston's syndromes. Collapsing the two forms of corruption ("oligarchs and clans" and "official moguls") marked by weak economies and weak states/societies, the correlation increases to −.788. The developed countries with "influence markets" (mostly campaign contributions from businesses to elected officials) had substantially less petty corruption than other countries ($r = .757, N = 41$) and less grand corruption ($r = .705$), based upon perceptions from the Global Corruption Barometer discussed below.

West (see Figure A1-3) but far more prevalent elsewhere, and this difference is highly significant with a strong correlation ($r^2 = .638$).

The variations among types of corruption are essential to understanding the inequality trap. Dishonesty bothers people more when it is pervasive, when they see people getting rich from it – and they themselves remain poor – and when it is inescapable. Petty corruption doesn't cause people to lose faith in their fellow citizens or to become envious as grand corruption does (see Chapters 5, 6, and 7). Yet petty corruption is one step away from street crime such as pickpocketing (see Chapter 3), which is strongly linked to corruption. Petty corruption only occurs where there is a lot of higher-level malfeasance. So, even though people learn to live with small gift payments and not judge others negatively because they are all part of a corrupt system (Karklins, 2005), petty corruption drags ordinary people into the web of dishonesty – and ultimately points the way to the inequality trap.

Plan of the Book

Here is a brief tour of the arguments to come:

In Chapter 2, I present the theoretical framework of the "inequality trap": how high inequality leads to low out-group (generalized) trust and then to high corruption – and back to more inequality. I show that all three are sticky over time – they change little. The predominant accounts of corruption are institutional and I show that governmental structures, especially in the past three decades, have been far more malleable. So it is difficult to explain things that don't change much (corruption) with structures that do change (democratization). There is, however, one key institution that shapes corruption: the *fairness*, not the effectiveness, of the legal system.

In Chapter 3, I present aggregate cross-national tests of the inequality trap thesis, focusing on a six-equation model of corruption, trust, inequality, regulation of business, the riskiness of a nation's economy, and a new measure of government effectiveness (derived from business executives' perceptions of the effectiveness of government institutions). I find strong support for the inequality trap. While I find a weak relationship between inequality and corruption, the links from inequality to trust and from trust to corruption are strong – and there is a reciprocal link from corruption back to inequality. The fairness of the legal system, strangling regulations of business, wealth, and a measure of particularized trust (restrictions on conversions to minority religions) all lead to higher levels of corruption. Neither democratization nor effective government is a significant predictor of corruption.

I also show that corruption, far more than effective government, leads to public policies that produce better quality of life, stronger market performance, and less inequality. Higher levels of corruption are also associated with property crimes (but not crimes of violence), especially pickpocketing. A simultaneous equation model shows that corruption leads to more crime (leaders set a bad example), but reducing crime will have a minor effect on corruption.

I also show a more direct connection of corruption with the Failed States measure of uneven economic development, which measures inequality among different groups in a society (and is thus the basis for particularized trust). Perceptions of corruption are linked to aggregate measures of inequality in hierarchical linear models of cross-national surveys: the Gallup Millennium Survey of 2004 and the 2004 Global Corruption Barometer of Transparency International.[9]

Next I consider (in Chapters 4, 5, and 6) corruption in countries that prior to 1989 were ruled by Communist governments. Communist societies had high levels of corruption and low levels of trust. Contrary to the inequality trap thesis, they had *low* levels of economic inequality. Such lower inequality was imposed from above rather than reflecting the sense of social solidarity that we see in the Nordic countries (see Chapter 8). The transition to democracy and a market economy brought great instability and rising levels of inequality. This "new" inequality triggered old social tensions among ethnic groups. Higher inequality, low out-group trust, a sense of pessimism for the future, and jealousy for those who succeeded in the new economy was a strong recipe for even more corruption than in the past. The transition countries provide a good testing ground for the inequality trap since surveys indicate that people in these nations largely do not believe that you can get rich without being corrupt. There are strong linkages between inequality and corruption, both in aggregate data and in surveys.

In Chapter 4, I present aggregate portraits of trends in inequality and corruption as well as aggregate analyses of the determinants of corruption, inequality change, state failure, service deterioration, sales on credit, the sources of gift payments, and the persistence of voting for the Communist party in these states. I also estimate an individual-level model of businesspeoples' decisions (from the 2005 European Bank for Reconstruction and Development/World Bank BEEPS survey) to make sales on credit. The results provide strong support for the inequality trap argument.

In Chapter 5, I focus on Romania. Romania is an excellent case study for the inequality trap among transition countries. It has historically high levels of corruption and it also has strong ethnic conflict, leading to low generalized trust. Inequality has also been rising sharply since transition. Using a 2003 survey, I examine the linkages among perceptions of inequality, trust, and corruption and find strong support for my argument – especially the notion that grand corruption leads to social strains and to perceptions of rising inequality, low trust in other people and in government, and in support for political and market

---

[9] The 2004 Global Corruption Barometer is a cross-national survey (of 62 nations) conducted by Transparency International and was provided to me by Robin Hodess and Marie Wolkers of Transparency International. Details are available at http://www.transparency.org/policy_research/surveys_indices/gcb/2004_1. The Gallup Millennium Survey was conducted by Gallup International in 2000 for 61 nations and was provided to me by Merrill James of Gallup International. Details are available at http://www.gallup-international.com/ (follow the link to the Millennium Survey).

reforms, while petty corruption (except for the legal system) does not lead to social strains.

In Chapter 6, I focus on how the general public and elites see corruption differently in transition countries, using data from one country that seems to have reduced corruption the most (Estonia), another that has relatively high corruption but almost no increase in inequality (Slovakia), and another with high corruption and rising inequality (Romania again). In all three countries people worry about the linkage between inequality and corruption, but businesspeople and government officials are less likely to make this connection than are ordinary people (especially in Estonia) and that where inequality has risen less (in Slovakia), both the public and elites are less likely to make the connection than where it has risen more sharply. In Estonia, which now ranks as relatively honest according to Transparency International, elites see little corruption, while ordinary citizens continue to see widespread malfeasance – suggesting a variation on the inequality trap.

In Chapter 7, I examine cases that are strong tests for the inequality trap thesis. Africa is one of the best test cases for the inequality trap argument, since it is marked by high inequality, low trust, and high levels of corruption. Singapore and Hong Kong stand out as strong exceptions to my argument, since they have relatively high inequality, low trust, but rank as among the least corrupt countries in the world. Using Afrobarometer data for 14 African countries and specifically country-level surveys in Mali and Nigeria, I find strong support for linkages between inequality and corruption as people perceive them. There are strong linkages between beliefs about inequality in society and perceptions of corruption, almost exclusively grand (not petty) corruption. In Botswana, where government has become more honest, the linkages are not significant. Singapore and Hong Kong once were marked by high levels of corruption, but now have very little malfeasance. In both countries, independent anti-corruption commissions played a key role in combating dishonesty. Similar institutions in Africa (and elsewhere) have failed.

Singapore and Hong Kong succeeded in reducing corruption because they were both relatively wealthy. While both nation-states used strong legal sanctions against corrupt officials and businesspeople, each also relied heavily upon public education, socialization of young people into a sense of civic morality, and especially in a program that linked anti-corruption drives to rising living standards and less inequality. The external threats facing both countries from China helped to provide the initial motivation for curbing corruption – so that Singapore and Hong Kong would not be dominated by China – and public support for the anti-corruption drives. Perceptions of corruption in Hong Kong (using the 2004 Asian Barometer) are *not* related to beliefs about the extent of inequality. The social conditions that gave rise to strong efforts to combat malfeasance in public life are not easily transferred to other countries' experiences.

In Chapter 8, I focus on the Nordic countries and on the United States. The Nordic countries constitute another key test. They rank high on equality and trust and low on corruption. Analysis of survey data from wave 3 of the

World Values Survey show that Nordic perceptions on corruption rest on trust and confidence in key institutions, especially the police and the civil service. Attitudes about inequality and poverty are not significant. The United States is a relatively low corruption country but with mid-level rankings on trust and inequality (trust has been falling, inequality rising). Survey data do not provide much support for an inequality trap in the United States, either for people in general (the 1987 General Social Survey) or for believing whether most politicians are crooked (the 2004 American National Election Studies), although there is a greater effect for leaders than ordinary citizens. Corruption varies widely across the American states. A cross-state analysis of reporters' perceptions of corruption in state legislatures leads to strong support for the inequality trap argument, however. Both overall inequality and the ratio of African-Americans to whites in poverty are strong predictors of corruption perceptions (as is generalized trust). Reporters' perceptions of corruption are related to the vote for Progressive Presidential candidate Robert LaFollette in 1924, and both corruption perceptions in 1999 and the LaFollette vote are strongly predicted by the white-collar share in 1920 as well as the share of a state's population born to Scandinavian parents in 1880. This strongly supports my argument that corruption is sticky over time.

In Chapter 9, I reconsider the question: How can we eliminate corruption? Following Wilson and Kelling's (1982) argument on "broken windows," starting at the ground level may be the right course. Yet the considerable evidence that petty corruption is largely unrelated to trust in either other people, in government, or even in the market suggests that working from the ground up won't alleviate people's concerns about – or perceptions of – corruption. Nor would focusing on street-level crime (pickpocketing), as I argue in Chapter 3, lead to greater honesty in government. So we must look elsewhere. This brings us back to programs that reduce inequality and I speculate on how political leaders in New York City may have created the conditions for their own demise by providing free public university education for a large number of students. I conclude with some thoughts on the political difficulties of tackling inequality, which I see as the central step in the battle against corruption.

The countries I examine reflect a mixture of theory and good fortune, with a bit of personal interest thrown in. My interest in corruption was stimulated by some work on trust in transition nations, especially Romania, with Gabriel Badescu and Paul Sum (Badescu, Sum, and Uslaner, 2004) that readily spilled over into corruption research (Uslaner and Badescu, 2004). The strains of transition, especially the rise of inequality in societies where egalitarianism was the state religion and corruption was taken for granted, makes transition countries a natural test for the inequality trap (Chapter 4). My interest in Romania and the centrality of corruption, low trust, and ethnic conflict – together with an excellent survey that provides an opportunity to examine my central ideas – makes that country a natural choice (Chapter 5). Chapter 6 was motivated by a desire to examine whether the general public and elites in transition see corruption differently (they do) and how this reflects their linkages of corruption and inequality. The choice of countries was based upon these theoretical concerns. Fortunately, the surveys I was able to obtain reflected a variety of circumstances: lower corruption in Estonia, lower inequality in Slovakia, and both increasing corruption and inequality in Romania.

Chapter 7 came about when I presented my aggregate model at the City University of Hong Kong in March 2006. People in the audience were excited about the model but they told me that it just didn't seem to apply to Hong Kong. Conversations with friends in Singapore led to the same conclusion. So I became committed to understanding why these cases were such outliers (and like each other). In contrast, African nations seemed to be a central test of my overall thesis because most African states have been marked by high inequality, low trust, and a great deal of corruption. Botswana was a notable exception and its pattern of curbing corruption seemed to reflect many of the same forces as those in Singapore and Hong Kong. The availability of survey data for both Hong Kong (Asian Barometer) and for Africa (the Afrobarometer) helped in testing my claims. My proposed "solution" to the inequality trap – universal social welfare programs focusing on education – is rooted in the Nordic model and my work with my Swedish colleague Bo Rothstein (Rothstein and Uslaner, 2005). So it became important to test the inequality trap where it was *least* likely to be found – and then to replicate it, to the extent possible, in another setting (the United States) with relatively low corruption but increasing inequality – as well as great variations within the country.

A Motif for the Book

I begin each chapter – and focus more in the concluding chapter – on a musical tale that reflects my theme of the inequality trap. The 1928 musical by Berthold Brecht (play) and Kurt Weill (music), *The Threepenny Opera*, an adaptation of John Gay's *Beggar's Opera* (1728), is a story of a petty thief (Macheath, also known as "Mack the Knife") who runs afoul of the law and especially of Jonathan Jeremiah Peachum, the "boss" of London's beggars, who receives a percentage of whatever they can beg. Macheath becomes engaged to Peachum's daughter, Polly, much against her parents' wishes, since Macheath has a long history of failed love affairs (and many other marriages). Peachum has Macheath arrested, convicted, and sentenced to death. Polly's friends help Macheath escape, but he is rearrested and cannot raise enough money to bribe the guards to free him before his scheduled execution. At the end of the play, Macheath suddenly is given a reprieve by a messenger from the queen and is rewarded with vast riches.[10]

---

[10] On *The Threepenny Opera*, see http:www.threepennyopera.org, and for a summary, see http: www.threepennyopera.org/story/Synopsis.php. The lyrics at the head of each chapter all come from the 1954 Mark Blitzstein production (see http://www.threepennyopera.org/ histAmerica.php and especially http://www.threepennyopera.org/histOffBway.php), accessed January 31, 2007.

As my father was my mentor about corruption, my mother introduced me to the recording of *The Threepenny Opera*. I have her original cast album today and find its lyrics haunting. The play, like most of Brecht's work, is dark and pessimistic. The story is one of how poverty and especially inequality lead people to live on the edge of the law, often well past the edge. The "Ballad of the Easy Life" (see the head of this chapter) sets out the universal temptation to live well rather than to live honestly and "How to Survive" makes the link with inequality: "Now those among you full of pious teaching [w]ho teach us to renounce the major sins should know before you do your heavy preaching, our middle's empty, there it all begins.... For even honest folk [m]ay act like sinners unless they've had their customary dinners" (see Chapters 7 and 8).

Songs from *The Threepenny Opera* set the theme for each chapter. They tell a story of poverty, an unfair legal system, and especially how those at the bottom have little choice but to engage in corrupt behavior because the real villains are those at the top. The inequality trap tells much the same story. In *The Threepenny Opera*, Macheath is suddenly rescued and given great wealth just as he is about to be hung. Yet Brecht's real message is that such happy endings don't happen in real life, only on the stage, and he is far more pessimistic than I am: "...in real life the ending isn't quite so fine" (see Chapter 9). My story has a happy ending for Singapore and Hong Kong – and, to a considerable extent, for Botswana. (The Nordic countries have happy beginnings, so there is no need to focus on happy endings.) We come face-to-face with Brecht's pessimism when we realize that the successes of Hong Kong and Singapore (and likely Botswana) are not easy to replicate. The inequality trap is not easy to escape.

2

Corruption and the Inequality Trap

We pray to be more kindly than we are.
But sad to say the chances happen never.
You have to reach up high and man is low.
We'd all be glad to live in peace forever.
It seems that circumstance won't have it so. . . .
Of course, I'm telling you the truth –
the world is mean and man uncouth. . . .
To be aglow instead of low.
But you know circumstance won't have it so.
And nothing much will help a lot and you can toss it in the pot.
The world is mean and man uncouth.
And sad to say I tell the truth.
It always happens that way. It always happens that way.
And nothing much will help a lot and you can toss it in the pot.

> From "Circumstance," Berthold Brecht and Kurt Weill,
> *The Threepenny Opera*

"I think," said Martin Lomasny, "that there's got to be in every ward somebody that any bloke can come to – no matter what's done – and get help. Help, you understand, none of your law and your justice, but help."

So the Boston ward leader for the Democratic party told political reformer (or "muckraker") Lincoln Steffens (1931, 618) in the 1920s. Lomasny's constituents were poor immigrants who often found themselves on the wrong side of the law. They had little faith in the legal system, which was clearly biased in favor of people with money who could hire high-priced lawyers. They had to feed their families. Sure, Lomasny was corrupt himself, but he was the lifeline against a system that was stacked against his poor constituents.

Lomasny had a commodity – the ability to intervene on behalf of a citizen – that ordinary people did not possess. Lomasny, like other *patrons*, was not merely one among equals with his *clients*. Patron-client relations rest upon a foundation of inequality. The corruption of the leaders was simply their fee for providing services to the poor – and often undeserving: After all, if you came to Martin Lomasny to ask him to get a family member out of jail, you were usually not in a position to claim moral superiority. The problems of corruption arise, paraphrasing Wittgenstein (1953), when morality goes on holiday.[1] The lines of virtue and vice were blurred in Lomasny's Boston. Both the churches and Lomasny's political machine "provided help and counsel and a hiding place in emergencies for friendless men, women, and children who were in dire need, who were in guilty need, with the mob of justice after them" (Steffens, 1931, 618).

Economic inequality creates political leaders such as Martin Lomasny, who will "take care" of his constituents, and New York City boss George Washington Plunkitt, who made patronage a virtue rather than a vice, since it provided jobs for ordinary citizens. These leaders *help* their constituents, but more critically *they help themselves*. Perhaps the most famous line from Plunkitt's autobiography (as told to a political reporter) explained how the nineteenth-century political boss who had only a small salary from his post got rich: "I seen my opportunities and I took 'em" (Riordan, 1948, 4). Inequality leads to *clientelism* – leaders establish themselves as monopoly providers of benefits for average citizens. These leaders are not accountable to their constituents as democratic theory would have us believe. As Xin and Rudel (2004, 298) argue, "A culture of corruption emerges in these impoverished settings...." Corruption is thus part of an *inequality trap* that saps people (especially at the bottom) of the belief that it is safe to trust others.

Corruption gives some people advantages that others don't have. Corruption transfers resources from the mass public to the elites – and generally from the poor to the rich (Tanzi, 1998). It acts as an extra tax on citizens, leaving less money for public expenditures (Mauro, 1997, 7). Corrupt governments have less money to spend on their own projects, pushing down the salaries of public employees. In turn, these lower-level staffers will be more likely to extort funds from the public purse. Government employees in corrupt societies will thus spend more time lining their own pockets than serving the public. Corruption thus leads to lower levels of economic growth and to ineffective government (Mauro, 1997, 5). The inequality trap is hard to break. I posit a model in which inequality, mistrust, and corruption are mutually reinforcing:[2]

inequality → low trust → corruption → more inequality

My argument on the roots of corruption is largely pessimistic: Corruption is not easy to eradicate if it is largely based upon the distribution of resources (economic inequality) and a society's culture (trust in people who may be different from yourself). Changing institutions may not be easy, but its difficulty pales by

[1] Ludwig Wittgenstein (1953, 19e) wrote that "...philosophical problems arise when language *goes on holiday*" (emphasis in original).
[2] For a similar perspective, developed independently, see You (2005b).

comparison with reshaping a society's culture or its distribution of wealth (and power). Changes in income distribution clearly come about through institutions such as legislatures or unions representing workers, and I do not denigrate their importance in policy formation. My essential point is that institutions are not autonomous, so that changes in political structures alone are not sufficient for reducing either inequality or corruption. Corruption is based upon a social and economic foundation that must be recognized if we hope to reduce its deleterious effects.

I draw a sharper distinction between institutions and culture than others might. I recognize that there is an interplay between the two and that concepts such as democracy are more than a set of structural rules. Dahl (1971, 2) defines democracy as a political system that is "completely or almost completely responsive to all its citizens." Warren (2004, 333) argues that democracy means the maximization of "rule by and for the people" and that people are "of equal moral worth" and should have an equal right to participate in decision-making. On this account, corruption and democracy are closely connected (Warren, 2004). My emphasis on economic equality and legal fairness fit in well with Warren's "moral" conception of democracy and I shall argue in the chapters to follow that "good" institutions that combat corruption have their roots in such egalitarian ideals of democracy.

Most of the literature on corruption is not so nuanced. The most common accounts of corruption focus on what I might call "institutional shells," so that if you change structures, you change outcomes. Moving from totalitarian government to parliamentary democracy, from one electoral system to another, from a Presidential to a parliamentary system, from centralized to decentralized government, and the like will be sufficient to increase/decrease corruption. These shells have no "soul" or "moral" component demanding equality, as Warren's democracy does. The literature largely treats them as mere pieces of machinery, almost as malleable as when a plumber replaces a worn screw on a leaky faucet with a new one to stop a leak. Change Romania from a Communist state to a parliamentary democracy, adopt an open-list electoral system, decentralize power to localities, and select a Prime Minister instead of a President and Romania becomes another Switzerland. I don't find such arguments compelling and they don't stand up in my statistical model (see below and Chapter 3). If such structural forces determined corruption, there would be no inequality trap. They don't, and I think that it is important to draw a line between such institutional shells and culture/economics, even if the distinction is less nuanced.

My argument is not that (democratic) institutions don't matter for curbing corruption. Rather, they are not "unmoved movers." Strong institutions were essential in the battle to reduce corruption, as the cases of Hong Kong and Singapore (Chapter 7) show. Reducing inequality requires state action and specific policies (universalistic social welfare programs). The success of anti-corruption commissions in Hong Kong and Singapore did *not* require formal democratic institutions – since neither city-state is a democracy as traditionally

defined. However, leaders in both Hong Kong and Singapore engaged the public in their fights against malfeasance through public campaigns and socialization in the schools, as well as through policies designed to increase economic
equality through universal social welfare. Warren (2004) would certainly see
this involvement of the citizenries as reflecting democratic values, if not formal
structures.

Similarly, I find institutional effects elsewhere, but always connected to a
wider conception of democracy and democratization. The more "democratic"
transition countries also have less inequality (cf. Dahl, 1971, 82–8), even though
changes in democratization do not lead to changes in inequality (Chapter 4).
An unfair legal system is a key determinant of corruption, both in my aggregate
model (Chapter 3) and in perceptions of the publics in Romania and throughout
Africa, especially in Nigeria (Chapters 5 and 7). Africans also link corruption
to poor governance and the lack of freedom of speech (Chapter 7). Throughout
the story that follows, strong institutions, most notably equal justice for all, play
a key role in combating corruption. And authoritarian governance, especially
Communism, generally leads to high levels of corruption.

There seems to be an asymmetry in the institutional effects on corruption.
"Bad" governance is strongly associated with corruption (though the causal
direction is unclear; see Chapter 3), while democratic institutions have a tendency – though not significant in a multivariate model (see Chapter 3) – toward
greater honesty in government.[3] There are notable exceptions such as Hong
Kong and Singapore and there is little evidence that *democratization*, a change
to democratic structures, can overcome a legacy of corruption. And this is cause
for caution about expecting too much from political institutions by themselves.
Strong institutions must be linked with strong, especially egalitarian, societies.

Why an Inequality Trap?

The most compelling argument for the notion of an inequality trap is that corruption is *sticky*. There is little evidence that countries can escape the curse of
corruption easily – or at all. The r^2 between the 2004 Transparency International estimates of corruption and the historical estimates for 1980–5 across
52 countries is .742. Any theoretical perspective on corruption must take into
account its persistence over time. Just as corruption is "sticky," inequality and
trust do not change much over time either. The r^2 for the most commonly used
measures of economic inequality (Deininger and Squire, 1996) between 1980
and 1990 is substantial at .676 for a sample of 42 countries.

A new inequality database developed by James Galbraith extends measures
of inequality further back in time and across more countries. The r^2 between
economic inequality in *1963* and economic inequality in *1996* is .706 (for 37
countries). The r^2 between generalized trust World Values Surveys between
1980 and 1990 is .81 for the 22 nations included in both waves – the r^2 between

---

[3] I found the same pattern for generalized trust in Uslaner (2002, 222–9).

generalized trust in 1990 and 1995 is also robust (.851, N = 28). The stickiness of corruption, inequality, and trust are the heart of the inequality trap. *Inequality, low trust, and corruption are all sticky because they form a vicious cycle.* Each persists over time and it is difficult to break the chain.

Our actions reflect not only our own desires and beliefs, but also how we feel that others will act. People pattern their actions on what they believe others will do and what others think is acceptable (Hedstrom, 2005, ch. 3). If you believe that "everyone is corrupt," you will follow the herd and act corruptly yourself (Tavits, 2005). Even if you feel uncomfortable in behaving corruptly, you may feel that there is no alternative to following the crowd if you are to survive (see Chapters 5 and 7), so corrupt behavior becomes a "self-fulfilling prophecy" (Merton, 1968). There is a similar dynamic in evolutionary game theory models: When "nice" (trusting) people are in the majority in a society, they will "crowd out" miscreants so cooperative (honest) behavior will be the rule. Where "mean" (mistrusting) people are in the majority, cooperators will "die out" and defection (corruption) will be the norm (Bendor and Swistak, 1997).

The reinforcing nature of the inequality trap reflects a "path dependent" relationship among inequality, trust, and corruption. Path dependency is a historical pattern in which initial conditions persist over long periods of time. "Long movement down a particular path," Pierson (2001, 261) argues, "will increase the costs of switching to some previously foregone alternative . . . in politics the pursuit of such change faces two additional obstacles: the short time horizons of political actors and the strong status quo bias associated with the decision rules that govern most political institutions." The undesirable equilibrium of high inequality, low trust, and high corruption is not readily upset. The short-term horizons of politicians – to enrich themselves but also to respond to demands from the public – both work against the sorts of policies that can reduce inequality and combat corruption.

These analytical models suggest why the inequality trap is so hard to break. They do not account for the factors that give rise to dishonest behavior. Social interaction models tell us that we mimic the behavior of others, but they can't explain why others act the way they do. Arguments that highlight path dependence generally focus on an initial event, such as the adoption of a policy alternative, that may persist over long periods of time, even though its initiators did not have such great foresight. Some path dependent decisions – such as the adoption of the QWERTY typewriter keyboard – may endure for long periods of time simply because no better alternative emerged (Pierson, 2004, 23, 44–8). While path dependence offers a compelling story about how patterns persist, it is of limited help in explaining the roots of corruption. Dishonesty in government, business, and society did not arise from choices, either planned or unanticipated (Pierson, 2004, 115–19).

I shall propose a model of the forces that lead to corrupt (or dishonest) behavior. I do not offer an account that traces corruption back to its historical roots, so my argument is mostly static. So are most accounts of corruption.

However, the reinforcing nature of the inequality trap helps to explain why corruption persists, and I turn in Chapters 7, 8, and 9 to a discussion of how some societies fought corruption and won – as well as how others put up more meager battles and "lost" (if they were really trying to end malfeasance).

While it is difficult to escape the inequality trap, it is not impossible. Universal social welfare policies both increase trust and reduce inequality (Rothstein and Uslaner, 2005). Reducing inequality also frees people from being dependent upon corrupt patrons and makes them masters of their own fates. Education is also strongly associated with higher levels of trust in outsiders (Uslaner, 2002, ch. 4), so increasing the level of education will also foster honesty in government indirectly. The adoption of such policies, notably universal education, seems to underlie the stories of successful battles against corruption in such diverse places as Sweden, Denmark, Singapore, Hong Kong, South Korea, Botswana, and New York City (see Chapter 9). Universal education is not an easy policy to implement and the evidence for its role in the battle against corruption seems compelling but is not firmly established.

If my claim is correct, we may find a very different recipe for fighting corruption than others have offered. It will also resolve a key issue of causality. The inequality trap reflects a vicious cycle – with inequality at both the start and the end of the chain. In any causal link, it is difficult to know where to begin. Do we need to curb corruption to end inequality or must we focus on reducing inequality to combat corruption? If education is the key, the "trap" begins with inequality – or at least we know where the intervention must take place.

The Roots of Corruption

Economic inequality provides a fertile breeding ground for corruption – and, in turn, it leads to further inequalities. The connection between inequality and the honesty of government is not necessarily so simple: As the former Communist nations of Central and Eastern Europe show, you can have plenty of corruption without economic inequality – at least as inequality has been conventionally measured. This statistical disjunction between inequality and corruption should not lead us to dismiss the link between the two.

High levels of inequality go hand in hand with high in-group trust and low out-group trust. The struggle to make do and to help one's family and friends may take moral precedence over engaging in corrupt activities that people would prefer to shun.

While there may be a weak relationship between inequality and corruption, this may reflect the way we measure the former. The conventional way of measuring inequality – the Gini index – may be too blunt an indicator to tap the connection between disparities of wealth and corruption. I shall also examine an alternative measure of inequality – uneven economic development along group lines, as measured in the Failed States Index project of the Fund for Peace.[4] This measure, which reflects the economic stratification of a society

---

[4] For the index, see http://www.fundforpeace.org/programs/fsi/fsindex2006.php.

by group is more strongly linked to my argument that corruption rests upon a foundation of strong in-group trust and low out-group trust. The measure of uneven economic development is much more strongly related to corruption than are any of the standard Gini indices available.

However, uneven economic development is also very strongly related to *all of the other determinants of corruption – so that adding it to a statistical model gives me no extra leverage – and indeed, the tight relationships among the many parts of the syndrome of corruption lead to a less satisfactory statistical model.* Nonetheless, some simple portraits of the linkage among uneven economic development, corruption, and its determinants make for a telling story that supports my overall thesis (see below).

Even though aggregate statistical models may not show a direct linkage between economic inequality and corruption, ordinary people do see such a tie. The aggregate models provide the key test of the inequality trap argument, because they cover a wide range of countries and are based upon measures that are central to my argument.

In cross-national surveys, perceptions of corruption are higher in countries that have higher levels of economic inequality (see Chapter 3). Surveys indicate that where corruption is high, as in the former Communist nations of Central and Eastern Europe and in most of Africa, people see clear connections between malfeasance and inequality. The general public is also more likely to see such a tie than are elites, which suggests another type of inequality – a difference in perceptions between those who have more resources and those with less. Where corruption is lower – as in Botswana, Hong Kong, the United States, and the Nordic countries – people do not perceive such a connection (Chapters 5 through 8). Survey evidence may not provide as comprehensive a test as aggregate data analysis, but it provides strong support for the argument that *people perceive a link between corruption and inequality.*

The historically low levels of inequality in the formerly Communist countries of Central and Eastern Europe as well as the former Soviet Union confound the linkage between inequality and corruption in the overall aggregate model. Since transition, inequality has increased, often dramatically, in most of these countries. As the nations became democratic, their governments did *not* become more honest. Since transition, both aggregate and survey data indicate that people in some transition countries see a link between inequality and corruption.

There is one key institutional structure that I posit to affect corruption, both directly and indirectly. It is the *fairness of the legal system.* The fairness of the legal system reflects the belief, as stated by Martin Lomasny, that people without resources don't expect equal treatment from the legal system. A fair legal system is *not* the same thing as economic inequality – indeed, the two are only modestly related, as I show below. Yet, a fair legal system may be as troubling to many poor people as the overall distribution of wealth itself. An unfair legal system makes corruption work and multiplies the advantages of the wealthy.

The fairness of the legal system is distinct from the *efficiency* of the legal system (Rothstein and Stolle, 2002). You can have a system of courts in which trials are conducted expeditiously and the courts can be nominally – or even practically – independent of the other branches of government. But this does not mean that the proceedings are fair – or that the beneficiaries of corruption will face justice at all. Even if you put all of the bad guys on trial, they may not be convicted.

I present in Chapter 3 a cross-national model of inequality, trust, corruption, regulation, a country's risk rating (for potential investors), and the quality of government. I find no direct effect for inequality, but rather an indirect one through generalized trust. The fairness of the legal system has both direct and indirect effects on corruption. The indirect effects come through the impact of the fairness of the legal system on strangling regulation – which, in turn, leads to greater corruption. Regulation is a policy choice that affects corruption, but reforming such procedures will be insufficient to reduce corruption significantly.

More traditional institutional accounts of corruption often suggest that the cure for malfeasance is to put the bad guys in jail. If we do so (and we ought to do so), they will be replaced by other corrupt leaders. Nor do we need a reformed system of government that either centralizes power to herd in independent "entrepreneurs" who extort businesses or average citizens (Treisman, 1999) or decentralizes power to prevent an all-powerful "grabbing hand" (DiFrancesco and Gitelman, 1984, 618; Fisman and Gatti, 2000; Kunicova and Rose-Ackerman, 2005).

Corruption has consequences: Dishonesty leads to a less stable economic and political environment – as reflected in the ratings of overall risk by forecasting firms. These ratings guide decisions by investors and lending agencies. Governments considered very risky overcompensate by trying to control too much, enacting regulations that are so strict that they provide greater opportunities for state capture and further corruption.

Even more critically, corruption leads to less effective government, *but effective government does not lead to less corruption, more trust, or less inequality*. I present a new measure of government effectiveness derived from cross-national surveys of business executives (the 2004 Executive Opinion Survey of the World Economic Forum). "Effective governments" are efficient – they get things done and do not waste taxpayers' money. Their decision-making processes are open and the courts are structurally independent from the other branches of government (see Chapter 3). These "effective" or "good" governments are far less corrupt or more "honest" than poorly performing states – but the causal arrow seems to go from corruption to bad government rather than the other way around. Equally critical is the lack of a direct connection between institutional design – using a wide range of indicators – and corruption.

Corruption leads to less effective government, less trust, and greater inequality (Rose-Ackerman, 2004, 6, 14). The path backward from corruption to greater inequality is direct, even though the path forward is not (through trust). Gyimah-Brempong (2002, 186) finds that a 1-point increase in the Transparency International Corruption Perceptions Index is associated with an increase of 7 points on a 100-point Gini index in Africa. Rose-Ackerman

(2004, 6) argues that corrupt officials spend too much on big projects (infrastructure) where they can channel contracts to their cronies. As corrupt officials empty the treasury, there is less money available for investments in programs, such as education, that benefit those at the bottom of the economic ladder.

While there is no path from ineffective government to larger disparities in wealth, effective government might lead to policy choices that promote policies that can break the poverty trap – if we could only get good government. Yet the idealized path from good government to greater equality is, as Samuel Johnson said of second marriages, the triumph of hope over experience.[5] Good government, I shall show, has lots of positive effects, but policies promoting greater equality are not among them.

Corruption and Institutional Design

Why is corruption pervasive in some societies and not in others? Can we reform our political systems to reduce corruption? What lessons can we learn from the experiences of transition countries about the causes and consequences of Communism?

Most studies of corruption focus on its institutional roots and many discussions treat corruption as a measure of ineffective government (Rothstein and Teorell, 2005). The institutional argument takes place on three levels: (1) the overall structure of government; (2) specific institutional forms such as centralized versus decentralized authority, types of electoral structures, the nature of the legal system, and the like; and (3) extra-governmental institutions such as the media.

Institutional accounts are attractive for two reasons. First, corruption is all about the lack of transparency and the inability of ordinary citizens to hold leaders to account if they abuse the public trust. Except in the most extraordinary circumstances, political leaders do not make public their illicit dealings – and generally go to great lengths to hide such actions. Autocrats are not accountable to the public; democratic politicians are. Recall the regimes of Mobutu Sese Seku of Zaire (now the Democratic Republic of Congo), "Papa Doc" Duvalier of Haiti, and leaders of Communist regimes too numerous to name. All ran "kleptocracies" and there was no trace of their wealth until after they had been ousted from office. Officials in democracies are subject to public scrutiny, so democracy should help to reduce corruption (Adsera, Boix, and Payne, 2000, 19; Lederman, Loayza, and Soares, 2005, 16–17, 23; You and Khagram, 2005), as would greater political stability (Leite and Weidmann, 1999, 20; Treisman, 2000). Klitgaard (1988, 75) famously offered an equation on the roots of corruption as "monopoly plus discretion minus accountability."

Second, anti-corruption organizations such as Transparency International place great emphasis on structural reform because it seems to be more feasible.

---

[5] From Boswell's *Life of Johnson*, cited at http://www.samueljohnson.com/popular.html, accessed October 21, 2005.

In some arguments, it is simply a matter of putting the evildoers in jail and a stronger court system or fewer temptations for the "grabbing class" such as higher salaries for public employees (LaPorta et al., 1999; Mauro, 1997, 5; Tanzi, 1998, 573; Treisman, 2000; but cf. Rose-Ackerman, 1978, 90–1).

Institutions come and go, but corruption persists – so it seems hazardous to assume that a change in political structures will lead to a reduction in corruption (Johnston, 2005, 22). For many institutions – especially centralized versus decentralized authority – there are conflicting arguments about the effects on corruption. Some think that a centralized authority makes corruption more likely, while others say that the multiplicity of "grabbing hands" in a decentralized system leads to more dishonesty.

Some institutionalists pay little attention to social or cultural factors, thus granting too much explanatory power to structure. In some cases, the link between corruption and institutional structures may be spurious – the effects vanish when societal and economic factors are considered: Paldam (2002) shows that the impact of democratic governance on corruption becomes insignificant when he controls for per capita income.

Some institutional accounts are simply too blunt. Many students of corruption believe that we can solve many of the problems of dishonesty by strengthening the legal system. They are on to something important, but it is *not* the power of the legal system, the number of courts, or even the connection between the courts and other institutions of government that matters. Instead, it is the *fairness* of the legal system – and you can't get impartiality by tinkering with institutions.

How do institutionalist arguments fare? Democratic governments are less corrupt. On Transparency International's (TI) 2005 Corruption Perceptions Index, countries that were "fully free" on Freedom House's 2003 index had a mean score of 5.87, while partially free countries had a mean of 3.18, and the "not free" countries averaged 2.97. The simple correlation between corruption and democracy is .523, reasonably robust if not overwhelming. Authoritarian countries have a great deal of corruption. Every "not free" country has a corruption score below the mid-point on TI's scale and all but Tunisia rank close to the bottom. Yet democracy is hardly a guarantee of honesty. Democracies are all over the place on the corruption index, with almost half below the mid-point.

As Mueller (2001) argues, creating democratic institutions is not difficult. Freedom House assesses the democratic character of governments annually, measuring both political rights and civil liberties indices. The last 20 to 30 years have been boom times for democracy. New political institutions emerged and people in formerly authoritarian states exercised rights that they had long been denied. There is only modest consistency from 1973 to 2003 in either political rights ($r^2 = .165$) or civil liberties ($r^2 = .263$, both N = 77). Even excluding countries that were Communist in 1973, the respective r^2 values increase only to .264 and .375 (N = 67).

If we restrict the comparison period to begin in 1988, the year before the revolutions in Central and Eastern Europe, the picture does not look much brighter. The political rights index of Freedom House showed considerable change from 1988 to 2003: On the 7-point scale (with lower scores indicating greater political rights), the mean score improved from 3.138 in 1988 to 2.554 in 2003. For former and present Communist nations, the score moved from 5.789 to 2.917. More critically, there was virtually no correlation between the 1988 and 2003 scores. For 62 nations, there is a significant, though not powerful, coefficient of earlier scores on the later ones ($t = 2.22$, $r^2 = .076$). For the 17 Eastern bloc countries, the coefficient is not at all significant ($t = -.05$, $r^2 = .0001$).

The changes in political rights and civil liberties from 1973 to 2003 are unrelated to changes in corruption from 1980–5 to 2004 ($r^2 = .007$ and .038, respectively, $N = 38$). Moving the democratization measures forward to 1988 does not improve the fit with changes in corruption ($r^2 = .004$ and .0005 for political rights and civil liberties, $N = 39$). *Institutions are not nearly as sticky as corruption – and structural change does not track the level of transparency* (cf. Uslaner, 2004a).

Democracy is not the cure-all for corruption because elected officials can entrap their followers in patron-client relationships, often called (at least in the United States) "political machines." These organizations tightly control access to government jobs and even to justice. In Chicago at the turn of the century, political leaders made a powerful show of force in what seems like a routine larceny trial (Martin, 1936, 300, quoted in Gosnell, 1968, 79–80):

During the pendency of the case there appeared before Mr. Austin (the person robbed) in behalf of the defendant, whose guilt was unquestioned, two state senators, a member of the lower house (the defendant's attorney, who later was a Democratic candidate for judge of the Municipal Court), a chief clerk of the Appellate Court, two deputy clerks of the Municipal Court, the [party] club president and party committee chairman, and six others, citizens of more or less prominence, all of whom urged Mr. Austin to drop the case. In addition, Mr. Austin's principal witness, a youth of fifteen years, was threatened with kidnaping by gangsters, resulting in policemen being assigned to guard his home.

This show of political force did not reflect the severity of the crime or a concern that justice might not be served. Instead, it was a demonstration to the community that Chicago's political leaders had the power to "protect" the accused party – and in turn, they demanded complete political loyalty.

Newer democratic systems, stemming from political transitions, are particularly prone to corruption, and elections may even provide the opportunity for *increased* corruption (Andvig, n.d., 56–8; Johnston, 2005, 196). Where corruption has been widespread for many years, creating *effective institutions* rather than simply new forms of government may be particularly difficult since dishonesty may be strongly entrenched in existing structures (Hopkin, 2002, 583–4).

Even in long-standing democracies, elections may not deter corrupt politicians. Machine leaders can "buy" the support of people who depend upon their largesse for jobs, other resources, and even justice – especially of minority group members who have few resources of their own (Rose-Ackerman, 1978, 212–13; You and Khagram, 2005, 138; Wilson, 1960, 54–5). Corrupt leaders can expect, or extort, the support of the public in elections. In post–World War II Italy, despite widespread allegations of dishonesty by legislators, deputies who faced charges of corruption were no more likely to lose their reelection bids than members who were not indicted. And these findings parallel those for the United States (Chang and Golden, 2004; Golden and Chang, 2001). In Brazil, President Luiz Inacio Lula de Silva won reelection with more than 60 percent of the vote even though he was implicated in major scandals, including extorting contractors to provide an illegal multi-million-dollar fund that financed his 2002 election and that paid off members of minority parties to support his government. A 56-year-old maid commented after voting: "Lula cares about the poor, and that's what matters to me, more than all this talk about corruption, which we've always had. . . . thanks to him, my salary has gone up $20 a month and the price of food has gone down enough that I'm eating a lot more meat than in the past" (Rohter, 2006, A6).

Democratic institutions may not be sufficient to reduce malfeasance. Every transition country except Serbia and Montenegro and Belarus became more "free" between 1988 and 1998, according to the Freedom House scores, yet the 10 of the 11 transition countries for which there are data became *more* corrupt from 1998 to 2003. Even allowing for a time lag, democratization doesn't seem to produce more honest government.

Democracy may be too blunt an instrument to be the "cure-all" for kleptomania in civic life. I shall consider several of the most prominent institutions in the corruption literature, including the structure of governing institutions, the electoral system, the quality of the bureaucracy, and the legal system.

Democracy doesn't guarantee accountability because leaders can centralize power and act very much like autocrats even where there are elections. Klitgaard's (1988) equation for corruption puts monopoly power at the heart of his account of political dishonesty. In a decentralized or federal system of government, it is easier for both ordinary citizens and other politicians to monitor the honesty of leaders (Lederman, Loayza, and Soares, 2005, 5). Andvig (n.d., 85) adds: "Since everyone knows everyone else's business in decentralized settings . . . it is harder to conduct under-the-table deals" (cf. Fisman and Gatti, 2000; Karklins, 2005, 109). Centralized authority, represented by both unitary governments and Presidential regimes (Kunicova, 2005; Kunicova and Rose-Ackerman, 2005; Lederman, Loayza, and Soares, 2005, 17), have higher levels of corruption. When you put a lot of power in a central authority – be it democratic or autocratic – you reduce accountability and make corruption more likely.

Or do you? Treisman (1999, 1) argues that decentralized (federal) states are *more* corrupt than unitary ones. He claims that bureaucrats in such states will not coordinate their illicit activities with each other and will thus "overgraze the commons." Corrupt deals depend upon personal relations between the guilty parties – which are more likely to occur in smaller settings. Conflicting legal systems may also make enforcement against mercenary officials more difficult. Bennett and Estrin (2005) offer a formal model that establishes essentially similar results. Yet, Rose-Ackerman (1978, 212), deMello and Barenstein (2002, 353), and You and Khagram (2005, 150) reject *either a positive or a negative linkage* between centralization and corruption.

Both positive and negative effects of decentralization on corruption seem reasonable. They are clearly inconsistent, so a would-be reformer could throw up her hands in despair when thinking about how to remake governmental institutions in the fight to reduce malfeasance in office. There is no balance of compelling evidence on either side – and the impact of governmental structure (both centralization and Presidential systems) vanishes in the model I present in the next chapter.

If we cannot fix responsibility on governmental structure or electoral accountability more generally, can we gain some leverage by focusing on electoral arrangements that give advantage to potential malfeasants? Politicians, Kunicova and Rose-Ackerman (2005) argue, should represent their constituents rather than special interests; political parties are more tied to such corrupt interests than individual legislators. Constituents can hold individual members responsible for actions, whether they are based upon policy choices or stealing from the public purse.

A closed-list proportional representation (PR) electoral system breaks down this system of direct constituency representation in two ways. First, a PR system is based upon multi-member rather than single-member districts – in the extreme, in Israel, the entire nation is one electoral district. This disrupts the linkage between legislators and their districts. Second, a closed-list system means that voters cannot vote for a specific candidate, but can only chose among competing political parties. A closed-list proportional representation system gives power to the parties and disrupts the representational link between legislators and their constituents – and makes corruption more likely. When a closed-list system is combined with centralized authority (as in Presidential systems), the opportunities for corruption are much greater (Kunicova and Rose-Ackerman, 2005, 577; but see Persson, Talbellini, and Trebbi, 2000, 11–12).

Yet this argument is problematic on three grounds. First, Golden and Chang (2001, 677) make precisely the *opposite* claim for Italy: "Italy's use of the [open-list] preference vote appears to have contributed significantly to the development of extensive, high-level political corruption in the postwar era." Second, it is far from clear that political parties promote some notion of a broader interest than do individual legislators. Political parties in many parts of the world – especially in the United States – have been as closely associated with corruption as have individual politicians. Martin Lomasny was not a lone wolf in political life. He was the leader of a corrupt "political machine." Olivier de Sardan (1999, 42) makes much the same point about democratic transitions in Africa: "The change to democracy seems...merely to have introduced the possibility of openly attacking [corrupt] practices (by means of a denunciation of 'prebend' and 'racket'), without modifying them."

Third, this disagreement may be much ado about little. The simple correlation between corruption (the 2005 TI index) and closed-list PR electoral systems (from Kunicova and Rose-Ackerman, 2005) is only −.038; for open-list systems, it is only a bit higher (.167). Even this modest relationship is complicated by the fact that almost 60 percent of the Presidential systems with closed party lists in the analysis of Kunicova and Rose-Ackerman are in Latin America or in transition countries. This institutional factor may reflect something common to these polities – and of importance to corruption, the low levels of generalized trust in these countries.[6]

Another institution that fosters accountability is the media. While the press is not a government institution, it can play a vital role in exposing corrupt behavior. The media can publicize malfeasance and put an end to it. Freedom of the press is sometimes linked to less corruption (Brunetti and Weder, 2003), but at least one study finds that this relationship really reflects the higher level of media autonomy in wealthier countries (Lederman, Loayza, and Soares, 2005, 24). Countries with high newspaper readership and democracy have less corruption (Adsera, Boix, and Payne, 2000). Yet, Rose-Ackerman (1999, 167) cautions that the potentially powerful effects of the media are less likely to strike at corruption where it is most needed – in poor countries with high levels of illiteracy.

Press campaigns against corruption are like crabgrass control. Crabgrass is, in the American vernacular, a weed that grows in lawns. You can pull it out, but new growth will come back before you know it. Quick fixes get rid of a handful of corrupt officials or businesspeople, but they don't "solve" the problem of endemic corruption.

McMillan and Zoido (2004) tell a fascinating story of how Vladimiro Montesinos Torres, chief of Peru's secret police and the right-hand man of President Alberto Fujimori, bribed judges, politicians, and especially the owners of television stations in the 1990s. (Rose-Ackerman, 1999, 166, worried that the media might be too closely tied to political organizations to investigate corruption.) Montesinos not only kept meticulous records of these bribes – and the written receipts that he insisted each recipient give him – but he also videotaped the negotiations. Ultimately, an opposition politician was able to get a copy of one of these videos and played it at a press conference in 2000. One small cable channel, which Montesinos had not bribed, began playing the video again and again. Other networks soon followed suit, even though they

---

[6] The simple correlation between corruption (using either the Transparency International measure or the World Bank measure that Kunicova and Rose-Ackerman employ) and their measure of closed-list proportional representation systems is just −.02 to −.03; their Presidential system variable loses significance in a multivariate regression including trust and dummies for Latin America and former Communist nations.

had been part of the conspiracy. Montesinos and Fujimori were soon indicted, and Montesinos's corrupt circle of more than 1600 people collapsed (McMillan and Zoido, 2004). These revelations toppled Fujimori's government as the President fled to Japan, the home of his ancestors.

Did the revelations lead to cleaner government? McMillan and Zoido (2004, 89–91) caution that media exposure of misdeeds may not itself be sufficient to end corruption, as shown by the failure of press exposés in Ukraine and Russia in the 1990s. Peruvians had already begun to sour on the Fujimori administration's poor performance on the economy. Yet they still argue (McMillan and Zoido, 2004, 91): "Safeguards for the media – ensuring they are protected from political influence and are credible to the public – may be the crucial policies for shoring up democracy."

The media revelations seem to have had little effect in either the short or the immediate term. In 1998, while Montesinos's operations were in full swing, Peru's score on TI Corruption Perceptions Index was 4.5 (with higher scores indicating greater "transparency" or honesty) – about the level of Italy or Uruguay. Peru ranked 41st out of 88 countries in the TI ratings. By 2002, its score fell to 4.0 (more corrupt), ranking 45th out of 102 and tied with Brazil, Bulgaria, Poland, and Jamaica. By 2005, the index had fallen again to 3.5, tied for 65th out of 160 countries rated (and tied with Mexico, Panama, Turkey, and Ghana). *The increase in corruption from 1998 to 2005 for Peru was the seventh greatest among the 85 countries sampled in both years – ranking behind only Zimbabwe, Costa Rica, Belarus, Malawi, Côte d'Ivoire, and Poland (tied with Namibia).* The ratio of the 2005 to the 1998 score was the ninth smallest of 85 countries. The exposure of corrupt media and the ensuing media campaign that felled the government failed to have lasting effects. Five years later, corruption seems to have gotten worse rather than better. The videos of the chief of secret police negotiating bribe prices seem to be no more lasting than episodes of *CSI*, the highly popular American police action program that "solves" many different crimes each week, always moving on to new territory.

If it is difficult to establish a linkage between democratic, especially electoral, accountability and corruption, a more likely prospect is the bureaucracy. Bureaucrats can withhold basic public services unless they receive "gift payments" from ordinary citizens and companies doing business with the state. Bureaucrats can also "grease the wheels" of a slow-moving process by granting special favors to people or firms that pay them off – from the police officer who "saves" the speeding driver a trip to traffic court by collecting a "fine" on the spot, to the doctor who lets a paying patient advance to the head of the queue, to the clerk at the customs office who won't release a firm's goods until he receives an "extra" "gift" payment. Bureaucrats extract such payments from ordinary citizens and businesses because their salaries are too low (Andvig, n.d., 31; LaPorta et al., 1999; Mauro, 1997, 5; Weder, 1999, 107). If we paid bureaucrats more, they would not have to extort money. Higher incomes would lead them away from temptation, and the fear of losing their jobs – which are now more valuable – if caught would deter them from cheating the public (Tanzi, 2002, 35).

Yet they might do so anyway. Treisman (2000) finds no evidence that higher wages for bureaucrats decrease corruption. Tanzi (1998, 573) holds that "high wages do not eliminate the greed on the part of some officials." The total amount of money extorted is not likely to fall even if fewer people demand payments (Tanzi, 2002, 35). Rose-Ackerman (1999, 130) argues: "Systems that are based on the exchange of narrow political favors cannot be cured by reforms in civil service and procurement systems." Even if higher wages could stop bureaucrats from acting as bandits, this would have only limited effect on the overall level of corruption in a country, with almost no effect on the grand corruption of higher-level politicians and business firms (Rose-Ackerman, 2004, 27).

Ironically, the correlation between bureaucratic wages and corruption is only significant in bivariate tests in the West – not in the developing countries (where the zero-order correlation is .01) nor in transition countries (where it is .22). The modest relationship in the West ($r = .36$, significant in a bivariate regression at $p < .10$) gives us pause if we hope to reduce corruption by raising bureaucrats' wages. The only effect at all comes in countries that already have the most honest governments (and even this effect vanishes when I control for per capita income). Paying more in high-corruption, low-wages countries seems to have little effect. In Romania there is no statistical relationship between salaries paid to public bureaucrats and the estimated levels of corruption in World Bank Diagnostic surveys (Anderson et al., 2001, 25). The most likely explanations are (1) if a high salary would deter corruption, the increase in wages would have to be substantial to make a bureaucrat unconcerned with "topping up"; and (2) there would need to be some real likelihood that a corrupt official would lose her job – and be unable to find alternative employment. Evidence that any country with high levels of corruption could dramatically increase wages or would fire more than a handful of dishonest officials is lacking.

No Justice, No Peace?

Perhaps the most convincing institutional link is through the judicial system. The law determines which acts are corrupt and which are acceptable. Institutions of justice – the police and the courts – differ from other branches of government. People expect the police and especially the courts to be neutral (Rothstein, 2000, 492–3; Tyler, 1990) as well as honest. This neutrality is reflected in the refrain, "Justice is blind" and in the statues outside courthouses of Lady Justice wearing a blindfold.

The fairness of the legal system is critical *because no other political institution is predicated upon equality to such an extent*. Elections are formally about equal access and power: Each of us has one vote. But many people do not vote, at least in some countries, and the distribution of participation is not equal across the population. Even more critically, elections are not determined by atomized individuals casting ballots in isolation. Elections require mobilization and in many parts of the world lots of money – and certainly neither of these are distributed equitably (Verba, Schlozman, and Brady, 1995, 190–2).

The system of justice should not only be neutral, but also a bulwark against arbitrary treatment. A system of property rights means that government officials cannot confiscate people's possessions – and demand bribes for returning it. Russian citizens are deluged with fake goods on sale everywhere – from vacations complete with photos (so that errant husbands might convince their wives that they are on "fishing trips") to bogus caviar, phony diplomas and term papers (including portions of President Vladimir Putin's doctoral dissertation), and fake VIP stickers and flashing blue lights for your car so that other cars will let you avoid Moscow's traffic. About half of all consumer goods are bogus in Russia (Murphy, 2006). It should hardly be surprising that the annual value of bribes in Russia increased by a factor of 11 from 2001 to 2005 – and that the market for corruption in business is 2.66 times the size of the federal budget (Indem, 2006).

Without the rule of law, the state – or the mob – can arbitrarily determine who possesses property (Ledeneva, 2005, 9). A country with a weak rule of law, such as contemporary Russia, is a funnel for corruption. Mauro (1998a, 12) argues:

You live in a society where everybody steals. Do you choose to steal? The probability that you will be caught is low, because the police are very busy chasing other thieves, and, even if you do get caught, the chances of your being punished severely for a crime that is so common are low. Therefore, you too steal. By contrast, if you live in a society where theft is rare, the chances of your being caught and punished are high, so you choose not to steal.

Rothstein (2000) argues that a strong legal system would create a sense of social insurance for ordinary citizens. If the courts are corrupt, people will solve their problems outside the law – and use whatever resources they can muster to do so (Rose-Ackerman, 1999, 153).

A well-ordered society is run through the rule of law. The key to less corruption is an effective system of property rights and the rule of law (Lambsdorff, 1999; Leite and Weidmann, 1999, 20, 23; Rawls, 1971, 454; Treisman, 2000; You, 2005b, ch. 2). Tyler (1990, chs. 4–5) argues that people respect – and obey – the law because they believe that the justice system is fair and that they have been treated fairly. If people feel that they have been treated unfairly by the police or in the courts, they are less likely to have faith in the legal system. Inequality before the law is part of the larger theme of inequality more generally. *People are more troubled by corruption when it promotes inequality than when it simply takes their money.* Scott (1972, 33) argues even more pointedly: "Much of what we consider as corruption is simply the 'uninstitutionalized' influence of wealth in a political system."

The English legal tradition is often held out as providing among the strongest protections of property rights in the world and thus as a strong barrier to corruption. Eight countries with British legal heritage rank in the top 20 (out of 160 nations) in Transparency International's 2005 Corruption Perceptions Index and seven rank in the top 20 (out of 123 nations) in the ratings of legal and property rights of the Economic Freedom Network.[7] Treisman (2000) and Singer (2005) find that countries with a British legal tradition have lower levels of corruption, but Lederman, Loayza, and Soares (2005, 26) find no such effect.

Leite and Weidmann (1999, 20) and Dreher and Schneider (2006) argue that countries with a strong rule of law have less corruption. Such findings should be taken with some caution, however. It is difficult to disentangle the rule of law from corruption; the most commonly used measure of the rule of law, from the World Bank's Governance data set (Kaufmann, Kraay, and Mastruzzi, 2005), includes corruption as one of its components.[8]

Institutions of the law have major impacts on corruption. Street-level crime and corruption go together (see Chapter 3). The justice system is susceptible to corruption and cooptation by dishonest leaders.

della Porta and Vannucci (1999, 142) argue that the Italian judiciary in the 1980s and 1990s protected corrupt officials – and took part in bribery. The legal system took an active and public role in protecting a corrupt deal. *Raccomandazione* is the Italian practice of soliciting favors from people in high places. In October 2000, the director of a civil court in Southern Italy received 88 pounds of fish in return for helping to expedite the case of a plaintiff. A lower court convicted the director of corruption, but a higher court overruled the verdict. The director could only be convicted of *pretending* to influence higher authorities; punishment would be warranted only if the official *couldn't* deliver. Even direct evidence of pay-offs (what *New York Times* reporter Alessandra Stanley, 2001, called "squid pro quo") was insufficient to convict.

This case is surely exceptional. Courts do not generally enforce corrupt deals. Yet the case was not unique: *Raccomandazione* "is by now so deeply rooted in our culture that most people believe it is an indispensable tool when seeking even that to which they are entitled," a court wrote in 1992 as it overturned yet another conviction for influence peddling (Stanley, 2001). Former Italian Prime Minister Giulio Andreotti was acquitted in 1999 of a charge that he tried to influence the Mafia; a judge in Palermo postponed a new trial, arguing that the court had more important business.

The judiciary is especially likely to be linked to corruption in transition countries. When Russian entrepreneur Mikhail Khorodovsky confessed his sins of relying on "beeznissmeny" (stealing, lying, and sometimes killing) and promised to become scrupulously honest in early 2003, Russians regarded this pledge as

[7] The TI measures can be downloaded at http://www.transparency.org and the Economic Freedom Network's data can be downloaded at http://www.freetheworld.org. The eight countries with British legal traditions with the lowest levels of corruption and rankings (in parentheses) are New Zealand (3), Singapore (8), Australia (9), the United Kingdom (11), Canada (14), Hong Kong (15), the United States (17), and Ireland (20). The seven countries ranked highest on legal and property rights are Australia (3), the United Kingdom (6), Canada (8), the United States (9), New Zealand (11), Ireland (14), and Singapore (17).

[8] I am grateful to Carter Johnson for bringing this to my attention.

"startling." When he was arrested and charged with tax evasion and extortion under orders from President Vladimir Putin ten months later, the average Russian was unfazed: About the same share of people approved of his arrest as disapproved of it (Schmemann, 2003; Tavernise, 2003). The arrest of Khorodovsky stands out as exceptional: Corrupt officials and business people are rarely held to account. While crime spiraled in Russia after the fall of Communism, *conviction rates plummeted* (Varese, 1997). Ninety percent of Russian businesspeople held that vague laws gave government officials leeway in interpreting regulations, thus leading to demands for bribes (Popov, 2006). The biggest problem facing business in relatively clean Slovakia is poor law enforcement, according to a recent survey of the country's economic elite (Gyarfasova, 2002, 14).

Too few police or too few courts is not the critical issue. Nor is the quality of training for the police or for judges – or even how swiftly justice is meted out. The judicial system seems problematic when it is perceived as *unfair* (Tyler, 1990, chs. 4–5). People at the top are less likely to face the strong arm of the law, while those with fewer resources will face much harsher justice. The very branch of government that is supposed to be *the most neutral* often turns out to be *the most biased*. An unfair judicial system will protect the corrupt and punish people who must cope with corruption.

As Lomasny and the political bosses in Chicago showed, control over the courts gave politicians leverage over their constituents. They could, in many cases, determine who went to jail and who went free. Such power not only insured political loyalty, but it also served to ensure that minority groups, notably African-Americans in the United States, remained beholden to political bosses and did not pose a threat to rule by political bosses (Wilson, 1960, 54–5). Even as African-Americans have become enfranchised, they still face unequal justice – being more likely to be stopped by the police for "speeding" than whites in what has become known as "driving while black." The biased justice system keeps those with fewer resources dependent upon the powerful.

In transition countries and in developing nations more generally, unequal justice penalizes the poor. They fear the justice system, rather than respect it. The police may extort "fines" for speeding, jaywalking, or other moving violations whether the accused is guilty or not. Poor people have neither the time nor the resources to fight such charges, so they have little choice but to pay. Many poor people work in the underground economy, where they have no legal rights (Djankov et al., 2003, 71).

Dishonest politicians and business people may be shielded from the wrath of justice in highly corrupt societies. A bribe to the right judicial authorities is likely to prevent criminal prosecution of corrupt officials. Tanzi (1998, 574) writes: "In the real world, relatively few people are punished for acts of corruption." The periodic anti-corruption campaigns in Russia have done little to reduce malfeasance – and are aimed at punishing individuals out of favor (Coulloudon, 2002, 187–8). When political leaders are tried and convicted, people are skeptical since "Russia is a place that perfected the show trial for those who fall out of political favor – and "it is always the case some people are found [guilty] at the lower or intermediate level, while no one at the top is" (Myers, 2006a, C5). Ordinary Russians believe that the police are the public institution *least likely to give them fair treatment*. Almost half of crime victims won't turn to the police for help – and ordinary Russians are more afraid of the police than they are of the Mafia (Varese, 2001, 39–41).

Corrupt officials aren't prosecuted because there are too few courts or because the judiciary's agenda is too crowded. The legacy of a judicial system is not a guarantee that the legal system will be fair (the correlation between an English law tradition and the measure of legal fairness discussed in Chapter 3 is only .08). The Italian court's claim that it was too busy to retry former Prime Minister Andreotti was not credible. Corrupt officials don't face the wrath of the law because the courts treat them differently than they do ordinary citizens – and they treat poor people worst of all. Legal fairness is less about institutional design than about inequality. Making a country's legal system more fair is a lot more difficult than training the police better and appointing more judges.

Corruption and the Inequality Trap

Corruption reflects low levels of generalized trust and high levels of economic inequality. Even the one institutionalist component of my argument – the fairness of the legal system – is not a straightforward measure of institutional design. First, this argument suggests strong limits on what institutional engineering (such as anti-corruption campaigns to put unscrupulous politicians in jail or to increase the penalties for malfeasance) can accomplish. Second, it creates a clear link among perceptions of corruption and increasing inequality, pessimism for the future, declining trust in other people (and in government), and opposition to market reforms in the transition countries that I find in public opinion surveys in succeeding chapters.

The poor become trapped as clients to their patrons in corrupt societies. The well off "redistribute" society's resources to themselves and entrench themselves in power by controlling all of society's institutions (Glaeser, Scheinkman, and Shleifer, 2003, 200–1). The poor who depend upon powerful leaders for their livelihood – and for justice – have almost no opportunity to challenge the balance of power (Scott, 1972, 149). Corruption stems from inequality and reinforces it.

Glaeser, Scheinkman, and Schleifer (2003, 200; see also You, 2005b, 45–6) argue:

... inequality is detrimental to the security of property rights, and therefore to growth, because it enables the rich to subvert the political, regulatory, and legal institutions of society for their own benefit. If one person is sufficiently richer than another, and courts are corruptible, then the legal system will favor the rich, not the just. Likewise, if political and regulatory institutions can be moved by wealth or influence, they will favor the established, not the efficient. This in turn leads the initially well situated to pursue socially harmful acts, recognizing that the legal, political, and regulatory systems will not hold them accountable. Inequality can encourage institutional subversion in two distinct ways. First, the havenots can redistribute from the haves through violence, the political process, or other means. Such Robin Hood redistribution jeopardizes property rights, and deters investment by the rich.

Similarly, You and Khagram (2005, 138) argue: "The rich, as interest groups, firms, or individuals may use bribery or connections to influence law-implementing processes (*bureaucratic corruption*) and to buy favorable inter-pretations of the law (*judicial corruption*)."

Inequality breeds corruption by (1) leading ordinary citizens to see the system as stacked against them (Uslaner, 2002, 181–3); (2) creating a sense of dependency of ordinary citizens and a sense of pessimism for the future, which in turn undermines the moral dictates of treating your neighbors honestly; and (3) distorting the key institutions of fairness in society, the courts, which ordinary citizens see as their protectors against evildoers, especially those with more influence than they have (see also Glaeser, Scheinkman, and Schleifer, 2003; and You and Khagram, 2005).

Corruption and inequality wreak havoc with our moral sense. della Porta and Vannucci (1999, 146) argue that pervasive corruption makes people less willing to condemn it as immoral. As corruption becomes widespread, it becomes deeply entrenched in a society (Mauro, 2004, 16). In an unequal world, people of the dominant group may not see cheating those with fewer resources (Gambetta, 1993; Mauro, 1998b, 12; Scott, 1972, 12) or evading taxes (Mauro, 2002, 343; Owsiak, 2003, 73; Uslaner, 2006a) as immoral. People at the bottom of the economic ladder will have little choice but to play the same game even as they may resent the advantages of the well off (Gambetta, 2002, 55).

Where corruption is widespread, people realize that they are not the masters of their own fate – and they lose faith that their future will be bright. People become resigned to their fate. In the World Values Survey waves 1–3 (1981, 1990, 1995–7), respondents who believed that corruption was widespread in their country were significantly *less likely to believe they could get ahead by hard work rather than by luck or having connections*. The zero-order correlation is modest (as we might expect with a sample of almost 60,000, tau-b = .061) – but 34 percent of people in societies where corruption was seen as widespread thought the only way you could get ahead was by luck, compared to 29 percent in honest societies. In turn, 59 percent of respondents who said that they could get ahead by hard work said that the future looked bright, compared to 45 percent who said that you need luck or connections (tau-b = .116). And people living in honest societies are considerably more likely to have a high level of life satisfaction (r = −.179, for a difference of a full point on a 10-point scale).

People who believe that the future looked bright were significantly less likely to condone buying stolen goods or taking bribes.[9] If you believe that you need

[9] The simple correlations, based upon samples of about 120,000, are about .06.

luck to get ahead, your probability of saying that cheating on taxes is never justified is .52, compared to .62 if you believe that hard work pays off.

Dishonest government demoralizes people – but it does not rob them of their moral sense. People come to terms with petty corruption – the small payments they make to doctors, police officers, clerks, and even professors (see Chapter 5). These "gift payments" have become part of day-to-day life and they can help people overcome the bureaucratic delays and trips to the courts (Huntington, 2002, 257). Ordinary people are not so blasé about grand corruption, where politicians and business people make big money through illicit deals.

Even for smaller "gift payments," there is moral ambiguity. People all over the world, in different cultures, see corruption as a moral evil. Yet when they face persistently high levels of corruption, people may become fatalistic about controlling dishonesty. They come to terms with petty corruption, seeing benefits from the small bribes that they must pay to get by and recognizing that life would be more difficult without these lapses of civic virtue. Barely more than a third of Hungarians see a moral problem when doctors demand "gratitude payments" for medical services (Kornai, 2000, 3, 7, 9). This system of "gift giving" is so widespread that almost all doctors accept "gratitude money": 62 percent of physicians' total income came off the books. A majority of public officials in the Czech Republic, Slovakia, Bulgaria, and Ukraine in 1997–8 found it acceptable to receive extra payments from clients. Between 11 and 39 percent of citizens of those countries (in that order) reported offering a "small present" to officials and between 6 and 24 percent offered "money or an expensive present" (Miller et al., 2001, 217, 241).

Two-thirds of respondents to a Polish survey said that giving gift payments was inevitable, more than half said that such extra charges were simply signs of respect, and little more than a third would refuse to give a bribe. However, over two-thirds say that both giving and receiving such payments was morally reprehensible (Kolarska-Bobinska, 2002, 323–4). State Department surveys of attitudes toward corruption in Bulgaria, the Czech Republic, Hungary, Poland, Romania, and Slovakia found that between 75 and 86 percent of their publics said that "accepting a bribe in the course of a person's duties" was never justified – comparable to, or even greater than, corresponding shares of the public in Britain, France, Germany, and Italy (Office of Research, 1999, 9).

People in countries with high levels of corruption think that such payments are wrong but not nearly as bad as grand corruption – and they see little way out of demands for petty corruption (Mungiu-Pippidi, 2003, 268–70). When people have little choice but to pay, they tend to blame the "system" rather than themselves, others, or human nature (Karklins, 2005, 59).

Grand corruption is all about inequality – officials and entrepreneurs getting rich illegitimately. Petty corruption doesn't create a big income gap. My wife, my son, and I vacationed in Croatia in the summer of 2005. On a tram in Zagreb, a young man inquired what I did and when I told him I was writing on corruption and inequality, he responded: "Yes, we all know about that. If you steal a video recorder, you're a criminal. If a politician steals a hundred million dollars, he's a respected citizen."[10]

If people became inured to all forms of corruption and lost their moral sense, then we would not expect outrage at leaders who line their pockets and send their country's wealth to Switzerland or the Cayman Islands. A view of corruption that sees it as varying from one culture to another might not be surprised by the toleration of malfeasance. Such tolerance is nuanced by the recognition that grand and petty corruption are fundamentally different.

Inequality is not simply economic. Glaeser, Scheinkman, and Schleifer (2003, 200–1) see the distortion of the legal system as the most damaging consequence of economic inequality. The rich can buy influence in the courts and get away with it since they will not be held accountable.

In a corrupt polity, honesty is the exception to the norm – and professions of midnight conversions bring a mixture of derision and incredulousness. No one who has profited so immensely from a corrupt system could possibly change course so drastically – and pity the poor citizen who took him at his word. Where corruption is rampant, people have little hope for justice – thus they don't even seek it. Martin Lomasny's constituents did *not come to him for justice, only help*. Lomasny could not run a political machine dispensing justice.

Some Preliminary Evidence

Fairness of the legal system is not as strongly connected to economic inequality as we might suppose. In Figure A2-1, I present a plot of a cross-national indicator of fairness of the legal system and economic inequality in 2004. The legal fairness indicator was developed by the Economist Intelligence Unit (EIU); the EIU only estimated fairness for 60 countries, so I derived estimated values for other countries by imputation.[11] The EIU measure of legal fairness is distinctive in that it does *not* incorporate corruption (in contrast to the World Bank measure of "rule of law"). While corruption rests upon a foundation of an unfair legal system – where the wealthy and powerful are less likely to face justice than the poor – they are distinct concepts. Corruption can persist even when the legal system is perceived to be fair (as in the more "successful" transition countries of Hungary, the Czech Republic, and Poland), while other countries seem to have reduced corruption even without legal fairness (Estonia and Spain).

---

[10] Similarly, the Russian magazine *Argumenty I Fakty* editorialized in 2006: "A person who steals a chicken might go to jail, of course, but a person who steals millions is welcome to become a member of the Federation Council or the Duma" (quoted in Myers, 2006a).

[11] The variables I used for the imputation are gross national product per capita (from the State Failure Data Set), the tenure of the executive and a dummy variable for having a parliamentary system (from the Data Base of Political Institutions), the Freedom House composite indicator of democracy trichotomized for 2003, and the distance of a country from the equator (from Jong-sung You). All variables had positive coefficients. The R^2 is .769; the standard error of the estimate is .647 (N = 53).

Economic inequality is measured by the Gini index from Deininger and Squire (1996). There are too many countries (especially with values close to each other) to label each one on the graph. Instead, the points are denoted by W for developed Western nations, E for present and former Communist nations, and * for other countries. Overall, the fit between these two indicators of equality (equal treatment before the law and equal distribution of wealth) is not strong. For 88 nations, $r^2 = .131$. The correlation is depressed by the former and present Communist nations that largely have unfair legal systems but more equitable distributions of income.[12] For many years, this equality was imposed from above by a command economy – but even as inequality has grown sharply, it has not approached the level of capitalist economies. Overall, we see relatively high economic equality matched with both low and high levels of judicial fairness. When I remove the East bloc countries, the r^2 rises to .279 – still rather modest. Fairness of the legal system is *not* the same as economic inequality.

What, then, can we make of the connection between inequality and corruption? I shall offer a multiple-equation estimation focusing on corruption below, but for now, I focus on bivariate plots of inequality and corruption. Measuring corruption is tricky, but there is general agreement that the best measure is that of Transparency International. The TI scores for a wide sample of countries (here I use the measure for 2004) come from a "poll of polls" of business executives and the public, as well as rankings by risk analysts and experts on the politics and economics of each country (Treisman, 2000). The ratings range from zero (most corrupt) to 10 (least corrupt).[13] I use the Deininger-Squire Gini indices to measure economic inequality.[14]

The plot of inequality and corruption (see Figure 2-1) is striking: Across 85 countries, the r^2 is a paltry .082, suggesting no relationship at all between inequality and corruption. In Figure A2-2, I present a lowess plot of inequality and corruption. The lowess curve suggests a slight downward slope – more inequality leads to more corruption (or less transparency). But the pattern is not clear and two groups of countries stand out: the former and present Communist nations, which have lots of corruption and relatively equitable distributions of income (lower left part of the graph), and the Western industrialized nations, which have relatively low inequality and even less corruption than we might

---

[12] Within the former and present Communist countries, there is also a negative relationship between economic inequality and legal fairness ($r = -.357$, $N = 23$, $r = -.526$, $N = 17$ for the original, non-imputed data). The East bloc nations reduce the overall goodness of fit since they lie on a separate and less steep regression line.

[13] The choice of year matters little, since the *minimum* correlation I found in ratings from 1996 to 2004 is .945 (between 1996 and 2003). The rankings can be found at http://www.transparency.org.

[14] The more recent estimates by James Galbraith, which are more controversial, available at http://utip.gov.utexas.edu/data.html, and WIDER, available at http://www.wider.unu.edu/wiid/wiid.htm, do not cover as many countries with acceptable data as the Deininger-Squire data.

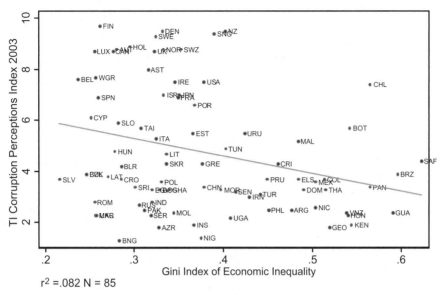

$r^2 = .082$ N = 85

FIGURE 2-1. Corruption by Economic Inequality.

expect based upon their distribution of wealth. Figures 2-1 and A2-2 suggest no clear relationship between economic inequality and corruption, but they also point to the former and present Communist regimes as outliers.

What happens when I remove the former and present Communist regimes? The lowess plot in Figure A2-3 indicates a moderate relationship between inequality and corruption. There is a gently tapering off downward slope in the connection between trust and corruption. The lowess plot becomes flat at moderate levels of inequality (a Gini of .4) and then rises a bit at the more extreme values. Overall, there is a moderate fit between the two indicators ($r^2 = .246$, N = 62) when the former and present Communist countries are excluded. With a bivariate r^2 of this magnitude, it should not take much effort to see it vanish in a multivariate analysis.

You and Khagram (2005, 144–8) find stronger effects for measures of corruption and inequality with a larger sample of countries (N = 129) and corruption indicators averaged from 1996 to 2002. They estimate a simpler model than I do in Chapter 3, but even so, the simple correlation between inequality and corruption is modest ($r^2 = .140$),[15] so it would not be surprising to see this modest connection vanish in a more complex model. You and Khagram argue that inequality matters more in democratic countries. They are correct, but this still doesn't resolve the problem. Regressions predicting corruption by economic inequality yield insignificant coefficients for countries classified as

---

[15] From my own estimation of data provided by Jong-sung You.

"not free" or "partially free" by Freedom House – and a significant (at p <
.01) negative coefficient for the 55 "free" nations: The nation with the highest
level of inequality ranks 2.8 points lower on the 10-point corruption index
compared to the most equal democracy – *but the fit of the regression is rather
meager* ($r^2 = .10$). Democracy does not seem to be the mechanism that makes
inequality increase corruption.[16]

The connection of corruption with fairness of the legal system is far stronger –
and this is hardly surprising. While I took care to find an indicator of the fairness
of the legal system that is *not* based upon an underlying measure, it is hardly
surprising that corruption flourishes where the courts give special treatment to
some over others – and where court procedures are not transparent. The least
fair legal systems have a mean corruption score of 2.82, while the most fair
systems have a mean of 8.78 (high scores indicate greater transparency, less
corruption; see Figure A2-4). The fit between legal fairness and corruption is
very strong: $r^2 = .722$ for the 55 cases of the original EIU data and .733 for the
86 cases including the imputed scores.[17]

There is some evidence that inequality of treatment by the courts is strongly
associated with corruption, but the support for a link with economic inequality
is modest at best. There are good theoretical reasons to believe that corruption
stems from economic inequality as well as the fairness of the legal system but
the evidence does not seem compelling. Have we reached a dead end?

Trust, Inequality, and Corruption

Not at all. There *is* a link between inequality and corruption in the aggregate
data, but it is not direct. Inequality leads to corruption because it leads to
resentment of out-groups and enhanced in-group identity. Generalized trust,
the value that is predicated upon the belief that many others are part of your
moral community, is the foundation of the "well-ordered society." When we
believe that "most people can be trusted," we are more likely to give of ourselves
and to look out for the welfare of others. When we believe that "you can't be
too careful in dealing with people," we are likely to be on our guard and to feel
little compunction in taking advantage of others who may not have our best
interests in mind.

Generalized trust is predicated on the notion of a common bond between
classes and races and on egalitarian values (Putnam, 1993, 88, 174; Seligman,

---

[16] The Galbraith inequality data for 1994 show a much stronger connection between inequality
and corruption, especially when I omit countries with a legacy of Communism. Now the r^2 rises
to .528, but for fewer countries (N = 56). The Galbraith data (see n. 17) only cover household
income, rather than wealth more generally, and the smaller number of cases covered would limit
the applicability of the model to be estimated below. The Galbraith data are useful for some
comparisons, but the Deininger-Squire data set is generally considered to be the most reliable.

[17] I plot only the original scores, which are integer values. The imputed scores are not generally
integer values and the plot was unreadable.

1997, 36–7, 41).[18] Faith in others leads to empathy for those who do not fare well, and ultimately to a redistribution of resources from the well-off to the poor. If we believe that we have a shared fate with others, and especially people who are different from ourselves, then gross inequalities in wealth and status will seem to violate norms of fairness. Generalized trust rests upon the psychological foundations of optimism and control, and on the economic foundation of an equitable distribution of resources. Optimism and control lead people to believe that the world is a good place, it is going to get better, and that they can make it better. Economic equality promotes both optimism and the belief that we all have a shared fate across races, ethnic groups, and *classes*.

Corruption, of course, depends upon trust – or "honor among thieves." As it takes two to tango, it takes *at least two to bribe*. Corrupt officials need to be sure that their "partners" *will deliver* on their promises (Lambsdorff, 2002a, 2002b). Lambsdorff (2002a) argues: " . . . if corrupt deals cannot be enforced, this can act as a deterrent to corruption itself." Corruption thrives upon trust, but it cannot be based upon the notion of widespread goodwill and common interests in a society underlying generalized trust. If you believe that the world is a good place and we should do our best to help those with less, we shouldn't be willing to exploit others through corrupt deals. Entrance into a corruption network is not easy. Members of a conspiracy of graft cannot simply assume that others are trustworthy (as generalized trusters do). Treating strangers *as if* they were trustworthy (also as trusters do) can be hazardous at best. And believing that people without any ties to the conspiracy are trustworthy (as generalized trusters do) threatens the integrity of the cabal.

Instead, corruption thrives on *particularized trust*, where people only have faith in their own kind (or their own small circle of malefactors). Particularized trusters strongly distrust outsiders. They fear that people of different backgrounds will exploit them – and in a dog-eat-dog world, you have little choice to strike first before someone exploits you. Gambetta (1993) argues that the Mafia took root in Southern Italy because there were strong in-group ties and weak generalized trust there. Varese (2001, 2) makes much the same argument about the Russian Mafia: "If trust is scarce, and the state is not able or willing to protect property rights, it is sensible to expect a high demand for non-state, private protection. The existence of a demand for protection does not, however, necessarily imply that a supply of protectors will emerge."

Low levels of generalized trust should lead to greater corruption. When people don't trust people who are different from themselves – and reserve their trust for their own kind (particularized trust) – they will feel less guilty about acting dishonestly to people who are not part of their moral community. Where inequality is high, people do not see a common fate with members of out-groups, whether they define these groups in economic, ethnic, or racial terms. If we don't share interests or a fate in common, acting dishonestly to you will not trouble

---

[18] The following section is derived from Uslaner (2004a), which in turn summarizes Uslaner (2002).

me as behaving badly toward those whose destiny I share. Leys (2002, 67) argues that "...corruption seems to be inseparable from great inequality."

Scott (1972, 11–12) presaged this argument more than three decades ago:

> It is not just the strength of...parochial ties that creates many occasions for corruption, but rather their strength in relation to ties of loyalty to the nation. Although the citizen who asks an illegal favor from a relative in the civil service may be forgetting his responsibilities as a citizen, the civil servant in granting the request is acting against the norms of his public position. In all except the most traditional contexts he faces a conflict of values; on the one hand, there are the public values of his government post and, on the other, the compelling obligations he owes to his family. This conflict is often an unequal one. In most traditional societies the plunder of outsiders was approved, even encouraged, while such behavior within the community was punished severely....The compelling nation of parochial ties together with traditional gift-giving practices...account for a portion of the corruption found in underdeveloped nations.

Cheating the out-group does not raise the same moral approbation as behaving badly toward your own in-group.

High inequality makes people wary of out-groups and more likely to seek protection from people who are different from themselves – and strong leaders who reinforce in-group ties, or patrons, will flourish. Clientelism reinforces strong in-group ties and hostility toward out-groups, paving the way for corruption (Xin and Rudel, 2004, 298). In clientelistic societies, the poor may be forced into the informal economy – where they have no legal protection and where they will also be forced to "turn to their ethnic communities...for the provision of public goods and this process can initiate a vicious cycle in which ethnic communalism 'breeds attitudes of illegitimacy'" (Lassen, 2003, 8). Corruption will reinforce strong in-group ties and the belief that out-groups cannot be trusted. Inequality, especially when stratified along group lines, creates dependence upon strong leaders who reinforce in-group ties.

Engaging in petty corruption to help one's in-group may not result in the same moral disapprobation in a highly unequal society as it would in a more prosperous, more egalitarian country. The giving of "little gifts" (or "kola") in Africa is a "moral duty" and refusal to do so "is not only a sign of avarice or of bad manners, but also carries the risk of attracting misfortune" (Olivier de Sardan, 1999, 38–9). Such "gift giving" is an alternative to paying small bribes available to people whose in-groups have connections that will enable them to get by in daily life (Olivier de Sardan, 1999, 41). When a society has strong in-group ties, low trust of out-groups, and either a high degree of inequality (as in Africa and many other societies) or engineered shortages (as in Communist societies), petty corruption becomes morally ambiguous. People don't like it, but they learn to accept it as inevitable and as a way of providing for themselves and their families.

The tradition of giving small gifts to people who have been, or who could be, helpful may make it easier for people to engage in petty corruption. This does not mean that people believe that such payments are morally justified, but only that the means to support your in-group, especially if you see a dominant out-group as privileged, become less troublesome – and the difference between giving small gifts to your in-group and making payments to others also becomes less problematic. In societies with higher generalized trust, people will be more likely to expect fair and equitable treatment, so the immorality of petty corruption is more straightforward.

The relationship between trust and corruption is not simply one way. Highly corrupt societies lead people to mistrust their fellow citizens and to withdraw to their own in-group. Rothstein (2000, 491–2; cf. You, 2005a, 5–7) argues:

In a civilized society, institutions of law and order have one particularly important task: to detect and punish people who are "traitors," that is, those who break contracts, steal, murder, and do other such non-cooperative things and therefore should not be trusted. Thus, if you think that particular institutions do what they are supposed to do in a fair and efficient manner, then you also have reason to believe...that people will refrain from acting in a treacherous manner and you will therefore believe that "most people can be trusted."

Rothstein is almost right. You can't generate trust by the strong arm of the law. Simply rounding up the usual suspects and putting the person(s) who broke into my house some years ago when we were on vacation will not affect my level of trust in out-groups (Uslaner, 2002, 44–7, 242–4). However, an unfair legal system can, at least indirectly, lead to less trust. In the statistical model I shall present in the next chapter, I argue that an unfair legal system will lead to more corruption – and, in turn, to less trust. People don't lose faith in others simply because they exploit the system by being corrupt. Corruption leads to less trust *because it leads to more inequality* (see Chapter 5).

Where is generalized trust high and where is it low? *Across a wide set of nations, across the American states, and over time in the United States – the only country with a long enough time series on the standard survey question on trust[19] – the strongest predictor of trust is the level of economic inequality.* As economic inequality increases, trust declines (Uslaner, 2002, chs. 6, 8; Uslaner and Brown, 2005). Optimism for the future makes less sense when there is more economic inequality. People at the bottom of the income distribution will be less sanguine that they too share in society's bounty. The distribution of resources plays a key role in establishing the belief that people share a common destiny – and have similar fundamental values. When resources are distributed

[19] The question, "Generally speaking, do you believe that most people can be trusted, or can't you be too careful in dealing with people?" was asked first in cross-national samples in *The Civic Culture* in 1960 (Almond and Verba, 1963). It has been regularly asked in the General Social Survey in the United States and periodically in the American National Election Studies. Cross-nationally, it has been asked in each wave of the World Values Survey. The measure here comes from the 1990 and 1995 waves (most recent figure used). For an analysis of why the question refers to trust in strangers and a more general defense of the question, see Uslaner (2002, ch. 3). The cross-national analysis omits countries with a legacy of Communism. I do not do so here, but I do omit China, since it has an anomalously high trust value (see Uslaner, 2002, 226, n. 6).

more equally, people are more likely to perceive a common stake with others. If there is a strong skew in wealth, people at each end may feel that they have little in common with others. In highly unequal societies, people will stick with their own kind. Perceptions of injustice will reinforce negative stereotypes of other groups, making trust and accommodation more difficult (Boix and Posner, 1998, 693).

Putnam (1993, 88, 174) argues that trust will not develop in a highly stratified society. And Seligman (1997, 36–7, 41) goes further: Trust *cannot* take root in a hierarchal culture. Such societies have rigid social orders marked by strong class divisions that persist across generations. Feudal systems and societies based on castes dictate what people can and cannot do based upon the circumstances of their birth. Social relations are based on expectations of what people must do, not on their talents or personalities. Trust is not the lubricant of cooperation in such traditional societies. The assumption that others share your beliefs is counterintuitive, since strict class divisions make it unlikely that others actually have the same values as people in other classes.

A history of poverty with little likelihood of any improvement led to social distrust in a Sicilian village that Edward Banfield (1958, 110) described in the 1950s: "...any advantage that may be given to another is necessarily at the expense of one's own family. Therefore, one cannot afford the luxury of charity, which is giving others more than their due, or even justice, which is giving them their due." The village is a mean world, where daily life is "brutal and senseless" (Banfield, 1958, 109). All who stand outside the immediate family are "potential enemies," battling for the meager bounty that nature has provided. People seek to protect themselves from the "threat of calamity" (Banfield, 1958, 110).

Inequality leads to low levels of trust in strangers. What trust remains is entirely within your group, so there are few moral sanctions for cheating people of a different background. Inequality thus breeds corruption indirectly – by turning people inward and reducing the sanctions, both external and internal, of taking advantage of others. Trust and corruption *are* linked. I show the connection in Figure A2-5 (see also Uslaner, 2004a).[20] Here we see a more robust fit than in the connection between inequality and corruption: $r^2 = .420$ for 83 cases.[21]

---

[20] The graph is a bit difficult to read, because it is difficult to fit the country abbreviations into the graph since many countries have similar values on both variables. The trust question comes from the World Values Survey (see n. 11) – and to increase the number of cases, I imputed values on this measure as well. The variables used to impute trust are gross national product per capita, the value of imports of goods and services, legislative effectiveness, head of state type, tenure of executive (all from the State Failure Data Set), distance from the equator (from Jong-sung You of Harvard University), and openness of the economy (from Sachs and Warner, 1997; data available at http://www.cid.harvard.edu/ciddata/ciddata.html). The $R^2 = .657$, and the standard error of the estimate = .087, N = 63.

[21] Three outliers stand out – Saudi Arabia, Morocco, and Greece – all of which likely have estimates of trust that seem unrealistically high. The Greek estimate of trust is from the World Values Survey, which places it between Canada and Finland and far ahead of more similar states such

The linkages between inequality and low out-group trust and high in-group trust makes the relationship between inequality and corruption more complex. When some groups in a society are considerably worse off than others, they may feel more reliant on corrupt behavior to get their "fair share." The Failed States measure of uneven economic development reflects the relative inequality of resources for different groups within a society – so it is even more theoretically linked to both trust and corruption than is a simple Gini index. If inequality were distributed equally across groups within a society, there would be less reason for in-group trust to dominate over faith in out-groups – and it would not seem so justifiable to cheat an outsider if there were not an economic caste system. This measure *is* strongly related to corruption ($r^2 = .636$, $N = 139$; see Figure A2-6).

The countries with the greatest deviations tend to have relatively high levels of uneven economic development but less corruption than we might expect – and these are countries that have either ethnic tensions (Israel, Jordan, Cyprus, the United States) or have moderate-to-low levels of group inequality but still greater honesty than we might expect. These countries tend to have a large number of native populations (New Zealand, Australia, and Canada), immigrants (France, the United Kingdom, the Netherlands), or guest workers (Germany and France). There is a similar pattern of legal fairness against uneven economic development ($r^2 = .581$, $N = 87$).

The Gini index is only weakly related to the uneven economic development measure ($r^2 = .122$, $N = 85$). When I exclude present and former Communist nations, $r^2 = .208$ and $N = 63$. So it seems that the Failed States measure is a superior measure of inequality. The difficulty in using the measure of uneven economic development to present a direct linkage with corruption is that it works too well. Substituting this measure into the six-equation model I estimate in Chapter 3 leads to insignificant coefficients for many of the variables in the model, including uneven economic development itself – because of multicollinearity among the variables. On the one hand, this high degree of intercorrelation indicates considerable support for the claim of an inequality trap. It suggests a tightly connected syndrome of unequal distribution of wealth by groups, an unfair legal system, low trust, low income and a risky economy, and bad policy choices. However, using this measure gives me little leverage in explicating how each of these factors contributes directly or indirectly to corruption, so I stick with the more conventional Gini index of inequality in the estimates in Chapter 3.

In the next chapter, I shall show the empirical foundation of the inequality trap: inequality leads to low trust; low generalized and high particularized trust lead to high levels of corruption, which in turn produces more inequality.

as Italy, Turkey, and Spain. Greek scholars have told me that they question this score. The values for Saudi Arabia and Morocco are close to New Zealand and Finland, on the one hand, and West Germany and Great Britain on the other. These values are imputed and thus may not be as reliable. Without these countries, the R^2 rises to .478.

Closing the Loop: From Corruption to Inequality

Why worry about inequality? Isn't corruption more of a problem for poor countries than where the distributions of income are unequal (Paldam, 2002)? After all, the simple correlation between inequality and corruption is minuscule, while the relationship between wealth (as measured by the gross domestic product adjusted for purchasing power parity) and corruption is very robust ($r = .888$, $N = 80$).[22] Yes, wealth matters, and corruption both feeds on poverty and keeps poor people poor. But it also contributes to inequality, even if the route from an unequal distribution of income to corruption is indirect. Wealth and inequality are not simply two terms for the same economic result. Three different measures of inequality – the standard World Bank measure (Deininger and Squire, 1996) that I employ in Chapter 3, the more controversial Galbraith measures, and the new United Nations University World Institute for Development Economics Research (WIDER) estimates[23] – all have modest correlations with income, as measured by Penn World Tables as per capita GDP adjusted for purchasing power parity ($r^2 = .144$, .343, and .246, respectively).

Inequality matters because *people think it matters*. When I look at public opinion data on corruption in the next four chapters, I show a direct link with inequality. Even where inequality has been relatively low in the recent past – in transition countries – people see growing inequality as the major consequence of dishonesty by politicians and business leaders. Poverty isn't sufficient to make people lose faith in others and become envious.

Inequality will lead to such jealousy – and the effect is particularly strong for an unfair justice system (Tyler, 1990, chs. 4–5). Chinese peasants have launched many protests and riots against corruption by the rich and their own poverty. A porter carried a bag that brushed against the pants of a government official's wife in 2004; the politician then grabbed the porter's carrying stick, beat him with it, and threatened to have him killed. Local peasants in turn mobbed the provincial capital, overturned cars, and set the town hall on fire. The porter explained the riot: "People can see how corrupt the government is while they barely have enough to eat" (Kahn, 2004, A1). In Northern Kenya, as poor people faced the worst drought in 20 years in 2006, high-level officials were reported to have stolen $1.3 billion in money that was to be allocated to irrigation and road projects to alleviate the effects of the drought. "Look at us selling fruits at intersections while our leaders are feathering their nests and filling their stomachs," a Kenyan woman said (Wax, 2006).

---

[22] The GDP measure comes from the Penn World Tables at http://pwt.econ.upenn.edu/php_site/pwt_index.php.

[23] The Galbraith data can be accessed at http://utip.gov.utexas.edu/data.html. They are more controversial because they are based only on salaries rather than on total income. The WIDER World Economic Inequality Database can be accessed at http://www.wider.unu.edu/wiid/wiid.htm. Here I use the 1994 Galbraith estimates since they cover the largest number of countries. The N's for the three regressions are 78, 64, and 71, respectively.

In Nigeria, where corrupt officials have reportedly pilfered $400 billion over 40 years, one leader, Diepreye Alamieyeseigha, reportedly stole at least $3 billion. He found himself on the wrong side of a political fight within Nigeria and was indicted for money-laundering, arrested in London, and forced to surrender his passport. He mysteriously escaped, disguised as a woman, and fled back to his home province. As a member of the princely class, he claimed immunity from prosecution. Alamieyeseigha's story is but one of many about leaders who have faced justice – real or illusory – in Nigeria. Yet little has changed. Nigeria ranked first on the corruption ratings in 1980–5 and tied for third in the TI rankings in 2005.[24] Nigeria's poverty Eradication Committee was allocated $23,000 in the 2005 state budget, about half that spent on toiletries for public officials (Polgreen, 2005).

No wonder, then, that people look at life fatalistically. In the 1999 State Department surveys in transition countries, no more than 12 percent of any public (Romania) believed that corruption could be eliminated – and only 3 percent in the *most honest countries* (the Czech Republic, Slovakia, and Hungary) agreed with this statement. Barely more than a third of the people in any country believed that malfeasance could be eliminated *or* substantially reduced (Office of Research, 1999, 10). Even where there is a democratic revolution where new leaders promised a clean sweep of miscreants, as in Kyrgyzstan and Georgia in recent years, corruption persists. "There is too much evidence for too many cases.... We could arrest everyone," a Georgia prosecutor said (Greenberg, 2004, 39; Vick, 2005).

Putting the bad guys in jail, holding corrupt leaders accountable through elections, media campaigns, more efficient courts, and anti-corruption campaigns are all worth the effort. Anti-corruption campaigns *can* work – and have succeeded in Singapore and especially in Hong Kong, as I shall discuss in Chapter 7. However, each of these "success stories" rests on specific social conditions that may not be easily replicable. Accountability works best where corruption is already low and punishing the relatively small number of miscreants is easy. Anti-corruption campaigns proved most successful in two small and relatively wealthy states/territories that faced external threats. Corrupt officials *do* lose elections – though punishment at the polls is much more likely where malfeasance is the exception rather than the norm.

Less bureaucratic red tape is one way to reduce corruption, as I show in Chapter 3, and this may be doable. But it won't be easy since strangling regulation stems largely from a weak and risky economy, which rests upon a bed of social tensions.

We ultimately fall back on two dimensions of equality – economic and legal. If we ultimately need to focus on reducing inequality to build up the trust necessary to curb corruption, we come head on to the problem that corruption leads to more inequality. The political power of elites will give them the power

---

[24] Chad and Bangladesh, which tied for first in the 2005 rankings, were not rated in the 1980–5 survey.

to target government spending to programs that will make them even better off. Corrupt governments invest more in big buildings and the military, where contracts can be awarded to those paying the highest price, and less on social services, where there are fewer opportunities to bribe (Gupta, Davoodi, and Alonso-Terme, 2002, 461–2; Gupta, deMello, and Sharan, 2002, 325; Rose-Ackerman, 2004, 6). Education spending, the social policy that may have the greatest potential to reduce inequalities (Rothstein and Uslaner, 2005), will be dramatically lower in highly corrupt countries (Mauro, 1998a, 267) – and educational inequality is much greater where dishonesty is greater (see Chapter 3).

Transfer payments, social insurance, and health spending will also be lower where corruption is high (Mauro, 2002, 349) – all reinforcing inequality. Not only is there less money to spend on social programs such as health and education, but where corruption is rampant, the poor will likely have to make extra "gift" payments to receive routine services – thus imposing extra costs on people who are least able to afford them (Gupta, Davoodi, and Tiongson, 2002, 255). Poor people in Zambia pay 17 percent of their incomes in bribes for medical care, while the middle class pays just 3 percent. These payments are ubiquitous. In India new parents must pay $12 to see their newborn boys and $7 to see a just-born girl, while the poor earn just $1 a day; 90 percent of families with newborns report paying such duties (Dugger, 2005). More than 60 percent of Indians report offering bribes to get a job done. Economist Arun Kumar argues: "Anything to do with the police, anything to do with the judiciary, the poor people have to pay bribes for getting their rights so that poverty becomes more entrenched. Illegal dealings beginning from the top may seep down to those in the bottom rungs, but then it affects them much more than it would affect the top" (Marketplace, 2005). Many low-income people cannot afford even these small bribes, so they go without government services altogether (Kaufmann, Montoriol-Garriga, and Recanatini, 2005). Many people in India reportedly die of malaria and diarrhea because they either can't or won't pay bribes to be admitted to hospitals (Marketplace, 2005). In Romania poor households were twice as likely not to seek medical attention (Anderson et al., 2001, 15) – because they could not afford it.

People are also more likely to confront demands for "extra" payments when they face misfortune, especially when they are victims of crimes (Hunt, 2006, 2, 19). A public radio broadcast in the United States told of how police extorted a large amount of money ($1000 US) from a widow in India whose husband committed suicide. The officers at first refused to release the dead man's body to his widow, then threatened to charge her with murder, and kept demanding more money after the woman's brother paid the asking price (Marketplace, 2005).

Even people who get medical care and an education are "robbed," since in highly corrupt countries the theft of medicines and textbooks is common, the rates of infant mortality and low birthweight babies are twice as high as in countries with more honest governments, and the school dropout rate is five times as great (Gupta, Davoodi, and Tiongson, 2002, 251, 271–2).

Dishonest governments have lower economic growth. The accumulating costs of bribes reduce the overall productivity of business. Foreign firms may be reluctant to pay bribes, so fewer new businesses will get off the ground. In corrupt societies, more business is done off the books, so governments get less money to spend on social programs (Mauro, 1995, 701; Rose-Ackerman, 2004, 4–6). Lower growth in turn means even less money to spend on social programs, thus reinforcing inequality even beyond the direct effects of resources stolen from the treasury (Gupta, Davoodi, and Alonso-Terme, 2002, 460).

Corruption is a curse, then, not just because it is a violation of the law. Corruption rests upon a foundation of inequality and leads to more inequality in turn. And the policies that might redress inequality are less likely to be enacted in corrupt states. This is the inequality trap. In the next chapter, I provide empirical support for these claims.

3

Corruption, Inequality, and Trust

The Linkages Across Nations

> You warn us with appropriate caresses
> That virtue, humble virtue always wins.
> Now please before your moral verve oppresses
> Our middle's empty there it all begins....
> For even honest folk may act like sinners
> unless they've had their customary dinners.
>> From "How to Survive," Berthold Brecht
>> and Kurt Weill, *The Threepenny Opera*[1]

Is there really an inequality trap? And does corruption rest more upon social strains – high inequality and low trust – than upon strong institutions? I present evidence in this chapter for the framework that I have outlined in Chapter 2. I also show that there may be direct linkages between inequality and corruption – first by introducing a new measure of inequality that also reflects in-group trust and second by examining cross-national surveys on people's perceptions of corruption. Where some groups fare much better than others in a society, corruption will be much higher. This measure of uneven economic development encompasses both economic inequality and the social strains that lead to high in-group trust and low out-group faith in others. This new measure is strongly related to corruption, but also to almost all of the other determinants of corruption, leading to problems in estimating either direct or indirect effects in a statistical model, but suggesting very strong support for an inequality trap.

The inequality trap forms a syndrome, not just a single factor leading to corruption. It is a push-me, pull-you dynamic, where there seem to be only two exogenous "fixes" to the problem of corruption, legal fairness, and economic growth. Beyond high inequality and in-group trust and low out-group trust, the regulatory regime contributes to high levels of corruption.

---

[1] The full text is available at http://www.amateurgourmet.com/the_amateur_gourmet/2006/05/how_to_survive.html.

Strangling regulations involve many steps in gaining approval for contracts or policy implementation, involving lots of bureaucrats who can hold their hands out for a "gift" payment. However, a smothering regulatory regime has its roots in a shaky economy and an unfair legal system. An economy at risk in turn reflects internal conflicts and ethnic tensions, as well as . . . inequality. It is far from clear that an unfair legal system can be created through straight-forward institutional design. We can create more courts, we can make justice more efficient (more trials in less time, more judges appointed), and we can train the police force to perform better. Yet it is not so easy to make the legal system *fair*. We may be able to generate strong economic growth in our drive to reduce corruption. While economic growth is essential to reducing inequality, rapid development of an economy creates winners and losers – thus increasing inequality at least in the short run. A strong economy *is* a stimulant to the reduction of corruption, but the stickiness of corruption and the weak relationship between economic growth and malfeasance suggest that good economic policy alone will not suffice to end the legacy of corruption.[2]

I show that an honest government, more so than an effective state, will be more likely to achieve positive outcomes and policies – especially on the sorts of social policies that are most likely to reduce inequality and boost trust. Then I point to another important consequence of corruption: high levels of street crime, especially pickpocketing. Malfeasance at the top encourages street crime far more than delinquency promotes dishonesty at the top.

The inequality trap is more than a set of aggregate statistical relationships. It reflects *how people think about corruption*. I show later in this chapter, as well as more explicitly in Chapters 5, 6, and 7, that where inequality is high, or increasing, people see corruption as both stemming from unequal relationships and reinforcing inequality. I examine two cross-national surveys in this chapter, the Gallup International Millennium survey and Transparency International's Global Corruption Barometer. While the evidence is not uniform, there is support, in two-level (individual- and country-level effects) models, that higher degrees of inequality and low out-group trust lead to greater public worries about corruption.

The Aggregate Model

The inequality trap is not a simple question of what leads to higher corruption. A simultaneous equation model is necessary to untangle the effects of inequality,

---

[2] Using several measures of real growth in GDP and multiple measures of inequality and economic growth, I found almost no correlation between growth and inequality or growth and corruption. GDP per capita adjusted for purchasing power parity (from Penn World Tables) is more strongly related to inequality, but even here the relationship is only moderate: $r^2 = .144$ for the World Bank Ginis from Deininger and Squire (1996) and .251 for the average Ginis from You and Khagram (2005). Using measures of economic growth from the International Country Risk Guide (ICRG) and from the United Nations (http://hdr.undp.org/statistics/data), the r^2 values for regressions on growth and corruption vary from .05 to .10.

trust, and corruption upon each other. I shall outline the model below, to be estimated by two-stage least squares, which permits me to estimate what is called a non-recursive system of equations. Simply put, such a system allows for inequality to affect corruption (indirectly through trust) and then for corruption to lead back to more inequality. I focus on what factors shape each of these parts of the syndrome – inequality, trust, and corruption – as well as three other variables that are key elements in my model: strangling regulation, the riskiness of the economy, and government effectiveness. I shall discuss the model below, as well as the measurement of variables. Effective government is particularly difficult to measure, so I focus on my new indicator for it in some detail.

I treat legal fairness as exogenous. I don't believe that legal fairness is in any sense an "unmoved mover" or an institution that is easily designed. I do not include it as a part of the model to be explained for two reasons. First, if I used the same predictors for legal fairness that I did for corruption or strangling regulation or economic inequality, everything would be connected to everything else and it would be difficult to disentangle what shaped what. When I examine an alternative measure of economic inequality, uneven economic development, this is exactly what happens. Uneven economic development is strongly related to many other parts of the syndrome – and this high degree of interrelationships makes statistical relationships difficult to estimate. Second, outside of the same factors that shape corruption, it is unclear how we can get a more fair legal system. The theory about the effects of legal fairness is strong (see Tyler, 1990), but much weaker on how to get institutions to "behave better."

I now move to a more comprehensive model of the determinants of corruption, trust, and inequality. I add three other factors to the mix: the level of regulation in a society, the overall risk rating by the International Country Risk Guide (ICRG), and a measure of government effectiveness.

A highly regulated economy can lead to greater corruption in two ways. First, when the government takes a dominant role in the economy, it creates many access points for entrepreneurs to "seize the state." Business leaders "capture" the state by paying off public officials to provide them with private benefits. Businesspeople and bureaucrats work together to profit at the expense of the rest of those in society (by cutting growth rates). Second, high regulation leads business leaders to evade taxes (Friedman, Johnson, Kaufmann, and Zoido-Lobaton, 2000; Hellman, Jones, and Kaufmann, 2003). Since regulation is also endogenous to the institutions and policies of the state, I need an equation for the extent of state regulation.

The regulation measure comes from the World Bank governance indicators for 2004 (Kaufmann, Kraay, and Mastruzzi, 2005). Strangling regulation is different from steering economic or environmental policy. The World Bank measure is a composite index including restrictions on imports, exports, ownership of business by non-residents, discriminatory tariffs and protections, burdensome regulations in conducting and starting businesses, wage and price controls, foreign investment restrictions, unfair competition and trade, the efficiency of the tax system, price stability, distortionary taxes, and restrictions on competition (Kaufmann, Kraay, and Mastruzzi, 2005, 106–7). Zimbabwe, Belarus, and Iran rank as having the most intrusive regulation, while Luxembourg, Singapore, Iceland, and Finland have the least. Such strangling regulation is the product of an unfair legal system as well as a high level of risk.

Investors will be wary of doing business in countries with high levels of corruption. When countries receive a high risk rating, they will rely more upon the unofficial economy, on the one hand (Rose-Ackerman, 2004, 6) and on strangling regulations that make it difficult for firms out of favor to do business in a country. Risk is endogenous since I expect it to stem from corruption – and, through encouraging strangling regulation, to lead to further corruption. But risk depends upon more than corruption. Inequality should produce social strains that make investing risky – and ethnic tensions and other internal conflicts should also make investors wary.

Effective government is important for two reasons. First, an ineffective government is likely to adopt policies that may be less responsive to pressing problems than to pressure from powerful groups (Rothstein and Teorell, 2005, 6). Second, governments must deliver the services they promise – and do so fairly (Rothstein and Teorell, 2005, 5). This is *not* simply reiterating that effective governments are free from corruption. Effective government includes making laws; enforcing them; and making sure that service delivery is fair, efficient, and open to influence by all citizens.

There have been several attempts to measure effective government, mostly in the United States. The most prominent is David R. Mayhew's (1991) measure of the number of important laws passed by the United States Congress over time. Another set of measures of effective government in the American states is performance rankings on financial management, capital management, human resources, "managing for results," and information technology in a study by the Government Performance Project (GPP) of Governing magazine and the Maxwell School of Citizenship at Syracuse University. The GPP used program information, a survey, and "interviews [with] budget officers, auditors, public managers, auditors, academics, and legislative aides in every state" (Knack, 2002, 775). An additional measure for the states is the number of Ford Foundation/Kennedy School of Government (Harvard University) awards for innovation a state has won (King, Zeckhauser, and Kim, 2001).

These measures have gotten considerable currency in work on American politics – especially Mayhew's measure of major laws enacted and variations on it. However, the measure of important laws is too specific to the American system of dispersed powers, which allow small numbers of legislators (sometimes even a single individual) to become obstructionists, thus making it difficult to enact legislation. Most other democracies are parliamentary systems, where enacting legislation is far easier. The GPP project is a rather thin measure of the quality of government. Surely, information technology and financial management are important for a government agency – but they are hardly the defining characteristics of what makes one government "effective" and another "ineffective."

Cross-nationally, the World Bank Governance project has a much broader indicator of government effectiveness (Kaufmann, Kraay, and Mastruzzi, 2005, 104–5). The World Bank measure includes, among other items: ratings of administrative and technical skills of the civil service, government instability, the quality of the bureaucracy, policy consistency, management of public debt, the effectiveness of the executive, "consensus building," debt management, trust in government, the consistency of policy-making, global e-government, and debt management. This measure is a remarkable achievement, but it may be too inclusive. Instability and trust in government, for example, are better considered as consequences of effective government rather than as components.

I propose a new measure of effective government focusing on government capacity, efficiency, and inclusiveness. The measure is the factor scores from a factor analysis of six questions asked in a cross-national survey of business executives. The 2004 Executive Opinion Survey of the World Economic Forum asked businesspeople to rate their country on judicial independence, the efficiency of the legal and legislative systems, the wastefulness of government spending, the favoritism of government decision-making, and the transparency of government decision-making.

Surveys of businesspeople are not the same as surveys of the public – but they have been widely used in research, especially on corruption. Kaufmann, Kraay, and Mastruzzi (2007b) admit that businesspeople may be more likely to rate government more favorably than the mass public – and in Chapter 6, I provide strong evidence for this when I examine surveys of the mass public, business entrepreneurs, and public officials in Estonia, Romania, and Slovakia. However, their comparison of mass and public responses to questions of good governance show that mass and elite responses are highly correlated across countries (Kaufmann, Kraay, and Mastruzzi, 2007b). I present the full question wordings and scorings in the appendix to this chapter. The government effectiveness measure is a factor score of these six measures. All six measures loaded very highly on a single factor. Five of the six indicators had loadings of .90 or higher; the wastefulness of government spending had a marginally lower loading (.876). All six of the measures had communalities of .8 or greater (see Table A3-1).

This measure is attractive since it focuses on the capacity and fairness of government policy-making: An independent judiciary is critical to the rule of law, but independence is not sufficient. The efficiency of the court system matters as well. Long delays in legal affairs can lead to inequities in justice and make firms reluctant to enter into contracts. They may also punish those out of favor with the state. A strong parliament will be more likely to represent a larger number of interests than we might expect from an all-powerful executive.

Wastefulness of government spending and favoritism of government decision-making seem close to corruption – but they are not identical to it and are closer to the other measures in this index than to the TI measure of corruption. Government spending can be wasteful even in the absence of corruption – and favoritism in decision-making is at best a weak indicator of corruption. In some contexts, this may be quite acceptable – and hardly illegal. Finally, the transparency of government decision-making is important for corruption – but as defined here, it is also central for effective government. People cannot influence their government if they do not know what it is doing and how it is doing it.

Perhaps surprising is the modest correlation of these six indicators with a question on red tape in the bureaucracy: How much time does your firm spend in negotiating with government officials? The red tape question correlates only at $-.364$ (N $=$ 84) and does not load on the same factor. A measure of bureaucratic quality from the ICRG has a higher correlation (r $= .734$, N $- 81$), but even this measure is not so strongly related to the other quality of governments as the other six measures are to each other. Effective government is not the same thing as service delivery – and this should be reassuring. The quality of government ought to reflect more than filling out forms and fighting with petty bureaucrats – and by this measure, it does.

My measure of government effectiveness is related to both fairness and corruption, but it is not based upon such measures. The indicators for the legal system are conceptually distinct from the fairness of the legal system as measured by the Executive Intelligence Unit.[3] The new measure is strongly related to the World Bank effectiveness measure for 2004 (r $= .870$), but it seems more straightforward in interpretation. I present the country scores for the government effectiveness index in Figure A3-1. I move now to a discussion of the model.

The Corruption Model

I estimate a six-equation model of corruption across 62 countries – the number of countries on which I have data on all variables in the model.[4] The six endogenous variables are corruption (the TI index), generalized trust (with imputed values), the level of regulation in a country (from the World Bank Governance data set for 2004), economic inequality, the overall stability and credit worthiness of a country,[5] and how effective a country's government is. The key questions I pose are:

- Is there a direct relationship between trust and corruption?
- Is there a direct relationship between economic inequality and trust – and does it flow from inequality to trust (Uslaner, 2002, ch. 8), trust to inequality

---

[3] The simple correlations with the (imputed) measure of legal fairness are .754 for legal efficiency and .762 for judicial independence. These two measures have a correlation of .943 (all N $=$ 84).

[4] The results are very similar to those for a simpler instrumental variable estimation with 73 cases focusing solely on corruption. I use the TI Corruption Perceptions Index for 2004 in this analysis.

[5] The International Country Risk Guide of Political Risk Services is an index of 22 indicators of the overall level of risk in a country's economic and political systems. The ICRG overall risk index is composed of 12 political components, 5 financial, and 5 economic risk factors. Higher scores indicate greater risk. The June 2005 data I employ rank Norway (1), Luxembourg (2), and Switzerland (2) as the most stable/least risky countries in this sample, with Zimbabwe (137), Serbia (131), and Nigeria (124) as the most troubled countries. The measures are used by international organizations, export credit agencies, banks, and other commercial lenders – as well as private businesses – to determine the creditworthiness of a country. The measure is thus an indication of the financial and political stability of a country. See http://www.prsgroup. com/commonhtml/methods.html and http://www.prsgroup.com/commonhtml/methods.html#_ International_Country_Risk.

(Knack and Keefer, 1997), or both ways? A direct relationship between inequality and trust and a similar connection between trust and corruption would provide support for my argument that inequality has an *indirect* impact on corruption.

- Does corruption in turn lead to more inequality? Corruption slows economic growth (Leite and Weidmann, 1999; Mauro, 1995, 701; Tanzi, 1998, 585). It reduces the amount of money available for various government programs, including the government share of the gross domestic product and expenditures on the public sector, for education, and transfers from the rich to the poor (Mauro, 1998b, 269; Tanzi, 1998, 582–6). So corruption should lead to more inequality – *even if there is not a direct link from inequality to corruption.*

- Is the fairness of the legal system an important determinant of corruption? The fairness of the legal system should also shape the level of regulation in a society. An independent and fair judiciary should also lead to less regulation. Political leaders would not attempt to control business if they believe that the courts would step in and challenge attempts to capture the state.

- Does corruption lead to less stable and less effective government? Corruption should lead investors to shy away from a country, for fear of expropriation or being compelled to function in a weak legal environment (Rose-Ackerman, 2004, 6). Corruption should also lead to less effective government. When leaders steal from the public purse, they should be less responsive to the broader public.

- Does ineffective government lead to greater corruption? Does effective government lead to better policy choices – especially policies that reduce inequality and create greater support for the regime?

- Do higher risk ratings lead to less effective government or to poor policy choices? Countries with higher risk ratings should be likely to adopt strangling regulations that distort market competition. These regulations in turn should lead to greater corruption in a vicious cycle.

- Do trust, corruption, a country's risk rating, and effective government rest upon institutional foundations – or upon cleavages within society? I expect that institutional factors should *not* be the key determinants of trust, corruption, a country's risk rating, or effective government – except for the fairness of the legal system. Rather, corruption should depend upon trust and policy choices; risk ratings and government effectiveness should depend upon corruption and the health of a country's economy – and on its domestic conflicts. And trust, in turn, depends on economic equality and its historical legacies of culture and conflict.

- Putnam (1993, 111, 180) argues that trust and good government go hand in hand: Good government promotes trust (cf. Levi, 1998; Rothstein, 2000) and trust promotes good government. Is there a reciprocal relationship or does it only go one way – and, if so, which way? I expect that trust will encourage good government, but that good government should not lead to greater trust (Uslaner, 2002, chs. 2, 7).

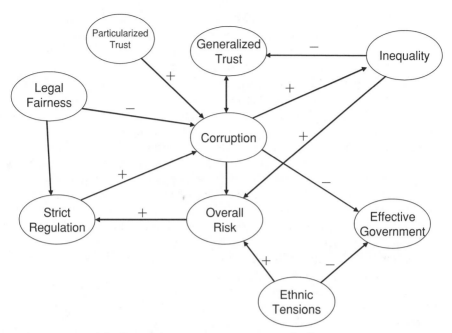

FIGURE 3-1. Model of Inequality, Trust, Corruption, and Effective Government.

The endogenous relationships I test are from (see Figure 3-1 for a diagrammatic presentation of this model):

- trust → corruption
- inequality → trust → inequality
- government regulation → corruption
- inequality → overall risk
- corruption → effective government → policy choices
- trust → effective government → trust

Some key connections involving exogenous factors are:

- legal fairness → corruption → overall risk → strict regulation → corruption
- legal fairness → strict regulation → corruption
- internal conflicts → trust, overall risk, effective government

For both corruption and effective government, I estimated both basic and extended equations. The extended equations add structural factors that might loom large in the effectiveness of government institutions. Higher levels of democracy, as reflected in Freedom House's index of civil and political rights, should lead to less corruption and more effective government (Adsera, Boix, and Payne, 2000; Treisman, 2000). Higher levels of bureaucratic quality (ICRG) should also be associated with better government and less corruption. So should a proportional representation electoral system and a parliamentary, as opposed to a Presidential, legislative system. Linz (1990) has argued that Presidential systems lead to chief executives to centralize power – and to become more corrupt (cf. Kunicova and Rose-Ackerman, 2005, Lambsdorff, 2005a). Proportional representation systems disperse accountability, compared to plurality systems, where there is a direct connection between a representative and her constituency. Voters who must choose from a list of candidates, rather than voting for one individual, will have fewer opportunities to punish corruption (Persson, Talbellini, and Trebbi, 2000, 4, 11–12; Rose-Ackerman, 2004, 12).

The extended equations test for the impact of structural factors. I shall not report them for a simple reason: The structural factors failed to reach statistical significance. In neither equation do the form of electoral or legislative system matter. Nor are there effects for the quality of the bureaucracy. Democracy does not matter, perhaps surprisingly, for effective government. For completeness, I include the Freedom House measure in the basic model for corruption – and "move" the other variables to the list of instruments used for the system. Yet, the simple institutional measure of democracy *does not lead to less corruption*. The coefficient has the wrong sign.

For the corruption equation, I include the Freedom House democracy measure,[6] trust (imputed), the level of regulation, the fairness of the legal system (imputed), ethnic fractionalization, and following Paldam (2002, see also Lambsdorff, 1999, 7; Mauro, 1995, 701), the wealth of a country, measured as GDP per capita. I also include a measure of particularized trust. It is not easy to get measures of in-group trust that are distinct from generalized faith in others. Surveys that have multiple questions on whom we trust – or how we evaluate in- and out-groups – offer a way to measure these two forms of trust separately (Uslaner, 2002, 52–6). However, there are no comparable data available cross-nationally. So I must rely upon a proxy for particularized trust: whether a state restricts members of minority religions from converting others to their faith. This measure comes from the State and Religion data set of Fox (2006). While at best an approximation – perhaps a crude one – it does tap the idea of only trusting one's own in-group. Religious fundamentalists tend to trust only people of their own faith – and when they do participate in civic life, they join exclusively religious organizations (Schoenfeld, 1978, 64; Uslaner, 2002, 87–8; 2001). Restrictions on conversion are the mark of fundamentalist domination of the state – and I use this measure as a proxy for particularized trust. Such restrictions are indicative of high in-group trust and low tolerance toward out-groups.

Ethnic diversity may lead to a strong sense of ethnic identity, which in turn, Lassen (2003, 8) argues, may result in "the political process allocat[ing] excludable public goods and transfers based on ethnic characteristics (favoritism)." Lassen (2003) and Alesina, Devleeschauwer, Easterly, Kurlat, and Wacziarg (2003) find strong support for the argument, though Treisman (1999) and Leite and Weidmann (1999) failed to find significant effects for ethnic diversity upon corruption. I thus include the Alesina et al. (2003) measure of ethnic

---

[6] I use a trichotomized measure of free (+1), partially free (0), and not free (−1) countries.

fractionalization in the equation. In the equations for overall risk and govern-ment effectiveness, I use a measure of ethnic tensions in a society, but here I follow the existing literature and employ a measure of ethnic fractionalization.

The model for corruption may appear thin and different from many in the literature. However, I did many sensitivity tests for variables discussed in the literature and have found no reason to add any of them to my model. Specifi-cally, I did not find significant relationships for the level of public sector wages (LaPorta et al., 1999; Mauro, 1997, 5; Tanzi, 1998, 573; Treisman, 2000; but cf. Rose-Ackerman, 1978, 90–1); the extractive resource (oil) base (Leite and Weidmann, 1999); the size of the unofficial economy (Lambsdorff, 1999); the level of newspaper readership (Adsera, Boix, and Payne, 2000); federal versus unitary governments or the share of government revenues spent at the local level (Treisman, 1999; Fisman and Gatti, 2000); the level of political stability (Leite and Weidmann, 1999, 20; Treisman, 2000); the level of democracy in a country (You and Khagram, 2005); or the use of closed- or open-list pro-portional representation systems (Kunicova and Rose-Ackerman, 2005). All of these variables faded into insignificance within the model I present below. At the bottom of Table 3-1, I also list the exogenous variables used as instruments.

I do not include inequality in the corruption model. The weak relationships between the standard measures (Gini indices) of inequality and corruption led me to argue that the relationship should be indirect – through trust. This is the model I posit here.

The story of legal fairness can be repeated for the other determinants of corruption, both direct and indirect. Uneven economic development is strongly related to trust ($r^2 = .421, N = 80$), strangling regulation ($r^2 = .580, N = 87$), the riskiness of the economy ($r^2 = .587, N = 84$), and per capita GDP ($r^2 = .620, N = 84$). It is also strongly related to a dummy variable for mem-ber countries of the Organization for Economic Cooperation and Development (OECD; $r^2 = .472, N = 87$), which in turn is highly correlated with all of the other measures.

For the trust model, I largely follow the cross-national model in Uslaner (2002, ch. 8) in arguing that the level of economic inequality and the share of the population that is Protestant should be key factors shaping trust. I have already laid out the argument on inequality. The "Protestant ethic" is an indi-vidualistic creed: To succeed in a competitive world, we need to rely upon other people. In collectivist societies, people can rely upon their peer groups and get by with particularized trust. In individualistic societies, generalized trust becomes essential. Trust is higher in individualistic societies (Triandis, 1995, 126) and Protestant societies are more individualistic (Uslaner, 2002, 232, n. 21) and less hierarchical (Inglehart, 1999, 92–3) than other countries.

Civil war can tear a country apart, so I expect that countries that have had civil wars are less likely to be less trusting.[7] While there is little evidence

---

[7] This relationship is clearly endogenous, but it is beyond the present work to examine the endo-geneity.

that democracy leads to greater trust, there is ample support for the claim that Communism depresses trust. The repressive Communist system made it treacherous for ordinary citizens to trust each other – at best people had faith in their close friends and family members, and even then there were often risks (Gibson, 2001). I thus include a dummy variable for former and present Communist regimes. Finally, I test whether there is a link from government effectiveness to trust. While this is a prominent theme in much of the literature on trust (see the citations above), I do not expect to find such a connection. Generalized trust develops early in life and is largely resistant to experiences, including those with the government (Uslaner, 2002, chs. 2, 4–5).

The equation for business regulations includes the fairness of the legal system, the openness of the economy to external trade,[8] the growth rate of the gross domestic product, and the overall risk rating by the ICRG. An economy open to foreign trade, on the other hand, would give foreign investors more of a say in how companies are run. To be able to export to foreign countries, a firm must be free of tight control from above. Imports also lessen central control over the economy. Open markets are widely considered to be both a cause and an effect of low corruption (Leite and Weidmann, 1999, 20; Mauro, 1997, 4; Rose-Ackerman, 2004, 10–11; Treisman, 2000; You and Khagram, 2005). Instead of a direct link, I posit an indirect connection beginning with strangling regulations. Open markets will pressure countries to have more transparent regulatory regimes – which in turn will lead to less corruption.

When the economy is growing at a fast pace, political leaders might be more wary about scaring investors away with strangling regulations. On the other hand, the more a country is perceived to be a bad risk, the more the leadership may try to regulate the economy. A country that already is at risk is likely to overcompensate its regulations – and to make things more complicated than they already are. Leaders may adopt such strangling regulations either to appear to be putting some order into a chaotic economy – or simply as reacting defensively to prevent foreign creditors from gaining too much power in their countries.

The equation for inequality includes trust and corruption – and also the dummy variable for former and present Communist countries and the shares of the population that are Muslim and Protestant. Eastern bloc countries should have lower levels of inequality, as should both countries with large Muslim and large Protestant populations. Protestantism stresses individual achievement. Achievement-oriented values stress equality of opportunity rather than equality of results. The greater wealth of Protestant nations and the higher levels of trust in individualistic nations lead to the expectation that Protestant countries will have lower levels of inequality. Islam has placed greater emphasis on collective goals, especially on one's economic responsibility to the larger community (as reflected in the prohibition on charging interest on loans). So it should not

---

[8] The measure of the openness of the economy was provided by Jong-sung You. In the Gini equation, the Muslim share of population comes from http://www.islamicpopulation.com.

be surprising to find a powerful coefficient on percent Muslim for economic equality (Esposito and Voll, 1996, 25).

The model for overall risk includes economic inequality, corruption, and measures of internal conflict and ethnic tensions, both from the ICRG. Here my argument is straightforward: The creditworthiness of a country reflects its social conflicts as well as the misdeeds of its public officials. Corruption should have the greatest impact on risk ratings, but social conflicts should not be far behind. A country should be a bad risk if its social fabric is torn. Economic inequality clearly contributes to such strains. I also use two other measures, both from the ICRG, that should contribute to risk: the level of internal conflicts and ethnic tensions.

Finally, the government effectiveness includes trust (imputed), corruption, ethnic tensions, the poverty level (from the ICRG), and a legacy of Communism. The extended equation also includes structural factors that have played a prominent role in the literature: the level of democracy (from Freedom House), the quality of the bureaucracy (from the ICRG), whether a country has a Presidential or parliamentary system, and whether a country has a proportional representation or plurality electoral system.

Putnam (1993, 103) argues that "civic regions" in Italy, which are marked by high levels of trust, have better government: "Political leaders in civic regions are...readier to compromise than their counterparts in less civic regions....leaders there are readier to resolve their conflicts." Uslaner (1993, ch. 6; 2002, 212–15) links the increasing contentiousness and use of obstructionist tactics in the United States Congress to declining levels of trust. I expect that trust should be a key factor in shaping effective government, *even if there is no evidence for a linkage going from government effectiveness to trust.*

The linkage between corruption and ineffective government needs no elaboration. Similarly, the transition from Communism has not been smooth for most countries in Central and Eastern Europe. Not only does corruption remain high and trust remain low, but governments are not generally considered effective. The difficulties in governing that plague transition countries were expressed by an academic from the region, who commented at a conference I attended: "There are two types of governments in Europe, those that always get reelected (Western Europe) and those that never get reelected (Central and Eastern Europe)." The measures of ethnic tensions and poverty from the ICRG are indicators of the social strains that make effective government difficult. High poverty rates place additional demands on government and add to the social strains in a society – so poverty should lead to less effective government.

Evaluating the Model

All six of the equations perform very well in accounting for corruption, trust, regulation of the economy, and inequality. Even though R^2 is not strictly appropriate for two-stage least squares estimation, the high values for R^2 and the low values of the standard error of the estimate (see Table 3-1) give us confidence

TABLE 3-1. *Simultaneous Equation Estimation of Corruption*

Variable	Coefficient	Std. Error	t Ratio
Corruption equation			
Trust (imputed)	5.810****	1.612	3.60
Regulation of business	.933***	.358	2.60
Fairness of legal system	.626***	.211	2.96
GDP per capita (ICRG)	.405***	.156	2.60
Ethnic fractionalization (Alesina)	1.256	.573	2.19
Restrictions on conversions minority religions	−.483**	.280	−1.73
Freedom House 2003 democratization	−.426	.327	−1.30
Constant	−.482	.773	−.62
Trust equation			
Economic inequality (Gini index)	−.515***	.191	−2.70
Civil war	−.091****	.025	−3.62
Protestant share of population 1980	.200****	.059	3.40
Former Communist nation	−.110***	.042	−2.60
Government effectiveness	.014	.021	.68
Constant	.502****	.075	6.70
Regulation equation			
Fairness of legal system	.239***	.082	2.91
Openness of economy to trade	.229***	.092	2.48
Real growth in gross domestic product	−.083	.068	−1.21
Overall country risk (ICRG)	−.014****	.003	−4.71
Constant	.378	.848	.44
Inequality equation			
Trust (imputed)	−.135	.190	−.71
Corruption	−.028***	.009	−3.26
Former Communist nation	−.163****	.026	−6.38
Protestant share of population 1980	.119	.052	2.28
Muslim percent of population	−.001****	.000	−3.70
Constant	.575****	.036	15.76
Overall risk equation			
Economic inequality (Gini index)	31.580	25.424	1.24
Corruption	−8.378****	.958	−8.74
Internal conflicts (ICRG)	7.066****	1.500	4.71
Ethnic tensions (ICRG)	3.898***	1.628	−2.39
Constant	168.766****	15.924	10.60
Government effectiveness equation			
Trust (imputed)	.761	.946	.80
Corruption	.498****	.064	7.80
Ethnic tensions (ICRG)	−.093**	.047	−2.00
Poverty level 2005 (ICRG)	−.355****	.090	−3.94
Former Communist nation	−.397***	.144	−2.76
Constant	−1.425****	.227	−6.28

* p < .10; ** p < .05; *** p < .01; **** p < .0001 (all tests one-tailed except for constants)

TABLE 3-1 (*continued*)

Summary of Models

Equation	R²	S.E.E.	Mean	F Statistic
Corruption	.900	.855	5.276	68.51
Trust	.653	.081	.299	19.73
Regulation of business	.818	.392	.624	65.95
Inequality (Gini index)	.518	.072	.358	11.27
Overall risk (ICRG)	.850	13.756	50.839	80.57
Government effectiveness	.835	.428	.158	54.91
		N = 62		

Instrumental variables: Religious fractionalization (from Alesina, Devleeschauwer, Easterly, Kurlat, and Wacziarg, 2003); English legal tradition (from the Levine-Loyaza-Beck data set at http://www.worldbank.org/research/growth/llbdata.htm); GNP per capita (State Failure Data); constraints on the executive branch of government (Glaeser, LaPorta, Lopez-de-Silanes, and Shleifer, 2004); military in politics (at www.freetheworld.com); terrorism risk (ICRG); bureaucratic quality (ICRG); and parliamentary system and proportional representation (from the Data Base of Political Institutions at http://www.worldbank.org/wbi/governance/pubs/wps2283.html).

in the models. The R² values range from .518 (for inequality) to .900 (for corruption) and the standard errors of the estimates are, relative to the means, generally quite small. The models fit the data well.

The most important result is that there is an indirect linkage between inequality and corruption and it goes through trust. As we move from the low level of inequality in Switzerland to the very high level in South Africa, trust declines by 20 percent. As we move from the least trusting country (Brazil) to the most trusting (Norway), corruption decreases on the 10-point TI scale by 3.6 units. This is equivalent to moving from the low transparency of Panama to that of the United States or Belgium. The impact of inequality on trust is sufficient to produce a considerable effect on corruption. A shift from a country ranking highest on legal fairness to one at the bottom corresponds to a shift of 3.1 on the TI index – from Poland to the level of Portugal or Israel.

A rise in particularized trust would lead to a 1.5-unit decrease in the TI index – making Cyprus almost as corrupt as Brazil. A shift from the most strict regulatory regime to the least (from Nigeria to Luxembourg) would bring a country to the level of Israel or Japan (6.36 on the 10-point scale), while moving from a "not free" to a "free" country has a more modest shift of .85 points *in the wrong direction*. Ethnic diversity seems to lead to *less* corruption rather than more: The coefficient is positive rather than negative (the simple correlation is −.386). But income matters: The richest group of countries in the ICRG per capita GDP measure are 2.05 units "more honest" than the poorest.

Trust has the greatest impact on corruption, as measured by the change in the TI index as we move from the least to the most trusting nation. The other effects, in order, are the regulatory regime, the fairness of the legal system, a nation's GDP per capita, and particularized trust. Democratic regimes are no more likely to be honest than non-democracies. *Institutional factors do not loom large in determining the level of corruption in a country except insofar as they lead to more or less equitable treatment of citizens before the law or except insofar as they promote economic equality and an economic system free of political interference.* This does *not* imply that governments cannot regulate the economy – the Western European countries that have the least "regulation" are all welfare states. It *does* suggest that politicians must take care in *how* they regulate. The equation for corruption performs extremely well *without any standard institutional variables such as centralization, parliamentary system, type of electoral list, type of executive – each of which fell to insignificance when added.*

The model for trust confirms the results in Uslaner (2002, ch. 8): Eastern bloc countries are far less trusting (by an average of 11 percent) – so that if Estonia did not have a legacy of Communism, its citizens might be as trusting as the Austrians. Protestant societies are more trusting: The difference in trust between the country with the largest Protestant population (Norway) and the smallest (among them Turkey) is 20 percent. Countries that have experienced civil wars are 9 percent less trusting. But the largest effect comes from economic inequality. As we move from low values on the Gini index (Belgium) to the highest (South Africa), trust declines by 21 percent – the difference between Switzerland and South Africa. The coefficient for government effectiveness on trust is insignificant.

In the model for regulation, the levels of risk and the fairness of the legal system are the most important predictors. The state with the greatest risk level will be very likely to have a strangling regulatory regime – going from the lowest risk level to the highest leads to a change in regulatory quality equivalent to the distance from Norway to Indonesia. The gap in legal fairness is considerably smaller (.956 on the standardized scale rather than 1.722), but still equal to the gap between Japan and Uganda. An open economy also makes strangling regulation less likely – but here the effect is half that of overall risk. Closing Japanese markets would "only" take that state down to the regulatory level of Pakistan – but still quite a bit better than the Ukraine or Kenya. A growing economy leads to less strangling regulation. The fastest growing economy will rank .29 lower on the standardized regulation scale.

The model for inequality suggests that economic inequality shapes trust rather than the other way around (cf. Uslaner, 2002, 232–6). Present and former Communist countries are considerably more egalitarian, by an average of .16. The Muslim share of the population is significantly associated with reduced inequality.[9] *The share of Protestants in a society is incorrectly signed.* Finally, corruption leads to more inequality: The difference between the most and the least corrupt country leads to a change in Gini coefficients of .23 – which is the difference in inequality between Belgium and the Philippines or Costa Rica.

---

[9] The inequality gap between countries with no Muslims and the largest Muslim share (Indonesia) is .194; Indonesia is an outlier in this sample (which does not include many Muslim countries). Less extreme is Turkey, and here the difference in effects is reduced to .07.

The equation for inequality is the least successful of the four, according to three different criteria: the lower (though still far from modest) R^2, the low F ratio, and the high t-value of the constant. Nevertheless, the equation still performs well and the other estimations all support my overall framework.

Corruption has the strongest effect on the overall risk rating: The most "honest" country ranks 68.7 points lower on the ICRG ranking than does the most corrupt. Finland would be as risky for investors as Argentina if it were as corrupt as Bangladesh. But internal conflicts also have a powerful effect on risk. The highest levels of conflict lead to a 42-point shift in risk ratings – the equivalent of a shift from Germany to Israel or Ukraine. The effects of inequality (13 points) and ethnic tensions (18 points) are smaller, but still significant.

As with corruption, the structural variables (Presidential versus parliamentary system, proportional representation versus plurality elections, quality of the bureaucracy, and status as a democracy) are all insignificant in the model for government effectiveness. If the most corrupt country (Bangladesh) were to become as honest as Finland, it would have a government as efficient (or even more so) as Denmark. Trust and poverty are also very important. Raising the trust level of Brazil, the least trusting country, to Norway's top rating would raise its quality of government to midway between Spain and Thailand. Reducing poverty would have a dramatic effect on government effectiveness – a 1.42-unit change on the standardized scale. Changing Bangladesh's poverty level to that of the Nordic countries would not give it as effective a government as we find in Northern Europe, but would move it up to the level of the United States. Low trust and high poverty may not be quite as important as corruption, but they have a major effect on the quality of government. Ethnic tensions are also a significant factor shaping the quality of government: Higher tensions mean less effective government, but the impact is more modest at .47 on the standardized scale. This effect is slightly larger than I find for former Communist countries (−.40).

The effectiveness of government, then, mostly reflects corruption and societal forces. Corrupt governments are by far the least effective. Yet there are powerful effects, both direct and indirect (through corruption), for generalized trust. Trusting countries have better governments, even though there is no evidence of a direct link *back from effective government to generalized trust*. Moreover, trust works not only directly but also as the most significant predictor of corruption. In 1976, American Presidential candidate Jimmy Carter promised the public "a government as good as its people." Seemingly, it is difficult to give the people a government much better than they are.

Escaping the Inequality Trap?

Overall, there is considerable support for my thesis: Inequality leads to lower trust, which in turn is associated with greater corruption. The fairness of the legal system also shapes corruption, both directly and indirectly through the regulatory regime. Social bonds and the distribution of wealth – and justice – play key roles in determining whether a country will be corrupt or transparent. Institutional factors do not matter as much as social bonds, policy choices, and equity.

Not only does inequality lead to greater corruption (albeit indirectly), but corruption leads back to more inequality. This *inequality trap* works both directly – from corruption to inequality – and indirectly, through an unfair legal system, strangling regulation, a risky credit environment, and ineffective governments. This model shows that it is not simply societal factors that constitute the inequality trap. Bad policy choices – economic policies that lead to high risk ratings and strangling regulation – are part of this same syndrome. It would be nice if a simple shift in policy choices could get us out of the trap. In theory, it could. But the same forces that lead from high levels of inequality to low trust to high corruption also lead to strangling regulation, high risk ratings, unfair legal systems, and ineffective government.

There are other routes out of corruption. Wealthy countries are less corrupt (see Chapter 7 on Hong Kong and Singapore). Economic growth leads to less strangling regulation, as do open markets, so there are policy choices that can help in the fight against corruption. Yet, even here, fighting malfeasance is not as simple as selecting better policies that will promote growth, reduce inequality, and lead to more trust and less corruption. Low trust countries close their markets, at least in part because particularized trust makes people wary of dealing with strangers and worried that open markets could lead to threats to their own industries (Uslaner, 2002, 193–7, 245).

Corrupt countries close their markets. Protectionism is another form of protection that businesses buy from politicians. So it seems that we may need honest government to open markets so that we can fight corruption. In the model I have estimated, the link from free trade to less corruption is indirect – by reducing strangling regulations. Open markets lead to demands for less red tape and thus to lower levels of corruption. More critically, the impact of wealth, economic growth, and trade is considerably less than that for other, less malleable factors such as trust and both legal and economic inequality. Treisman (2000) notes, with more than a bit of pessimism, that "huge, effective trade liberalizations" might make "a dent" in corruption. Indeed, this is in part how Singapore and Hong Kong were transformed from high-corruption societies to the top ranking states in the TI index (S. Quah, 1997, 306). Yet these cases are exceptional, unlikely to be mimicked by other nations with great malfeasance among officeholders and businesspeople.

Is It Better to Be Efficient or Clean?

Inequality can be combated by government programs (see Chapter 8 for specific advice), both directly and indirectly. Governments can enact policies that make the poor better off and they can promote policies that stimulate the economy. A growing economy leads to less poverty and inequality (Gupta, Davoodi, and

Alonso-Terme, 2002, 460, 478–9; Mauro, 1995, 706). There is a long literature on how corruption restricts economic growth (see among others Leite and Weidmann, 1999, 25; Mauro, 2002, 342; Rose-Ackerman, 2004, 4–6; Tanzi, 2002, 45–6) as well as support for the claim that corruption increases inequality (see Chapter 2).

How effective is government – specifically effective government – in producing policies that either directly or indirectly reduce inequality and make people's lives better? The insignificant effects of effective government on inequality may not be so consequential if good government is more likely to enact policies that will ameliorate the effects of poverty and inequality. Can effective government do the job or do reductions in poverty and inequality depend more on clean government than an efficient state?

I examine 15 policies and outcomes for which there are good cross-national data and their determinants. These policies and outcomes reflect a range of options and outcomes that enhance markets and especially that improve the quality of life. While the policies and outcomes I examine all refer to laudable goals for the state and society – ranging from free markets to ethical business people – it is social welfare policies that provide benefits for large numbers of people (education, health, and to a lesser extent transfer payments) that offer the greatest potential to combat inequality. These policies, however, depend upon government performance. The adoption of universalistic social welfare policies in Sweden in the 1930s depended upon the public perception that public officials would spend the money honestly (Rothstein and Uslaner, 2005, 53–8).

Does effectiveness or honesty in government matter more in leading to positive policies and outcomes across countries? I estimate models for each of the policies, once including the TI corruption index and once the effective government measure. Which is more powerful in producing policies that reduce inequality directly; lead to greater growth or citizen satisfaction with policies; or promote open markets, tax compliance, and better labor-management relations? These measures come from a variety of sources, including the World Economic Forum (WEF in Table 3-2), the Gallup International Millennium Survey, the United Nations Development Programme, the Economic Freedom in the World Network, and a variety of published or unpublished papers cited in Table 3-3.

The policies and outcomes I consider cover a wide range, including citizen satisfaction with the environment. I also focus on policies that either directly or indirectly encourage economic growth: the WEF growth competitiveness index, market capitalization, opening markets to small and medium firms, the extent of government control of the economy, the extent to which the government rather than the private sector dominates economic consumption, good labor-management relations, how ethical business firms are, and the extent of business involvement in charitable donations. Ethical firms and companies involved in charity should provide a more fertile climate for economic growth by making the business environment safer for investment and more linked to

TABLE 3-2. *Summary of Regressions for Government Effectiveness and Corruption*

Variable	N	Government Effectiveness			Corruption		
		Coefficient	Std. Error	t Ratio	Coefficient	Std. Error	t Ratio
Growth competitiveness ranking 2003 (WEF)	75/76	−9.493****	1.794	−5.29	−14.358****	2.358	−6.17
Tax compliance (WEF)	45	.095**	.055	1.72	.226**	.131	1.74
Expropriations risk 1982–97 (Glaeser et al., 2004)+	64/66	.785****	.201	3.90	1.169****	.181	6.47
Market capitalization (LaPorta, et al., in press)+	43	.111*	.073	1.53	.113**	.042	1.91
Markets open to small/medium firms (LaPorta, et al., in press)+	40	.592****	.128	4.61	.427***	.123	3.47
Index of state-owned enterprises (LaPorta et al., 1999)	35	.443*	.279	1.59	.653**	.274	2.39
Government consumption/GDP(freetheworld.org)	72/74	−.581***	.203	−2.86	−.802***	.305	−2.63
Good labor-management relations (WEF)	70	.365****	.089	4.12	.320**	.155	2.07
How ethical are business firms (WEF)	81	.602****	.044	13.83	.887****	.070	12.61
Executives involved in charitable causes (WEF)	68	.106****	.031	3.31	.252****	.080	3.75
Satisfied with state of environment (Gallup Millennium)	49	.187****	.036	5.18	.167****	.040	4.17
Education spending (LaPorta et al., 1999)	43	.437***	.172	2.54	.663***	.205	3.24
Education Gini 1990 (Thomas, Wang, Fan, 2001)	47/48	−.030*	.022	−1.39	−.065****	.019	−3.35
Education standard deviation (Lederman)++	60/62	−.002	.027	−.06	−.087***	.035	−2.48
Secondary school enrollment (UN Development Program)	70/75	.021	2.056	.01	7.752***	2.648	2.91
Public health expenditures (UN Development Program)	74/81	.206	.217	.95	.770***	.254	3.04
Transfer payments (LaPorta et al., 1999)	55/56	2.520***	.930	2.71	4.502****	.919	4.90
UN Human Development Index (UN Development Program)	76/69	.008	.015	.54	.069****	.016	4.32

* p < .10; ** p < .05; *** p < .01; **** p < .0001
+ Estimated by 2SLS with instrumental variables
++ Data provided by Daniel Lederman, World Bank
Bold outcomes: corruption impact stronger; *italicized outcomes: effectiveness outcome stronger.*
Corruption index standardized.

76

TABLE 3-3. *Summary of Models for Variables Shaped by Corruption and Effective Government*

Variable	N	Other Variables in the Model and Significance (Corruption, Effectiveness)	R^2
Growth competitiveness ranking 2003 (WEF)	75/76	Openness of economy (**, **), regulation of business (−, ***, ****)	.85, .86
Tax compliance (WEF)	45	Informal sector (−, ***, **), English law tradition (***, ***), education (NS, **)	.67, .50
Expropriations risk 1982–97 (Glaeser et al., 2004)	64/66	Informal sector (−, NS, ***), Gini index (−, ***, ***)	.67, .69
Market capitalization (LaPorta, et al., in press)	43	Ease of starting new business, freetheworld.org (**, ***)	.50, .52
Markets open to small/medium firms (LaPorta, et al., in press)	40	Courts have independent procedural powers, LaPorta et al. (2003) (****, ***)	.73,
Index of state-owned enterprises (LaPorta et al., 1999)	35	Rightist parliament (***, ***), East bloc (−, **, ***), ethnic polarization (NS, NS)	.49, .44
Government consumption/GDP (freetheworld.org)	72/74	GDP per capita PPP (−, ** ****), East bloc (−, ****, **)	.50, .51
Good labor-management relations (WEF)	70	Ethnic tensions (−, NS, *), union density (NS, **), business regulation (−, NS, *)	.44, .51
How ethical are business firms (WEF)	81	Legal fairness (NS, ****), ethnic tensions (NS, *), East bloc (−, *, **)	.87, .86
Executives involved in charitable causes (WEF)	68	East bloc (−, ****, ****), Jewish share population (****, ****)	.48, .51
Satisfied with state of environment (Gallup Millennium)	49	Openness of economy (***, ***), government run by will of people (****, ****)	.66, .71
Education spending (LaPorta et al., 1999)	43	Rightist parliament (−, **, ***), internal conflict (−, ****, ****)	.58, .50
Education Gini 1990 (Thomas, Wang, Fan, 2001)	47/48	Internal conflict (−, **, ***), rightist parliament (NS, NS)	.31, .22
Education standard deviation (Lederman)++	60/62	Poverty rate (−, ***, NS), East bloc (−, **, **), ethnic polarization (**, *)	.54, .51
Secondary school enrollment (UN Development Program)	70/75	Poverty rate (−, ***, ****), East bloc (***, ****), ethnic fractionalization (−, **, ***)	.74, .74
Public health expenditures (UN Development Program)	74/81	Internal conflict (−, ***), ethnic fractionalization (−, NS, **), Freedom House democracy (***, ****), rightist parliament (−, *, ***)	.49, .56
Transfer payments (LaPorta et al., 1999)	55/56	Internal conflict (−, ***), rightist parliament (−, *, **)	.46, .32
UN Human Development Index (UN Development Program)	76/69	Internal conflict (NS, **), East bloc (*, NS), ethnic fractionalization (−, ****, ****), informal economy (−, NS, **), Freedom House democracy (**, ****)	.70, .65

Effects in equation with corruption listed first, followed by equation for effectiveness; − indicates negative coefficients;
* p < .10; ** p < .05; *** p < .01; **** p < .0001

the community. Policies and outcomes linked to the reduction of poverty and inequality focus on education and health, two areas that offer hope for reducing inequality and are also plagued by corruption in many countries: how much money per capita a country spends on education and the level of secondary school enrollment – two indicators of educational inequality (a Gini index and the standard deviation of educational attainment) – as well as public health expenditures per capita. Finally, I consider the level of transfer payments to the poor in a country and how well people do overall – as reflected in the United Nations Human Development Index.

In the larger picture of the 15 policies and outcomes considered, *corruption matters more than effective government, especially on policies and outcomes that reflect reductions in poverty and inequality.* The coefficients, standard errors, and t ratios for corruption and government effectiveness are in Table 3-2, while details of the models (including other predictors employed) are in Table 3-3. For the models in Table 3-2, I standardized the corruption scores so that they are directly comparable to those for effective government.

Of the 15 policies and outcomes I consider, effective government has stronger effects (as measured by the regression coefficients) for 3, corruption for 11, and 1 policy (market capitalization) has essentially equal coefficients. Good government matters for three policies/outcomes that we would not ordinarily associate with reducing inequality (at least directly): opening markets to small and medium size firms, good labor-management relations, and public satisfaction with the state of the environment. In each of these three areas, effective government has a modest advantage over clean government. The differences are not large so it seems that either effective or clean government would lead to better policy outcomes. Effective government and corruption matter about equally for the ability of firms to get established in a market (market capitalization).

Clean government matters much more, often substantially. The corruption coefficient on the WEF growth competitiveness index is 1.5 times larger than the impact for effective government (the regression coefficients are negative since the scores are ranks). The corruption coefficient for tax compliance is more than twice as great as the impact for effective government. Businesses are less at risk for state expropriations in clean governments than in effective ones. And the state is substantially more likely to give way to the private sector where there is clean government compared to an effective regime. An honest government, much more than a good one, will lead firms to behave ethically (by a factor of 1.5) and to be involved in charitable causes (by almost 2.4 to 1). This is not surprising, since trust is one of the strongest predictors of charitable contributions (Uslaner, 2002, chs. 5, 7) and the honest state rests upon a foundation of generalized trust.

The biggest differences between effective and clean governments come on policies and outcomes that directly reflect or are targeted to reduce inequality. On only three of the seven measures (education spending and transfer payments) is government effectiveness significant. Every coefficient for clean government is significant at least at $p < .01$. Even for the three policies where there is a significant effect for effective government, the coefficient for corruption is considerably higher – by a factor of 1.5 for education spending, 1.8 for transfer payments, and 2.2 for the education Gini index. The coefficient for corruption on secondary school enrollment is 369 times as large as that for effective government, while the coefficient for the standard deviation of education achievement is "only" 44 times as great as it is for good government. The effect for the Human Development Index is 8.6 times as great for honest government.

Either good government or an honest state will enact policies that may promote economic growth. If there is a direct link between growth and equality, this may offer a way to get from an efficient regime to a more just one. But there is little direct evidence that effective government is sufficient to reduce poverty or to enhance equality. An honest state is critical to those goals.

Corruption is also far more critical to overall state capacity than is effective government. My measures of state capacity are the 12 indicators from the Failed States Project (see n. 3, Chapter 2, for the source). A failed state is a government that cannot deliver essential services and cannot guarantee its citizens security from threats within and without. The project includes 11 specific measures and an overall index. I present the simple zero-order correlations between each variable and the 2005 TI Corruption Perception Index, on the one hand, and the effective government measure on the other (see Table A3-2). The 11 measures include uneven economic development, mounting demographic pressures, massive movement of refugees, a legacy of vengeance (group grievances), severe economic decline, criminalization and delegitimization of the state, the progressive deterioration of public services, widespread violations of human rights, the security apparatus as a "state within a state," the rise of factionalized elites, and the intervention of other states. In the sample used to estimate the simultaneous equation model in Table 3-1, the most troubled nations are Pakistan, Bangladesh, Uganda, and Nigeria, while the best functioning countries are Norway, Sweden, Finland, Ireland, and Switzerland.[10]

For every indicator of state failure, corruption matters a lot more than does governmental effectiveness. I present correlations for both the full sample of countries for which there are Corruption Perceptions indices and for the sample in the data set for this project (N = 139 and 87, respectively). The simple correlations are all considerably greater for corruption than for effective government – except for severe economic decline, where the differences are smaller. The differences are on the order of 30 percent for uneven economic development, deterioration of public services, delegitimization of the state, and a legacy of vengeance. Failed states are unequal states – and they do not have the capacity to develop public services sufficient to reduce inequality. Citizens know that corrupt governments cannot deliver essential services and they will resist paying the taxes needed to support a welfare regime since they have little confidence that the money will actually be used for the common weal.

---

[10] For the full 146 countries in the Failed States project, the greatest failures occur in the Sudan, the Democratic Republic of the Congo, the Cote D'Ivoire, and Iraq.

Cops, Robbers, and Grand Theft

Corrupt governments have consequences that reach down to the level of the street. Corruption is often linked to organized crime, to tax evasion, and to the informal economy. I have argued that it rests upon the foundation of an unfair legal system. Each of these "aspects" of corruption can be linked, in turn, to street-level crime. *The Threepenny Opera* is a play that juxtaposes the justice meted out to a petty thief compared to the great profits reaped by the real criminals, the bankers and industrialists who prey upon the poor.

All crime is not the same. Corruption is more of an economic crime than a violent one: The link between assault or rape and corruption is unclear at best – and it is empirically weak.[11] Property crimes, ranging from theft to (especially) pickpocketing, have a much stronger connection to high-level malfeasance. The direction of causality is unclear.

Using data from the International Crime Victimization Surveys (ICVS) of the United Nations Interregional Crime and Justice Research Institute[12] aggregated to the country level, I show a strong relationship between corruption and the perceived extent of pickpocketing in a society. Corruption is not merely bad behavior by elites, be they in government or in business. Corruption and street-level economic crime go hand in hand. So, if we put all of the pickpockets in jail, can we curb corruption? Alas, no. Street-level crime has a very modest effect on corruption. However, high-level malfeasance sends a strong signal to petty thieves that there is little respect for the law in their countries. This close link between corruption and street-level crime parallels the strong relationship between grand and petty corruption (see Chapter 1). Corruption not only leads to fewer social programs but it also leads to less order on the street.

The route from street crime to higher-level corruption seems puzzling. Did a Russian oligarch, Romania's Nicolai Ceausescu, Nigeria's former President Sani Abacha, or the chieftains of industry in the Enron or Tyco cases in the United States in the early twenty-first century decide to pillage their nations' (companies') treasuries because someone broke into their car – or even because they read about an epidemic of burglaries? Hardly. Maybe crime on the street is simply an indication of a lack of law and order in a society, as I argued above. But it seems even more likely that a man or woman on the street might look up and see leaders validating thievery – and *then* conclude that if it is acceptable for the rich and powerful to steal, it cannot be any less moral for the poor petty criminal to lift the wallet of a wealthier person not minding her purse.

Hunt (2004, 17) shows, using data from the ICVS, that people are more likely to engage in petty corruption ("offer a bribe") if they have been the victim of a fraud, been robbed, or been assaulted. Azfar (2005) and Azfar

---

[11] Corruption may involve violence, as in the actions of the Mafia or in some coercive attempts to extort bribes, but my general point is that there is a difference between ordinary economic crimes and violent ones.

[12] See http://www.unicri.it/wwd/analysis/icvs/index.php.

and Gurgur (2005) report that high rates of corruption lead to more thefts from personal property, more homicides, more car theft, more burglaries, and a lesser willingness to report crimes to the police, but not contact crime (cf. Soares, 2004). These two arguments are not necessarily inconsistent, since Hunt focuses on petty corruption and Azfar and Gurgur on grand corruption.

I first consider the bivariate linkages between corruption and a variety of types of crime to support my claim that corruption is linked to economic crimes and not to violent crimes. This is strong evidence against the argument that corruption reflects a general sense of lawlessness – that venal leaders and even petty criminals are the first step on a slippery slope to a more general decline of morality. Of course, both corruption and street crime are assaults on morality, but they are not assaults on other people. I then estimate a simultaneous equation model of corruption and street crime (pickpocketing) and show, as I argued above, that the relationship between the two is largely top down – from corruption to pickpocketing. There is a weak tie in the opposite direction, but it is barely significant and likely reflects a weak rule of law in corrupt societies.

Citizen estimates of crime from the ICVS are hardly the same as actual figures on violations of the law. However, it is notoriously difficult to get comprehensive comparative data on a wide variety of crimes and the ICVS citizen estimates seem to have considerable face validity. The ICVS surveys are national surveys in many nations, especially the West and some transition nations. In other former Communist states and in African nations, the surveys only cover urban areas. This is not ideal, but without using the urban samples, there would be too few cases for aggregate analysis and the results for those countries with only urban samples seem to have face validity as well. Not all questions are asked in every country, so ultimately the sample size is less than 50 nations. The same questions are asked of often small samples over multiple years. I aggregated the responses to each of the survey questions from 1992 to 2000 to conduct aggregate cross-national analyses.

Pickpocketing in many ways is like corruption. It is a theft of money without violence – and without people even knowing that they have been victims.[13] Of all of the measures of crime in the ICVS, pickpocketing has the strongest relationship to corruption (see Figure A3-2). The relationship is very powerful ($r^2 = .659$, $N = 48$) with the 2005 TI Corruption Perceptions Index. Where corruption is high, so is pickpocketing.

Pickpocketing, like corruption, is also sticky. Some countries had sufficient data to estimate levels of pickpocketing at two separate time points. I estimated earlier and later levels of pickpocketing by adding data from 2001 and 2002 and setting a breakpoint at 1996. For the 26 countries for which I could obtain earlier and later estimates, the two series are reasonably strongly related ($r^2 = .506$). However, the estimates for Japan in the second time series is a

[13] In 1990, my wife's purse was stolen on the subway (tube) of her native city, London, and she didn't realize that it was gone until the thief had left the train.

strong outlier and very different from the earlier estimates. Removing Japan, the r² increases to .712.[14]

Corruption is also linked to a variety of other economic crimes, though not as strongly as to pickpocketing: It leads to high levels of damage to cars (r² = .540, N = 48), greater fraud (r² = .474, N = 46), personal theft (r² = .343, N = 48), and reporting of personal theft to the police (r² = .581, N = 48). However, corruption is *not* associated with either the frequency of assault (r² = .000, N = 48, see Figure A3-3), the current level of sexual assaults (r² = .000, N = 48), or the frequency of sexual assaults over the past five years (r² = .094, N = 48). *Corruption is linked to economic crime, not to violent crime.* There is no evidence supporting a general syndrome of criminality that is connected to corruption.

There is a modest relationship (r² = .244, N = 31) between pickpocketing and economic inequality *when present and former Communist countries are excluded* (see Figure A3-4). Lederman, Loayza, and Menendez (2000, 22) report strong relationships between trust and homicide rates, and trust is a powerful predictor of pickpocketing (r² = .441, N = 48). Pickpocketing, like corruption, seems to follow the path from high inequality to low trust to disrespect for the law.

Pickpocketing is less frequent when people see the legal system and especially the police as fair, though, as I shall show shortly, not when people fear the consequences of illegal behavior. There is also a strong relationship between the extent of pickpocketing and positive evaluations of police performance (also from the ICVS, r² = .653, N = 48; see Figure A3-5).[15] *It is not* simple police presence that matters; the relationship of pickpocketing with the average number of police per capita is weak (r² = .050, N = 40). Rather, it is fairness that matters. Legal fairness (r² = .572, N = 48), the reliability of the police according to business executives responding to the World Economic Forum's Executive Opinion Survey (r² = .458, N = 47), and the perceived corruption of the police in both the TI Global Corruption Barometer (r² = .522, N = 33) and the Gallup International Millennium survey (r² = .485, N = 26). The fairness of the legal system and the respect for even-handed treatment by the police reduces the incentives for people to disobey the law (cf. Tyler, 1990).

Corruption and pickpocketing have common foundations in the bivariate plots. How are they interrelated and which matters most for the other? I expect that corruption will have a strong impact on pickpocketing, but that the effect of pickpocketing on corruption should be modest at best. I present the simultaneous equation model of pickpocketing and corruption in Table 3-4. The

[14] The estimate for the Phillipines is also an outlier (.780 compared to .471), though not as wildly off as the Japan estimate (.902 compared to .278). Removing the Phillipines as well increases the r² to .781.

[15] China is a strong outlier, with both high levels of approval for the police (perhaps reflective of a reluctance to make negative comments to strangers) and high levels of pickpocketing. Without China, the r² falls to .522.

TABLE 3-4. *Simultaneous Equation Model of Corruption and Pickpocketing*

Variable	Coefficient	Std. Error	t Ratio
Corruption equation			
Pickpocketing frequent	−1.659*	1.282	−1.29
Trust (imputed)	3.294***	1.151	2.86
Particularized trust: Restrictions on conversions to minority religions	−1.216**	.579	−2.10
Regulation of business	.999****	.232	4.30
GDP per capita (ICRG)	.528****	.130	4.06
Eastern bloc	−.712***	.286	−2.48
Constant	3.407**	1.103	3.09
Pickpocketing equation			
Corruption	−.032**	.015	−2.18
Police job satisfaction (ICVS)	−.532****	.146	−3.65
Freedom House 2003 democratization	−.062**	.036	−1.70
Average sentence length (perceived, ICVS)	−.016	.017	−.95
Frequency suspended sentences (perceived, CVS)	.120	.619	.19
Constant	1.163****	.132	8.84

For estimaton using pickpocketing measure multiplied by 10 for comparability with corruption measure: Coefficient of pickpocketing frequency on corruption: −.166; coefficient of corruption on pickpocketing: −.324.

* $p < .10$; ** $p < .05$; *** $p < .01$; **** $p < .0001$ (all tests one-tailed except for constants)

Summary of Models

Equation	R^2	S.E.E.	Mean	F Statistic
Corruption	.929	.710	5.716	80.52
Pickpocketing	.737	.118	.573	20.59
	N = 44			

Instrumental variables: Religious and ethnic fractionalization (from Alesina, Devleeschauwer, Easterly, Kurlat, and Wacziarg, 2003); English legal tradition; fairness of legal system; and don't report crime because police won't do anything (ICVS).

model for corruption is essentially the same as the one in Table 3-2. Since the number of cases is now only 44, I eliminate ethnic fractionalization (which was not significant) and legal fairness (because collinearity with the other variables became too strong when I added pickpocketing). The model for pickpocketing includes corruption, satisfaction with police job performance, the Freedom House measure of democratization, and two measures of potential punishment for offenders as perceived by ICVS respondents: the average length of sentences for criminals and the frequency of suspended sentences. Both are indicators of the severity of the criminal justice system and tougher penalties should lead to lower rates of pickpocketing.

The corruption equation largely replicates the findings in Chapter 3: generalized trust and higher levels of GDP per capita lead to less corruption;

particularized trust, strangling regulations, and being a present or former Communist country are associated with higher corruption. So do high rates of pick-pocketing, though the coefficient is only significant at p < .10. The difference in corruption between the highest (Ukraine) and lowest (New Zealand) levels of pickpocketing is 1.29 – about the difference in corruption between Indonesia and Egypt. GDP per capita has a much stronger effect on corruption, 2.64, which would raise Indonesia's rating to that of Italy or Hungary. Trust's impact is also considerably greater – 2.06. The pickpocketing equation indicates that institutions do matter: Democracies have, on average, 12 percent lower rates of pickpocketing than authoritarian nations. This impact is quite modest compared to the almost 40 percent difference in pickpocketing rates predicted by comparing Canadians' strong satisfaction with their officers of the law and the disdain of Russians. Corruption matters a great deal: Pickpocketing rates are 24 percent higher in the most corrupt nation in this sample (Indonesia) compared to the least (New Zealand). Neither average sentence length nor the frequency of sentences significantly shapes levels of pickpocketing.

High levels of corruption send signals to ordinary citizens: Elites have little respect for the law, so people on the streets follow the leaders. When I rescale the pickpocketing variable so that it has the same range as the TI Corruption Perceptions Index, the coefficient of corruption on pickpocketing is twice as large as the one for pickpocketing on corruption. Leaders don't pilfer from the treasury because they see crime on the street, but petty thieves seem to take a message from dishonesty at the top. Corruption not only leads to poorer policies and worse social outcomes, it leads to less order on the street, which is also tied to a lower quality of life.[16]

The link between pickpocketing and corruption provides support for a top-down explanation. High-level corruption "trickles down" to the street level and greater levels of democracy are associated with lesser property crimes. Institutions seem, perhaps ironically, to matter more for "facts on the ground" than for higher-level misconduct.

How People Think About Corruption

The aggregate models support my link from inequality to low trust to high levels of corruption and to more inequality. The connection between inequality and corruption is indirect, through trust. Yet, as I argued in Chapter 2, the connection between inequality and corruption is important at least in part because *people think about corruption as stemming from inequality.* I analyze responses to cross-national surveys below; to polls conducted in transition countries in Chapter 4; and to country-level surveys in Romania, Estonia, and Slovakia in Chapters 5 and 6.

---

[16] The relationship between pickpocketing and the United Nations Human Development Index is moderately strong (r^2 = .417, N = 31), with India excluded as a strong outlier (with India, r^2 = .218).

I consider here surveys conducted by Gallup International, first for the firm itself in 2000 (the Gallup International Millennium Survey) and second for Transparency International in 2004 (the Global Corruption Barometer). For each survey, I estimate regression models with both individual- and aggregate-level predictors. To control for variation at the country level – both for the survey data and the aggregate measures included – I estimate standard errors clustered at the country level. The two surveys encompass large numbers of respondents across many countries. The models I estimate encompass 42 nations in the Gallup International Millennium Survey and 47 in the Global Corruption Barometer.[17]

The Gallup International Millennium Survey asked people how they described their government. They could answer yes or no to any of the following alternatives: corrupt, efficient, just, or responds to the will of the people. I focus on responses to the corruption response. For the Global Corruption Barometer, I examine how big a problem (on a four-point scale) people see both grand and petty corruption.

Hierarchical linear models are very sensitive to model specification and may often fail to achieve statistical convergence.[18] For the Gallup International Millennium Survey, I estimate all of the countries in a single model with country-level indicators for separate Gini index variables (using the measures from Jong-sung You) for former and present (Vietnam) Communist nations, and "other" countries (outside the Eastern and Western blocs). For the Global Corruption Barometer, I estimated three separate models for each grand and petty corruption: one for the West, one for transition countries, and one for other (largely developing countries) using only the Gini index at the country level.

The predictors are limited by the available variables in the surveys. I report the model for the Gallup International Millennium Survey in Table A3-3. The individual-level variables include perceptions of government representation and fairness: The country is governed by the will of the people, all are equal before the law, and the government does a good job handling crime. The first two indicators are measures of political and legal fairness and equality. The third reflects a commitment to honesty, which should be lacking if the country is highly corrupt (see Chapter 7). Also in the model is a rough indicator, the best in the survey, of a respondent's personal economic situation: whether having a good standard of living is the most important goal in life. There are no questions on inequality in the survey. I also employ a surrogate measure of in-group/out-group trust: whether there is discrimination in the society on the basis

[17] The number of countries is smaller than the full samples because of missing data on inequality for some nations. The models were estimated using the xtmixed procedure of Stata 9.

[18] The Gini index I employ for the Gallup International Millennium Survey is the average Gini from 1947–96 and comes from a data set graciously provided by Jong-sung You (see You and Khagram, 2005). For the TI Global Corruption Barometer, I employ Gini indices from the United Nations Development Programme. These two Gini indices are highly correlated at the aggregate level ($r = .831$, $N = 81$). I employ different Ginis for the two surveys to maximize the number of countries that I can retain in the analyses.

of political beliefs (no other measure of discrimination was included). Finally, I include two demographic measures: age and education (attended college or university). Young people may be less likely to be jaundiced by corruption than their elders, while more highly educated people might be less skeptical of the motivations of politicians.

The strongest determinants of perceived corruption are the measures of government fairness and effectiveness, but both surrogates for trust are also significant. People who see discrimination as common are more likely to say that corruption is common. Believing that your standard of living matters most in life leads people to see more corruption. Younger people are less likely to perceive the government as corrupt, but college educated respondents do not have different perceptions of corruption levels.

People living in countries with high levels of inequality do indeed see their governments as less honest, the country-level (random) effects show. *In both transition countries and in the "other" (mostly developing) countries, greater inequality leads people to perceive more corruption.* The effect, as measured by the regression coefficients, is stronger for the transition countries, though the t ratio is higher for developing nations. Where corruption is high, inequality matters. There is no significant effect for inequality in the West when I substitute it for maldistribution in either of the other regions.

The corruption model for the Gallup International Millennium survey provides strong support for the argument that perceptions of fairness – from the legal system and the government more generally – strongly shape the belief that governments are corrupt. People who see discrimination in society are also more likely to say that their polity is corrupt – at least indirect evidence that particularized trust promotes malfeasance. People who live in more corrupt countries quite reasonably see more dishonesty in government. Personal economic goals and status (through education) are either insignificant or have modest effects.

The models for the Global Corruption Barometer tell a more nuanced story: Inequality (as measured by the You average scores) matters most for the transition nations – and, perhaps surprisingly, not at all for the developing nations or for the West. Also, presaging results to come (see Chapters 5, 6, and 7), inequality matters more for grand corruption than for petty corruption. I estimate separate models for grand and petty corruption for each bloc, again clustering the standard errors at the country level.

The predictors for the corruption models include two measures of how people believe that corruption affects them: a general measure of whether corruption affects your own life and whether anyone in your family has offered a bribe in the past 12 months. The first question is rather general and may reflect a general distaste for dishonesty in civic life. The second question is far more specific and should be tied more to petty corruption than to grand malfeasance – since large-scale corruption is beyond the reach of the vast majority of people and few would likely admit to either paying or receiving large amounts of money in return for favors. However, smaller bribes are common in many countries: Close to 40 percent of Kenyans and Moldovans answered yes, while over 30 percent assented in Nicaragua, Ghana, Lithuania, Romania, and Ukraine.[19] Less than 1 percent of respondents in Austria, Ireland, and the United States admitted to a bribe. I expect that people who admit that a family member has paid a bribe would be more likely to see high levels of petty corruption – but they should not be especially more likely to say that there is grand corruption.

The survey has two questions that tap dimensions of fairness: whether poverty and human rights are big problems. The importance of poverty taps the economic roots of corruption. It is not clear whether concern over poverty reflects worries about inequality or economic deprivation more generally: The aggregate correlation with the Penn World Table measure of GDP per capita is $-.775$ ($N = 53$), while the correlation with various Gini indices is much lower, even when excluding present and former Communist countries (ranging from .361 for the full set of World Bank Ginis to .618 for the average inequality scores from You and Khagram [2005] excluding present and former Communist countries). However, the correlation with uneven economic development is about as strong ($r = .733$, $N = 53$) as it is for GDP per capita. Concern for human rights reflects both high out-group trust (aggregate correlation with generalized trust is .667, $N = 55$) and greater equality among groups (aggregate correlation with uneven economic development is .682, $N = 52$).

The models also include demographics, including age, income, education, gender, and three religious identification measures – Muslim, Catholic, and Jewish. Religious identification may encompass social networks that help people get around corruption: Muslims and Catholics in transition countries and Jewish respondents in almost all cases are less likely to see higher levels of corruption. Otherwise, demographic variables do not matter much and sometimes their signs flip from one model to another.

The models show that the sources of grand and petty corruption are largely similar, which is not surprising since countries where people see one type of corruption as problematic are also those where they see big problems for the other type ($r^2 = .917$, $N = 62$). People who believe that corruption affects their own life are likely to see both grand and petty corruption as serious – and the regression coefficients for the two models are almost identical (see Table A3-4). Human rights concerns matter mightily for *both* types of corruption and are the strongest determinant of corruption perceptions.

The models also suggest that the public recognizes that *both* grand and petty corruption affects their own lives. The perception that corruption affects your life is significant everywhere and perhaps, somewhat ironically, the coefficients are highest where corruption is *least* common (in the West). For grand corruption, the coefficient is smallest in the transition nations – but these are

---

[19] Sixty-one percent of respondents from Cameroon gave positive responses, but Cameroon was not included in the hierarchical linear models.

the only states where offering a bribe in the past 12 months shapes corruption perceptions. So there may be a substitution effect in the model for grand corruption for transition countries, with offering a bribe taking up some of the explanatory power of corruption affecting one's own life. The corrupt dealings of political leaders and business people may be beyond the direct experience of ordinary people, but they recognize that it takes a toll on their own fortunes, much as the more direct involvement with petty corruption does.

The aggregate measure of inequality matters most for the transition nations – perhaps because the other or "no bloc" group of nations includes Hong Kong and Singapore, two countries that have sucessfully combated corruption (see Chapter 7), and thus this group may be too heterogeneous. At least for transition countries, there is a clear link between inequality and perceptions of corruption – and the effect is much stronger (as measured by the t ratio) for grand corruption compared to petty corruption.

There are more powerful effects of economic perceptions at both the individual and country levels – and of a corrupt legal system – for people who believe that corruption affects their own lives in the 2004 Global Corruption Barometer (see the estimates in Table A3-5). People who see poverty or human rights as big problems and the unemployed are far more likely to say that corruption affects their own lives. People who live in countries with higher levels of inequality (as measured by the Gini index from the United Nations Development Programme are slightly more likely to see that corruption affects them directly, so that people living in the most unequal country in the sample (Guatemala) are predicted to see .352 units (on a 1–4 scale) more "corruption affecting their lives" than are people in Denmark (with the lowest Gini). This amounts to the difference between living in Singapore and Bulgaria (or Afghanistan).

More critical is legal fairness. People living in countries with the most fair legal systems are substantially more likely to see less corruption in their own lives – a difference in corruption perceptions of .544, or hypothetically moving from Singapore to Albania. While the effects of economic inequality are limited, legal fairness, another form of inequality, is a more powerful determinant of corruption perceptions.

Beyond these economic perceptions are perceptions of the levels of corruption of different social institutions. The strongest effects come from beliefs that the education and medical systems are corrupt – since people are more likely to come into direct contact with these institutions. Yet, there are also powerful effects for perceptions of corruption in business and in the legal system. Even though the question of whether you have offered a bribe in the last 12 months may not be the best measure of the level of corruption (see Chapter 1) in a society, people who say that they have made such payments are more likely to say that corruption affects their own lives. Residents of present or former Communist countries are no more likely to say that malfeasance affects them directly, though the simple dummy variable's effects are captured in virtually all of the other independent variables. Most critically, being unemployed, seeing poverty as a problem, and the level of inequality in respondents' countries lead people to see direct impacts of corruption.[20] This model shows a direct link between perceptions of corruption and economic problems as well as actual economic distress (unemployment and country-level inequality).

There is support for this linkage at the aggregate level as well: Higher levels of economic inequality lead more people to say that corruption affects their own lives, as do lower levels of trust, more strangling regulations, and a larger share of the economy in the informal sector (although the latter two predictors are significant only at $p < .10$; see Table A3-6). Moving from the lowest to the highest level of inequality leads to a change in the perceived level of corruption of .432 (somewhat higher than in the individual-level model) – or the difference between middle-ranked countries such as the United States and Canada to Venezuela. The effect for trust is even stronger at −.608: Moving from the highest to the lowest level of generalized trust leads to large shifts in perceived corruption – the difference between the United States and Canada, on the one hand, and India, on the other.

The strong significance of the country-level inequality coefficients may be partially explained by the need to omit the country-level corruption estimates. However, these measures are only modestly correlated, so that cannot be a large part of the story. These multi-level models suggest that inequality *does* shape perceptions of corruption. In both cases, I also included per capita GDP as a country-level predictor and it was never significant. The models I have estimated suggest that the public is more concerned with both grand and petty corruption where there is greater inequality – except in present and former Communist states, but even here there is a significant effect of inequality on perceptions of grand corruption.

Where the distribution of resources is unequal, people are more likely to see corruption as problematic. It may seem curious that the level of inequality shapes both grand and petty corruption in the Global Corruption Barometer surveys. Petty corruption does not make people rich and it does not shape people's levels of trust in their fellow citizens, their government, the workings of democracy, or even the market (see especially Chapter 5). So how can I account for the generally greater country-level effects for petty corruption than for grand corruption?

The explanation for these seemingly anomalous findings – and for the greater effects of inequality on corruption perceptions in the West – is that people in the West are substantially less likely to see high levels of day-to-day dishonesty, but not so ready to count their governments as clean. I created dichotomous variables for perceiving grand and petty corruption. While almost 90 percent of people outside the West saw petty corruption as problematic, only 61 percent of Westerners agree. Fewer than 20 percent of respondents in Denmark, Finland,

---

[20] More educated people are less likely to say that corruption affects them, as are older people. The incorrect signs for the East bloc and legal fairness likely reflect the fact that the perceptions of corruption in the model are much higher in East bloc countries and nations with unfair legal systems.

and Norway express concern for petty corruption – and even these figures seem surprisingly high for the Nordic countries – but over 85 percent of people in Italy, Japan, and Greece, and 93 percent of Portuguese, are bothered by small-scale corruption.

In the West, fewer people are bothered by petty corruption – but the range is much greater than we see in other countries. Outside the West, fewer than 80 percent are concerned about petty corruption in only five countries: Singapore at 18 percent, Hong Kong at 45 percent (about the same as the Netherlands), and three other nations that had between 70 and 80 percent (the Czech Republic, Taiwan, and Uruguay). There is less concern for petty corruption in the West and there is more variation among Western publics: The standard deviation for these countries is .489, compared to .314 for other countries, excluding the exceptional cases of Hong Kong and Singapore (see Chapter 7).

People in the West as well as in transition and developing countries are more likely to be concerned with grand corruption. Outside the Nordic countries, almost 80 percent of Westerners see grand corruption as problematic. For the rest of the world, at least 80 percent in each country see grand corruption as troublesome, for an average share of 92 percent, with Singapore (22 percent), Hong Kong (53 percent), and Estonia (71 percent) as exceptions.

Westerners are not likely to have to pay extra to get to the head of the queue in a doctor's office, nor will they be stopped by a police officer for "speeding" or crossing the street against a traffic light. Westerners largely see justice as fair: Their average score on the imputed measure of impartial justice is 4.3 on a 1–5 scale, compared to 2.4 for other countries (with no significant differences between transition and deploring nations).

The estimates of petty corruption by Western publics are likely too high when measured against actual experience (though we have no way to measure this). And this overestimation may be particularly great where inequality is high. Westerners are also prone to overestimating grand corruption: The French and the Japanese believe that grand corruption is just as troublesome as do Kenyans and Bulgarians. Yet there is undoubtedly more high-level corruption in the West than street-level dishonesty. Petty corruption, then, should be found primarily where inequality is high, while grand corruption exists in every society. Johnston (2005) makes a similar claim in his "syndromes of corruption" argument: Developed, wealthy (and more equal) societies are not corruption-free. Rather, they have *primarily* grand corruption.

There is no direct way to test this claim. However, there is some circumstantial evidence that supports my argument. While perceptions of grand and petty corruption are almost perfectly correlated at the aggregate level, the individual-level survey data permit me to break down concerns over the two types of corruption. Only a handful of people in any country saw only petty corruption, but an average of 10 percent across nations saw only grand malfeasance. The share was almost twice as great in the West (17 percent) as in the former and present Communist countries (10 percent) and even more than in the developing nations (7 percent). More critically, the share of people who were only troubled by grand corruption was *lower* in countries with higher levels of economic inequality, with larger informal economies, and where people must make "gift" payments to make do.[21]

People in highly unequal societies, where a lot of people must make do outside the market system, are particularly likely to worry about both large-scale and small-time corruption. People in more equal nations with well-developed markets and few demands for "extra" fees to get things done see mostly grand corruption. This is why we see stronger individual-level effects of social status on petty corruption – and why the country-level effects of inequality on petty corruption are greatest for countries with high levels of corruption and inequality (the "other" nations).

Corruption and Inequality Reconsidered

The aggregate models show strong support for the notion of an inequality trap. There is no direct linkage between inequality and corruption using the traditional Gini index measures of economic inequity. There is, however, an indirect link from inequality to corruption through strong in-group (particularized) trust and low out-group (generalized) trust, leading back to more inequality. This inequality trap is compounded by even stronger effects for two other forms of inequality: an unfair legal system and uneven economic development among groups in a society. There seems to be little hope for a quick institutional fix for corruption. An honest state seems more likely to adopt the sorts of policies that will lead to economic growth and more equality than an effective state.

You can get better government if you end corruption, but you can't get rid of corruption by changing institutional structures. Enhancing democracy works – but its impacts are less than those of policy choices and cultural factors such as trust. An Indian journalist commented on the sharp cleavages that led to a cycle of unstable coalitions, none of which could form a government: "We have the hardware of democracy, but not the software, and that can't be borrowed or mimicked" (Constable, 1999, A19).

Perhaps equally critically, in highly unequal societies people perceive more corruption. I have presented some evidence of this in two-level models of cross-national survey data above. The evidence is mixed and the two surveys yield somewhat inconsistent even if supportive conclusions. There seems to be considerable evidence that people see higher levels of corruption where there is considerable inequality and corruption. There are also weaker ties, especially for petty corruption, where inequality is lower (in transition countries). But the

---

[21] Here I use the measure of economic inequality from You and Khagram (2006) and the estimate of the size of the informal economy from the Executive Opinion Survey of the World Economic Forum. The regression equation (with robust standard errors in parentheses) is $-.002^*$Gini $-.020^*$Informal Sector $-.123^*$(Offer Bribe), $R^2 = .388$, $N = 51$.

effects for the West are not so easily reconciled. There is also evidence in these surveys that perceptions of unfairness – the legal fairness and representation of all questions in the Gallup International Millennium Surveys and the concern for poverty in the Global Corruption Barometer – lead people to become more worried about corruption. And low out-group trust – as measured by proxies including perceptions of discrimination in the belief in one true God in the Gallup International Millennium survey and seeing human rights as a big problem in the Global Corruption Barometer – also make people more concerned about dishonesty. These "trust" measures are at best surrogates, they do not measure "trust." Yet they are highly related, both at the aggregate level and, theoretically, to generalized trust. The strong effects for these measures on corruption perceptions support the argument that when there are strong group conflicts in a society, cheating others loses some of its moral approbation.

The solution to this problem is to look for more direct evidence. I cannot resolve the issue of perceptions in the West, but in the chapters to follow I shall confront perceptions of inequality in transition countries, especially Romania, Estonia, and Slovakia. Through analyses of attitudes from the public, entrepreneurs, and government officials, I shall show that (1) people do make a connection between inequality and corruption, both indirectly through trust and directly; (2) grand corruption makes people less trusting of others and more envious of those who have become wealthy by dishonest means, while petty corruption has little effect on people's attitudes; (3) ordinary citizens are more likely to see corruption linked to inequality than are either business or governmental elites; and (4) the link between perceived corruption and mistrust will generally be stronger for ordinary citizens than for elites.

The inequality trap is not simply an issue of making causal inferences from aggregate statistical models (which many would say is very risky). It is also rooted in how people think about corruption. When people see corruption as rooted in unequal distributions of wealth and justice, they are likely to become cynical about the world around them. This cynicism will lead to greater in-group loyalty, to believing that out-groups (including the wealthy) are not to be trusted, and a greater willingness to do whatever is necessary to get by in a corrupt world. These perceptions of inequality feed upon themselves – and people feel that they are trapped in a corrupt world where the rich get richer and the poor depend upon their patrons.

Appendix

World Economic Forum Government Effectiveness Indicators: Question Wording and Coding

Judicial independence:
The judiciary in your country is independent from political influences of members of government, citizens, or firms (1 = no, heavily influenced, 7 = yes, entirely independent)

Efficiency of legal system:
The legal framework in your country for private businesses to settle disputes and challenge the legality of government actions and/or regulations (1 = is inefficient and subject to manipulation, 7 = is efficient and follows a clear, neutral process)

Efficiency of legislative system:
How effective is your national Parliament/Congress as a law-making and oversight institution? (1 = very ineffective, 7 = very effective, equal to the best in the world)

Wastefulness of government spending:
The composition of public spending in your country (1 = is wasteful, 7 = provides necessary goods and services not provided by the market)

Favoritism of government decision-making:
When deciding upon policies and contracts, government officials (1 = usually favor well-connected firms and individuals, 7 = are neutral among firms and individuals)

Transparency of government decision-making:
Firms in your country are usually informed clearly and transparently by the government on changes in policies and regulations affecting your industry (1 = never informed, 7 = always fully and clearly informed)

4

Transition and the Road to the Inequality Trap

> What keeps a man alive?
> What keeps a man alive? He lives on others.
> He likes to taste them first then eat them whole if he can.
> Forgets that they're supposed to be his brothers,
> That he himself was ever called a man.
> Remember if you wish to stay alive
> For once do something bad and you'll survive.
> > From "How to Survive," Berthold Brecht and Kurt
> > Weill, *The Threepenny Opera*[1]

When Bo Rothstein (2000, 479) was invited to Moscow to lecture about the Swedish civil service, a Russian bureaucrat asked him: "'How do you go from a situation such as Russia's to the situation which exists in Sweden?' That is, how do you move a society (or an organization) from a low trust situation with massive tax fraud and corruption to a high trust situation where these problems, while still in existence, are much less severe?"

Is there a way out of this misrule, this lawlessness, and low trust? The inequality trap suggests not. Yet Russia and other countries that made the transition from Communism to democracy – in Central and Eastern Europe and in the former Soviet Union – are the major exceptions to my argument linking high inequality through low generalized trust to much corruption. Yes, they have high levels of corruption – the former and the handful of still Communist countries on average are more corrupt than either the West (by far) or the developing nations. And yes, they have low levels of trust – slightly higher than developing countries but much lower than the West. Yet they have on average *the lowest levels of inequality* – marginally less than the West but far lower

---

[1] The full text is available at http://www.amateurgourmet.com/the_amateur_gourmet/2006/05/how_to_survive.html.

levels than developing countries.[2] In the aggregate model testing the inequality trap, I included a dummy variable for transition countries since they had high levels of corruption *and largely did not fit the overall model*.

So will transition countries escape the inequality trap? Alas, no. The fall of socialism and totalitarianism did not mean the emergence of well-ordered states with strong markets layered on top of the already existing egalitarian distribution of wealth. New democratic institutions did not ensure smoothly functioning states and reduced corruption. Parliamentary elections and promises of the rule of law did not turn Romania or Russia into Sweden (Uslaner and Badescu, 2004). The march to market democracy has been a mixed success: Most formerly Communist countries had free elections and freedom of speech, but virtually all had to confront two troubling consequences of transition – **rising, sometimes sharply increasing, inequality and greater corruption**. The distinctiveness of the transition countries becomes less compelling when (1) they are compared among themselves, rather than with other nations, especially the West; (2) when considering more recent data on inequality, which has been rising significantly in most former Communist countries; and (3) when I examine survey evidence about *how people think about corruption and inequality*. I take up trend data in this chapter, focusing only on transition countries and survey data in the two chapters to follow.

A decade and a half after the Berlin Wall fell and Communist governments throughout Central and Eastern Europe and in the former Soviet Union crumbled with it, the transition to democracy remains very much a work in progress. In some countries the transition has worked well: You can walk down the streets of Budapest and Prague and see little evidence of the Communist past in the expensive boutiques and the elegant older buildings. Yet you can also drive through rural Transylvania and pass Roma women sitting on the side of highways peddling doilies; their husbands and children tug their produce to market in carts pulled by donkeys. You can walk through the streets of Belgrade and see bombed-out government buildings from the United States attacks in 1999 to stop the genocide in Kosovo and take a turn around any corner to see crumbling Communist-era cement apartment buildings. You take the Metro in Novosobirsk, Siberia, and put your hands over your face so as not to breathe the gasoline fumes from the trains.

There is another side to both stories. You can dine well at the fancy new restaurants in the "big city" of Cluj-Napoca, Romania. The pedestrian mall in Belgrade sells widescreen Sony LCD television sets and the gourmet

---

[2] For the full set of nations ranked by Transparency International in 2005, former and present Communist countries averaged 3.42 on the Corruption Perception Index, compared to 7.97 for the West and 3.50 for developing (other) nations (N = 29, 21, and 110, respectively). On trust (imputed), the East bloc averaged .234, developing nations .220, and the West .388 (N = 25, 39, and 30, respectively). For the World Bank Gini index, the present and former Communist countries average .308, the West mean is .319, and developing nations average .443 (N = 23, 23, and 42, respectively).

supermarket in Novosobirsk offers cans of Japanese beer for five dollars each, as well as all manner of attractively presented imported foods.

As some people prospered in the capitalist economy and could afford to buy the fancy goods in the Gianni Versace, Givenchy, and Burberry boutiques, many more could not keep up with the new economy where jobs were no longer guaranteed for life. Many people were forced into the informal economy, in which they earned less than in state enterprises and had no legal protection against exploitation by corrupt employers. In China, which is making the transition to capitalism, if not to democracy, you can buy three scoops of the American gourmet ice cream Häagen Dazs for $6.50 two blocks away from Beijing's Tiananmen Square, home of the Great Hall of the People: The ice cream parlor is right next to the Rolex store and around the corner from the Rolls Royce dealership. A 15-minute walk away from the main square, that same $6.50 will buy you a pair of shoes.

Even the "success stories" struggle with the legacies of the past. As much as Budapest and Prague may resemble Vienna, Hungarian politics is wracked by ethnic conflicts. Two days before the 2006 Prague parliamentary elections, the opposition party (leading in many polls) charged the leaders of the governing party with blocking an investigation of a murdered business executive who reputedly collaborated with state officials and the Mafia in defrauding the state energy company (among other alleged crimes).[3] The governing party did not suffer major losses and the Czech anti-corruption party received 2.6 percent of the vote and no seats in the Parliament.

Democracy is not a cure-all, argues Mueller (2001). But, then, neither is his preferred route to success, the market. Almost all transition states became *more* corrupt as they became democratic, and almost all transition states saw sharp rises in economic inequality over the past decade and a half.

This chapter is about the rise of the inequality trap in transition countries, in societies where inequality ranked very low on the list of problems in Communist societies. Increasing inequality may not be the only problem in transition countries, but it is the source of grievances for other issues. The market economy forces many people into the informal sector, where they earn at best subsistence wages and have no legal protection. The "owners" of the informal economy have no legal protection either, but they have the resources to bribe public officials not to interfere with their businesses and to evade taxes and other regulations, making them even richer. Many people felt cheated by the transition – and repeated double-crossing is a signpost of unequal wealth and power (Howard, 2002, 29).

People in transition countries see a clear link between corruption and inequality. As Anderson et al. (2001, 25) argue,

The poor often blame the government for their impoverishment and report widespread corruption and helplessness. In Georgia, poor farmers equate privatization with theft

---

[3] See http://www.praguemonitor.com/ctk/print_friendly.php?id = 33144, accessed May 30, 2006. I am indebted to Petr Mateju of the Czech Academy of Sciences for the citation.

and complain that the best land is distributed to those who work for the police, courts, school directors, and business people. In Moldova poor people equate independence, democracy, and the transition to market with lack of social justice. Workers on collective farms report being cheated out of their share of grains and denied access to equipment by those in control.

Jack Blum, who formerly worked for the Senate Foreign Relations Committee, commented on a multimillion scandal in Kazakhstan involving an American consultant, multinational oil companies, and many Kazakh officials, reportedly including President Nurultan A. Nazarbayev: "Corruption is at the heart of what causes poverty in third world countries. We tell ourselves that in the short term, we can buy these guys who will serve the national interest, but in the long run it always turns into a disaster" (Stodghill, 2006, BU9). Former Kazakh Prime Minister Akezhan Kazhegeldin said of corruption: "There is a small group of people getting rich – and I mean really rich – in Kazakhstan while the rest of society remains really poor. The leadership is not interested in pushing a market economy. They keep two sets of books, one for themselves and another for everyone else" (Stodghill, 2006, BU9).

The great promises of transition are democracy, equal justice under the law, and opportunities for prosperity and access to the material goods that were denied to all but the elite under Communism. Both justice and prosperity are still distributed unequally – and people with less will naturally envy those with much more, especially in societies where economic equality was a central tenet of official ideology. The rapid and often steep rise in inequality underlies many of the problems that people see in their transition nations.

Corruption and inequality are the talk of most transition countries. People see them as the biggest obstacles to making the grade in transition. They speak of corruption and inequality as if they were two sides of the same coin, as if the inequality trap were something distinctive to former (and present, in the case of China) Communist regimes, rather than seeing themselves as the exception to the larger pattern. As inequality and corruption have both grown, ordinary people look at wealthy people and are convinced that they must be corrupt. Much of the time, they are right. But even when they aren't, those who have not fared well from transition look with envy upon the consumer goods, fancy cars, and the flouting of the law by people who have become rich.

Communist economies could not deliver the goods, so people had to use whatever means they could to get by – and petty corruption was at the top of the list. Party and government leaders and their close associates did not live by the same rules as everyone else, so grand corruption flourished as well. There were few people at the top, so the economic statistics showed very modest levels of inequality. The advent of capitalism widened the gap between the newly rich and the poor. For many countries, the result was a vicious circle entwined in the low trust among people that was the hallmark of the Communist regimes – in brief, the inequality trap.

Part of the inequality trap is an unfair legal system, and the former (and present) Communist countries score poorly on legal fairness, though slightly better than developing nations.[4] On average, 42 percent of people in transition countries believe that their court system was not fair – ranging from 28 percent in Estonia to 68 percent in Georgia.[5] Totalitarian systems were based upon eternal vigilance against enemies of the regime, and their secret police intimidated people to testify against their acquaintances, their friends, and even their families. This system of legal repression took especially high tolls on people who had no friends in high places, who were otherwise powerless, making the legal system not only brutal but also unfair. It also makes trusting anyone beyond your closest friends and family hazardous – and irrational. What ties that develop are intensely personal. Trusting strangers involves a leap of faith that is too dangerous in Communist regimes.

Rothstein suggested that Russians could reduce corruption and build trust by creating a stronger legal system, but the Russians have seemingly paid him little heed. In 2005, over 1400 "takeover artists" seized control of Russian private businesses, owned by locals and foreigners alike, by forging sales agreements, voting out the rightful owners, and often using violence to take over factories. By either bribing authorities or stealing the ownership documents, these con men are outside the reach of the law (Kramer, 2006). Starbucks, Kodak, Forbes, Audi, and the H&M clothing chain have all been the targets of trademark "squatters," who have registered the company names and extort up to $60,000 from the rightful owners to reclaim their brands as the courts stand idly by. The Starbucks brand name was far more coveted, with an asking price of $600,000 (Kramer, 2004, C1, C4).

Many ordinary people still face a justice system biased against them. A Russian court convicted a railway worker in a closed trial in 2006 after his car was hit from behind by a vehicle carrying one of the country's most prominent politicians, causing an accident that ended in the death of the official. The court ruled that the worker should have seen the leader's car coming and sentenced the worker to four years hard labor, provoking widespread protests (Finn, 2006). Russia is hardly unique: Poor people in China who challenge government policy and their attorneys are regularly jailed and denied counselors who would argue on their behalf (Fan, 2006; Kahn, 2005).

The growing economic inequality across transition countries gives people little reason to be optimistic for the future, much less to believe that they are the masters of their own fate – two of the most critical determinants of generalized trust. Many of the totalitarian regimes also prohibited long-standing ethnic tensions from coming to the fore. Democracy gave voice to these conflicts, sometimes violently (as in Bosnia, Serbia, Croatia, Armenia, Azerbaijan,

---

[4] On the 1–5 scale (with higher scores indicating better performance), the mean score for the imputed legal fairness index is 2.49 for the transition countries, 2.36 for developing nations, and 4.30 for the West (N = 24, 43, and 26, respectively).

[5] These data come from the 2002 BEEPS (Business Environment and Enterprise Performance Survey) by the World Bank at http://info.worldbank.org/governance/beeps2002/. The BEEPS 2005 data (see below) were graciously provided by Utku Teksoz of the European Bank for Reconstruction and Development.

Macedonia, and Russia) and sometimes in a political party system based upon ethnic ties (Hungary, Romania, Bulgaria, Ukraine). These ethnic conflicts reinforced the low level of generalized trust in former Communist states. They were not simply issues of identity, but of control over land and of the distribution of wealth: Present and former Communist countries have much higher levels of uneven economic development than we see in the West (an average score of 6.64 out of 10 compared to 4.1 for the West).[6]

My primary task in this chapter is to examine aggregate evidence on the increases in inequality and corruption in transition nations and to show how they are related to each other: to demonstrate that the aggregate linkages from inequality – both economic and legal – to low trust to high corruption hold for transition countries as well. I could not demonstrate this with the model in Chapter 3 because I needed to use measures of economic inequality (from the World Bank) that are clearly comparable to each other. Because of the salience of rising inequality in transition countries, there are multiple measures of wealth distribution in these countries that permit me to track changes over time and there are multiple measures for more transition countries than are in the cross-national data sets.

I shall present aggregate analyses of the consequences of inequality among countries in transition in Central and Eastern Europe and the former Soviet Union in this chapter. However, there are only 27 transition countries and the availability of data for my desired measures is often sparse, so most of these analyses (mostly confined to simple graphs) may not be conclusive.

I will offer three multivariate models of corruption, inequality change, and the change in the Communist vote, recognizing that they are based upon small samples. Nevertheless, they support my argument of an inequality trap with data from countries where economic inequality has historically not been a major issue.

Inequality and an unfair legal system are key determinants of corruption – but there is hope as well. Wealth and an open economy also lead to less corruption, so a country's fate may be somewhat more optimistic than first thought. Inequality, in turn, stems from corruption, a growing informal economy, and a general sense of disorder (street crime) – though democracy does lead to greater equality. Inequality, corruption, and a weak legal system all lead to higher shares of voting for the Communist party – the natural enemy of the reconstructed market economy and perhaps of democracy itself. They are also key determinants of state failure and the interruption of public services (using both the Failed States and BEEPS data sets). In most of the analyses, I consider changes in inequality, rather than (or in addition to) the absolute levels of inequality. Rising inequality may make people even more disappointed with transition than the actual amount of inequity, since it gives them little reason to be optimistic over the longer run.

---

[6] Developing countries had an average score of 7.40, higher than any other group. The sample sizes are 22 for the West, 42 for developing nations, and 23 for the East bloc.

Next I turn to both individual-level analyses (including some hierarchical models) and aggregate regressions on business practices, service delivery, and gift payments in transition countries using the 2005 Business Environment and Enterprise Performance Survey (BEEPS) of the European Bank for Reconstruction and Development and the World Bank. BEEPS 2005 is a survey of business people in 26 transition countries (all except Turkmenistan).[7] I investigate the effects of inequality and generalized trust on the shares of business sales on credit at both the individual and aggregate level.

Raiser, Rousso, and Steves (2004) argue that the share of sales on credit is a good proxy for trust in economies where people have long had little faith in strangers – and just as little experience in extending credit. Both mistrust and corruption, in a hierarchical model, and perceptions of corruption and the lack of a respect for law, lead business people to deny credit to strangers. So do strong in-group ties – but a willingness to engage in organizations with other business people promotes selling on credit. At the aggregate level, corruption and inequality both lead to less reliance on credit. Increasing inequality and a corrupt legal system lead to more gift payments in a wide range of business dealings, but strong financial regulations can overcome some of the demands for bribes. Increasing inequality, corruption, and weak legal systems all have deleterious effects on perceived service delivery for water supply, phone service, and power outages.

The story of the aggregate analyses is straightforward: Inequality matters in a region where it has historically not been seen as a critical problem. It leads to more corruption, a greater willingness to vote for the Communist party (and hence to restrict the market), to mistrust in business (as reflected in sales on credit), to more demands for gift payments by business people, and to problems in the delivery of basic services. The transition countries are not immune from the inequality trap. The situation is not completely dire. In most cases, policy choices or institutional design can mediate the negative effects of inequality and corruption. Yet they are not sufficient to overcome the trap completely. Institutions such as democratic government matter too, but the trap seems inescapable.

The Inequality Trap and the Transition from Communism

Under Communism, all people (animals) were equal, George Orwell (1946, 123) wrote in *Animal Farm*, though some were more equal than others. This "equality" meant that most people faced the same problems of scarcity of goods and had to resort to informal connections – petty corruption – to get by in daily life: to stand in line for food, to help run errands, or to use a friend or relative to cut through the bureaucracy was common practice under Communism (Flap and Völker, 2003; Ledeneva, 1998). In Romania the system was called *pila*. It

---

[7] There are 9,655 respondents in total, including 557 in Turkey, which I have excluded from these analyses since it is not a transition country.

was so pervasive in Russia that, like snow for northern peoples, it had multiple names: *blat* (pull), *pomochi* (mutual aid), *sviazy* and *znakomstvo* (connections), and *protektsiia* (patronage) (DiFrancesco and Gitelman, 1984, 603; Hosking, 2004, 52).

These techniques of mutual assistance were essential to getting by in a system where everything was in short supply. Bureaucrats' control over scarce goods and their freedom to treat people arbitrarily and with abuse gave them considerable power over ordinary people – and this power translated into demands for bribes for every manner of goods and services. Sixty-four percent of Soviet citizens who emigrated to Israel, West Germany, and the United States in the late 1970s through 1980 held that having connections was the best way to get things done; 46 percent said that they would offer a bribe as a matter of *first* resort if a public official lied to them or refused to give them their due (DiFrancesco and Gitelman, 1984, 611).

People see the bureaucratic system as stacked against them and see few alternatives to paying bribes or using connections:

[T]he average citizen is without influence over policy-making and has little legal protection against administrative arbitrariness or even the mindless application of what is construed as the law. He is left to devise individual strategies and tactics, which will not change the making of the law, but will, he hopes, turn its implementation in his favor. Each person, then, is reduced to being a special pleader, and not with those who make the rules but with those who are charged with applying and enforcing them (DiFrancesco and Gitelman, 1984, 618).

Communist countries had less inequality based upon official data (which may not have been measured or reported with precision) than the West or developing nations.[8] Yet this statistical inequality hid the great wealth of a handful of officials at the top, the *nomenclatura* in Russian, who had privileges unavailable to ordinary citizens – and who used their state positions to enrich their private lives. Communist countries were filled with corrupt officials, even as they preached equality and kept the overwhelming share of their populations poor. There were perpetual shortages because of the centralized means of production, but also because of the imbalance of demand and supply and the large bureaucracy that provided many opportunities for extortion.

Communist regimes rested upon unwritten rules rather than legal fairness. Rules were always open to interpretation – thus providing opportunities for officials to blackmail and intimidate ordinary citizens (Ledeneva, 2005, 9). Corrupt officials were mostly immune from charges of malfeasance, since they were part of the same state apparatus as the courts. Communism also rested upon a "culture of dependency and low levels of initiative," which provided fertile

---

[8] The results are largely the same, whether one looks at the World Bank Ginis (available for only eight Communist countries in 1980) or the Galbraith data (in 1987, available for 9 countries, or in 1990, for 12 nations): The East bloc countries averaged Gini indices of 26.7, 27.0, and 28.2, respectively, compared to the low- to mid-30s for the West and the mid-40s for developing nations.

grounds for corruption. So did the fuzzy dividing line between what was public and what was private and the high level of secrecy (Holmes, 2006, 183–5).

The transition to democracy that began in 1989, especially with the fall of the Berlin Wall, and culminated with the demise of the Soviet Union in 1991 was one of the most striking transformations in centuries. Democratic institutions took hold: Political parties bloomed – in some countries such as Romania and Poland the number of parties right after the transition was dizzyingly large: more than 200 in Romania and over 100 in Poland.

The transition raised both hopes and expectations for millions of people (Howard, 2002, 136–40; Sztompka, 1999, 160; Vasecka, 1999, chs. 2, 7). Yet six years later, when Rothstein visited Moscow, government officials and the public alike still saw the society as plagued by corruption, tax evasion, an unfair legal system, and low trust. Perhaps above all, it was less equal.

In 2006, almost all of the countries in Central and Eastern Europe as well as Estonia, Latvia, and Lithuania had become "developed democracies," according to the Bertelsmann Transformation Index (Bertelsmann Stiftung, 2006, 234–5), although some countries, especially the Asian nations formerly part of the Soviet Union, lagged behind. People throughout transition countries presumed that democratic government and markets would transform former Communist nations into modern market democracies, complete with the rule of law and economic prosperity (Sztompka, 1999, 179). When this did not occur immediately, optimism gave way to disappointment.

The disappointments of transition reflected much more than unrealistic expectations. The end of the all-powerful state meant "shock therapy" for many ordinary workers, who lost their guaranteed jobs and had to find their own way in economies with few opportunities. State enterprises hired far too many people and their private successors could not afford such large workforces. As many people struggled to find alternative employment – often in the informal economy – corruption persisted. Dishonesty became more prevalent as former Communist party members were often able to secure control of the privatized companies at a fraction of their market value – and with few legal checks on how they ran their businesses (Johnston, 2005, 196). Many of the old bosses were still around – and they seemed to be among the few who really prospered in the new order. For many, the authoritarian regime was thankfully gone, but in its place was a free-for-all grab for money and power marked by "uncertainty and devoid of moral guidance" so that "people feel isolated and lonely, and turn their resentments against others" (Sztompka, 1999, 174).

Transition countries' publics see wealth as a sign of strong connections and especially of dishonesty. While most Westerners believe that the path to wealth stems from hard work, 80 percent of Bulgarians, Hungarians, and Russians say that high incomes reflect dishonesty (Kluegel and Mason, 2000a, 167; cf. Orkeny, 2000, 109). Even in countries such as Estonia, Slovenia, Slovakia, and Poland – the "success stories" among transition countries – ordinary people expressed suspicion of how people became rich in the early 1990s. By later in the decade, such feelings had subsided in countries where people were doing well (especially in the Czech Republic), but became more intense where inequality had increased (Orkeny and Szejelyi, 2000, 208).

Mateju (1997, 4–5) argues

...the long-lasting presence of an egalitarian socialist ideology and a functioning "nomenclatura system" associated with various social and economic privileges mean that those countries undergoing the post-communist transformation will show a low tolerance for the growth of inequality ... individuals who feel that life-chances for their group or class are declining in relation to those of other groups or classes may tend to consider such changes as the result of social injustice ...

Stoyanov et al. (2000, 35) report survey data on Bulgaria showing that

the reasons for being wealthy ... have to do mainly with the unfair social system ensuring better opportunities for the "well connected" and the unscrupulous....the negative image of wealthy people does not represent only the communist socialization stereotype, but results also from recent ... experiences of corruption, organized crime, and "illegal" wealth.

People in transition were substantially less likely than Western publics to believe that "people get what they need" and that "people have equal opportunities to get ahead" (Orkeny and Szejelyi, 2000, 206).

In the 1999 International Social Survey Programme (ISSP) focusing on inequality, 51.8 percent of the respondents in the 9 transition countries surveyed believed that to get to the top, you must be corrupt, compared to 28.3 percent on average in the other 18 countries (mostly Western democracies).[9] Perceptions linking inequality to corrupt behavior are particularly severe in countries where corruption is most severe, both in the handful of transition countries in the sample and in the full set of countries in the ISSP sample. Eighty-one percent of Russians and 68 percent of Bulgarians agree, compared to 32 percent of Hungarians and 39 percent of Czechs. These perceptions also strongly track inequality and especially changes in inequality in the transition countries but *not* in other nations.[10]

---

[9] For details on the ISSP, see www.issp.org. The transition countries surveyed are Bulgaria, the Czech Republic, East Germany, Hungary, Latvia, Poland, Russia, Slovenia, and Slovakia. The Western countries are Austria, Australia, Canada, Cyprus, France, Israel, Japan, New Zealand, Northern Ireland, Norway, Portugal, Spain, Sweden, the United Kingdom, the United States, and West Germany. Also included are Chile and the Philippines. The percentages I report are the shares of respondents who answered "strongly agree" or "agree."

[10] For the eight transition countries – there is no separate corruption measure for East Germany – the r^2 between the 2005 TI corruption measure and perceptions that you must be corrupt to reach the top is .588. For the full 25 countries, the $r^2 = .385$, but the Philippines is a strong outlier and without it, the r^2 rises to .595. For the WIDER 2000 Gini the r^2 values are .665 (for 8 transition nations) and .035 (for 15 other countries) and for the WIDER change in Gini from 1989 to 2000, the r^2 values are .775 (for 8 transition nations) and .166 (for 10 other countries with the wrong sign).

Even though the World Bank Gini index is 25 percent lower for the transition countries, people in those nations see far more inequality than those in other countries: 39 percent say that it is important to come from a wealthy family to succeed (compared to 29 percent elsewhere). Only 18 percent (compared to 25 percent) say that income differences are necessary for a country's prosperity, while 93 percent (compared to 78 percent) say that income differences are too large. People in transition countries are more likely (by 63 to 57 percent) to see a conflict between the top and bottom rungs of society and by an even larger margin (55.1 to 42.6 percent) to see a struggle between the rich and the poor. Eighty percent (compared to 63 percent) believe that government has a responsibility to reduce income gaps – which is hardly surprising since few people believe that people get rewarded for their skills and intelligence (20.5 percent compared to 50.4 percent elsewhere) or especially the efforts they expend (13.6 versus 42.3 percent). Western respondents see far less economic inequality and far greater opportunities for advancement through one's own efforts. People in transition countries see far more inequity and link it to corruption.

The strong arm of the state, the perception of an unfair legal system, and of unequal access to basic consumer goods made generalized trust a scarce commodity in Communist countries. Yes, there were social networks in Communist states. They were not the "bridging" ties that connect us to people who are different from ourselves. Instead, they consisted of two types of connections that either substituted for wider ties – families and intimate friends – or that may even have inhibited generalized trust – purely instrumental networks that existed "to secure resources from state authorities which controlled everything from political life to personal careers to food and housing" (Rutland, 2005, 9–10; Howard, 2002, 27–8).

The helping networks that played such a key role in the Communist regimes were *substitutes* for the wider social networks that were simply not possible under repressive governments (Flap and Völker, 2003; Gibson, 2001; Ledeneva, 1998, ch. 5). The responsibility of people to help each other reach subsistence led to a strong sense of particularized trust within the group – a distinction between us (*svol*) and them (*chuzhie*) in Russia. Ledeneva (2004, 85–6) argues: "Personal networks undermine formal institutions and thus damage impersonal systems of trust." These mutual aid networks are based upon a notion of solidarity, *krugovaya poruka* or *pomochi* in Russian, where people assume a sense of collective responsibility for each other by a wide variety of means, including coopting (bribing) bureaucrats and police officers. They also enforce community "norms" by ensuring that people in a community do not shirk their responsibilities – or behave in a manner that some in the community find objectionable (Hosking, 2004, 52; Ledeneva, 2004, 86–7, 105).

The roots of low generalized trust include the strong arm of the regime, the dense social networks that formed to help people get by in daily life, and the widespread perception that most government officials extorted considerable amounts of money from both ordinary citizens and state enterprises (DiFrancesco and Gitelman, 1984, 611).

I move now to an examination of the emergence of the inequality trap in formerly Communist nations. I will first offer some descriptive graphs on the key elements of the inequality trap in transition countries and then examine how they are related to each other in simple bivariate graphs. Then I will consider both aggregate and survey evidence on the impact of inequality in transition countries.

Inequality, Social Solidarity, and the Transition to a Market Democracy

Some countries have fared better in transition than others. I shall present some evidence (preliminary because of sample sizes) that economic inequality makes transition rocky. Then I move to multivariate analyses on the determinants of corruption and inequality change – and to a consideration of the consequences of inequality.

Two different databases tell largely the same story. The Rosser, Rosser, and Ahmed (2000) data on income distribution show an increase in economic inequality from 1989 to the mid-1990s for every country save one (Slovakia). The more recent WIDER estimates indicate substantial increases in inequality – an average change of 78 percent from 1989 to 1999 – for each of 21 countries (see Figure A4-1).

The rise in inequality was accompanied by an increase in the shadow economy (Schneider, 2003). Even the best performing economies, Slovakia and the Czech Republic, had almost 20 percent of their revenue off the books. Three countries had a majority of their revenue in the informal sector (Ukraine, Azerbaijan, and Georgia) and 15 of 21 countries for which there are data have at least a third of their income in the shadow economy (see Figure A4-2). Even more distressing is that 16 of the 18 countries for which there are data experienced increases of between 10 and 42 percent in the shadow economy only one country (Hungary) had a (very slight) decrease while another (Slovenia) experienced no change (see Figure A4-3). Not only did inequality increase, but more people had to rely upon the informal sector.

The greater the share of the economy beyond the reach of the state, the more difficult it will be for a government to marshall the resources to gain public confidence that the state can provide essential services. And here we see part of the inequality trap: If people have no confidence that politicians can pursue policies that will lead to prosperity and economic justice, they will hide their income from the tax collectors (Uslaner, 2006a; Torgler, 2003). Overall, the average share of the shadow economy more than doubled from 1989 to 1999–2000 (from 17 to 38 percent) and the average increase in the Gini index of inequality was 33 percent. I shall show below that these two trends are strongly related to each other.

Corruption remains a persistent problem (see Figure A4-4). In 2004, every transition country had a higher level of corruption than *any Western country.*

The 2005 scores show sharp leaps in honesty for Estonia and Slovenia (atypical for this index) – outranking Greece and Italy and tied with Israel among Western nations. However, excluding Estonia and Slovenia, the mean for East bloc countries is *lower* than for developing nations. Every one of the countries in Figure A4-5 became more corrupt from 1998 to 2004. Since the corruption figures vary from 2004 to 2005, the direction of change is not as critical as is the persistent high level of corruption in the transition countries. Even differences in some scores do not disrupt overall patterns: the correlation between the 2004 and 2005 scores for the 27 transition countries is .959.[11]

Corruption is sticky over time in transition countries, as elsewhere, though there are not sufficient cases for a meaningful comparison over time until 1998. There is only a moderate amount of consistency from 1998 to 2005 ($r^2 = .543$, $N = 12$), but far greater for the larger sample between 1999 and 2005 ($r^2 = .832$, $N = 24$). The public in transition countries sees corruption as a long-term, insoluble problem: In a 2005 survey, just 8 percent of Russians held that corruption can be eliminated "if dishonest leaders are replaced with honest ones," while 26 percent hold that "Russia has always been characterized by bribery and embezzlement, and nothing can be done about it" (Popov, 2006; cf. Karklins, 2005, 59 for a more general statement on transition countries). In Chapters 5 and 6, I examine survey evidence that shows how people link inequality and corruption in Romania, Estonia, and Slovakia and find strong support for this connection – and more so among ordinary people than for elites (businesspeople and government officials).

The increases in inequality might lead us to think about the inequality trap as something that emerged from the shock therapy of transition, disrupting the legacy of more egalitarian societies. Yet here, too, the countries that became more equal after transition had less egalitarian income distributions *before transition*: $r^2 = .592$, $N = 14$ using the WIDER measures for 1989 and 1999 and a more impressive .801, $N = 13$ for the 1999 WIDER measure and a new estimate for 1987–8 also developed at WIDER (Mikhalev, 2005). *The levels of inequality have clearly risen substantially since transition, but the foundations for the inequality trap were in place even before the fall of Communism.*

Increasing inequality and high levels of corruption are a perfect recipe for low levels of generalized trust – and Figure A4-6 shows the levels of trust for the 1995 World Values Survey. The relatively high levels of trust in Ukraine, Serbia, Bulgaria, and Bosnia seem anomalous and perhaps reflect imperfect survey conditions after transition, be they in survey design or in translation. Nevertheless, the transition countries are less trusting – often by quite a lot – than Western nations, except for two countries with their own

---

[11] The regression coefficient is 1.092, indicating that the 2005 scores are virtually a one-to-one correspondence with those from 2004. A t-test that this coefficient is significantly different from 1 (which would indicate a perfect correspondence between the 2004 and 2005 scores) yields an F ratio of 2.06, with (1, 25) degrees of freedom and $p < .164$, so the coefficient is not significantly different from 1.

democratic transitions (though many years earlier), Portugal and Spain, as well as France.

Inequality, corruption, and low trust go hand in hand with an unfair legal system, so it is not surprising that over a third of businesspeople thought that the courts were not fair in 21 of the 26 countries in the 2002 BEEPS – and that over a quarter of the respondents in every country agreed with this claim (see Figure A4-7). These figures are broadly consistent with the low rankings of transition countries compared to the West on the (imputed) Economist Intelligence Unit measure of legal fairness (see n. 4 above).

How Inequality and Corruption Matter

What are the links among inequality, corruption, the shadow economy, trust, and legal fairness? I begin with some aggregate results on how inequality matters in transition economies. I express my results simply, through graphs, because of data limitations. For some of my analyses, limited data restricts my number of cases to as few as ten, so clearly any complicated modeling is impossible.

First, corruption and inequality *are* related across transition countries. There is no way to track the relationship either at or shortly after transition since there have been only a handful of nations rated on the TI scale until recently. By 1997, there is a modest relationship between inequality and corruption ($r^2 = .202, N = 11$), which increases slightly in 2004 ($r^2 = .221, N = 15$), using the WIDER inequality indicators. The Dutta-Mishra measure of inequality is more strongly related to corruption ($r^2 = .349, N = 22$; see Figure A4-8). There is a stronger relationship between corruption and unequal economic development ($r^2 = .370, N = 27$).

More telling is the relationship between corruption and *change in economic inequality* (Figure A4-9): Countries in which economic inequality has increased substantially since transition are more corrupt, though the strength of the relationship is modest. If I exclude the two "most honest" transition countries – Slovenia and Estonia – the r^2 almost doubles (to $r^2 = .431, N = 19$). A lowess plot (not reported) shows that the relationship is particularly pronounced for countries with relatively high levels of increments in economic inequality.

Inequality is often linked to the shadow economy and there is clear evidence for this in the transition countries (see Figures A4-10 and A4-11). The Dutta-Mishra inequality indicators (used to maximize the number of cases) are strongly related to the size of the shadow economy ($r^2 = .509, N = 19$): As the informal sector increases, so does economic inequality (see also the analysis in Table 4-1 below). The causal relationship might go the other way (from inequality to a larger informal sector), but the number of cases is too small to tease out which way(s) the relationship might go. However, there is clear evidence that the relationship is not spurious, since changes in the size of the shadow economy are also clearly related to changes in economic inequality ($r^2 = .503, N = 16$;

see Figure A4-11) using the WIDER estimates for inequality.[12] As the size of the informal sector grows over time, so does the level of inequality.

The cross-sectional results (Figure A4-10) show two outliers: Uzbekistan, which has more inequality than one would expect from the size of its shadow economy, and Belarus, which has far less inequality than we might expect. Existing data do not provide much evidence on whether the observations for Uzbekistan are out of line, but the Dutta-Mishra estimates of inequality for Belarus are significantly lower than those from WIDER.[13] Without these two outliers, the r^2 rises to .886.

The informal sector thrives under an unfair legal system (using the BEEPS 2002 aggregate score for "the courts are generally not fair," $r^2 = .616$, N = 21, Figure A4-12). An unfair legal system also leads to an increasing share of the economy in the informal sector since transition (Figure A4-13; $r^2 = .580$, N = 18). The tight connections between inequality and the shadow economy and the moderate connection of inequality with corruption would lead us to expect that the shadow economy would be strongly associated with corruption. Dreher and Schneider (2006) argue forcefully that the shadow economy is not simply a form of corruption. It is difficult to imagine a high level of corruption without a large informal sector. There is evidence supporting this argument in Figure A4-14, where the size of the informal sector is clearly related to the level of corruption in 2004 ($r^2 = .504$, N = 21).

Even more powerful is the relationship between the *change in the size of the shadow economy* and the level of corruption: Countries where the informal sector has grown the most have the highest levels of corruption ($r^2 = .643$, N = 18; see Figure A4-15). Finally, there is also a strong relationship between the *change* in a country's level of corruption from 1998 to 2004 and the *change* in the shadow economy from transition to 2000 (see Figure A4-16). This relationship is very strong ($r^2 = .659$), even though it based upon the small number of cases (10) rated by Transparency International prior to 1999.

As with the larger sample of countries, there is a clear connection between the fairness of the legal system and corruption. Countries where businesspeople are more likely to believe that the courts are not fair have higher levels of corruption ($r^2 = .464$, N = 25; see Figure A4-17). An unfair legal system also goes hand in hand with economic inequality: perceptions that the courts are not fair track *increases in economic inequality* (data not shown, $r^2 = .500$, N = 16). Growing inequality clearly threatens both the ability to raise revenue and the perception that justice is tilted toward the rich.

Inequality, the shadow economy, an unfair legal system, and corruption form a syndrome. The missing link in the inequality trap is generalized trust. There is no aggregate connection between inequality and generalized trust ($r^2 = .0006$).

---

[12] The Dutta/Mishra figures are not time series estimates and the Rosser, Rosser, and Ahmed (2000) estimates have many fewer cases.

[13] The Dutta/Mishra estimate of inequality for Belarus is 21.7 (transformed to a 0–100 scale), compared to the WIDER estimate of 29.4 for 1997 and 33.7 for 1999.

TABLE 4-1. *Determinants of Corruption in Transition Countries*

Variable	Coefficient	Std. Error	t Ratio
Gini (Dutta/Mishra, 2005)	−3.012***	1.263	−2.38
Courts not fair (BEEPS 2002)	−4.689****	1.572	−2.98
GDP per capita PPP (Penn World Tables)	.0001****	.0000	4.24
Openness of economy (Penn World Tables)	.009**	.005	1.91
Constant	.849	.846	1.00

RMSE $= .473$; $R^2 = .855$; $N = 21$
* $p < .10$; ** $p < .05$; *** $p < .01$; **** $p < .0001$

The link between trust and corruption is also non-existent ($r^2 = .001$ for the 2004 TI index, .005 for the 2005 measure). This may reflect problems in some surveys or it may reflect the fact that trust was so dangerous in Communist societies that generalized trust may not mean quite the same thing as in other countries. There is some evidence that this is the case in China, where many surveys show high levels of generalized trust (Tang, 2005, 105–11). When my analysis shifts from the aggregate to the individual level (see Chapters 5 and 6), trust in Romania and Estonia is related to perceptions of both corruption and inequality.

There is a more *direct* inequality trap in the transition countries from an unequal distribution of wealth and an unfair legal system to corruption. There are not sufficient cases to test this in a model similar to that in Chapter 3. However, I present a much more truncated model in Table 4-1, where I examine the determinants of corruption in 21 transition countries. Overall, the model fares quite well ($R^2 = .855$) and it leads to reasons to be both optimistic and pessimistic about corruption after the fall of Communism. Economic inequality and an unfair legal system are important determinants of corruption. Moving from the lowest level of inequality (Belarus) to the highest (Georgia) leads to a shift of .84 units on the 2004 TI scale – the difference between Croatia or Poland, on the one hand, and Macedonia on the other: The .84 increment amounts to almost a 25 percent shift in the level of corruption. The impacts are substantially larger for legal fairness and especially for GDP per capita (adjusted for purchasing power parity). A growing economy and more open markets also lead to less corruption, so corruption does seem responsive to policy choices.

Getting rich seems to be a powerful – perhaps the strongest – determinant of malfeasance in Table 4-1. Can countries grow their way out of corruption? The cross-sectional evidence suggests so. Yet, as in much of life, the rich get richer and the poor get poorer. Nations faring well in 1993 were the same ones that prospered in 2000: The r^2 between the gross domestic product (Penn World Tables) in 1993 and 2000 is .871 ($N = 16$). *Much of the reason for the deviation from a perfect linear relationship lies in the extraordinary growth rates of countries with the lowest levels of corruption – Estonia and Slovenia.*

Perhaps honest government is more essential to economic growth than wealth is to low corruption.

Growth has been highly uneven: Of the 16 transition countries for which there are data on GDP change from 1993 to 2000 in the Penn World Tables data, half showed *declines* in income since early in the transition and only Poland, Slovenia, Estonia, and Albania have experienced growth rates of more than 10 percent over eight years. Of the 26 transition countries for which there are data on GDP growth from 1990 to 2003 from the United Nations Development Programme, 10 (all in the former Soviet Union) had *negative* growth rates, 5 grew at less than 1 percent, and only 1 at a rate more than 10 percent (Bosnia, which nevertheless remains one of the more corrupt countries even among transition states. Transition states cannot count on growing their way out of dishonesty).

Opening the economy is a policy choice that seems to reduce corruption. When a country opens its market to foreign investment, it is inviting participation in the economy by firms that may not be so willing to bribe public officials to gain access to markets and even to government contracts.

We do not see the stickiness for open markets between 1993 and 2000 that we do for inequality, wealth, and corruption ($r^2 = .418, N = 16$). Most transition countries had more permeable markets in 2000 than they did seven years earlier; five had exceptional records in this regard: Hungary, Poland, the Czech Republic, Romania, and Moldova. Once more, contemporaneous levels of market openness have stronger relationships with corruption than do changes in liberalization. The correlations between the TI index in 2005 and market liberalization in 2000 are .708 ($N = 23$) and .577 with openness in 1993($N = 19$). How free the markets were to foreign competition shortly after transition matters more than whether a country has become more open over time ($r = .169, N = 19$). Opening markets is a useful tool in fighting corruption, but its impact seems considerably smaller than other variables – and why it doesn't have a greater effect over time is unclear.

If inequality is a key factor in shaping corruption, what leads to increases in the unequal distribution of wealth in a society? I estimate a model for changes in equality from 1989 to 1999 (WIDER) in transition countries in Table 4-2 – and it is clear that corruption matters. Three of the four factors shaping rises in economic inequality reflect either corruption or the failure of the legal system more generally ($R^2 = .730, N = 18$). More corrupt countries have greater increases in inequality.[14] The greatest effect comes from a growing shadow economy: As more and more people are forced into the informal sector, inequality rises. The level of disorder from street crime (from World Bank estimates, Hellman et al., 2003) also leads to growing inequality. Disorder from street crime penalizes the poor more than the wealthy (who can afford to hire protection). It dissuades businesses from investing in communities with high levels of lawlessness, further limiting the economic development of poor neighborhoods.

---

[14] To get sufficient cases for analysis, I had to use the 2004 Transparency International Corruptions Perceptions Index here, but, as noted above, corruption is very stable over time.

TABLE 4-2. *Determinants of Inequality Change in Transition Countries*

Variable	Coefficient	Std. Error	t Ratio
Corruption	−.117**	.064	1.83
Change in shadow economy 1989–94	.969***	.307	3.16
Disorder from street crime (Hellman et al., 2003)	.225***	.095	2.37
Freedom House democratization index 2003	−.180***	.056	−3.21
Constant	1.572*	.865	1.82

RMSE = .141; R^2 = .730; N = 18
* p < .10; ** p < .05; *** p < .01; **** p < .0001

There is a positive message in this estimation: Democratic countries had significantly smaller increases in inequality than those countries where political institutions are less free. This is heartening news, both for institutionalists and for citizens of transition countries where democratization has not progressed so rapidly. Democracy is *not* sticky: The correlation between the Freedom House index of democratization before transition (1988) and in 2003 is only .080 (N = 15). Even as recently as 1993, the correlation with the 2003 index was just moderate (r = .558). The level of democratization is related to the level of inequality, but once more, *change in democratization* is not related to increases in inequality; the correlation is even slightly negative (r = −.129, N = 19). Many "partially free" countries in 1993 had become fully democratic by 2003, but there were six "not free" countries in 2003 compared to five seven years earlier. Democratization has the potential to reduce inequality, yet stronger institutions haven't emerged where they are most needed – in the least equal societies.

The Consequences of Inequality and Corruption

Inequality and corruption threaten transition not just because they threaten social solidarity. They also limit the capacity of the state to maintain order and to provide essential services – and they make some people wonder whether the transition is an empty promise.

The Failed States index is a measure of the capacity of a polity to maintain order and to deliver essential services (see Chapter 2), of the "vulnerability to collapse or conflict."[15] A key component of the index is the deterioration of public services, which is essential both for ordinary citizens and for businesses in a newly privatized economy. There is strong evidence that both corruption and inequality lead to weak states. High levels of corruption are powerfully related to both overall state failure (r^2 = .722, N = 27) and to the deterioration of public services (r^2 = .693, N = 27). Increasing inequality (more so than the present level of inequity) also shapes both state failure (r^2 = .429, N = 21) and poor service delivery (r^2 = .475, N = 21). (See Figures A4-18 and A4-19).

[15] http://www.fundforpeace.org/programs/fsi/fsifaq.php

Inequality change seems less powerful than corruption in shaping state failure. Corruption directly leads to state failure and to inadequate public services. The state will have fewer resources to deliver services and people will lose faith in its honesty and fairness. They will try to avoid taxes and will have low expectations of being treated fairly. Compliance with the law becomes less compelling and the state will be less able to establish its authority. The effect of inequality on state failure is less straightforward. Rising inequality creates social strains and leads to less faith in the state as well as other citizens – ultimately with the potential to lead to create severe conflicts within the society. In a highly unequal society, service delivery is likely to be targeted more at those who can pay, either directly or through bribes. The poor may lack access to basic services and even when they do, they may not be able to afford the "gift payments" for hook-ups or for "customer service."

Democratization also matters for both state failure and public service deterioration (Table A4-1). Democracy makes a state better able to govern and to provide better public services. Yet honest government seems to matter at least as much. The most honest government will lead to a 1.80 change in the public service deterioration scale (from Slovenia's top-ranking 3.5 score among transition countries to Romania's level) compared to a change of 1.55 for democratic governments (to the level of Serbia at 5.0). Inequality matters a bit less, accounting for 1.2 units on the deterioration scale. Each factor makes a significant contribution to both state failure and poor public services, with the models accounting for 90 percent of the variance in each measure. Corruption, inequality, and a lack of democracy all contribute to poor public performance.

We see the same story with a different database – the 2005 BEEPS. BEEPS asked its business respondents to indicate whether they have experienced service interruptions such as low water supply, lack of phone service, or power outages. I estimate identical regression models for the three measures of service interruption in Table A4-2 and, overall, the three models are quite successful (with R^2 values ranging from .424 for lack of phone service to .684 for low water supply). The models include three predictors: change in inequality (WIDER), confident that the legal system will enforce contracts and property rights, and corruption. Changes in inequality and levels of corruption lead to poor service delivery in all three areas. Inequality increases are particularly powerful for low water supply. Even though power outages are more common than low water supply problems, they may be less problematic, since poor people may find ways to tap into the power grid even when they are not formally connected.

The impact of both increases in inequality and the level of corruption is sharpest where the poor are most severely affected. Lack of phone service is an issue only to people who can afford a phone – or who try to get a phone without success. Many people in transition countries, as in the West, have cellular (mobile) phones and pay by the call, so service delivery is not as critical an issue. They do not seek legal redress if their service is cut off, as they might with a low water supply or power outages, so an effective court system is less critical – and is not significant. The BEEPS data support the results from the

TABLE 4-3. *Determinants of Change in Vote for Communist Parties from 1989 to 2004 for Transition Nations*[+]

Variable	Coefficient	Std. Error	t Ratio
Change in economic inequality (WIDER)	35.153[****]	8.768	4.01
Gift payments consume 36–40 percent of business income (BEEPS 2002)	732.923[**]	407.782	1.80
Mafia not an obstacle to business (BEEPS 2002)	−22.777[**]	12.597	−1.81
Courts enforce laws: strongly disagree (BEEPS 2002)	−89.357[**]	46.652	−1.92
Constant	−27.908[*]	14.779	−1.89

RMSE = 7.832; R^2 = .766; N = 20
[*] p < .10; [**] p < .05; [***] p < .01; [****] p < .0001
[+] Data from the Comparative Political Data Sets at http://www.ipw.unibe.ch/mitarbeiter/ru_armingeon/CPD_Set_en.asp

Failed States index – changes in inequality and corruption lead to poor service delivery. There is no impact for democratization in these estimates.

The logical outcome of poor performance stemming from inequality and corruption is disappointment with the transition itself among many citizens. There is more than a little nostalgia for the "old regime," especially in countries that have not fared as well in transition. In the 1995 World Values Survey, the average rating of the current regime in transition countries on a 10-point scale is 4.23, compared to 5.81 for the previous regime. People had positive views of the old regime in 10 of 18 countries, but in only 2 (Croatia and Azerbaijan) were the mean scores above 5 for the new system. In only 6 of 18 countries did people have a more positive view of the new system than the old, with the most upbeat scores occurring in Croatia and Poland and the most negative views in Russia, Moldova, Macedonia, and Ukraine.

DiTella and McCulloch (2003, 6) argue that people who are fed up with corruption and who wish "to return to the profits proposed by the social contract" will vote for left-wing parties in an attempt to redistribute some of the ill-gotten gains from corruption back to the poor. Corruption breeds envy and especially lower-income voters will demonstrate their unhappiness with inequality by supporting parties of the left. Inequality and corruption lead voters in transition states to become more likely to support Communist parties (see Table 4-3). Increases in inequality are the strongest determinant of change in the vote for Communist parties across 20 transition countries. These findings are bolstered by the powerful aggregate relationships between the share of voters in transition countries identifying with left-wing parties in the 1999 ISSP and the 2005 TI Corruption Perceptions Index (r^2 = .858) and the 2000 WIDER Gini index (r^2 = .782). These results are based upon very small samples (N = 7), but they corroborate the findings in Table 4-3.

Voters punish more establishment parties by supporting the Communists and their promises to redistribute income back to those who have suffered during transition. Three measures of corruption from the BEEPS 2002 survey also play a key role in increasing support for the Communists: when gift payments constitute a significant share of business income, when the Mafia is (not) seen as an obstacle to business, and when businesspeople believe that the courts are not enforcing the laws.

All three measures reflect the view that the new regimes have failed to curb the abuses of the past. Gift payments by businesspeople will be reflected in "extra payments" that ordinary citizens must make for public services. Mafia power is a sign that the rule of law is weak, as is the unwillingness of courts to enforce the law. Each aspect of corruption puts burdens on businesspeople, but even more on ordinary citizens, who do not have as many resources to deal with the costs of corruption. (Clearly people who look to the Communists because they are upset with corruption have short memories.) Dishonest leaders will lead to resentment that some people are getting rich by illegitimate means – and to attempts to redress the situation through elections. In the next chapter, I shall show that perceived increases in inequality and corruption in Romania leads people to demand that the state limit incomes of the rich.

Once more corruption and high levels of inequality push ordinary citizens to support the left. They lead businesspeople to be ever more cautious in dealing with each other. In the United States (and other Western societies) in the 1960s, before the decline of generalized trust and the rise of the litigious society, people in enterprises did "business on a handshake" (Macauley, 1963, 63). Your word was your bond and no legal protection was necessary, a sign of the high level of trust in society (Uslaner, 2002, 46). Back then, there were no enterprises in transition countries, but the lack of trust that characterized (post-)Communist publics was a great barrier to such informality in finance once markets came to transition countries. While the strong arm of the law may help obtain order when trust is lacking, an effective legal system ultimately depends upon a sense of social solidarity (Uslaner, 2002, 221).

In countries with low generalized trust and a weak and unfair legal system, relying upon the good intentions of others or the rule of law involves a leap of faith. Raiser, Rousso, and Steves (2004, 58) argue that accepting credit from clients who may be strangers is an indicator of trust: "A firm's willingness to forego prepayment may be seen as an indication that its directors believe they will be paid fully and on time, either due to trust in the customer's reliability or in the legal system's ability to fairly adjudicate business disputes." Across 26 transition countries, firms accepted about a third of their revenue from clients on credit, ranging from 6.5 percent in Uzbekistan and 10 percent in Tajikistan to 63 percent in Slovenia, according to the 2005 BEEPS.

What factors lead to such trust in business partners? I examine this question in two ways. First, I present a cross-national aggregate analysis (Table A4-3) and then an analysis of individual responses from businesspeople in the survey including aggregate measures of corruption and change in inequality from 1989 to the present (Table 4-4). The aggregate model shows that the same factors that drive voters to support Communist parties – increases in inequality

TABLE 4-4. *Determinants of Shares of Business Sales on Credit in Transition Countries: BEEPS 2005*

Variable	Coefficient	Std. Error	t Ratio
Courts are fair	.069	.338	.21
Confident legal system will enforce contracts and property rights	−.324	.451	−.72
How many cases plaintiff in civil or commercial courts in three years	.541****	.128	4.22
Street crime obstacle to business	−2.235***	.891	−2.51
Common in business for firms to make gift payments to officials	2.250****	.524	4.29
How often make gift payments to tax officials	−.746**	.576	−1.30
Number of customs inspections in past 12 months	.141	.088	1.63
Share of sales to multinational firms	.122***	.047	2.62
Share of sales to small firms	−.167****	.027	−6.25
Member chamber of commerce	5.967***	2.329	2.56
Family/friends important information sources on new customers	−1.156***	.376	−3.07
TI Corruption Perceptions Index 2004	6.952****	1.700	4.10
Change in Gini 1989–present (WIDER)	−25.616****	5.802	−4.41
Constant	67.688****	11.177	6.07

Estimates are regression coefficients with standard errors clustered by country.
Number of countries: 21; Number of observations: 3964
R^2 = .199; RMSE = 33.402
* p < .10; ** p < .05; *** p < .01; **** p < .0001 (all tests one-tailed except for constants)

and corruption – make business people wary of giving credit to their clients. Increasing inequality and the perception of high levels of corruption lead to a smaller share of sales on credit.

When businesspeople see the system as corrupt, they are unlikely to believe that their fellow citizens will be honest either – and that they could not get justice if they had to go through the courts. The social strains that accompany increasing inequality make it less likely that businesspeople will adhere to norms of honesty and reciprocity. Businesspeople *are* more likely to offer sales on credit if they are members of the local Chamber of Commerce. Such membership may help sellers get to know potential clients – and thus reduce the uncertainty of dealing with strangers that is essential to generalized trust. Businesspeople may either meet their clients directly or gain information about their reliability from other Chamber members. Rather than rely upon a generalized faith in others or in the courts, transition businesspeople may fall back on the old Russian dictat (popularized by American President Ronald Reagan), "Trust but verify."

I examine the survey responses to BEEPS 2005. The individual-level variables include perceptions of the legal system, corruption, bureaucratic regulations, social networks, and who the clients are. Neither the perception that the courts are fair nor that the legal system will enforce contracts is significant, but they may be reflected in the willingness of people to take their cases to court if need be. While it may seem counterintuitive that businesspeople would grant credit to clients if they had to go to court frequently, willingness to use the legal system often indicates a high level of satisfaction with the judiciary. The number of cases is also a measure of the total number of contracts a firm has. So businesspeople who have many clients will be more likely to go to court often – but also to accept a larger share of total revenue on credit.

Street crime leads business people to be wary about the security of their own business – and to be less likely to offer sales on credit. Making gift payments to officials could lead to fewer sales on credit, but the opposite seems to be the case. Gift payments may ease the regulatory burden for businesspeople – and perhaps to establish a close connection with the police and judges – which might reduce the risk in giving clients credit. However, gift payments to tax officials reduces the likelihood of extending credit: Perhaps people believe that if they have to bribe tax officials, they will have *fewer* rights protected in the legal system should creditors default. Customs inspectors are widely regarded as among the more corrupt officials, yet customs inspections have no impact on sales on credit.

Social and business networks are also critically important and both speak to how in-group and out-group ties shape business relationships. The more you rely upon friends and family as sources of information, the less likely you are to make sales on credit. When you rely upon very close associates, you will be wary of letting customers you may not know buy goods without prepayment. As in the aggregate model, membership in the Chamber of Commerce seems to provide the "right" amount of information about potential clients to permit more credit. Multinational firms may be based in the West, where trust levels are higher and where demands for prepayment may indicate a lack of good faith.

Businesspeople dealing with foreign firms are exposing themselves to a more trusting environment. Businesspeople are wary of giving credit when they deal mostly with small firms. Small businesses may lack market capitalization – and, in a shaky business environment, may come and go, leaving creditors with large debts. Dealing with multinational firms – in essence, opening markets – forces businesspeople to sell on credit. Yet few firms are in the international marketplace. Overall, less than 4 percent of sales across the 26 countries in BEEPS 2005 are with multinationals. Most business (64 percent of sales) is with small firms, which still predominate in transition countries.

The country-level variables included in the model are corruption and changes in inequality since transition. Both are highly significant, with among the highest t ratios in the model. Where government is corrupt, businesspeople find giving credit to be risky. Increasing inequality makes entrepreneurs more likely to demand prepayment. If inequality leads to a less stable and less trusting political, social, and economic environment, businesspeople may insist upon payment up front.

Businesses give credit, then, when they deal with citizens and governments they believe to be honest, when the environment is both more certain and favorable to stability and trust, where they can either trust the courts or gain access to them through "gift payments," and when they are in strong positions to obtain information on their clients. Where such information is lacking – when people mostly rely upon friends and family to tell them about potential clients and when they deal with small firms that may not have well-established reputations – they will be more likely to demand prepayment.

Businesspeople in transition states are not prone to give their clients the benefit of the doubt. Only a third are willing to make sales on credit. They will be reluctant to grant credit unless they have strong evidence that they will be repaid. This itself is not unusual, but in the West, firms worry less about what might happen if their clients default. There is less uncertainty about the fairness of the legal system – so giving credit is less risky. In the less secure and fair legal environment of transition countries, businesspeople verify first, then trust.

Corruption seems to be at the heart of problems at both ends of the economic spectrum: It leads some people – presumably those at the bottom of the income distribution – to vote for Communists. It leads others at the higher end of the income distribution – businesspeople – to withdraw from extending credit to clients. It affects people daily – when they hear about big corruption in the media or when they experience it in gift payments.

Demands for bribes are a constant annoyance to entrepreneurs and a mark of the corruption that inhibits the development of a market economy in transition (and other) societies. In BEEPS 2005, businesspeople were asked how common various "gift payments" are (on a six-point scale) in a wide variety of contexts. Overall, most respondents did *not* report that extra fees were the norm – the highest scores came from "my line of business" (2.37 out of 6), getting business licenses (2.02), and obtaining government contracts (1.97), while the lowest score is for getting public services connected (1.47).

What shapes these extra payments? I estimate 10 identical aggregate regressions for different forms of gift payments in Table 4-5 across 20 countries. For each regression, I include three predictors: (1) the change in inequality (WIDER), (2) the belief of businesspeople (in BEEPS 2005) that the court system is uncorrupt, and (3) how extensive the system of financial regulations in a country is (from the European Bank of Reconstruction and Development). A lower rate of increase in inequality and an uncorrupt legal system should lead to less frequent gift payments. So should extensive financial regulations. When businesses are forced to keep their books straight, they cannot have entries for "bribes." So when countries adopt regulations proposed by international banking firms, they are accepting the argument that businesses in transition countries follow the same rules as those in the West.

The three variables perform well in predicting the level of gift payments in eight of ten models, with R^2 values ranging from .426 (gifts to fire inspectors) to .702 (gifts for business licenses). The exceptions are for gifts to get government contracts and to safety inspectors ($R^2 = .088$ and .193, respectively). In the

TABLE 4-5. *Determinants of Gift Payments in Transition: Aggregate Models from BEEPS 2005 (Robust Standard Errors)*

Variable		Change in Gini	Court System Uncorrupt	Financial Regulation EBRD	Constant	R^2	RMSE
How common are gift payments in my business?	b	**.532****	**.314*****	**−.280****	**4.172*****	.635	.364
	S.E.	.314	.177	.095	.831		
How common are gifts for business licenses?	b	**.549****	**−.299*****	**−.200*****	**2.621*****	.702	.209
	S.E.	.175	.066	.039	.301		
How common are gift payments to courts?	b	**.230****	**−.346*****	**.017**	**2.172*****	.500	.185
	S.E.	.138	.094	.069	.312		
How common are gift payments to customs?	b	**.334****	**−.395*****	**−.087***	**2.573*****	.587	.216
	S.E.	.195	.100	.058	.360		
How common are gifts to environmental inspectors?	b	**.310****	**−.149****	**−.046**	**1.671*****	.447	.154
	S.E.	.126	.056	.037	.273		
How common are gifts to fire inspectors?	b	**.479****	**−.313****	**−.031**	**2.039*****	.426	.267
	S.E.	.227	.120	−.35	5.880		
How common are gifts to get government contracts?	b	**−.296**	**−.181**	**−.011**	**2.905*****	.088	.287
	S.E.	.332	.153	.065	.833		
How common are gifts to get public services connected?	b	**.280****	**−.154***	**−.118****	**1.796*****	.527	.165
	S.E.	.170	.074	.039	.407		
How common are gifts to safety inspectors?	b	**−.033**	**−.222****	**.011**	**2.333*****	.193	.200
	S.E.	.192	.087	.047	.441		
How common are gifts to tax authorities?	b	**1.117*****	**−.468***	**−.340****	**2.636*****	.692	.378
	S.E.	.324	.201	.120	.701		

* p < .10; ** p < .05; *** p < .01; **** p < .0001

N = 20

Regression coefficients in **bold**

other eight equations, the change in inequality and the corruptibility of the court system are significant predictors of extra payments. The honesty of the court system also matters for gifts to safety inspectors. Financial regulations are only sporadically significant – in 5 of the 10 models (and one – for customs officials – at p < .10).

Changes in inequality matter most for those extra payments that are most common – in "my line of business," for business licenses, and to tax authorities. Inequality change matters for these three areas, especially to tax authorities (by the values of the unstandardized regression coefficients) where opportunities to "soak" the wealthy are greatest. Business licenses are the province of the wealthy, who also are most likely to offer bribes to tax collectors. These are also (together with customs officers) the same areas where the honesty of the court system and the extent of financial regulations matter most. Rising inequality, a corrupt court system, and weak financial regulations make it more likely that officials will demand bribes from those who can afford to pay. Smaller shifts in the income distribution, more honest courts, and stronger financial regulations protect (wealthy) businesspeople from predatory government officials. *Lower rates of increase in inequality, a fair legal system, and strong regulations all work to make markets unfettered by demands for extra payments. Greater increases in inequality, corrupt courts, and weak regulations hurt the development of markets.*

Reprise

Inequality and corruption affect the day-to-day lives of people at both the bottom of the income distribution and at the top. Corruption robs the state of vital resources and makes less money available for public services. It also extracts a tax, in the form of extra payments, on people who can least afford to pay them (Kaufmann, Montoriol-Garriga, and Recanatini, 2005). It gives advantages to those who can pay, and, as I shall show in the next chapters, corruption becomes most salient when people associate dishonesty with great wealth. Lack of access to essential public services will anger the poor, but the real "costs" of corruption come in areas where the wealthy can buy benefits that make them richer: in business and with tax collectors.

Just as the gap between the rich and the poor has grown in many societies – and especially in transition countries, the former Communist nations are becoming divided between those that seem to be on the path to becoming successful market democracies and those that are growing even farther away. There are now the makings of an inequality trap for the countries that are marked by high inequality and strong corruption. Some of the former Soviet republics have inequality levels at or above those of the least equitable developing countries, and their levels of corruption are also among the worst in the world.

The story is not quite so simple. While Georgia, Moldova, Tajikistan, and Azerbaijan (among other former Soviet republics) face daunting odds in combating corruption, even the most "successful" countries – Slovenia, Estonia, and the Czech Republic – are not little Swedens or Finlands guiding the way to transparency and egalitarianism (much less high trust). Corruption is still very much an issue in these countries.

Growing inequality and persistent corruption makes the transition to market democracy difficult. Many transition countries – especially those caught in the inequality trap – are also mired in weak institutions, having less than fully developed democratic institutions and especially with unfair legal systems. Inequality and corruption also are associated with a larger informal economy, less willingness of businesspeople to extend credit, deteriorating public service, and greater support of voters for Communist parties. The inequality trap takes a strong toll on the societies that have had the most troubled transitions – and it makes future "improvements" in either institutional structures or public policies more difficult. Dysfunctional governments are unlikely to "heal themselves" or to adopt policies such as open markets and universalistic social policies that may be unpopular (see Chapter 5).

Even where there seems to be real progress toward a clean state, ordinary citizens don't always share this view. The Transparency International Corruption Perceptions Index shows that business elites in 2005 ranked Estonia as the 26th least corrupt country in the world (out of 160 nations). The Estonian business elite and government officials see their country as very honest as well, as the surveys I shall examine in Chapter 6 make clear. Yet the Estonian citizenry *sees widespread corruption* and associates this malfeasance with growing inequality.

It is not surprising that Romanians see corruption everywhere and make a clear connection with inequality (Chapter 5), but it is less clear why Estonian citizens might make the same linkage. The answer seems to lie in the inequality trap: Economic disparities between the rich and poor continue to increase and people in transition countries, as elsewhere, make the link between an unfair distribution of wealth and dishonest behavior by people who have gotten rich. The story is just as much about how people think about corruption – and inequality – as it is about who actually has their hands in the till.

5

The Rocky Road to Transition

The Case of Romania[1]

You all have heard of Solomon
The wisest man on earth
He understood humanity
And so he cursed the hour of his birth
And saw that all was vanity
How great and wise was Solomon!
And yet before the day was done
The world could see where it would end
His wisdom brought him to his bitter end
How fortunate the man with none
The next you see Julius Caesar, what became of him?
They showered praises on his name
And yet they tore him limb from limb
Just when he'd reached the height of his fame.
How loud he cried: "You too, my son!"
And yet before the day was done
The world could see where it would end
His courage brought him to his bitter end
How fortunate the man with none
And now at least you see MacHeath
His life hangs by a hair
Yet while his reason still commanded
There was no greater bandit
Known or feared in all the land
Then one day his heart was won
And see, the day is not yet done
And all can see where it will end

---

[1] Portions of this chapter were originally drafted as a paper with Gabriel Badescu of Babes-Bolyai University, Cluj-Napoca, Romania.

His lusts have brought him to his bitter end.
How fortunate the man with none.
   From "Solomon's Song," Berthold Brecht
   and Kurt Weill, *The Threepenny Opera*[2]

For many in European transition countries, a key measure of success is admission to the European Community. The "wealthier" countries gained early admission; the poorest and most strife-torn – including Albania, Belarus, Bosnia, Moldova, Montenegro, Serbia, and Ukraine – remain outside the community. Romania stood at the edge of the European Union (EU) as a candidate country looking in (together with Bulgaria). Both countries gained full membership in January 2007. Yet the EU remains concerned that the earlier stumbling blocks – especially the inconsistent application of the law and high levels of corruption – still plague Romania (Commission of the European Communities, 2006, 5): "[T]here needs to be a clear political will to demonstrate the sustainability and irreversibility of the recent positive progress in fighting corruption."

Romania's accession to the EU is a sign of great progress since citizens took to the streets in 1989 to overthrow what was clearly one of the most tyrannical Communist regimes. The demonstrations that started in Timisoara in December and quickly spread throughout the country, culminating in the overthrow of Nicolae Ceausescu and his regime, marked a striking turn toward a new vision of political and social life in Romania. The revolution was bloody – almost 5000 people were either killed or injured[3] – and Ceaucescu and his wife Elena were put on trial and executed, in contrast to the more peaceful transitions in most other Communist countries. As with most other transition countries, the new leaders and the new regime did not stem corruption and conflicts long buried under the banner of socialism resurfaced.

Since transition Romania has made considerable progress in many respects (see the transition indicators in Table A5-1 discussed below). Yet ordinary citizens are far from convinced that their lives have improved. They see, by an overwhelming margin, increased inequality (and they are correct) and persistent corruption and they have little faith either in their political institutions or in their fellow citizens. They fault both democracy and the market and link these failures of liberal democracy to rising inequality and to continuing corruption. Romanians do not see a *direct link* from inequality change to corruption – but they perceive corruption as both a key factor in why inequality has increased and as a reason to limit the incomes of the rich. Perceptions of rising inequality and of high-level corruption lead to less trust in other people – and low levels of trust also lead people to see more corruption.

---

[2] The lyrics are available at http://www.lyricskeeper.com/kurt_weill-lyrics/226991-solomons_song-lyrics.htm.
[3] See http://www.timisoara.com/timisoara/r.html.

Romanians' dissatisfaction with democracy, the market, their government, and especially other people rests strongly on perceptions of corruption – but *not all corruption*. Petty corruption does *not* lead to widespread pessimism. It is high-level corruption – among government officials and business people – that makes ordinary citizens disaffected from both other people and institutions. Payments to the courts are the only "gift" payments that bother people, since people expect the legal system to stand above the daily routines of bribery.

I examine the linkages among most of the key aspects of the inequality trap among the Romanian public in this chapter. A survey of the Romanian public conducted in 2003 allows me to consider most of the linkages I posited in the theoretical framework developed in Chapter 2 and the aggregate models in Chapter 3. There is strong support for the idea of an inequality trap in these data. Perceptions of rising inequality lead to less trust in other people, both directly and by making people more pessimistic about the future. Rising inequality also leads to less confidence in government. High-level corruption stems from low levels of generalized trust – and high levels of in-group trust – and in turn leads to less trust in others and, together with inequality, to demands for redistribution of wealth from the rich to the poor.[4]

I provide support for these claims by a simultaneous equation model (using two-stage least squares) of approval of government performance on improving the quality of life, generalized trust, perceptions of inequality change, the success of the government in handling corruption, and demands to limit the incomes of the wealthy. Then I present simpler models for trust in people, in government, in the market, and in democracy – and find that it is high-level corruption and not petty corruption that shapes people's views of their fellow citizens and their institutions.

I find that people who perceive increasing income inequality are less likely to approve of government performance or to trust other people and they are more likely to support limits on incomes of the rich. More generally, when people see the government as corrupt and the country moving in the wrong direction, social solidarity (trust in other people) and confidence in the state will decline – and there will be increasing demands for curtailing market forces and placing limits on incomes. People are largely inured to the petty corruption of everyday life; it is larger-scale corruption – by businesspeople and especially government officials – that threatens social solidarity and support for the state.

The pessimism of ordinary citizens is greater than that for elites (business-people and government bureaucrats), as I show in Chapter 6. I show a tight connection between perceptions of grand corruption and inequality among Romanians in this chapter – with similar results from a different survey in Chapter 6. Even though elites don't see as strong a connection, they are more pessimistic and more likely to make this linkage than elites in more successful transition countries (Estonia and Slovakia).

---

[4] You (2005b, 203) finds that perceptions of corruption also lead to lower generalized trust in South Korea, though he does not distinguish between grand and petty corruption.

I focus on Romania for three reasons. First, Romania has a long history of both corruption and low out-group trust. Romanians believe that their society is distinctive for its high level of corruption. They say of such malfeasance: "La no cal la nimeni," or "No one has it the way we do" (Sampson, 2005, 20). Romania has a long history of conflict between ethnic Romanians and its Hungarian, Jewish, and Roma minorities – and such low out-group trust is a breeding ground for corruption, especially when it is linked to inequality.

Second, Romania is an excellent test case for the idea of an inequality trap. Romanians have long been fatalistic. The renowned anthropologist Mircea Eliade wrote in 1953 that "few peoples can claim that they had so much ill fortune as the Romanian people" (quoted in Verdery, 1993, 196). Despondent attitudes about corruption and inequality persist, even as some indicators on economics, the quality of life, and corruption are either average or above average, both among transition countries and for all nations. Romania, even objectively, is hardly a success story. On some key measures, such as gross domestic product per capita, it ranks close to the bottom, and ethnic conflict and internal tensions persist. From 1975 to 2003, Romania experienced negative economic growth. Yet it is hardly the "basket case" of transition countries. In many ways, it is the "average" transition country – with a less successful transition than most other nations in Central and Eastern Europe (especially those already in the EU) but with considerably stronger performance than most former Soviet states.

I present a variety of indicators of a "successful" transition in Table A5-1. Romania's scores on a variety of measures – corruption, trust, the size of the shadow economy, economic inequality, the fairness of the legal system, democratization, wealth and well-being, uneven economic development, state capacity, and conflicts within the country – are generally far below the country's aspiration level – the European Union. The scores on corruption point to high levels of malfeasance that have been *increasing since the 1990s*. Romania's corruption scores in 2004 and 2005 suggest widespread dishonesty, yet these measures are hardly at the bottom of either transition countries or of all nations. Trust, as measured in the World Values Survey, is among the lowest in the world – but the share of trusting people in the survey I shall analyze below is considerably higher. Almost a third of the economy is in the informal sector – and the share has increased 16 percent since transition. Yet, again, Romania has middling performance, both among transition countries and among all nations.

The Gini index of economic inequality was .299 based upon WIDER estimates for 1999 and .311 for the more recent Dutta/Mishra measure. The 1999 figure represents a 26 percent increase since transition.[5] Yet both the absolute figures and the changes are mid-range among transition countries, though the rate of increase ranks quite high for the larger sample. The indicators of democracy, from BEEPS 2002 and the European Bank for Reconstruction and

---

[5] This estimate is far greater than the estimate for the mid-1990s by Rosser, Rosser, and Ahmed (2000).

Development's Nations in Transition measures, suggest that the legal system is still far from fair and the structural elements of democracy are weak (these measures are based upon a 1–10 score). Yet they are middling among transition countries. The two State Failure measures show substantial uneven economic development and modest state capacity – but these still represent above-average performance for transition countries and much better than average rankings for all countries. The same holds for the ICRG measure of internal conflicts, but the level of ethnic tensions is higher than most other countries.[6]

Romania's economic situation is less positive. Its gross domestic product per capita (adjusted for parity purchasing power) is close to the median for the world, but toward the lower end of transition countries. The growth in GDP from 1975 to 2003 is negative, close to the lower end of the world. Romania's economic performance has deteriorated since transition, when (in 1989) it ranked 57th out of 129 countries. By 2000, it had fallen to 77th of 136 nations and its growth rate was near the bottom of all countries. The overall quality of life, as measured by the United Nations Human Development Index, is not quite so bleak, but people's frustration with economic performance (see below) is understandable.

Romania's performance on many transition indicators, compared to other transition countries and the rest of the world (largely developing nations), is about average, sometimes better than that. Its economic numbers are not as reassuring. The public is likely to pass harsher judgment on corruption and inequality based upon the objective numbers – which is what they see – than on comparative measures. These factors make Romania a good case study for the economic psychology of transition, for looking at how people judge the performance of their government and how they evaluate their fellow citizens. Even as Romania has a long history of low out-group trust and corruption, under Communism it had a relatively equal distribution of wealth – at least as reflected in the Gini index (.23 to .24 prior to the fall of the Ceaucescu regime according to the WIDER estimates). While the more recent indices still reflect a *relatively* egalitarian society (with a Gini index of .31), the *rise in inequality* has been sharp – about 30 percent over slightly more than a decade. In the transition countries generally, both corruption and inequality increased since the fall of Communism. Romania offers an opportunity to examine how perceptions of corruption and inequality change are connected to each other – and to less trust both in fellow citizens and in government.

The third reason for selecting Romania is that I have access to a survey conducted in 2003 by a colleague with whom I collaborate, Gabriel Badescu of Babes-Bolyai University. This survey includes questions tapping most of the linkages in the inequality trap. In this chapter, I focus on this survey – and the analyses to follow provide strong support for the framework I have outlined.

---

[6] The range of the Failed States index is from 16.8 to 108.9, of uneven economic development from 2 to 9.2, of internal conflicts from 6 to 12, and of ethnic tensions from 1 to 6.

Romania: A Legacy of Low Trust and High Corruption

Corruption has a legacy in Romania at least as far back as the Ottoman empire (Sampson, 2005, 18). In Ottoman times, Romania was run by Greek princes (the Phanariotes) who bought their positions from the sultans, which they financed through extortion from ordinary citizens. Each local ruler could be challenged by other princes and bidding wars for power were common (Mungiu-Pippidi, 1997). The decline of the Ottoman empire and the independence of Romania did not lead to more honest government: "From the first king of Romania (and the concession of the first railroad) to the last king and government before [World War II], state property and the role of the state in developing Romania were accompanied by widespread influence-peddling and corruption" (Mungiu-Pippidi, 1997). Corruption flourished under Communism, where persistent shortages and dishonest officials made it impossible for ordinary people to get either staples or the "free" state services without bribes, connections, or both (Brubaker et al., 2006, 197; Jowitt, 1974, 1184).

The democratic transition seemed, if anything, to exacerbate malfeasance. Stan (2003, 4) argues: "Personal success had come to be measured in terms of 'stealing from the state,' the blatant use of public assets for private gains, and thus enrichment and entrepreneurship were met not with congratulations and praize (sic) but with condemnation." "There is a widespread sense," Brubaker et al. (2006, 197) write, "that everything can be had for a price."

Romania has long been marked by two key foundations for corruption: a Communist regime and low trust. Clearly these two factors are related: Communism strongly depresses faith in other people. The low level of generalized trust that is one of the key foundations of corruption can be traced to two other factors besides the legacy of Communism: (1) the long-standing poverty that has made Romanians so pessimistic and believing that they are not the masters of their own fates; and (2) the equally durable history of ethnic conflict between Romanians and other groups that make for a high degree of particularized trust and low generalized faith in strangers.

Romanian pessimism stems from the poverty in a traditional society before World War II and the Communist regime after the war. "Romanians," Stan (2003, 4) argues, "had come to view life and human interaction as a zero-sum game in which some individuals could benefit only at the expense of others." This is the same fatalism that Banfield (1958, 110) observed in a Sicilian village in the 1950s. Such a worldview reflects low generalized trust and faith only in your own kind – especially people close to you. Fatalistic attitudes also lead to a weakening of one's moral sensibility, what Banfield called "amoral familism," so that self-preservation dominates over other values.

This fatalism can lead people to take risks if they believe that the only ways you can get rich are by being corrupt or getting lucky. Most people have no hope to become wealthy by corrupt behavior. They are not on the receiving end of bribes. Getting lucky is the only other way to get rich: Hard work won't do it (Stan, 2003, 15).

When you walk through Metro stations in Russia, you see many people hoping to hit the jackpot by tossing coins into slot machines. Moscow has more casinos than any other city in the world except Las Vegas and Miami. One player estimated that " ... the new Russians – I would say that 80 percent are gamblers," even as the government threatened to shut them all down because gambling has become "legalized robbery" in the words of a billionaire businessman and member of Parliament (Myers, 2006b).

Romanians – as some others – wagered as well, and likely more of their income. Between 10 and 50 percent of the public gave considerable shares of money in 1992 to *Caritas*, an "investment" program started by nationalist parties. The perpetrators touted it as a sure way to get 800 percent returns within two years, to enhance social solidarity against "the immoral money of foreigners," and to enhance *incredere* or "trust" among Romanians (Verdery, 1995, 6, 7). *Caritas* collapsed in 1994 and large numbers of Romanians lost their savings, their hope for a better future, and their faith in institutions that could not protect them against their own instincts. Romanians were not alone: More than half of Albanians took part in multiple schemes in the 1990s and 2000 people were killed in riots when one scheme collapsed (Jarvis, 2000). This easy susceptibility to "get rich quick" plans points to the pessimism of ordinary citizens that transition is working – or will work.

The *Caritas* fiasco reinforced the views of ordinary Romanians that corruption is everywhere. "We are not in a normal world," a retired attorney said (quoted in Sampson, 2005, 19). Romanians don't see any evidence that anyone is trying to bring corruption under control and have little trust in their fellow citizens or in any government institutions except the army (followed by local government and the police), the 2003 survey shows (see Table A5-2). Fewer than 10 percent agree that corruption has decreased under the present government and barely that many are satisfied with the government's efforts to battle malfeasance. Only 18 percent of Romanians believe that the government is even trying to fight corruption – and overwhelming numbers say that most members of parliament, ministers, politicians, and businesspeople are corrupt.

Almost all Romanians believe (correctly) that inequality has been increasing – and few give the government much credit for improving the quality of life (25 percent), for advancing privatization (19 percent), or for improving public safety (14 percent). Most Romanians give little support to the workings of democracy (34 percent) and especially of the market (13 percent). Only a handful of people have any connections to help them deal with government, to find jobs, or to deal with banks. More people have ties to help with the police (16 percent) than with any other public or private officials.

There seems to be little evidence that people have to make many gift payments other than to the doctor (25 percent). The banks and county officials receive extra payments from less than 1 percent of respondents – and even the police and courts seem to extract bribes very infrequently (1.4 and 3.2 percent, respectively). However, these figures are deceptive since they reflect both who uses these public or private services and who pays.

More telling are the frequencies of bribes for people who have had contacts with professionals or officials. Thirty-five percent of respondents who had contact with doctors in the past five years admitted making "gift payments" to them, compared to 22 percent for the courts (for people with contact), 7 percent to city or county officials (for contact over the past five years), and 9 percent for the police (again for contact). *Even though these figures may be modest, most Romanians believe that professionals and government officials are corrupt.* Journalists are seen as the most honest (only 26 percent see them as corrupt), followed by professors (36 percent), government functionaries (56 percent), teachers (57 percent), local councilors (58 percent), doctors (65 percent), politicians (69 percent), judges (74 percent), businesspeople (75 percent), government ministers (79 percent), and members of parliament (85 percent).[7]

Another measure of extra payments comes from the World Bank's Diagnostic Survey of Romanians in 2000 in Table A5-3. Here there is much greater evidence of extra payments (*atentie* in Romanian), especially for medical services. Between half and two-thirds of Romanians report paying bribes, about a third saying that they did so voluntarily (to get better service).

From home repairs to schools to courts, at least one in five Romanians has to pay bribes. Basic services such as unemployment compensation and identity cards seem largely immune from demands for extra payments. However, the most common services – medical and gas installation – are the most likely to lead to extortion. And even though the courts and the police have low reported levels of bribery, most Romanians believe that the majority of jurists are corrupt and between 30 and 40 percent of crime victims simply don't report the incidents to the police, believing that they are not likely to get justice (Anderson et al., 2001, 16). Taking legal action against the state is even more daunting: The process is cumbersome and expensive and fraught with political favoritism biased against ordinary plaintiffs (Stan, 2003, 9). After the transition, the "new judiciary" behaved very much like the old legal system, but with even less zeal. Prosecutors and judges were easily intimidated by criminal gangs, so even when charges were pressed against corrupt politicians, almost none were convicted (Mungiu-Pippidi, 1997).

Even the media, the one institution most Romanians see as honest, is easily intimidated by threats of legal action (Sampson, 2005, 20). Mungiu-Pippidi (1997) wrote that in 1994 the media were complicit in corruption:

The Economist . . . published the prices required by Romanian journalists for various services, ranging from $500 to $1,500. In practice Romanian journalists can be bought for much less, since newspaper profits are paltry at best, and monthly salaries vary from $80 to $200 for an editor-in-chief. Newspaper owners have other businesses on the side, because dailies do not sell all that well. So they, too, are part of the network. . . . Of the three private Romanian television channels, one is run by a former spokesperson of the 1990 government, another by the director of Ceausescu's most prominent foreign-trade

---

[7] Here I report dichotomies for corruption; in the analyses below, I use the full four-point scale on how many members of each group are corrupt.

company, and the third by a personal friend of former President [Ion] Iliescu, [then] serving time in a German prison for tax evasion.

The Communist government espoused the standard East bloc line that ethnic identities were illegitimate. Such feelings countermanded the only real source of conflict in the world: the workers versus the capitalists. Brubaker et al. (2006, 88) argue: "The Romanian Communist regime was brutally homogenizing, and its rhetoric was often virulently anti-Hungarian as well as more generally xenophobic and nationalistic." Under the guise of the class struggle, the Communist government stressed national solidarity, so that ethnic institutions (schools, churches, voluntary organizations) were seen as threats to the unity of the people. The only "true" church was the Romanian Orthodox Church (which cooperated with the regime) and the only "true" identification was with the Romanian state.

There is considerable resentment toward people who have gotten rich from misdeeds, but at the same time people feel resigned to the belief that you can't get ahead in this world without being corrupt. King et al. (2003, 113) conducted focus groups with entrepreneurs in Cluj and one, whom they called "The Survivor," explained how he learned to come to terms with corruption:

It took me a very long time to discover this shortcut [corruption]. They saw me as an honest man, an idiot who saw the world through a horse's blinders and can only see the law. Nobody dared tell me until one day, exasperated, I asked somebody. I was told, "well, you are the honest one." OK, let me not be honest anymore. So I solved the problem.

People denounce corruption as the misdeeds of the rich and justify it as the defense against those who are undeserving.

Widespread corruption, from *Caritas* to the looting of the public purse by politicians and businesspeople and rising inequality, led to not only pessimism, but also to envy and the quest to assign blame for the system's failures. The post-Communist demons are the newly rich – and the sources of inequality are minority ethnic groups. Jews, Roma, and Hungarians are "strangers" in the state, "unacceptable others whom one excludes from one's moral community" (Verdery, 1993, 194), while generalized trust demands accepting strangers as part of your moral community (Uslaner, 2002, 1). Brubaker et al. (2006, 198, n. 17) argue: "... in an environment in which generalized trust remains exceptionally weak ... personal trust is important." As a Romanian woman named Sanda described her country to a young British couple walking across Central and Eastern Europe in 1993: "... nobody trusts nobody" (Goodwin, 2000, 152).

The histories of Jews, Roma, and Hungarians in Romania are hardly the same. The Jews and Roma were always outsiders throughout Romania. The Hungarians were the dominant power in Transylvania before World War II and ethnic Romanians had few rights in the province under Hungarian rule. The conflict between ethnic Hungarians and Romanians reflects a long-standing fight for political and economic dominance in shared territory.

Yet there is an underlying similarity in how dominant groups relate to ethnic minorities where resources are limited and people feel vulnerable. Majority groups who feel threatened will put the blame for their worries on minorities – whether they are numerous (as Hungarians are in Transylvania) or barely visible (as Jews and Roma are in most of Romania). Violence within Romania, local thieves say, is not their fault: The source of all bloodshed "in an otherwise peaceful country," they claimed, occurs *inside* "the Gypsy, Arab, or newly-arrived Chinese mafias" (Mungiu-Pippidi, 1997).

Anti-Jewish feelings became particularly acute in Romania, as in other European countries, after World War II and students led anti-Semitic riots; in 1937–8 the leaders of the nationalist Iron Guard movement established a strongly anti-Semitic government, even though it only lasted for six weeks (Brubaker et al., 2006, 50, 75). In the 1980s, Jews (and Germans) were forced to abandon their property and most left the country (Stan, 2003, 3). Even though there were barely any Jews left in Romania, many blamed Jews for both rising inequality, as agents of the West and private property, and for being the backbone of the early Communist movement in the country (Verdery, 1993, 199). The Roma, who lead insular lives of great poverty and work – if they do at all – in the informal economy, comprise a small share of the Romanian population (though considerably larger than the minuscule Jewish population remaining).

Hungarians are the largest minority ethnic group in Romania – and they are concentrated in Transylvania, which borders on Hungary. Transylvania was alternatively part of Hungary and Romania until the Hapsburg Empire collapsed after World War II – when it permanently became Romanian. After World War II, the Romanian government forced Hungarian civil servants to sign loyalty oaths and the Ceausescu regime was "violently anti-Hungarian as well as more generally xenophobic and nationalistic" (Brubaker et al., 2006, 88). Many Hungarians continued to harbor dreams of reuniting with the "mother country" and Romania took strong actions to limit the cultural, educational, and linguistic identity of ethnic Hungarians. A high trust society would place a strong emphasis on tolerance and acceptance of cultural differences. The Romanian state, however, took control of Hungarian primary schools and instituted Romanian-language instruction; before World War II, Romanian troops conducted a massacre of two Hungarian towns (Brubaker et al., 2006, 73, 76).

In post-Communist Romania, a Hungarian party (the Democratic Alliance of Hungarians of Romania) and two Romanian nationalist parties (the Party of Romanian National Unity and the Greater Romanian Party) became important players in democratic politics. The Hungarian party received the votes of the overwhelming share of ethnic Hungarians. Transylvania, where about a third of the population is Hungarian, saw a renewal of ethnic associations and schools for the minority population – leading to greater social segregation, demands for greater autonomy (and some say eventual reunification with the "mother country"), and perceptions of unequal treatment (Brubaker et al., 2006, 201,

274–89). One of the ethnic Romanian parties received 28 percent of the vote in the 2000 Presidential elections and the other elected a nationalist mayor, Gheorge Funar, three times in the largest city in Transylvania, Cluj-Napoca. Funar erected nationalistic statutes and plaques throughout the city and painted benches and trashbins with the colors of the Romanian flag (indicating that they were off limits to non-Romanians, especially Hungarians).[8]

Ethnic Hungarians see themselves as second-class citizens in Romania: 62 percent (in a 2000 survey) see relations with Romanians as marked by either conflict or mutual disregard, while only a third of Romanians agree. More than two-thirds of Romanians believe that ethnic background makes no difference when applying for a job, but only 41 percent of ethnic Hungarians agree. About three-quarters of Hungarians say that they greet their Romanian neighbors or sometimes ask Romanians for help – but only about 30 percent of Romanians admit interacting with Hungarians. Ethnic Hungarians are far more likely than Romanians to say that the latter are wealthier, more influential, and more respected (Culic, Horvath, and Rat, 2000, 291, 312–13, 330, 333). These tensions underlie the low trust that sustains corruption.

The Economic Psychology of Transition Dynamics

I use the survey of the Romanian population, carried out in October 2003, to examine a complex set of relationships linking economic inequality and corruption to the success of the democratic transition. The survey was carried out by the Center for Urban Sociology (CURS) as part of the Public Opinion Barometer program sponsored by the Soros Foundation for an Open Society – Romania.

I break the analysis into three parts. First, I examine a simultaneous equation model of how Romanian citizens link some core elements in the inequality trap. I examine the factors underlying performance of the government in improving the quality of life, generalized trust, the perceived increase (or decrease) in income inequality in 2003 compared to 1995–6, success of the government in handling corruption, and limiting the incomes of the rich. Then I offer a simultaneous equation aggregate model across 17 surveys in the same series from October 1996 to October 2003 with a far more limited set of variables common to all surveys: There are no questions about inequality and barely more than half of the surveys included the generalized trust question. I focus on perceptions of how well the Romanian government is handling corruption and optimism over the medium term (three years) for the Romanian economy. Then I turn

---

[8] Brubaker et al. (2006, chs. 5, 6, 8, and especially 10) argue that Hungarian and ethnic residents of Cluj mix freely with each other and pay little heed to nationalistic politics. However, three friends – two Americans who have lived there (Paul Sum of the University of North Dakota and Ronald King of San Diego State University) and a Romanian who is a native and who teaches there now (Gabriel Badescu of Babes-Bolyai University) – all see ethnic tensions at the individual level.

to simpler models of what people believe drives rising inequality, satisfaction with democracy and the market, trust in government, and generalized trust. These analyses focus on the different effects of grand corruption and both petty corruption and the need to use contacts to obtain basic services.

Perceptions of greater inequality should lead to less trust in others, less satisfaction with government performance, and demands to limit the incomes of the rich. Preliminary analyses did not provide any support for a direct linkage between inequality change and dissatisfaction with the government's handling of corruption. However, there is an indirect tie – through trust – and I shall show a strong connection from perceptions of corruption to demands for limiting the incomes of the rich and from approving the government's anti-corruption efforts to perceptions of inequality change; evaluations of how well the government is handling corruption should also shape attitudes on how well the government is performing on the quality of life – and the quality of people's lives should affect their views on corruption. Rising inequality, low generalized trust, and dissatisfaction with government performance in improving the quality of life and in fighting corruption form a syndrome of discontent and pessimism that ultimately lead to demands for restricting the incomes of the rich – and thus rolling back the march to a market economy.

The belief that income inequality is increasing is widespread in transition countries (Orkeny, 2000, 106; Stephenson and Khakhulina, 2000, 85; Stoyanov et al., 2000, 33; Vlachova, 2000, 63). Ninety-one percent of Romanians in the survey believed that inequality had increased from 1995–6 to 2003; 35 percent thought that it had become much greater.

Putting a limit on the incomes of the rich taps suspicion of the market and reflects the belief that ordinary people cannot become wealthy. Almost 70 percent of Romanians favor limits on income. Wealth is a sign of strong connections and especially of dishonesty. Fifty percent say that people become rich by breaking the law and another 24 percent say that wealth comes from having connections; an additional 6 percent cite luck, and just 8 percent say that hard work brings wealth. In a companion survey in May 2003, 55 percent proffered an "ideal" limit averaging $854 (United States) annually on wealth. Following a public debate on taxation, 66 percent favored such a limit in October, now averaging just $675. The demand for limiting income stems from growing inequality and the perceptions of corruption. In Romania, there is growing support for limiting the incomes of the rich.

There are measures of both "high-level"corruption among people with power and money (politicians, parliamentarians, ministers, judges, local council members, and businesspeople) and "low-level" corruption among ordinary professionals (journalists, professors, teachers, and doctors). The survey also has measures of both grand corruption (as measured by the "how corrupt" are different groups) and petty corruption, as reflected in "gift payments" that are necessary to get by in life (to doctors, banks, the police, the county, courts, the county, the city). Petty corruption is widespread in Romania; in my first visit, I bought some beautiful wine glasses in a state-run store, and the sales clerk wrapped them securely for me as carry-on "luggage" for the plane ride home. When the conference I was attending was over, I joined colleagues on a train to Budapest. At the border, customs officials wanted to confiscate the box. Fortunately, an American colleague who spoke Romanian scared them off.

I expect that *high-level corruption* and to a lesser extent *high-level gift payments* will lead people to have less trust in each other. People don't reason that dishonest doctors – or simply doctors who must supplement their income by "gift payments" – are a sign of a mistrusting society. Professionals' "gift payments" are not a sign of moral decay – and, apparently, not even "corrupt" professionals point to a failure of the social fabric or the state. To be sure, the measures in the survey of grand and petty corruption reflect different experiences. Evaluations of grand corruption are based upon perceptions – ordinary people are not in positions to pay big money to get favors from the state. Measures of petty corruption *do reflect personal experiences* – whether you have had to make payments or use connections to the police, the courts, the government, the bank, to get a job, or particularly at the doctor's office. These indicators may not be identical, but they represent how people experience different forms of malfeasance.

Government corruption and especially "gift payments" to the courts or other government officials should have greater impacts on people's evaluation of government performance, on trust in other people, and on demands for redistribution of income. Different measures of corruption may shape different components of my model, but they all follow a common pattern: Petty corruption (gift payments) does not shape trust, but it does shape optimism and evaluations of government performance. Larger-scale corruption has more pervasive effects – on both forms of trust, on government performance, and on demands for redistribution of income. Whenever corruption shapes people's evaluation of their state or their society, it is high-level corruption. The misdeeds of ordinary professionals don't matter.

The first model, summarized in the graph in Figure 5-1 and in Table 5-1, provides preliminary support for this claim, with much stronger support in the simpler models later in the chapter. The equations largely exclude demographics (age, gender, education) because there is no clear reason to include them – and this would reduce the sample size – there are 486 respondents with values on all variables across the five equations. I did test to see if any of these variables make a difference, and they do not. I include education in the corruption, perception equation since more highly educated people will be more likely to follow reports of corruption, and I thus expect that higher education levels will be associated with lower levels of satisfaction with government efforts to control corruption. Education is generally a strong predictor of generalized trust (Uslaner, 2002, ch. 4), but it did not prove to be so for Romanians (Uslaner and Badescu, 2004, 43–6). I also include wealth (can afford consumer goods since there is no simple income measure) only where it is clearly relevant (in the equations for government performance on the quality of life and on limiting incomes of the rich). While the predictive success of the models, as measured by R^2, does not

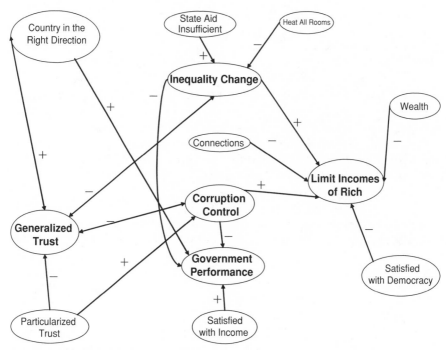

FIGURE 5-1. Model of the Inequality Trap Among the Romanian Public.

seem high, low R^2 values are common in survey analyses and are common in simultaneous equation estimations. In the discussion that follows, I focus only on the variables of relevance to the inequality trap in the text. I summarize the impacts of other variables in notes.

The first dependent variable in the inequality trap model is evaluations of government performance on the quality of life. Two of the other endogenous variables in the model – inequality change and especially the success of the government in controlling corruption – are key factors in shaping attitudes toward quality of life policies. People who see rising inequality and who are dissatisfied with efforts to control corruption are substantially less likely to approve of policies on the quality of life. Beyond these factors, both collective and personal well-being – "sociotropic" and "pocketbook" concerns (Kinder and Kiewiet, 1979) – lead people to approve of quality of life performance.

Simple wealth doesn't matter, but satisfaction with one's income makes people more satisfied with government efforts on the quality of life. So do positive evaluations of the market and democracy in Romania: When you believe that these institutions are working well, you will be more satisfied with efforts on the quality of life. I examined a variety of measures of petty corruption (gift payments) but only included payments to the courts, since it has the clearest theoretical link to satisfaction with government performance. However, even this measure of gift payments is not significant in shaping evaluations on the quality of life, so a mixture of personal factors (satisfaction with income) and

TABLE 5-I. *Simultaneous Equation Estimation of Inequality and Trust Models for Romanian Survey 2003*

Variable	Coefficient	Std. Error	t Ratio
Performance of government on quality of life			
Inequality change	−.427***	.164	−2.61
Government success in controlling corruption	.464****	.094	4.92
Make gift payments to courts	−.190	.197	−.97
Satisfied with democracy in Romania	.072**	.038	1.89
Satisfied with market economy in Romania	.093**	.043	2.15
Wealth (can afford consumer goods)	.015	.011	1.26
Satisfied with income	.133****	.040	3.33
Constant	−.370	.236	−1.57
Generalized trust			
Success of government in handling corruption	.066	.073	.90
Inequality change	−.276***	.115	−2.40
Most judges are corrupt	−.049*	.030	−1.63
Direction of country: right or wrong	.221****	.052	4.25
Have psychological link to Europe	.053**	.025	2.10
Number of connections	.012	.019	.64
Constant	−.101	.221	−.46
Inequality change			
Success of government in handling corruption	−.253***	.075	−3.37
Generalized trust	−.236*	.176	−1.34
Most doctors are corrupt	−.003	.036	−.08
Number of connections	.019	.026	.72
Homeless should receive housing from state	−.118**	.059	−1.99
Heated all rooms in house	−.138**	.066	2.09
Constant	1.266****	.210	6.03
Success of government in handling corruption			
Generalized trust	.315*	.194	1.63
Inequality change	.045	.185	.25
Performance of government on quality of life	.430****	.100	4.28
Support ethnic rights in a new constitution	.203***	.067	3.04
State of the economy in Romania	.078*	.050	1.54
Number of connections	−.040	.032	−1.23
Number of contacts to public and private institutions	.073***	.027	2.70
Education (highest degree received)	−.034**	.017	−1.93
Support PSD	.116****	.027	4.24
Constant	.821**	.331	2.48
State limit incomes of rich (agree)			
Inequality change	.500**	.276	1.81
Satisfied with Romanian democracy	−.178***	.054	−3.27
Most businesspeople are corrupt	.166***	.056	2.94
Trust in government scale	−.014	.065	−.21
People are poor because they don't get assistance from the state	.458****	.101	4.52

(continued)

TABLE 5-1 (*continued*)

Variable	Coefficient	Std. Error	t Ratio
Wealth (can afford consumer goods)	−.060****	.017	−3.47
Can afford holiday outside locality	−.224**	.129	−1.74
Own cellular phone	−.215**	.127	1.69
Number of connections	.022	.046	.47
Constant	2.827****	.595	4.75

* p < .10; ** p < .05; *** p < .01; **** p < .0001

N = 486

RMSE (R^2) by equation: Performance: .631 (.183); Inequality change: .645 (.014); Generalized trust: .477 (.034); Government success in handling corruption: .681 (.233); State limit incomes of rich: 1.039 (.012).

Endogenous variables in **bold**; endogenous dependent variables in ***bold italics***.

Exogenous variables: gender, church attendance, age, make gift payments to doctors, make gift payments to county, make gift payments to city, make gift payments to doctors, Hungarian ethnicity, tolerance of gays, government performance on jobs, government performance on agriculture, government performance on privatization, maximum salary that should be allowed, economic situation of country, life satisfaction, life quality next year, use e-mail, social protection increased/decreased in 5 years, have kitchen, work abroad last 10 years, state should help entrepreneurs, state should control media and parties, Romania needs strong leader.

approval of democratic and market reforms lead people to positive evaluations of government performance on quality of life issues. Just as important – perhaps more so – are the levels of corruption and increasing inequality. Rising gaps between the rich and the poor mean that government is not doing its job to provide for all, and a corrupt government will not have the resources to improve the quality of life, nor may it have the motivation to do so.

Surprisingly, there is no direct link between perceptions of government efforts on corruption and generalized trust. We should not be too quick to dismiss this linkage, since one of the main factors shaping generalized trust is believing that the direction of the country is right or wrong: Optimistic people are over 20 percent more likely to trust other people. There is also a strong relationship between the direction of the country and approval of the government's handling of corruption (tau-c = .282, gamma = .478), so there is at least an indirect relationship between perceptions of corruption and trust (through the direction of the country). Rising inequality has a strong effect on generalized trust: People who believe that inequality has dramatically increased are substantially less likely (by almost 30 percent) to trust their fellow citizens. There is one realm that is clearly associated with less trust: Believing that most judges, the arbiters of right and wrong, are corrupt makes people about 5 percent less trusting.

Putnam (2000, 288) argues that personal connections should lead to trust: These strong ties are the stepping stones to trust in strangers (but, see, among other contrary arguments, Newton, 1997, and Uslaner, 2002, ch. 4). The "helping" networks under Communism were, as I argued in Chapter 4, purely instrumental and substitutes for wider social networks. Such networks continued to be important in transition countries after the fall of Communism and they still reflect "'strong ties' that do not develop into the kind of cross-cutting 'weak ties' that...would open the door to a wider set of acquaintances, contacts, and opportunities" (Howard, 2002, 154). The survey asked respondents whether they have connections for finding jobs, in the business world, at city hall, to get a loan from the bank, at the county government, with courts or lawyers, with the police, or in a foreign country. I estimate the breadth of a helping circle by summing the number of connections. More connections do *not* lead to generalized trust – though they do not make people more insular either.

The survey has a good measure of out-group empathy, whether people have a psychological link to Europe. People with such a link will have a broader sense of their "moral community," while those without such ties will look inward and be more likely to be xenophobic. If you have such a connection, you will be more likely, by about 5 percent, to be a generalized truster.

There is modest direct support that corruption leads to less trust but more substantial indirect backing for this claim.[9] The path from corruption to low trust goes, at least part of the way, through perceptions of rising inequality. The strongest determinant (by far) of perceptions of inequality change is discontent with how the government handles corruption. There is strong support for the inequality trap here: Government corruption, people say, leads to greater inequality. However, this is only true for grand corruption at the level of the state. No gift payment, in preliminary tests, leads to perceptions of increasing inequality, as confirmed in the more elaborate analysis below. I represent low-level corruption by the claim that most doctors are corrupt since medical care extracts more "gift" payments than any other service (see Tables A5-2 and A5-3).

There is no support for the claim that people blame increasing inequality on low-level corruption or "gift payments" (not included in the equation). There may be something unfair when someone uses connections or makes a small payment to get a traffic ticket fixed, to jump in line at the doctor's office, or even to get a job. The police officer who demands a bribe for a speeding driver will ask for much less than the price of the traffic violation. The doctor who demands – or simply expects – an extra payment for services, or to advance in line, cannot charge too much. They will not be able to build large mansions or maintain accounts in the Cayman Islands. Instead, they can take their spouses out for a nice dinner. The inequalities are not large and there is less moral opprobrium in doing what others would do under similar circumstances. So there is less reason to believe that making gift payments would lead to either

---

[9] I do not include trust in government in the generalized trust model. Brehm and Rahn (1997) and Zmerli, Montero, and Newton (2003) argue that the two types of trust are strongly linked. Communist governments *did* seem to destroy generalized trust, yet there is little evidence that democratic governments can create it (Uslaner, 2002, chs. 5, 8) – and the relationship is particularly weak in transition countries in general and in Romania in particular (Badescu, 1999; Uslaner, 2006a; Uslaner and Badescu, 2004, 46).

perceptions of rising inequality or to a loss in faith in other people since neither the payment nor the acceptance of a small "gift" sets one apart from the larger community.

Both objective economic circumstances and beliefs about government responsibility also shape perceptions of inequality. People who face poverty directly – who cannot afford to heat all of the rooms in their houses – see inequality as rising more than those who have more resources. And those who believe that it is the state's responsibility to provide housing for the homeless are more likely to acknowledge increasing inequality. Finally, if you believe that most people can be trusted, you may be too optimistic, being less willing to acknowledge that inequality is actually rising. The effect from inequality to trust is far stronger than the tie from trust to perceptions of rising inequality, which is just barely significant (at $p < .10$).

What leads people to believe that the government is actually fighting corruption? First, there is a strong *reciprocal* relationship between believing the government is improving the quality of life and that it is fighting corruption (see the first equation above). If you believe that the government has improved the quality of life, you will also see it as fighting corruption. People who have upbeat views of the economy are also slightly more likely to approve of the efforts of the government to fight corruption, though this relationship is barely significant (at $p < .10$). Trusting people also are more likely to approve of efforts to combat dishonesty – but again this relationship is not strong.

More telling is the connection between particularized trust and corruption perceptions. The closest measure to particularized trust is opposition to ethnic rights in a new constitution. Romania's long history of group conflict has focused on the role of minority ethnic populations in the society. Hungarians have been particularly concerned with the repeated actions by successive governments to limit their rights. Almost 90 percent of Hungarians in Romania favor greater autonomy in areas where they are in the majority, while just 15 percent of ethnic Romanians agree (Culic, Horvath, and Rat, 2000, 320). Denying out-group rights, especially in a society that has so long been divided on ethnic lines, is a strong measure of particularized trust. And people who object to ethnic rights are far more critical of the government's role in fighting corruption. They seem to link their own hostility to minority groups to the entrenchment of corruption – and likely to the association of disliked groups with dishonest behavior. As with trust, having connections does not lead people to positive or negative judgments on fighting corruption. However, the more contacts people have with either public or private institutions, the more they approve of government efforts in combating corruption.[10]

---

[10] Frequent interaction with doctors, courts, lawyers, city and county officials, the police, and banks convince people lead people to see less corruption, not more. This may reflect the fact that wealthier people have more contacts – and poor people may simply have to do without such services. But it may also reflect two other dynamics: (1) wealthier people may be able to get things done without having to pay bribes (Kaufmann, Montoriol-Garriga, and Recanatini,

The last equation in the model is for supporting state limits on incomes of the rich. People with more resources – wealth, the ability to afford holidays outside your own town, and whether you own a cellular phone – are less likely to demand redistribution. These are people who are enjoying the benefits of the market economy, so it is not surprising that they do not favor radical redistribution. Having connections, on the other hand, does not lead people to either favor (or more likely) oppose redistribution (perhaps because having connections is strongly associated with wealth).

Romanians who believe that the state has failed to protect vulnerable citizens at the expense of the rich favor limiting incomes. If you believe that people are poor because they do not get assistance from the state and if you believe that inequality has gotten worse – positions held by large majorities of Romanians – you will be more likely to demand limits on incomes. The link is strong in Romania, even more than in some other transition countries (Kluegel and Mason, 2000a, 184). People who think that democracy has worked well are less likely to back redistribution, but those who say that most businesspeople are corrupt do want limits on incomes.[11]

The full model shows that there is a gulf in perceptions in Romania between

- people who see rising inequality, have low generalized trust and high particularized trust, see persistent and widespread grand corruption, see inequality resting on a foundation of grand corruption, and demand government action to level the economic playing field; and
- people who are less troubled by inequality (largely because they have benefitted from the new market economy), have higher levels of generalized trust and lower particularized trust, see progress in combating corruption (or can escape its grip by using connections), and fear tampering with market reforms.

This is the story of a divided society, but since the bulk of the public sees increasing inequality, has low trust, sees corruption as widespread, and favors redistribution, it is the saga of an inequality trap.

Growing inequality threatens the social fabric (generalized trust) directly and indirectly (through its effect on government performance on the quality of life) on faith in political institutions. Corruption also endangers social solidarity, but has even greater effects on government performance on the quality of life and on increasing inequality. It is corruption at the top not from below that matters – and even at the top, it seems concentrated in politicians, businesspeople, local

---

2005); and (2) service providers may be more reluctant to demand bribes from people with whom they interact frequently. However, more highly educated people view government efforts less positively. Finally and hardly surprisingly, supporters of the governing PSD party are more likely to rate the government's handling of corruption positively.

[11] Simple trust in government – based upon a factor analysis of confidence in the President, the parliament, political parties, the courts, the army, the police, and city hall – does not lead people to demand limits on incomes. Simple faith in institutional structures does not matter; specific performance does.

officials, and courts – precisely the officials most commonly cited when people discuss dishonesty in the transition countries. Lower-level professionals are not held blameworthy.

The individual-level model is buttressed by an aggregate model based upon 17 surveys from the same organization using a few of the same questions from October 1996 to October 2003. There are only 10 data points on generalized trust and there is no time series on inequality. However, I can estimate a model of the reciprocal effects of optimism (the key underlying factor behind trust) and evaluations of government control of corruption (as in the individual-level model). The two-stage least squares model in Table A5-4 also supports the idea of reinforcing effects between corruption and optimism (how well the economy of Romania will do in three years).

The equation for optimism includes control over corruption and the growth rate in the gross domestic product (from Penn World Tables). Both perceived success in fighting corruption and a growing economy lead to greater optimism. Fighting corruption matters more: The impact of controlling corruption is almost three times as great as the GDP growth rate.[12] When people are most optimistic, they are also predisposed to view government efforts at fighting corruption positively. When the informal economy (as estimated by the Heritage Foundation) looms larger, people are less likely to approve of the government's efforts on corruption. People may not be able to estimate the size of the informal economy and the Heritage Foundation measure is a simple index rather than a fine-tuned figure. They can see evidence of the informal sector on the street and when they see more of it, they conclude that the government is not fighting corruption.

An optimistic view of the future has a considerably greater impact – by a factor of almost four to one – on perceptions of corruption fighting. As the inequality trap model would suggest, there is a reciprocal relationship between corruption perceptions and optimism, which is the foundation of trust and which can be torn asunder by growing inequality, as the individual-level analysis showed above. Corruption and optimism are strongly linked ($r = .733$). Romanians are most upbeat for the country's future when they see success in fighting corruption – and most downbeat when they see rampant malfeasance.

Connections, Inequality, Trust, and Malfeasance: Big Corruption and Little Corruption

Ordinary citizens face petty corruption in both the public and private spheres. They still use connections to help them get by in daily life. Gift payments and using connections are signs of a still vibrant informal sector in Romania (and most other transition countries, though to varying degrees). I have provided some evidence that people don't become mistrusting or perceive rising inequality because of "gift payments" they must make or because they have to rely upon

---

[12] I calculated this by multiplying each variable's regression coefficient (see Table A5-4) by the range of its values.

connections. The October 2003 survey included a large number of questions on both the range of connections people have and the range of extra payments they make. The model above gives strong support to the overall notion of an inequality trap in Romania, but it cannot take full advantage of the range of questions in the surveys. The individual-level analysis suggests that grand corruption has much greater effects on perceptions of growing inequality and trust than does petty corruption. Is this true for all sorts of gift payments – or do some payments matter more than others? Similarly, having connections does not seem to have much effect on perceptions of inequality or on trust. Do different types of connections have varying consequences?

I focus now on the effects of big and little corruption as well as having connections on five key indicators of the success of transition: perceptions of increasing inequality, satisfaction with democracy and with the market in Romania, trust in government, and generalized trust. Does having informal connections make people feel more empowered – and thus less likely to argue that inequality has increased – or does it make them realize that they have advantages that others don't, so that they see more inequality? Do such connections increase confidence in the market, democracy, and in government because people know how to navigate the system? Or do they decrease faith in these institutions because people believe that they shouldn't need special ties to get things done? Are connections to get by still substitutes for wider social networks – and especially generalized trust? Or do they, under a democratic regime, play a more positive role in forming wider social bonds?

Similarly, does making gift payments make people envious of the public servants – and private employees such as doctors and bank clerks – who put the money in their pockets? Or are such payments "leveling devices," so that a small payment by ordinary folk will get them the same type of service that would cost rich people a lot more? Do such payments lead to perceptions of increasing or decreasing inequality? Do these bribes make people believe that they can make government – and the market – function better or do ordinary people see, as most academics do, petty corruption as examples of the failures of the market and the "honest" state? There is strong evidence (from aggregate models in Chapter 3 as well as earlier in this chapter) that grand corruption has powerful effects in reducing generalized trust (Uslaner, 2004a, 2006b; Uslaner and Badescu, 2004). And the model in Table 5-1 above suggests that petty corruption does not lead people to become mistrusting since it does not lead to greater inequality. Is this true for all types of petty corruption – or just for some?

I test these claims by probit, ordered probit, and regression models of survey responses to questions on trust in other people (generalized trust or social solidarity), trust in government institutions,[13] satisfaction with democracy, satisfaction with the market economy, and perceptions of changes in economic

---

[13] Trust in government is not the same as perceptions that politicians are honest (though I shall show that the two are related). Most models of trust in government (see especially Citrin, 1974) are based upon government performance on the economy and on war and peace, as well as on perceptions of honesty and how much faith people have in specific institutions and leaders.

TABLE 5-2. *Perceptions of Increasing Inequality in Romania: Ordered Probit*

Independent Variable	Coefficient	Std. Error	t Ratio
Quality of life next year	.054	.051	1.06
State of national economy in three years	.119**	.052	2.26
Wealth (can afford consumer goods)	.013	.013	1.04
Performance of government on quality of life	−.243****	.047	−5.13
Most government ministers are corrupt	.038	.058	.66
Most local officials are corrupt	.014	−.025	.25
Most politicians are corrupt	.164***	.070	2.36
Most judges are corrupt	−.029	.064	.46
Made "extra" payments when visiting doctor	−.085	.092	−.93
Made "extra" payments to court	.137	.217	.63
Made "extra" payments to city officials	.245	.252	.97
Made "extra" payments to county officials	.925	.770	1.20
Made "extra" payments to police	−.455	.310	1.47
Made "extra" payments to bank	.146	.434	.33
Have any connections to rely upon	.066**	.039	1.70
Have connections to rely upon for medical treatment	.164**	.084	1.96
Have any connections to rely upon in court/lawyer	.201**	.118	1.70
Have any connections to rely upon at city hall	.090	.093	.97
Have any connections to rely upon dealing with county	−.227	.158	−1.44
Have any connections to rely upon for bank loan	.025	.118	.22
Have any connections to rely upon for finding job	−.060	.117	−.51
Have any connections to rely upon in business world	−.896	.770	−1.16
Have any connections to rely upon in foreign country[+]	−.492***	.125	−3.94

* $p < .10$; ** $p < .05$; *** $p < .01$; **** $p < .0001$
−2*Log Likelihood Ratio = 1602.87; N = 971
Coefficients for variables other than "connections" are for "any connections." Cut points omitted.
[+]Two-tailed test of significance (all other tests one-tailed)

inequality in Romania. I present the results in Tables 5-2, 5-3, and A5-5 through A5-7. For the probit model for generalized trust (Table 5-3), I also include the "effect" of each predictor (the changes in probability of trust from the minimum to the maximum value of the predictor). I focus on measures related to the inequality trap and especially on the indicators of the informal sector – gift payments and connections.

Each equation includes the extra payments and one of the connection measures. Beyond that, the models for the four dependent variables reflect theoretical expectations for each. The tables present results for all of the connections measures (estimated separately) as well as a summary measure of the number of connections. The coefficients and standard errors for the other variables are from the equation for the total number of connections; the coefficients (and

TABLE 5-3. *Generalized Trust in Romania: Probit Analysis*

Independent Variable	Coefficient	Std. Error	t Ratio	Effect
Trust in government scale	.122**	.054	2.26	.197
Direction of country: right or wrong	.622****	.100	6.24	.218
State of national economy in three years	.091*	.059	1.53	.120
Inequality change	−.123**	.070	−1.75	.125
Level of social protection increased or decreased	−.113**	.066	1.72	.120
Wealth (can afford consumer goods)	.034**	.015	2.27	.144
Most ministers are corrupt	−.020	.064	−.31	−.020
Most local councilors are corrupt	−.019	.062	−.31	−.019
Most politicians are corrupt	−.181**	.077	−2.36	−.185
Most judges are corrupt	−.043	.071	−.61	−.043
Made "extra" payments when visiting doctor	−.014	.107	−.13	−.004
Made "extra" payments to court	−.530**	.304	−1.75	−.156
Made "extra" payments to city officials	−.231	.317	−.73	−.073
Made "extra" payments to police	−.139	.367	−.38	−.148
Made "extra" payments to bank	−.503	.511	−.99	−.056
Have any connections to rely upon	−.037	.045	−.08	−.055
Have any connections to rely upon for medical treatment	−.052	.096	−.05	−.016
Have any connections to rely upon in court/lawyer	−.170	.138	−1.23	−.054
Have any connections to rely upon at city hall	−.117	.113	−1.04	−.038
Have any connections to rely upon for police problem	.033	.120	.03	.011
Have any connections to rely upon for bank loan	.037	.141	.03	.012
Have any connections to rely upon for finding job	−.035	.131	−.27	−.011
Have any connections to rely upon in business world	−.165	.160	−1.03	−.057
Have any connections to rely upon in foreign country	−.194*	.139	1.39	−.062
Constant	−.288	.359	−.80	

* p < .10; ** p < .05; *** p < .01; **** p < .0001
Estimated R² = .341; −2*Log Likelihood Ratio = 1097.02; N = 948
Percent predicted correctly 70.4 (model); 64.7 (null)
Coefficients for variables other than "connections" are for "any connections."

standard errors) barely vary at all for the equations for each connection individually. I could not include multiple connections in single models because of high levels of collinearity: People with connections in one area tend to have ties in others. As in the simultaneous equation estimation above, variables tangential to the analysis are discussed in notes.

The models estimated reflect a balance of theoretical expectations about which factors should shape each measure of transition success and predictors that performed best in each equation. There is little reason to expect differences between satisfaction with the government's efforts at controlling corruption and the belief that "most politicians are corrupt." Yet the first question is a strong predictor (negatively) of satisfaction with the workings of democracy and the market, and with trust in government, while people who believe that most politicians are corrupt are more likely to see inequality as rising sharply and to lack faith in their fellow citizens. Where one measure is strong, the other does not achieve significance (and is not included in the final models). High-level corruption is consistently one of the most important predictors of each of the transition indicators, regardless of the measure. For generalized trust, believing that most politicians are corrupt leads to a 19 percent decline in the likelihood of having faith in your fellow citizens – an impact only exceeded by whether you believe that the country is heading in the right direction and whether you trust government.[14] Satisfaction with the market also reflects trust in the private sector and the belief that most businesspeople are *not* corrupt (one of the stronger determinants of positive evaluations of the market).

Do informal relations – "extra" (gift) payments or relying on connections – shape attitudes toward transition as does high-level corruption? *For each of the measures of transition success: (1) the informal sector plays a minor role in shaping public evaluations, and (2) the institutions that do have some impact are those that are perceived to be most fair and impartial: the courts and the police.* Gift payments are almost always *insignificant* predictors of trust in fellow citizens or government, satisfaction with democracy and the market, and even perceptions of rising inequality. Payments to the courts do *not* aggravate perception of inequality – they do have modest effects on satisfaction with democracy though much greater impacts on generalized trust. Note, however, the asymmetry in how gift payments shape trust. They have *no effect* on trust in government but there are strong impacts on faith in other citizens. Presumably people do not expect the same impartiality from the state as they do from the courts, but they do see making payments to the courts as undermining social solidarity, as Rothstein (2000) argues.

Making gift payments is not associated with increasing inequality. However, several of the measures of connections are, including the total number of ties,

---

[14] Trust in government is a significant predictor of generalized trust here and generalized trust also predicts trust in government. For the more comprehensive model above, I did not include trust in government as a predictor of generalized trust because the effects vanish in a simultaneous equation model (see n. 7 above).

connections for medical treatment, and influence with the courts. Medical and legal services are both essential; 71 percent of the sample had contacts with doctors or hospitals and 15 percent with the courts (and an additional 8 percent only with the police). If you don't have such contacts, you may get a lower level of service – or none at all – or your "gift" payment may be considerably higher. It is hardly surprising that using connections would lead to perceptions of rising inequality – though we might not expect that *people with influential ties would admit that these linkages increase disparities*. People who have connections for medical treatments or in courts realize that they have access lacking to most other citizens.

Yet these effects are not large. I dichotomized the inequality variable and computed effects for each type of connection: Court ties increased perceptions of growing inequality by 7 percent, medical intermediaries by only 1 percent, and any connections by 5 percent. Surprisingly, foreign connections led people to see lower levels of inequality (by 7 percent). This runs counter to expectations (so I use a two-tailed test), but the coefficient is large and the impact seems real. It may well be that people with foreign ties see themselves as climbing up the economic ladder – and therefore not as badly off as they once were. People with foreign contacts are more likely to see themselves as well off (the correlations with wealth are tau-c $= .213$, gamma $= .493$). But connections abroad do not breed satisfaction with democracy or the market. In both cases, international ties lead to lower levels of satisfaction with political and economic institutions. Foreign networks seem to point to success for individuals, but institutional failures. Democracy and the market should not be dependent upon foreign contacts.

Having connections seems to *increase* satisfaction with democracy rather than decrease it (again, using two-tailed tests). Any connections or connections with the police or for finding a job or getting a bank loan lead to more satisfaction with democratic performance. It seems that people who have connections may realize that this breeds inequality, but also that they make government function more smoothly. These effects are not small: Police connections raise satisfaction by 8.5 percent, bank ties by 7.8 percent, help in finding a job by 10.8 percent, and any connections by 19.5 percent (using a dichotomized measure of satisfaction with democracy). But relying on ties outside the country reduces satisfaction with democracy by 2.6 percent – perhaps reflecting the feeling that you need to rely upon friends abroad to get what you want from the system.

Connections, or *pile*, may shape positive views about government, but not about the market. Most of the time, as with gift payments, they are unrelated to views of capitalism. In the two instances of significant coefficients – ties with foreigners and any ties at all – the impact is negative, as initially expected. But these effects are not large (in the area of 1 percent for a dichotomized measure). And there are *no* significant effects for any forms of connections needed to get things done with generalized trust.

Using informal connections is sometimes associated with perceptions of rising inequality, but also with better performance of democratic government (where its effects are moderately strong). People see connections and gift payments as part of the routine of getting by in daily life in contemporary Romania. They do not condemn their fellow citizens for relying on these techniques for making life a little bit less difficult in most circumstances. Support from this argument comes from the *positive* effect (significant at p < .10 for a two-tailed test) of gift payments to city hall for trust in government. People with connections in foreign countries have less trust in their own government, perhaps having figured out ways to get around the local (unresponsive) bureaucracy.

What matters most to people in post-Communist societies is government performance – both in managing the economy and in curbing high-level corruption. The informal sector remains a key part of life in these societies, but it is mostly seen as a way of coping with a political and economic system rife with corruption. The informal sector does not destroy social cohesion. It does not make people less supportive of government or the market (except for the more "neutral" institutions of the courts and the police). Even as they realize that "gift payments" may be an unfair tax, they are generally minor irritants when political and business leaders may be plundering much larger amounts from the public purse. Citizens in transition countries have lived with the necessity of an informal sector for many years. They see it as a minor factor at best impeding the development of a market democracy. With increasing economic inequality and the harshness of the market, it may be a small price to pay to ensure coping with obtaining public and private services.

Romanian citizens clearly distinguish between grand and petty corruption, between malfeasance by politicians and businesspeople, on the one hand, and lower-level bureaucrats and service providers (doctors, banks, lawyers) on the other. Grand corruption bothers people greatly. Petty corruption violates notions of a well-functioning society but often brings benefits to the person who pays – and in any event, it does not make people rich. One of the entrepreneurs in the focus group interviewed by King et al. (2003, 145) commented on the demands of politicians:

We need to obtain some road clearances that give us the right to drive in the European countries. They give these to whom they like, though, in exchange for bribes . . . I, at first, thought that I may offend people by giving them money. They are not, on the contrary; they think they deserve all that money . . . and believe me, we're talking big money.

Bureaucrats tell businesspeople about the political leaders who are their bosses: "Keep out of there; you don't know that the guy is busy building himself a mansion" (King et al., 2003, 153).

King et al. (2003, 147) summarize the comments of their respondents:

. . . our focus group respondents considered small scale corruption without theft personally rational. Even those who refused to engage in it thought that it was useful, sometimes obligatory, to give a gift or little bribe in order to obtain the government services to which they were legally entitled. Necessity was commonly used to justify or excuse participation in his form of corruption, and to differentiate it from more severe forms of corruption which they did not regularly perform and which they generally considered much more dangerous.

People see a clear link from corrupt politicians to increased inequality (Table 5-2), and rising income disparities lead to less trust both in government and in fellow citizens. Yet gift payments do not seem to lead to perceptions of increasing inequality. While some connections do make people see rising disparities of wealth, the effects are not large and they do not spill over to less faith in other people, in the state, in democracy, or in the market.

In the equation for generalized trust, there are sharp distinctions among forms of corruption: Most venues of corruption do *not* lead to less trust. Even though having to make extra payments to courts leads to less trust, the 26 percent of Romanians who say that most judges are corrupt are not less trusting – nor likely to believe that inequality has increased. Apparently most people don't believe that judges are likely to get rich – nor do they lose faith in their fellow citizens because they see local councilors as corrupt or even government ministers as dishonest.[15] Nor does any form of "gift payments" other than to courts lead to less trust. And here the issue may not be how much people have to pay but rather being compelled to bribe for justice. The one venue of corruption that does undermine generalized trust is the belief that "most politicians are corrupt," since payments to higher-level officials involve larger amounts of money.

The key determinants of perceptions of rising inequality and satisfaction with both democracy and the market, beyond handling corruption, are people's evaluations of how well the government and the economy have worked. Both "pocketbook" (personal success) and "sociotropic" (societal prosperity) shape satisfaction with the transition. Yet how well you are doing matters *less* than perceptions of social progress. Neither the quality of life next year nor personal wealth shapes attitudes on increasing inequality – though how well the national economy will fare in three years does. Life satisfaction matters for approval of democracy and especially the market – and approval of the market also is tied to happiness with your income (though not to actual reported wealth). How well you are doing does not matter nearly as much as the most important variable across all three indicators: the performance of the government on the quality of life. For inequality, this is the only area (other than corruption) where government performance matters. Short-term prosperity (the quality of life next year) doesn't matter nearly as much as success over the longer term (three years). Immediate affluence doesn't matter at all for perceptions of increasing inequality and has only a moderate effect on support for democracy. It is, not surprisingly, more important for satisfaction with the economy.

For the market and especially for democracy, whether the government keeps the streets safe is also critical (and this is clearly related to Mafia influence and,

---

[15] Councilor and ministerial corruption may lead to less trust, but the effect may be dwarfed by perceptions that politicians are corrupt: The correlations with "most politicians are corrupt" are .301 (tau, gamma = .643) for local councilors and .286 (tau, gamma = .607) for ministers.

hence, corruption). How well the government handles public safety is the single most important factor explaining the trust in government scale.[16]

Perceptions of increasing inequality mostly reflect negative evaluations of government economic performance and of corrupt leaders. Support for democracy reflects expectations of economic performance and perceptions of how well the government is handling large-scale corruption. Support for the market economy reflects similar economic judgments as well as perceptions that private firms are trustworthy and large-scale corruption is being controlled. Trust in other people largely reflects optimism for the future,[17] the belief that politicians are *not* corrupt, and trust in government. People who have made gift payments to courts are less likely to have faith in others, as are people with connections in foreign countries (perhaps because they believe that in a well-ordered society, they should not have to rely upon people outside Romania). Two of the largest effects, amounting to drops in trust of about 12 percent each, are perceptions of rising inequality and the belief that the level of social protection from government programs has decreased. Less social protection and rising inequality both weaken social solidarity – and both point to increased disparities within Romanian society.

The Demands of a Successful Transition

The Romanian public clearly sees connections between high-level corruption and inequality – leading to low trust. Low trust is nothing new in Romania. Communism made faith in your fellow citizens hazardous and the long history of ethnic conflict is a sign that Romanians have been reluctant to reach out beyond their own in-groups.

The transition indicators in Table A5-1 also indicate that Romania is not faring as badly as it is sometimes portrayed. Why should the economic psychology of transition matter when people's opinions are simply too bleak given economic realities? This is a central question – since it applies with even greater force to Estonia and Slovakia, considered in Chapter 6, which are far more advanced in transition indicators than is Romania.

---

[16] Concern for disorder also leads to less confidence in democracy and trust in government: People who believe that Romania needs a strong leader (as in the past) are less satisfied with the state of democracy, as are people who believe that the state should control the media and political parties (who also have less trust in government). Supporters of the ruling (and former Communist) party, the PSD, have *more* confidence in government, while residents of the capital (Bucharest) are less likely to trust government. I expected that young people would have more faith in democracy and the market – this is barely supported (p < .10) for satisfaction with democracy, but young people are no more satisfied with market performance than others.

[17] Instead of the performance of government on the quality of life, I employ the measure of whether the country is heading in the right direction, which has the largest effect on trust. This measure is closer to indicators of optimism I have used elsewhere (Uslaner, 2002, chs. 3–4, 6). Wealthier people are also more likely to trust others.

Attitudes matter, perhaps more than actual economic statistics, because people's opinions shape their social and political world. Romanians have long been pessimistic and they continue to look to the future with trepidation. Some statistics, such as the growth rate, give them cause for great concern. Others may not seem so troublesome in the context of world rankings. However, Romanians are not (and should not be) content with comparisons with Bangladesh or even Mexico. Romania looks to Europe (and to the United States) as its future. Yes, for many people, the Western model is unattractive: It brings with it greater inequality and a lack of respect for traditional culture. But few, if any, want to go back to the Ceausescu era. Yet most Romanians have little faith that the future will lead to more equality and, especially, less corruption. In the World Bank Diagnostic survey, just 6 percent of Romanians believe that parliament wants very much to curb corruption – and 61 percent say "not at all."

Attitudes matter because they indicate that transition to a well-ordered society demands more than private enterprise and democratic institutions. The democratic transition in Romania is threatened by increasing inequality, persistent corruption, and especially by low out-group trust reflected in ethnic conflicts. These tensions between ethnic Hungarians and Romanians – and the continuing demonization of Jews even as only a handful of Jews remain in the country – hurt the transition in at least two ways. First, low out-group trust, especially combined with rising inequality, hurts the battle to control corruption. When people believe that "outsiders" receive more benefits or wealth than they deserve – as many Romanians believe about minority groups, including the Roma (who have very high levels of unemployment and are often forced into the informal sector) – then asserting the rights of your own group becomes paramount. People may complain about corrupt politicians, but they will continue to support public officials who steal from the public purse as long as they espouse the "right" positions on ethnic relations.

"Conspiring" within your own group becomes morally acceptable as people struggle to get by, so people come to accept using connections and even making "extra" payments to public servants, doctors, teachers, and bank clerks.

People see a moral dilemma in having to go outside what should be "normal channels." Sanda, the Romanian woman talking to the English walkers, said, "Everything in this country is black market. You must pay for everything" (Goodwin, 2000, 152). Yet they see also see the benefits of such petty corruption by giving them advantages in getting services, and these connections are largely all in the ethnic family: Only a quarter of Romanians ever ask ethnic Hungarians for help (Culic, Horvath, and Rat, 2000, 312–13).

Rising inequality and persistent low trust and high levels of corruption lead to envy and exacerbated social tensions among ethnic groups. There has been a long-standing conflict over maintaining Hungarian-language schools. These conflicts undermine support for universal social policies, which are the most likely to increase trust and combat inequality. Transition countries have now largely forsaken universal social welfare programs, many of which were mired in corruption anyway under Communism, for fee-based programs (European Commission Employment and Social Affairs, 2003). Romania will find it more difficult to escape the inequality trap and to reduce corruption. The long-standing pessimism of Romanians seems realistic.

6

Half Empty or Almost Full?

Mass and Elite Perceptions of Corruption in Estonia, Slovakia, and Romania

If at first you don't succeed, then try and try again.
And if you don't succeed again, just try and try and try.
Useless, it's useless.
Our kind of life is tough.
Take it from me it's useless. Trying ain't enough.
Since people ain't much good just hit 'em on the hood.
But though you hit 'em good and hard they're never out for good.
Useless, it's useless when they're playing rough.
Take it from me it's useless.
You're never rough enough.
From "The Useless Song," Berthold Brecht and Kurt Weill,
The Threepenny Opera

Romania's mixed success in the transition to a market economy, together with its legacy of ethnic conflict, poverty, and corruption, makes it easy to understand why its public is so pessimistic. Estonia and Slovakia have had a much more successful transition – especially to a market economy run under the rule of law, democracy, and relatively low levels of corruption. Estonia's capital, Tallinn, is a "boomtown," the surging economy called the "the Baltic tiger, the sequel to the Celtic tiger [Ireland] as Europe's success story," fueled by so many high-tech companies such as the Internet phone service Skype that outsiders call the country "E-stonia" (Tierney, 2006). Slovakia is a less prominent success, yet it has largely escaped the high levels of economic inequality that have been a hallmark of most transition countries and fares better than most former Communist states on corruption.

Yet citizens in Estonia and Slovakia remain pessimistic – and they see corruption all around them even as elites in these countries believe that government and business are much more honest. Not only do ordinary citizens see lots of malfeasance, but they link it – generally more than either government officials or entrepreneurs – to economic inequality.

I examine surveys of the public, entrepreneurs, and government officials in Estonia and Slovakia, and of the public and entrepreneurs in Romania in this chapter. The Slovakian and Romanian surveys were both conducted for the World Bank under their Corruption Diagnostic Survey program. The surveys had the same basic design so there are often (though not always) common variables in these polls – making direct comparisons possible. The Estonian survey was conducted for the Government of Estonia's Ministry of Justice under the auspices of the European Union. So while the surveys in the three countries included both masses and elites, only the Slovakian and Romanian studies have many questions in common. Even here, the surveys were not always as comparable as I would like: Government officials in Romania were not asked whether corruption increased inequality, so I cannot use the public officials survey here.

Despite the differences in design and question wording, one key result stands out: In all three countries, masses and elites see corruption differently. In Estonia, the public is far more likely to see malfeasance as pervasive, while the elites see themselves as far more honest. And the public links corruption more strongly to trust in other people than do either entrepreneurs or government officials. While there are no questions on inequality in the Estonian surveys, the very different perceptions of the extent of corruption in the country suggest a strong imbalance in how masses and elites perceive the fairness of their state and society.

The comparisons are more direct for Slovakia and Romania. Slovakia has the lowest level of inequality of any transition country – and has long been "a markedly egalitarian society, even by Eastern European standards" before the transition (Verwiebe and Wegener, 2000, 128; see also Table A6-1). Romania, as noted in Chapter 5, is relatively egalitarian but inequality has been increasing since transition – and almost all Romanians see this as threatening the already weak social fabric and most demand limits on the incomes of the rich. The informal sector plays a large role in Romania's economy, but considerably less in Slovakia's. Either using the transition countries or all nations as a base, Slovakia is relatively prosperous while Romania is not (see Tables A5-1 and A6-1).

Romanians are, not surprisingly, far more likely to link corruption to inequality and to explain the connection between corruption and inequality as reflecting worries about the security of the state and the transition to a functioning market economy, while the more "middle class" Slovaks see this tie as reflecting the society's moral failures. Slovakian citizens also lose faith in their government when they see it as corrupt and especially when they tie this dishonesty to increasing inequality. Slovakian elites who agree that corruption causes inequality do not necessarily lose faith in their government – and overall corruption matters much less to elites than to ordinary citizens.

Inequality matters in two distinct ways for corruption. First, in all three countries, masses see corruption differently from elites – in Estonia as more common, in Slovakia and Romania as more likely to lead to inequality. Masses are more likely to lose faith in other people (Estonia) and in their government (Slovakia) when they see corruption as widespread, especially grand corruption. Second, both masses and elites are more likely to see a tie between malfeasance and inequality where both corruption and inequality are higher – in Romania as opposed to Slovakia.

There are two key lessons from these findings. First, for a country that ranks somewhere in between honest and corrupt (Estonia), ordinary people see the "glass of corruption" as mostly full, while businesspeople and public officials – the key actors in honest versus corrupt dealings – have a more upbeat view of business-government ties. Citizens are bothered by even a "moderate" amount of corruption and may not be so willing to distinguish between a little bit of corruption and a lot. Second, Romanians and Slovaks may not make correct estimates about the total amount of corruption, but corruption and inequality matter more where they are bigger problems. Romanians see far more corruption and are more likely to tie it to inequality than Slovaks.

I show in this chapter that

- In each country, the mass public is considerably more likely to see widespread corruption than are the elites.
- In Estonia, the belief that corruption has increased leads ordinary citizens but *not the elite* to be less trusting of fellow citizens.
- The Estonian public sees increasing corruption as the result of malfeasance by elites, not by ordinary citizens.
- Ordinary citizens are far more likely to see corruption leading to greater inequality in both Slovakia and Romania than are elites – and Romanian citizens are considerably more likely to see inequality stemming from malfeasance than are Slovaks.
- Both Romanian and Slovakian citizens see the link between corruption and inequality as threatening the transition and especially a market economy. However, Romanians see the link between corruption and inequality as reflecting abuses of power as well as the pervasiveness of bribery, while Slovaks link it more to crime and human rights and not at all to petty corruption.
- Romanian entrepreneurs see the link between corruption and inequality in ways more similar to the Slovakian public than they do to their own fellow citizens. In Romania, the public is more likely to see corruption as tied to inequality, but there is no clear pattern in Slovakia. Yet the Slovakian citizenry and its elites are each less prone to make the connection than are the Romanian public and elites. The Romanian elite sees the tie much as the Slovakian public does.
- Slovakian entrepreneurs and government officials see the link between corruption and inequality as weakening the moral character of the society and threatening their own economic well-being; entrepreneurs are particularly likely to see the connection between corruption and inequality as stemming from the dishonesty of public officials *and* the mass public and of their own economic situation.

- Corruption causes ordinary Slovaks to lose faith in their government to a much greater extent than it does for either entrepreneurs or government officials. For Slovaks, the link between corruption and inequality leads to less trust in government *only for ordinary citizens, not for elites* – and only grand corruption, not petty dishonesty – leads ordinary citizens to lose faith in government.
- Slovakian entrepreneurs lose faith in government when they believe that public officials are dishonest, when the bureaucracy is unresponsive, and when public services are lacking. Slovakian officials only lose faith in government when they see direct evidence of dishonesty (bribes or embezzlement) among officials.

The Path to Transition in Estonia and Slovakia

Estonia and Slovakia are among the more successful transition countries (see Table A6-1). In 2004, when its Corruption Perceptions Index was only 4.0, Estonia still ranked first among transition countries on honesty. A year later Estonia's rating soared to 6.4, still relatively modest compared to most Western countries, but the best among transition countries. Slovakia was in the top quarter of transition countries, even as its TI index barely made the top third of all countries. Both countries nevertheless had increases in corruption compared to 1998, but Slovakia's improvement was among the best among all countries and Estonia also fared relatively well.

While neither country has a particularly trusting population, Slovakia has excelled in maintaining low levels of inequality – ranking first in the world (and, of course, among transition nations) by the WIDER and Rosser/Rosser/Ahmed measures and fourth among transition countries on the Dutta/Mishra index. Estonia has not fared so well on economic inequality. It ranks at or below the middle for transition countries and for all nations. Both countries stand out with relatively high gross domestic product per capita and GDP growth among transition countries – and they rank in the top third of all countries on GDP per capita but not for growth. Their citizens are living relatively well, according to the scores on the United Nations Human Development Index. Estonia stands out as a leader among transition countries in democratization and the rule of law – and for the fairness of its legal system. Slovakia does not rank quite so strongly, but it is still among the more successful of transition countries.

While both countries rank in the top quarter of transition states on the Failed States index, they stand in the bottom third of all nations on this measure of state capacity. Both fare much better on uneven economic development, though here Estonia far outpaces Slovakia, ranking third among transition nations and between 20th and 27th place (due to ties) among all nations. Given the overall higher level of economic inequality in Estonia, this result is somewhat surprising. It is reflected in the strong performance for Estonia, with Slovakia not far behind, on the ICRG measure of internal conflicts. Nevertheless, both countries have considerable ethnic conflict, even for transition nations. The relatively high level of ethnic conflict in Slovakia is echoed in the 1998 Ethnobarometer that showed Slovaks expressing the greatest concern among ten countries that ethnic minorities constitute a threat to peace in the country.[1]

Estonia has a relatively robust economy and has fared well on democratization – especially on the rule of law. It has less corruption than any other transition country (though Slovenia is virtually tied with it). Estonia and Slovakia stand out among transition countries on economic performance, even though their growth rates are modest. Other than Slovakia's low level of economic inequality, neither country ranks so highly that it is comparable with Western nations. Among Western European nations, Portugal and Malta in Europe have 2005 TI scores close to Estonia, with Greece far behind and tied with Slovakia and Italy somewhat higher. In both countries, then, there is still considerable corruption – even if they are relatively "clean" compared to other transition nations.

I focus first on Estonia and then on a comparative analysis of Slovakia and Romania. Of the three countries, Estonia stands out as the greatest success story – outpaced only among transition countries by Slovenia and the Czech Republic. Tierney (2006) attributes Estonia's success to the free-market policies of Prime Minister Mart Laar, who abolished almost all trade barriers, cut taxes, established a flat tax, and promoted business development and foreign investment with a zeal unheard of in transition countries – and indeed in most of the West. An unfettered market requires the rule of law, fair courts, and honest government and Laar worked hard to promote each. Estonia also had favorable economic conditions at its rebirth as an independent country: It was energy independent and did not depend upon large-scale heavy industry that led a European Union report to claim that the country has had "one of the world's fastest growing economies since mid-1997" (Panagiotou, 2001, 264). Estonians are more satisfied with their lives overall, according to the 2005 European Social Survey (wave 2), than are people in any transition country other than Slovenia (as well as more than the Portuguese), but the mean score of 5.89 is still considerably below the mean for the 25 European countries (including Israel) of 6.59.

If Tierney is correct, Estonia's success can be reproduced elsewhere in transition countries if the political will is strong enough. It would be strong testimony to the claim that policies matter – but so do honest and efficient institutions, such as a dominant executive branch. This structural account must be tempered by an explanation that gives more weight to history and culture. Estonia, like Slovenia, had a ready market for its exports in Western Europe. Its proximity to the Nordic nations gave it crucial advantages over other transition countries, as did its reform government prior to the break-up of the Soviet Union. The Soviet Union gave considerable autonomy, in both economic and social life, to

---

[1] The countries and the percentages saying that ethnic groups are a threat to peace are Belarus (14), Bulgaria (29), Croatia (39), Czech Republic (25), Hungary (19), Poland (17), Romania (32), Slovakia (43), Slovenia (10), and Ukraine (15). See Culic, Horvath, and Rat (2000, 293).

Estonia (and the other Baltic republics Latvia and Lithuania), permitting them a more liberal economy and contact with the West (Lauristin and Vihalemm, 1997, 75–6).

Most critically, Estonia was culturally tied to its closest neighbor, Finland, much more than it was to the Soviet Union. Panagiotou (2001, 274–5) argues that

most Estonians felt a strong affinity for Scandinavia, depicted...by the declaration of many Estonians that Finnish, and not Russian, was their second language. Moreover, Estonians' access to Finnish television and interaction with tourists from Scandinavia over the years had lent an important familiarity with western cultures and way of life....upon independence Estonia was better placed to shed the Soviet cultural legacy and deepen and enhance its links with western countries...

Ferries run almost hourly between Helsinki, the capital of Finland, and Estonia's capital, Tallinn, as Finns flock to Estonia for cheaper shopping (especially for liquor) – but also for family visits.

The Nordic countries rank very high on trust and low on both corruption and inequality, so the close ties between them and Estonia clearly shape post-Communist political and social life. The close ties with Finland (and other Nordic countries) lead to a more successful transition than most other countries, and especially those that were part of the former Soviet Union. Yet these ties do not make Estonia a little Finland. Corruption still persists in Estonia, trust is low, inequality is higher than it was under Communism and middle range by world standards, and ethnic relations are very tense.

The economic boom did not make everyone well off. Raun (2001, 255) argues that the transition in Estonia "...substantially heightened inequality of income and wealth as well as social divisions." Under Communism, Estonia (and the other Baltic states) had the lowest rates of inequality of any Soviet republic – but the Gini indices rapidly increased after independence to levels similar to Southern Europe; by the late 1990s, 37 percent of the population lived in poverty (Norgaard and Johannsen, 1996, 122, 124). Urban residents and especially young people prospered, while old people on pensions and in rural areas struggled to get by (Raun, 2001, 255). Seventy percent of people born since 1980 said that the economic situation in the past five years had gotten better, compared to about a quarter born in 1940 or earlier. Seventy-three percent of students said that the economy had improved, compared to about a fifth of pensioners.

The ethnic divide has long been a feature of Estonian life. Before the Soviet occupation, 88 percent of the population was ethnic Estonians and 8 percent was Russian. The Estonian birth rate fell precipitously in the 1940s; many Estonians were deported or fled to the West following the Soviet annexation, and 100,000 more were killed in World War II. The non-Estonian (mostly Russian) population increased by 2600 percent from 1940 to 1989 (Vetik, 2002, 74).

Estonia is marked by strong ethnic tensions between native Estonians and Russians. Estonians resented the deportations of their own and the resettlement of Russians by the Soviet authorities. At independence in 1989, only families who were citizens of Estonia prior to 1940 qualified automatically as citizens. Ethnic Estonians were considered "loyal by birth" or "by inheritance," even if they were not currently living in the country; non-Estonians were considered to be "born in disloyalty" and they had to demonstrate "signs of loyalty" by language proficiency and take legal steps to demonstrate that they were "Estonia-minded" and had an "Estonian mind-set" (Semjonov, 2002, 115, 119). Russians were stripped of their government positions (Kolsto, 2002, 252).

These ethnic tensions persist, as reflected in the low ranking for the country on the ICRG measure of ethnic tensions. Sixty-one percent of ethnic Estonians have high scores on a measure of "ethnic distress." Their "prevailing attitudes are related to political and social distrust together with indignation linked to ethnic issues and a fear of competition with non-Estonians" (Semjonov, 2002, 140). Estonians and non-Estonians live apart from each other, with Russians segregated mostly in the eastern part of the country (near Russia), encouraging thoughts of independence should tensions grow too strong (Fearon, 1998, 123). There is little interaction between the two groups and they have almost no contact with each other. People from both groups refrain from using the language of the other (Vetik, 2002, 78). Such residential segregation means that members of each group will not have the opportunity to interact with the other – and this promotes low generalized trust and high particularized trust.

Estonians fare better economically than Russians. In the public survey, 13.7 percent of ethnic Estonians earn more than $350 a month per person compared to 5.3 percent of Russians. While 45 percent of Estonians said that the economy had improved, only 39 percent of Russians agreed. In the European Social Survey 60 percent of ethnic Estonians expressed satisfaction with life overall, compared to 46 percent of Russians.

Growing inequality and ethnic tensions are recipes for low generalized trust – and the World Values Survey estimate for Estonia of 22 percent believing that "most people can be trusted" is in accord with this expectation (though the Ministry of Justice survey indicates far more trust). Yet Estonia ranks relatively well on the TI Corruption Perceptions Index. Can you have an inequality trap without a lot of corruption? What, then, is a high level of malfeasance – and who determines whether a society is corrupt or not? The TI Corruption Perceptions Index is an elite survey, based upon responses from businesspeople, academics, and other "experts."[2] The public may – and in Estonia does – see considerably more corruption than either businesspeople or government officials. Even a "successful" transition state such as Estonia may still be subject to an inequality trap. I cannot demonstrate this for Estonia as I did for Romania since the surveys

---

[2] See the Survey Sources for the 2004 CPI link at http://www.transparency.org/policy_research/ surveys_indices/global/cpi.

are not as comprehensive. Yet there is more than a bit of suggestion that Estonia has not escaped this syndrome.

Estonians' Views of Corruption: Masses and Elites

I examine surveys commissioned by the Government of Estonia and the World Bank and the United States Information Agency (for Slovakia and Romania).[3] The Estonian population survey used face-to-face interviews with a national probability sample in 2003 (N = 1002 respondents). The public officials and entrepreneurs surveys used Computer Assisted Web Interviewing. The public officials survey (N = 901) used a quota sample for (1) ministries, county governments, and constitutional institutions; (2) agencies and boards; (3) institutions of law and order, (4) politicians; and (5) local government officials (Tavits, 2005, 9). The entrepreneurs survey was stratified by region, size of business, and industry sector (N = 503; TNS EMOR, 2004, 7–8).

The Slovakian and Romanian surveys were conducted in 1999 and 2000, respectively. In Slovakia, the surveys included 350 public officials, 400 enterprise managers, and 1100 members of the public (Anderson, 2000, v). The enterprise survey oversampled corporations and the government officials survey balanced local, regional, and national officers in relatively equal proportions, with one manager for every six functionaries (Anderson, 2000, 2–3). The Romanian public sample of 1050 responses was stratified by region and size of community; the enterprise sample of 417 was stratified by region, type of enterprise, ownership type, size, and industry sector (Anderson, Cosmaciuc, Dininio, Spector, and Zoido-Lobaton, 2001, 38–9).

The 2003 surveys of the Estonian public, business entrepreneurs, and public officials were conducted by TNS EMOR by computer-assisted face-to-face design for the general public and by computer-assisted telephone design for the elites. The questions were largely, though not entirely, identical. Some questions were not asked of entrepreneurs. Here I focus on overall perceptions of corruption among each group (some questions were not asked of entrepreneurs) and a simultaneous equation model of perceptions of increasing corruption since the Soviet era and generalized trust.

I present basic descriptive data on perceptions of corruption as well as levels of both trust in people and support for political leaders and democracy in Table 6-1 below. The overall story is clear: The public is far more likely to

[3] Funding for the Estonian surveys (Ministry of Justice of the Republic of Estonia, 2005), conducted by TNS EMOR, was provided by the Ministry of Justice and the European Commission (Phare Project "Reducing Corruption in Estonia Number 2003/005–850.01.01). Response rates for the surveys for Estonia were 52 percent for the public survey, 36 percent for the government officials survey (Tavits, 2005, 9), and 29 percent for the enterprise survey (calculated from TNS EMOR, 2004, 7–8); for Slovakia, 52 percent for the public survey, 41 percent for the officials survey, and 38 percent for the entrepreneur survey (calculated from information provided by the Focus Center for Social and Market Analysis). No information is available on the response rates for the Romania surveys.

TABLE 6-1. *Perceptions of Estonians on Trust and Corruption: The Public, Business, and Public Officials*

Question	Public	Business	Officials	p Level
Corruption increased since Soviet times*	1.734	2.183	2.143	.0001
Corruption increased since 1990s*	1.837	2.575	2.316	.0001
Corruption inevitable in Estonia**	2.355	–	2.625	.0001
Courts in Estonia ensure fair trials**	2.232	2.201	2.199	n.s.
Trust most people in Estonia	.614	.693	.643	.01
Non-Estonians as trustworthy	.804	.774	.736	n.s.
Trust police**	2.294	2.078	2.162	.0001
Politicians do their best for the country	–	.469	.416	.10
Democracy best form of government**	1.940	1.524	1.664	.0001
Common: Offer bribe to avoid fine	.795	–	.078	.0001
Common: Offer bribe to change law	.466	–	.007	.0001
Common: Offer bribe for favorable ruling	.696	–	.040	.0001
Common: Entrepreneur offers bribe to expedite procedures	.745	–	.064	.0001
Common: Bribe offered to get job	.608	–	.005	.0001
Common: Civil servant uses state car	.917	–	.928	n.s.
Common: Civil servant lectures for pay	.650	–	.758	.0001
Common: Entrepreneur asks friend in civil service to expedite procedures	.799	–	.826	n.s.
Common: Entrepreneurs offer civil servants goods for help	.755	–	.651	.0002
Common: Civil servants order computers from relative's company	.694	–	.771	n.s.
Acceptable: Entrepreneur offers civil servants goods for help	.245	.127	.033	.0001
Acceptable: Patient jumps queue for operation because brother went to medical school with doctor	.342	.322	.145	.0001
Corruption if official accepts gift after service**	2.417	2.143	2.277	.0001
Corruption if official accepts bribe for service**	1.396	1.295	1.202	.0001
Corruption if get job through personal connection**	1.892	–	1.950	n.s.
Corruption if official takes money for providing information not publicly available**	1.392	1.252	1.212	.0001
Take bribes because it is polite	.277	.066	.081	.0001
Take bribes because civil servant pay is too low	.309	.170	.559	.0001
Take bribes because people are persistent	.300	–	.322	n.s.
Take bribes because everyone accepts them	.292	.147	.184	.0001
Take bribes because acceptance won't be punished	.624	.501	.548	.0001

All cell entries are proportions agreeing except where noted by:
* Range is 1–3, with higher values indicating decreased corruption.
** Range is 1–4 with lower values indicating greater trust in police, greater likelihood of fair trials, greater support for democracy, agreement that activity constitutes corruption, and that corruption is *not* inevitable in Estonia.

believe that high-level corruption is widespread, but there are fewer differences, if any, with low-level malfeasance. Even in a country that ranks relatively highly on the TI Corruption Perceptions Index, the mass public believes that grand corruption is common – and both the masses and elites see petty corruption as widespread.

Ordinary people and elites have very different perceptions of how common corruption is and what "dishonest" activities are tolerable. Across a series of measures, *the public is more likely to say that petty corruption is acceptable*. Ordinary people believe that they must be corrupt to get by, while entrepreneurs and government officials see themselves as part of a more "modern" and Western European society with different norms. The irony is that the public believes that petty corruption is widespread but inevitable, while the elites see low-level malfeasance as epidemic but unacceptable. We take the small gifts and use connections to gain favors, but we really shouldn't do so, government officials say.

Most telling is the simple question of whether corruption has increased or decreased since the Soviet era. The public is clearly more pessimistic: 48 percent of the public says that corruption has gotten worse, only 19 percent say the situation has gotten better. Public officials and entrepreneurs are far more optimistic: Only 30 and 25 percent, respectively, say that corruption has increased, while 47 and 53 percent say that it has gotten better. The public is convinced that there is more corruption than under Communism and the elites are just as certain that there is less.

All three groups are more likely to say that corruption has gotten better since the 1990s than to make a favorable comparison with Soviet times. Yet here the differences become even more stark. Just 25 percent of the public says that corruption has decreased since the 1990s – 43 percent say it is now worse – compared to 59 percent of bureaucrats and 73 percent of businesspeople.[4] The public, by 56 percent, agrees that corruption is inevitable in Estonia, while only 44 percent of government officials agree (the question was not asked of entrepreneurs). All of these differences are significant at p < .0001.

Elites are considerably more likely to trust the police. However, there is little difference in perceptions of the fairness of the courts. Two-thirds of the public believe that the courts ensure a fair trial, as one might expect in a country marked by high ratings for the rule of law and fair courts. Yet a significant minority of the general public, 20 percent, is not convinced that democracy is the best form of government, while fewer than 7 percent of either elite is so skeptical. The public is also less convinced than government officials that the economic situation in Estonia is better than it was five years ago. Both elite groups are torn as to whether politicians do their best for the country (a minority in each case). There are only modest differences in the share of people who trust most people and no significant gaps in perceiving people of different ethnic groups as just as trustworthy as Estonians. The generalized trust question

---

[4] The government officials survey include both elected and appointed officials, but I use the term "bureaucurats" to describe all.

in these surveys is not the same as in most other surveys (notably the World Values Survey) and it thus overestimates how trusting Estonians are (.22 in Table A6-1 from the World Values Survey).

Across the series of questions on how common corrupt acts are, the public is far more likely to see high-level corruption as common than are government officials (the questions were not asked of entrepreneurs). The public sees bribes as very common – for avoiding fines, to expedite procedures, to get a job,[5] for obtaining favorable rulings by administrators and judges, and to a lesser extent to change laws – while government officials say that such payments are rare. Less than 1 percent of officials say that it is common to bribe people to get jobs or to change laws. Both the public and government officials say that it is common for an entrepreneur to ask a friend in the civil service to expedite procedures or civil servants to order computers from relatives' companies. Are such actions corrupt or do they just represent using connections, which were part of everyday life in Communist (and other) societies where the market does not function well? The gray area in which entrepreneurs offer civil servants goods in turn for help – the value of the goods is not specified – is widespread, according to both the public and officials, but more so (by 76 to 65 percent, $p < .0002$) for the former.

While the public is more likely to see corruption as widespread, ironically it is less ready to characterize behavior as corruption or to condemn it as unacceptable. Just about half of the public says that corruption occurs when an official accepts a gift after performing a service, compared to 60 percent of officials and two-thirds of entrepreneurs. While all three groups strongly condemn taking a bribe (as opposed to a "gift") for performing a service (93, 98, and 97 percent, respectively), the difference is significant at $p < .0001$. All three groups also condemn an official taking money for providing information that is not publicly available, but again the officials and entrepreneurs are more critical than the mass public. Seventy-five percent of the public and officials condemn getting a job through a personal connection. Even though strong majorities of each group say that it is not acceptable for entrepreneurs to offer civil servants goods for assistance or for a patient to get faster service because his/her brother went to medical school with the doctor, the public is substantially more tolerant of such low-level corruption– perhaps because ordinary citizens confront such situations more often and may personally benefit from petty corruption.

Why do people take bribes? Ordinary citizens are considerably more likely to say that officials take bribes to be polite – not to offend the citizen who offers small "gifts – because everyone accepts money, and because officials will not be punished. The public sees these payments as part and parcel of daily life. They also say that people are persistent when they offer a bribe, so it is difficult for officials to say no. Here public officials agree with them. Officials say that they take bribes because their pay is too low – an argument that the public is less willing to accept and that entrepreneurs find even less convincing.

---

[5] Whether this is grand or petty corruption is unclear from the question.

TABLE 6-2. *Simultaneous Estimation of Trust and Perception of Increased Corruption: Estonian Public*

Variable	Coefficient	Std. Error	t Ratio
Generalized trust			
Corruption increased since Soviet era	−.269***	.084	−3.21
Most people are selfish	−.109****	.027	4.03
Strong leader better form of government	−.037*	.025	−1.42
Courts ensure a fair trial	.113***	.037	3.04
Economic welfare better than five years ago	.083***	.031	2.69
Unemployment serious problem	.093*	.061	1.51
Everyone accepts bribes	−.129***	.051	−2.54
Doctors request bribes	−.076	.074	−1.04
Age	.005****	.002	3.40
Estonian nationality	−.113**	.058	−1.97
Constant	−.142	.253	−.56
Corruption increased since Soviet era			
Generalized trust	−.266*	.201	−1.33
How guilty are entrepreneurs of corruption	.045**	.024	1.83
How guilty are ordinary citizens of corruption	−.029	.026	−1.13
Personally suffered from corruption	.056	.055	1.03
Speeder offers police officer bribe: how common	.194**	.084	2.31
Enterpreneur offers school official warm trip: how common	.162**	.080	2.02
Entrepreneur offers civil servant goods for favorable outcome: how common	.131*	.080	1.63
Civil servants take bribes because pay is too low	.209***	.080	2.59
Private sector employee	−.162**	.082	−1.97
Age	.008***	.002	3.69
Estonian nationality	−.250***	.086	−2.91
Constant	2.420****	.260	9.32

*p < .10; **p < .05; ***p < .01; ****p < .0001 (all tests one-tailed except for constants)
R^2 = .144 (trust), .192 (corruption increased); RMSE = .451 (trust), .712 (corruption); N = 391
Exogenous variables: trust in police, education, income, follow news, ever give a bribe, acceptable for official to accept warm trip, acceptable for official to accept state car, unemployed.

The larger story is that there is considerable inequality in perceptions of corruption. The public sees far more high-level corruption than either elite, though the differences for lower-level malfeasance are far smaller and generally not significant. The public is also far more likely to say that corruption has increased not only since Soviet times, but also in the past decade – and to say that corruption cannot be eradicated. This pessimism is reflected in the tolerance of much petty corruption. Elites see even small-time dishonesty as unacceptable. Ordinary people are more tolerant, perhaps because they have experienced petty corruption more often. They have fewer connections that might save them from having to pay bribes.

TABLE 6-3. *Simultaneous Estimation of Trust and Perception of Increased Corruption: Estonian Public Officials*

Variable	Coefficient	Std. Error	t Ratio
Generalized trust			
Corruption increased since Soviet era	−.130***	.055	2.34
Economic welfare better than five years ago	.017	.024	.74
Trust police	.148****	.042	3.52
Courts ensure a fair trial	.049	.048	1.03
People take bribes because they won't be punished	−.086**	.049	−1.74
Democracy best political system	.049*	.035	1.40
Constant	.903***	.236	3.82
Corruption increased since Soviet era			
Generalized trust	−.701**	.317	−2.21
Acceptable if speeder offers police favorable service	.512**	.288	1.78
Common for school official to accept warm trip for admitting student	.382**	.171	2.24
Personally have been offered bribes in last several years	.166***	.062	2.68
Never have faced conflict of interest	−.003	.051	.06
Common for civil servant to order computers from relative's firm	.333****	.092	3.61
Politicians do what is best for the country	−.162**	.090	−1.80
Income	−.026*	.016	−1.63
Age	.023****	.004	5.80
Constant	2.548***	.575	4.43

*p < .10; **p < .05; ***p < .01; ****p < .0001 (all tests one-tailed except for constants)
R^2 = .083 (trust), .209 (corruption increased); RMSE = .447 (trust), .781 (corruption); N = 350
Exogenous variables: Estonian nationality, education, everyone accepts bribes, satisfied with salary, corruption is inevitable, officials take bribes because pay is too low, acceptable for official to accept warm trip, acceptable for civil servant to use state car for personal use, acceptable for official to get operation through university friend, do not report corruption because it is no use, position is stable.

This inequality in perceptions, especially on grand corruption, may lead to strains in the society's social fabric. The social strains that come with increasing inequality and increased ethnic tensions should lead to less trust in fellow citizens, especially when people see high-level corruption as endemic.

I estimate models for generalized trust and perceptions of increased corruption since the Soviet era for the mass public, government officials, and entrepreneurs (see Tables 6-2, 6-3, and 6-4). The surveys did not have any measures of perceptions of inequality; the closest (asked in two of the three surveys) is whether economic welfare is better than five years ago. This is more of a measure of economic performance but it is as close as the surveys get to anything dealing with inequality. The three surveys had substantial overlap

TABLE 6-4. *Simultaneous Estimation of Trust and Perception of Increased Corruption: Estonian Entrepreneurs*

Variable	Coefficient	Std. Error	t Ratio
Generalized trust			
Corruption increased since Soviet era	−.153*	.089	−1.71
Everyone accepts bribes	.001	.071	.02
Trust police	.042	.042	1.00
Courts ensure a fair trial	.062	.054	1.14
Corruption if procurement given to relative	.028*	.020	1.39
Democracy best political system	.066*	.042	1.58
Education	.086**	.038	2.26
Age	−.001	.003	−.32
Constant	.189	.397	.49
Corruption increased since Soviet era			
Generalized trust	−.128	.632	−.20
Ever make extra payments to civil servants	.041*	.030	1.39
Ever made extra payments for state inspection	.142	.214	.67
Don't report corruption: No use in reporting	.294***	.112	2.63
Don't report corruption: Don't know where to report	.317**	.149	2.13
Expense of official proceedings an impediment to entrepreneurship	.098	.056	1.76
Democracy best political system	−.186**	.100	−1.85
Education	.024	.097	.25
Age	.015****	.005	3.28
Constant	3.288****	.661	4.98

*p < .10; **p < .05; ***p < .01; ****p < .0001 (all tests one-tailed except for constants)
R^2 = .080 (trust), .205 (corruption increased); RMSE = .366 (trust), .752 (corruption); N = 299
Exogenous variables: Corruption if official takes gift, officials take bribes because pay is too low, language spoken at home, acceptable for official to accept warm trip, follow news, complicated tax system impediment to entrepreneurship, would not report corruption because don't want to betray anybody, percentage of time in negotiations, get faster procedures from personal relationships.

in questions, but were not identical, so the models vary from one sample to another. Nevertheless, a clear pattern emerges and it is one of a stronger link between trust and corruption for the mass public than for elites, greater effects for economic variables on trust for ordinary citizens, and perceptions of rising corruption that largely reflect grand rather than petty malfeasance. As I summarize the results for each equation, I discuss variables that are not central to my main arguments in the endnotes.

For the mass public, perceptions of increasing corruption strongly reduce generalized trust – with a t ratio greater (in absolute value) than any variable other than the belief that most people are selfish and age (with older people being more trusting). Trusting people are also less likely to believe that corruption has increased since Soviet times, but this relationship is weak and barely significant even at p < .10. Public officials who believe that most people can be trusted are far less likely to see decreased corruption, but there is no significant effect for entrepreneurs. Public officials and entrepreneurs who see increased corruption are also less likely to have faith in their fellow citizens.

For each elite group, the size of the effect of perceived corruption on trust is markedly less than for the public. The regression coefficients for entrepreneurs and government officials are, respectively, 57 and 64 percent of the coefficient for the mass public. For entrepreneurs, there is a weak but marginally significant relationship between generalized trust and saying that procurement given to a relative constitutes corruption. Perceptions of increasing corruption, which are far more common for the mass public, have more powerful effects in shaping trust of fellow citizens among this group compared to elites.

Trust also leads people to say that corruption has fallen, especially for government employees (but not for entrepreneurs) and, to a lesser extent, for the mass public. Here my argument stands in contrast to Tavits (2005, 16), who finds no tie between generalized trust and another measure of corruption in this survey.[6] These results provide at best modest support for the idea of an inequality trap. The link from corruption to falling trust is considerably stronger and more supportive of the inequality trap thesis.

The perception of widespread bribery makes the general public less trusting. Petty corruption does not matter: Demands from doctors for "gift payments" do not lead to less trust. There is some evidence of an inequality of perceptions: Businesspeople who believe that everyone accepts bribes *are not less trusting of fellow citizens*, but widespread bribery does lead ordinary people to put less faith in their fellow citizens. Government officials were not asked if "everyone takes bribes." If they believe that bribe takers won't be punished, they will be less likely to trust others.[7] Government officials and the public trust others when they see the legal system as fair and efficient; entrepreneurs do not make this link. And only the public bases its trust on perceptions of economic well-being. For the mass public, there is a clear link between Estonian nationality and generalized trust. Ethnic Estonians are *less trusting* of people in general, a finding also reported by Kaplan (1995, 248). The lower levels of trust among Estonians reflect the view that other ethnicities, especially Russians, are outsiders in their country.

The corruption equation for the general public shows that perceptions of malfeasance depend more upon grand than petty misdeeds.[8] Ordinary

---

[6] Tavits (2005) argues that you will be more likely to engage in corrupt behavior if you believe that others will do so, rather than whether you are trusting. However, perceptions of others' motivations are endogenous to trust, so her claim that trust does not matter is not captured in her model.

[7] Support for democracy does lead to greater trust in people for entrepreneurs and for public officials, while the belief that government with a strong leader is a better form of government makes ordinary citizens less trusting. Age is significant only for the general public, while education leads to more trust only for entrepreneurs.

[8] Older people are more likely to see rising corruption, while employees in the private sector are less likely to see increased malfeasance.

citizens don't blame themselves for rising corruption – and personal experiences don't make them more likely to see rising dishonesty. Instead, they blame entrepreneurs for misdeeds. They see offering school officials expensive gifts such as trips to warm places as evidence that corruption has been increasing. If you believe that civil servants take bribes because their pay is too low or that it is common for entrepreneurs to trade goods for favorable rulings by bureaucrats, you are also more likely to see rising corruption: The grabbing hands of the bureaucrats and the entrepreneurs are the key sources of corruption, ordinary people say, and it is unfair to blame us. On the other hand, people who believe that it is common for people to pay bribes to police officers to fend off speeding tickets (58 percent of the public) are more likely to say that corruption is increasing. Petty corruption matters in how people evaluate malfeasance, but overall grand corruption seems to play a much larger role in shaping people's perceptions of dishonesty.

The model for the general public shows that ethnic Russians, rather than Estonians, see the greatest increase in corruption. Ethnic Estonians are *less likely to trust strangers, but also less likely to believe that corruption is increasing.* This may reflect the everyday experience of minority group members who are regarded as outsiders: They may not have the resources to obtain what they need in daily life through higher-level contacts without the need for bribes. Because Russians have lower incomes and largely live in ethnically homogenous neighborhoods, corruption may be more prevalent, as it is in societies that are both less affluent and marked by greater inequality.

On most measures of corruption in the survey, ethnic Russians are significantly more pessimistic and have had significantly more experience with corruption than people of Estonian heritage: whether you have ever offered a bribe (49 to 35 percent), whether corruption is inevitable in Estonia, whether corruption is a serious problem, whether it is common for a speeder to offer the police a bribe (72 to 54 percent), whether you have personally suffered from corruption (64 percent say no compared to 75 percent), whether you have bribed the police (16 to 8 percent), whether you have bribed your child's school (10 to 3 percent), and whether everyone takes bribes (36 to 26 percent). Ethnic Russians are more likely to consider acceptable acts such as offering a police officer a bribe for speeding (31 to 18 percent), entrepreneurs offering a school director a trip to a warm place (27 to 16 percent), and civil servants accepting fees for lectures (54 to 45 percent). Groups facing discrimination will see more corruption – and they will also develop a greater tolerance of misdeeds as the cost of getting by and doing business in an imperfect market.

These findings are not specific to this survey. In the 2005 European Social Survey, ethnic Russians were more likely to distrust public officials to treat you honestly (38 to 22 percent), to say that you can't always act honestly if you want to make money (45 to 34 percent). And they are less likely to agree that public officials asking for a bribe is seriously wrong (by 53 to 63 percent) and that making a false insurance claim is seriously wrong (by 31 to 42 percent).

The general story for government bureaucrats reflects a division between the majority who believe that corruption has fallen. They report never being offered a bribe nor facing a conflict of interest. Government officials believe that corruption is not common in Estonia. The majority of bureaucrats reflects the elite view (as reflected in TI's Corruption Perceptions Index) that Estonia is becoming a far more honest country – and very much in the Western European mainstream. The minority have perceptions that are much closer to the general public's views – that Estonia is still a state in transition.

For government officials, personal experience matters mightily and they do not make a clear distinction, as the general public does, between grand and petty corruption (see Table 6-3). If you have been offered a bribe, if you think that it is common for school officials to accept warm trips, if you believe that it is common for civil servants to order computers from a relative's firm, if you believe that it is common for a driver who speeds to offer the police favorable service, and if you don't believe that politicians do what is best for the country, you will be more likely to see rising dishonesty. Ironically, whether a government official has ever faced a conflict of interest has no effect on perceptions of rising corruption.

Entrepreneurs' perceptions of rising corruption reflect almost exclusively their willingness to deflect the blame for malfeasance away from themselves (see Table 6-4). If you don't know where to report corruption or believe that telling the police won't do any good, you are more likely to believe that malfeasance has been rising. Businesspeople who say that democracy is the best political system see decreasing corruption – also deflecting the responsibility for malfeasance from themselves to the political system. There is a tie between making a bribe to civil servants and perceiving rising dishonesty, but it is weak and barely significant (at $p < .10$). Payments for state inspections and believing that official proceedings are needlessly expensive have no effect on corruption perceptions.[9]

While these surveys are not ideal for testing for the inequality trap, there is support for some key elements in the mass public survey and less in the elite polls. For the public, economic distress leads to less trust, as does grand corruption, but not petty malfeasance. There is a modest link from generalized trust to perceptions of increasing corruption. Ethnic Russians perceive more corruption, are more tolerant of it, and are more likely to be involved in such activities. Trust also matters for public officials' perceptions of increasing corruption but not for entrepreneurs. There is support in two of the three surveyed groups that corruption perceptions rest upon a foundation of mistrust and that low out-group trust also leads people to see increasing levels of corruption.

Ordinary citizens are substantially more likely than elites to see grand corruption as widespread – and such misdeeds make them less willing to trust their

---

[9] For entrepreneurs, older people see rising corruption, but there is no effect for education. Higher-paid government officials are less likely to say that corruption is increasing, as are older bureaucrats.

fellow citizens. The difference in perceptions in itself suggests an inequality trap. Estonia may be relatively honest compared to other transition countries, but its corruption score still puts it below most Western countries. Even if the public misperceives the level of corruption, we cannot dismiss these perceptions. Especially when overlaid with strong ethnic conflicts and increasing inequality, the belief that corruption is widespread threatens social solidarity and may inhibit economic growth. Estonia ranks highly (third) on GDP growth among transition countries, yet it does not rank so highly among all nations.

Corruption and Inequality in Slovakia and Romania

Slovakia is another "success" story among transition countries, Romania somewhat less so. However, Slovakia's triumphs are relative. Compared to other transition nations, Slovakia generally ranks in the top third on most measures in Table A6-1; comparisons with the larger group of nations do not put Slovakia in such an exceptional light, especially when compared to its former "partner," the much wealthier Czech Republic. The key exception is the level of economic inequality, where Slovakia stands out. Slovakia is relatively uncorrupt compared to other transition nations, though hardly distinctive in more general comparisons. For Estonia, I asked if there can be an inequality trap without a lot of corruption – and concluded that the answer was largely positive. But Slovakia poses a more demanding test: Can there be an inequality trap without much inequality?

Alas, I cannot answer this question with the data at hand. The World Bank Diagnostic Surveys of corruption were not designed to test hypotheses about the determinants of corruption. Their aims were more modest, mostly to understand what people mean by the term "corruption," what evils people think malfeasance wrought, what specific steps people might take to report corruption, where and how often they encounter corruption in their daily lives (especially which agencies are more corrupt, which are more honest, and how much it costs for gift payments or bribes in various settings), and the quality of service provision. The latter questions are largely filled with missing data, since not everyone visits the doctor or health clinic often and not every doctor demands gift payments. The questions in the surveys that have sufficient responses for analysis are mostly those dealing with the consequences and "definitions" of corruption. The Slovakian surveys also included a question on trust in government that I shall examine as well.

The surveys are useful in three key ways. First, they include rising inequality as a possible consequence of corruption. So while there is no way to test for an inequality trap, I can examine whether people believe that corruption increases inequality – and what factors lead people to make this argument. Second, by comparing responses across masses and elites – entrepreneurs and government officials – I can examine *inequality in perceptions* as I did for Estonia. Are the masses more likely to say that corruption causes inequality than the elites? (Yes in Romania; no in Slovakia). Are the masses more likely to link the belief that corruption causes inequality to declining trust in government than are the elites? (Yes.) Third, although the Romanian survey has fewer relevant variables than the Slovakian polls (and Romanian government officials are not asked whether corruption increases inequality), the overlap in many questions allows comparisons between the two countries. Slovakia is the more successful transition country so far – both on levels of corruption and especially on inequality.

Slovakia's strong record on keeping inequality in check marks a continuation of the past and was widely considered to be among the best prepared nations for the transition. Czechoslovakia had a short-lived reformist government under Alexander Dubcek in 1968, who presided over the "Prague Spring" until Soviet troops toppled the regime. Most Westerners – and Czechs – were surprised when the Slovaks insisted upon having a separate state, especially since the Czechs were far more prosperous. A majority of Slovaks, however, saw the Czechoslovak republic as representing "oppression and exploitation" (Vasecka, 1999, chs. 3–4).

Slovakia was not only less prosperous than the Czech Republic. It also had, according to Vasecka (1999, chs. 2–4) a "feudal" social structure, with much of its population residing in small towns. Even though the level of economic inequality remained low (and by one account constant), a majority of the public resented the rising inequalities of the 1990s and saw the economic situation as worse than under Communism (Vasecka, 1999, chs. 3–12). Even as Slovakia ranks in the top third of transition countries on the TI Corruption Perceptions Index in both 2004 and 2005 and on legal fairness (BEEPS), the country's economic elite reported that poor law enforceability was the biggest obstacle to business. More than half of managers agreed with this and three-quarters of business analysts assented – and in 2002 they saw the problem as growing rather than receding (Gyarfasova, 2002, 7, 14).

While the basic descriptive questions are different in the Diagnostic Surveys in the two countries, there is clear support for the claim that the public is more likely to be more pessimistic about corruption than the elites. In Slovakia, there are few differences in the shares of the public (60.9 percent), public officials (62.9 percent), and entrepreneurs (66 percent) who say that corruption is a very serious problem in the country. The public is far more pessimistic about the control of corruption: Public officials are evenly divided about whether corruption will be higher (28.5 percent) or lower (29 percent) in three years. Entrepreneurs are more optimistic that malfeasance will be decreasing (34.9 percent compared to 22.4 percent for higher). Yet only 12.1 percent of the public expect dishonesty to decrease and 44.4 percent believe that it will grow.

The questions are different in the Romanian surveys, but the overall picture is the same (Anderson et al., 2001, 4). Almost equal shares of the public (67 percent) and businesspeople (70 percent) believe that all or almost all public officials are corrupt; not surprisingly, far fewer officials agree; still, 44 percent assert that this is true. Only a third of businesspeople agree that bribery is part of everyday life; 41 percent of entrepreneurs agree, but so do 60 percent of the mass public.

As in Estonia, there is a difference in perceptions on how widespread corruption is – and what the outlook for curbing it is. There are also divergent views on what the consequences of corruption are. Each survey asked respondents to rank up to three repercussions of dishonesty. I construct a measure of potential effects from the top two ranked answers.[10] I present the share of respondents choosing each consequence in Table A6-2, which shows

- Where inequality has been rising rapidly – in Romania – both the mass public and the entrepreneurs see rising inequality (and lowering incomes of the poor) as the major effects of corruption. No other effect even comes close: 53 percent of the Romanian public sees corruption as increasing inequality and a similar share as lowering incomes. Much smaller segments of the public worry that corruption endangers the security of the state (18 percent), infringes on human rights (17 percent), or contributes to moral decline (15 percent). Entrepreneurs do worry about moral decline (23 percent) and about corruption leading to less foreign investment (26 percent). Yet, even business-people are most worried about the distributional consequences of dishonesty (37 percent about inequality and 41 percent about lowered income).

- Where inequality is much lower, in Slovakia, there is not a significant gap in perceptions of effects between the mass public and the elite. The public is as much worried about the effects of corruption on public morality (38 percent) as it is about rising inequality (37 percent). Government officials are slightly *more concerned over economic distribution* than are ordinary citizens (43 percent) – and the levels of concern for lower income are half that of the Romanian samples. Instead, the Slovakian public's perceptions of negative consequences are not radically different from that country's elites. All samples of Slovaks are about equally worried that corruption will lead to a loss of confidence in one's own abilities and will threaten transition, and to a loss in foreign investment (with entrepreneurs naturally the most concerned), with human rights violations, to increasing dishonesty, moral decline, and crime. Elites are more worried about the effects on dishonesty, crime, and human rights, about maintaining order in society. But both the public and elites in Slovakia are worried that corruption will weaken the country's moral fiber. Overall, we don't see a sharp disjunction in views as we do in Romania. No group in Slovakia is primarily concerned with economic distribution to the exclusion of other worries. Public officials seem slightly more worried about inequality than are ordinary citizens.

- The Slovakian public is about as concerned that corruption increases inequality as the Romanian entrepreneurs, *not the Romanian public*. The Slovakian public looks upon corruption more as a threat to transition and as a moral issue and is less concerned about the distributional consequences. Slovaks have a far more nuanced view of corruption than Romanians do. While

---

[10] Many people did not give third choices and the responses were widely scattered, so I dropped third choices.

elites are more likely to see social problems arising from corruption than the general public, the gap is smaller than one might expect in a society where people see corruption as a major problem – and where ordinary citizens are far more pessimistic about controlling misdeeds.

What leads people to say that corruption increases inequality? I estimate models for Romanians and Slovaks in Tables 6-5 and A6-3 through A6-6. First, I present a model for the Romanian public and also estimate it for the Slovakian public (Table 6-5). The model that works for Romanians does not fare well for the Slovakian public. A very different model works far better (Table A6-3). Then I estimate models for Romanian and Slovakian entrepreneurs – which, again, are dissimilar (Tables A6-4 and A6-5) and finally for Slovakian government officials (Table A6-6).

The limited number of relevant questions in the diagnostic surveys means that I have to rely on two sets of predictors. First, I consider some definitions of what respondents say corruption means. Second, I include some other consequences of corruption. Respondents may give up to three responses for both what corruption is and what the consequences are, and the measures I have constructed represent positive replies to either the first or the second choice. While alternative consequences are part of the same overall questions, respondents are free to choose any two or three alternatives they choose from a list of between 10 and 12 alternatives for each question in different samples. People who see some consequences are unlikely to rate others as critical. In the Romanian public sample, I expect concern for the security of the state to be negatively related to saying that corruption increases inequality. The tie between corruption and economic distribution emphasizes distributional justice. The link between malfeasance and state security puts state power, rather than economic rights, as primary. I also expect that people who are primarily concerned with the effect of corruption on investment will be less worried about inequality. The transition to a market economy inevitably leads to some inequalities, since not everyone will prosper equally from a capitalist system, especially an emerging one. Worrying about losing investments should be negatively associated with concerns about the distribution of wealth.

I expect that people who say that corruption is an abuse of power and that it represents favoritism will be more likely to say that dishonesty leads to economic inequality. Both abuses of power and favoritism are associated with giving unfair advantage to some people. An unfair legal system should also lead to increasing inequality, as do perceptions that you can't get anything done without bribery (part of everyday life). Finally, wealthier people should be less bothered that corruption increases inequality.

The estimates in Table 6-5 largely support these predictions. I estimate equations for perceiving that corruption increases inequality by probit analysis, since the dependent variable is a dichotomy. Only one of the variables in the model for Romania is not significant: whether the courts are considered fair. The two variables with the greatest effects are whether you believe that corruption endangers

TABLE 6-5. *Probit Analysis of Perceptions of How Corruption Increases Economic Inequality: World Bank Corruption Diagnostic Survey of the Romanian and Slovakian Publics*

Variable	Romanian Public				Slovakian Public			
	Coefficient	Std. Error	MLE/SE	Effect	Coefficient	Std. Error	MLE/SE	Effect
Corruption is abuse of position	.313***	.115	2.73	.115	.017	.091	.19	.006
Corruption is favoritism to relatives or friends	.206*	.129	1.59	.076	.026	.096	.28	.010
Corruption leads investors to lose confidence	−.618****	.178	−3.47	−.224	−.025	.098	−.25	−.009
Corruption endangers security of state	−.683****	.144	−4.74	−.252	−.339***	.133	−2.56	−.122
Court decisions are not fair/Must bribe court+	.012	.053	.023	.018	−.014	.038	−.37	−.021
Bribe useless or part of everyday life	−.125**	.057	−2.21	.138	−.049	.043	−1.12	−.054
Income/Social class+	−.568**	−.280	−2.03	−.084	.021	.036	.59	.056
Constant	.400*	.184	2.18		−.237	.247	−.96	

* p < .10; ** p < .05; *** p < .01; **** p < .0001
Romania: Estimated R² = .150; −2*Log Likelihood Ratio = 692.193; N = 538
  Percent predicted correctly: 64.5 (model); 50.9 (null)
Slovakia: Estimated R² = .107; −2*Log Likelihood Ratio = 1092.048; N = 831
  Percent predicted correctly: 62.3 (model); 62.3 (null)
+First question wording in Romanian survey, second in Slovakian survey.

the security of the state and whether you think that misdeeds lead investors to lose confidence in the country. If you worry about the security of the state, you are 25 percent less likely to say that corruption increases inequality; being concerned about investor confidence makes you 22 percent less likely to fret about economic distribution. If you believe that bribery is a part of everyday life, you will be 14 percent more likely to say that corruption increases inequality – and there is a 12 percent greater likelihood that a person will worry about income distribution if she says that corruption is an abuse of position.

Saying that corruption means favoritism increases concern for inequality effects by 8 percent and the wealthiest individuals will be 8 percent less likely to worry about income distribution compared to those least well off. While the estimated probit R^2 is not high (.150), the model represents an almost 15 percent improvement in predictive power over random guessing. For Slovakia, only one variable – whether corruption endangers the security of the state – is significant in this model and even here its effect (12 percent) is half that for the Romanian public. The Slovakian model does not represent *any improvement over random guessing*.

The Slovakian public, which is substantially less likely to say that corruption increases inequality overall, does not use the same mental heuristic to link malfeasance to the economic distribution. Slovaks are 38 percent less likely to say that corruption increases economic inequality if they are worried that it causes crime, 36 percent less likely if they are concerned about human rights violations, 28 percent less likely if they worry most about transition, and 13 percent less likely if they link misdeeds with a weaker private sector. Whether bribery is a part of everyday life, whether courts are fair, and social class play no role in concerns over the distribution of wealth. The model performs very well (estimated probit R^2 = .520, percent predicted correctly = 75.4, compared to 62.1 percent for a null model).

Romanians link corruption to increasing inequality by the abuse of power and favoritism; the interests of the state and investors are seen as opposed to worries about inequality. This also holds in Slovakia, but people in Slovakia also place inequality in contrast to order and human rights. Slovaks make the sharpest distinctions between increasing inequality and worrying about social order (crime and human rights). Romanians do not make this distinction. Social order takes a secondary role to economic justice, which is juxtaposed against the state and entrepreneurs.

Entrepreneurs are less likely to see corruption as leading to inequality than are ordinary citizens. However, Romanian businesspeople have views that are closer to the general public in their country than they are to Slovakian entrepreneurs (see Table A6-2). The roots of perceptions of corruption's effects on income distribution are also different in the two countries, reflecting the greater perceptions of rising inequality in Romania. In Romania, entrepreneurs who say that corruption is an abuse of one's position is significant (at p < .10, just missing p < .05) are more likely to say that corruption leads to an inequitable distribution of wealth (see Table 6-4). Businesspeople who consider corruption as a form of abuse are 8 percent more likely to believe that malfeasance leads to unequal wealth, a somewhat smaller effect than for the mass public (12 percent). In Slovakia, believing that corruption is an abuse of position makes an entrepreneur 10 percent *less* likely to hold that it leads to inequality (see Table 6-5). Entrepreneurs in the two countries have a very different view of what abuse of position means – Romanians link it to economic injustice, Slovaks to misplaced business ethics.

Romanian entrepreneurs are more divided over the economic consequences of corruption than is the general public. Businesspeople are less likely to say that malfeasance leads to inequality if they believe that corruption slows the development of the private sector (by 32 percent) or if they say that it leads investors to lose confidence in the country (by 17 percent). Slovakian businesspeople are also divided along economic lines, but the impact of "corruption hurts the development of the private sector" is 15 percent, not very different from the mass public sample (13 percent) and substantially less than in Romania. As with the public, believing that corruption hurts transition also makes one less likely to make the link with inequality (by 20 percent, compared to 30 percent for ordinary citizens). Especially where inequality is greater (Romania), there is a trade-off in entrepreneurs' views on corruption and the private sector versus how it affects inequality.

Businesspeople in both countries shift the blame for corruption causing inequality. In Romania, they link this effect to competitors who don't pay their share of taxes (by 12 percent), presumably maintaining that tax evasion robs the state of resources to help the poor, and to the low pay for bureaucrats (by 9 percent), so lower-level officials supplement their meager wages by extorting money from the poor. Belonging to a business association seems to reinforce the belief that corruption doesn't cause inequality (by 10 percent) in Romania. Shifting the blame becomes easier if you have close contacts who agree with you.

In Slovakia, entrepreneurs blame the victims, ordinary citizens, for rising inequality (by 11 percent) – seemingly arguing that the public is the source of its own problems by tolerating petty corruption. Businesspeople don't limit their blame to the public. Anyone who demands petty corruption affects the income distribution. Entrepreneurs who say that gift payments are an obstacle to business are 21 percent more likely to worry about inequality.

In both countries, but especially in Romania, the link to inequality is stronger among people who see the government as responsible for handling corruption. The second greatest effect (31 percent) among Romanian entrepreneurs is the belief that the government has the greatest responsibility for fighting corruption and the fourth largest impact is the belief that political instability is harming your company (21 percent). In a society marked by a lot of corruption and rising inequality, the emerging economic elite puts the greatest blame for the link between corruption and inequality on state officials – the ones whom entrepreneurs see as getting rich through extorting the private sector (see Chapter 5). In Slovakia, businesspeople who believe that deputies don't want to solve the problem of dishonesty are more likely to make the connection to inequality – but the relationship is weaker (an effect of 13 percent and a barely significant coefficient at p < .10).

Romanian entrepreneurs who worry that dishonesty in government leads to moral decline throughout the society are considerably less likely to say that corruption increases inequality (28 percent), while their Slovakian counterparts who worry about human rights abuses similarly place less emphasis on the distributional consequences of corruption (by 26 percent). In both countries, businesspeople who worry most about what corruption does to the country's moral fiber are least likely to worry about the distributional consequences of misdeeds. Worrying about inequality stands, perhaps ironically, in contrast to concerns about the society's moral fiber. Morality is a worry of the middle and upper classes. Inequality is a concern of those with fewer resources.

This is evident in the strongest determinant of the link between inequality and corruption among Slovakian entrepreneurs. Entrepreneurs from businesses that have lost income over the past year are far more likely (40 percent) to worry that corruption causes inequality than businesspeople who have prospered. In Romania, if you think that competitors don't pay their fair share of taxes, you are 11 percent more likely to make the link between corruption and inequality.

Romanian entrepreneurs are far more likely to see the link between corruption and inequality as a conflict between claims on the distribution of wealth and the developing market economy. Slovakian entrepreneurs share these concerns, but they seem to be more worried about the behavior of their fellow businesspeople and the need to ensure human rights. They also blame ordinary citizens for their own plight, which we do not see in Romania.

Slovakian government officials, as the entrepreneurs, don't link inequality with abuse of position as Romanians do. Again, the coefficient is *negative* instead of positive as expected. The officials who worry most about inequality are least likely to be concerned about the effects of misdeeds on order in the state – crime (32 percent), human rights violations, and the security of the state (both by about 28 percent). They also are less concerned with loss of foreign investment (21 percent) or adjusting to transition more generally (29 percent). *Slovakian officials **are concerned about increasing inequality from misdeeds***: 43 percent agree that misdeeds do lead to economic injustice, more than any other sample other than the Romanian public. Yet there is a clear dichotomy among officials between worrying about the distribution of wealth, on the one hand, and order and the development of a market economy on the other. There is an especially strong trade-off between worrying that corruption causes inequality and that it leads to disorder. If you believe that corruption has been increasing, that it stems from a weak legal system, or that it plays a strong role in education, you are no more likely to make the link with inequality.[11]

---

[11] More highly educated officials are less likely to say that corruption causes inequality – most likely because they see themselves as part of an elite (who would have less reason to perceive inequality).

Though the patterns in these five estimations are not always straightforward – owing to the limited number of useful questions in the surveys and the variations in questions asked across the polls – it is not difficult to see a general pattern. Romanian citizens and entrepreneurs are more likely to see inequality as stemming from corruption as a system of abuse and favoritism. Slovakian citizens, entrepreneurs, and government officials are more likely to see corruption as causing inequality if they are less worried about its effects on business and civil order.

In Romania, where inequality has been rising, the public sees corruption as leading to more inequality and lower incomes. In Slovakia, where inequality has historically been low and has remained under control, ordinary citizens are similar to elites in the trade-offs they make on the effects of corruption: People either see corruption as leading to increased inequality or to less order in the society and a weakened market. While these data cannot test the idea of an inequality trap, they do lend support that the link between inequality and corruption is generally more salient for the mass public than for elites, especially where corruption is widespread and inequality is rising.

Corruption, Inequality, and Trust in Government

People trust government when they approve of its performance on the economy and on factors such as corruption (Citrin, 1974). Both play a large role in shaping Romanians' trust in government (Chapter 5). The Slovakian Diagnostic Surveys included a question on trust in government, specifically a five-point question on "how much faith you have in the honesty and integrity of the government of the Slovak Republic." This is not, of course, the standard trust in government question, but it will suffice to help understand the roots of faith in national institutions among the masses and elites in Slovakia.

The honesty and integrity of the government first and foremost depends upon the level of corruption overall and in specific institutions. Beyond malfeasance, performance also matters.

When governments deliver the goods, people have reason to believe that officials are honest – that they are using public funds for public purposes rather than lining their own pockets (Hanousek and Palda, 2006).

Since the trust in government question is a five-point scale, I estimate ordered probit analyses for the three samples in Tables 6-6, A6-7, and A6-8. I estimate effects, the differences in probabilities, as average changes across the categories.[12]

One result stands out: Perceiving that corruption causes inequality lowers trust in government by an average of 3 percent and is significant at $p < .05$, *but only for ordinary citizens.* The link between corruption and inequality does *not affect trust in government for entrepreneurs or for government officials.* There is some evidence of an inequality trap in these results. The belief that

---

[12] I estimated these changes using the spost package (prchange), from J. Scott Long, for Stata 9.

TABLE 6-6. *Ordered Probit Analysis of Trust in Government: World Bank Corruption Diagnostic Survey of the Slovakian Public*

Variable	Coefficient	Std. Error	MLE/SE	Effect
Corruption causes inequality	−.189**	.104	−1.82	.030
Corruption serious problem in Slovakia	−.185***	.095	−1.95	.029
Corruption increased in past three years	.423****	.055	−7.66	.233
Ministries are corrupt	−.326****	.083	−3.94	.100
Justice system is corrupt	−.147**	.082	−1.79	.046
Customs officials are corrupt	−.068	.074	−.91	.021
Education system is corrupt	−.002	.062	−.03	.001
Corruption means giving gifts	−.033	.114	−.29	.005
Bribe medical workers because asked to do so	−.011	.045	−.25	.007
Bribe education workers because asked to do so	−.033	.044	−.75	.021
Change in quality of health care by specialists	.157***	.054	2.91	.098
Education	−.083	.052	−1.59	.039

Cut points not reported. Effects are average changes in probabilities across the five categories of trust in government. The effects represent the changes from each value *to the next higher value.*
*p < .10; **p < .05; ***p < .01; ****p < .0001
Estimated R^2 = .116; −2*Log Likelihood Ratio = 1181.768; N = 486

"corruption causes inequality" leads to less trust in government only for the mass public. The effect for "corruption causes inequality" is not very strong (at 3 percent), but it is greater than most of the variables in the model.

The most important determinant of trust in government is the belief that corruption has increased in the past three years (23.3 percent), followed by the belief that government ministries are corrupt (10 percent) and that the justice system is corrupt (5 percent). Also significant is the belief that corruption is a serious problem (3 percent). *However, no measure of petty corruption – be it the education system, customs officials, giving gifts, or being asked by workers in the education or medical systems – leads ordinary citizens to be less likely to trust their government.* Instead, the quality of one key area of public service – health care – leads people to have more faith that their government is honest (by 10 percent).

As with the Romanian public (see Chapter 5), it is grand corruption – the type of malfeasance that leads to more inequality – that makes people trust their government less. Petty corruption, which does not increase inequality, has no effect on confidence in government. There is no evidence that attitudes toward government reflect social status (in the insignificant coefficient for education).

For entrepreneurs, trust in government reflects the belief that public officials are honest and that the state is delivering high-quality services. If you believe that parliament is corrupt, you will be 16 percent less likely to have faith in government. You will also be less likely to have confidence in the state if you think that corruption has increased in the past three years (by 7 percent), but not if you think that corruption causes inequality. The other factors shaping businesspeoples' faith in government all relate to how the state advances the cause of business: People who believe that bureaucrats stand in the way of business development (presumably by demanding "extra" payments) are 12 percent less likely to have faith in public officials. The quality of services also matters mightily: Believing that the infrastructure is an obstacle to business developments leads to a 9 percent drop in the average level of trust in government, while satisfaction with the quality of services from traffic police and in the energy sector lead to approximate gains of 10 percent in faith in state officials.

Entrepreneurs base their evaluations entirely on officials' conduct. Their own complicity, as reflected in whether clientelism is an obstacle to business development, is not significant. It may take two to make a corrupt deal – both entrepreneurs and state officials – but businesspeople don't seem willing to accept any blame.

Public officials don't accept this view. They base their own trust in government on how many dishonest officials they see in the bureaucracy – above their own level and at a distance from them. As with entrepreneurs, government officials do not link faith in the honesty of state officials to the belief that corruption causes inequality. The key factors leading to lower trust are the perception of increasing corruption (a decline on average of 15 percent), whether people in the central administration take bribes for influencing decisions (14 percent) or embezzle money (7 percent), and whether ministries are corrupt (7 percent). Each of these questions deflects responsibility from mid-level bureaucrats or lower level elected officials toward people at the top or to the administrators who take bribes or embezzle money – which respondents would certainly say does not include themselves.

Petty corruption is generally insignificant: The education system, traffic courts, being offered small gifts don't shape trust in government. Corruption in the health system and whether gift payments are common both lower trust in government (by 5 percent each), but both measures are barely significant at $p < .10$. The quality of bureaucrats in the central administration is also insignificant, as is the status (social class) of the officials.

An Inequality Trap?

While these data cannot establish an inequality trap in Estonia or Slovakia, they do suggest that there is an inequality in perceptions between the mass public and elites in these countries. The publics in Estonia and Slovakia are far more likely to see corruption as widespread and inevitable than are entrepreneurs or government officials. The publics in Estonia and especially in Slovakia are far more likely to have their trust in either their fellow citizens (Estonia) or the government (Slovakia) shaped by perceptions of high-level corruption and whether corruption increases inequality. For both masses and elites, perceptions of increasing corruption (Estonia) and whether corruption increases inequality (Slovakia) depend far more on grand corruption than on lower-level malfeasance.

Some countries, such as Slovakia and Estonia, may be doing a very good job in the march to transition by restraining either corruption or inequality or perhaps even both, at least relative to other nations in similar circumstances. Yet perceptions of corruption – and inequality – may persist even as elites see the world very differently. As long as there is corruption, ordinary citizens will perceive it as more troubling – and more linked to inequality – than elites. And they will be more likely to base their evaluations of the trustworthiness of fellow citizens and their government on the types of corruption that are most likely to increase inequality.

7

The Easy and Hard Cases

Africa and Singapore and Hong Kong

> Now those among you full of pious teaching
> Who teach us to renounce the major sins,
> Should know before you do your heavy preaching:
> Our middle's empty, there it all begins.
> Your vices and our virtues are so dear to you.
> So learn the simple truth from this our song.
> Wherever you aspire, whatever you may do,
> First feed the face and then talk right and wrong.
> > From "How to Survive," Berthold Brecht
> > and Kurt Weill, *The Threepenny Opera*[1]

The transition countries pose a challenge for the idea of an inequality trap. They rank high on corruption, low on generalized trust, but comparatively low on inequality – though income disparities have been rising, often sharply, in almost all of these countries. Despite this "challenge," I have generally found support for my argument linking perceptions of inequality, low trust, and high levels of grand corruption in transition countries. Especially in Romania, where perceptions of inequality are widespread and lead to demands for redistribution of wealth, the inequality trap argument receives strong support.

How well does the inequality trap account fare in a setting where all three conditions – high corruption, high inequality, and low out-group trust – all hold? African states largely, though hardly universally, meet all three conditions: high levels of corruption and inequality and low generalized trust. Such settings might qualify as a critical test of the framework. Strong support for the argument would bolster my account significantly while negative results would call it into question.

---

[1] The full text is available at http://www.amateurgourmet.com/the_amateur_gourmet/2006/05/how_to_survive.html.

On the other hand, Singapore and Hong Kong stand out as two glaring anomalies, with relatively high levels of inequality and low generalized trust.[2] Yet, Singapore (ranking 5th out of 160 countries, between Denmark and Sweden) and Hong Kong (ranking 15th, between Canada and Germany) are among the least corrupt countries in the world according to the 2005 Transparency International Corruption Perceptions Index. In the 2004 Global Corruption Barometer, Singapore's citizens were less likely than those of any other country (out of 63 sampled) to see grand corruption as a problem (with a mean score of 3.11 on a 4-point scale, with 4 indicating that grand corruption is not a problem at all). Hong Kong's citizens ranked ninth, at 2.31, between the Netherlands and Switzerland. Yet both Singapore and Hong Kong rank high on inequality and low on generalized trust. They are, in many ways, the polar opposite of the transition countries, yet they pose a severe challenge to the inequality trap argument. They have two of the key foundations for high levels of corruption, almost everything but malfeasance itself. Why, then, are Hong Kong and Singapore so honest?

Ironically, the most common arguments for why most African states are corrupt while Hong Kong and Singapore are so much more honest rest on very similar foundations: the strong state. African leaders after independence became all-powerful and all-grabbing, turning their new states into kleptocracies (Mbaku, 1998a, 249). Equally powerful and perhaps more autocratic leaders in Singapore and Hong Kong did not rob their countries' treasuries and deposit the riches in Switzerland or the Cayman Islands. Quite the contrary. *They used the strong arm of the law to impose honest and efficient government.*

I shall argue here that the "nanny state" is not, in and of itself, either the purloiner or the enforcer of morality. The inequality trap seems a more likely explanation. There are insufficient aggregate data to replicate tests such as those in Chapter 3 or even the more limited ones in Chapter 4. However, there is clear evidence in the Afrobarometer surveys that Africans see a clear link between inequality – both economic and legal – and corruption (though the connection to trust is less well supported). I will present models for how well the government handles corruption and how frequently people are treated unfairly from the 2002 (Round 2) Afrobarometer across the 14 countries surveyed.[3]

The data show strong support for linkages between perceptions of corruption and inequality across the 14 countries. A separate analysis of data for Mali in 2002 shows strong linkages between whether corruption is increasing or decreasing and perceptions of inequality, on the one hand, and support for

---

[2] Hong Kong is not an independent country, though its economic system and its political culture have largely been autonomous from its former and present rulers, the United Kingdom and China. For ease of language, I will often refer to Hong Kong as a "nation."

[3] The data are available at www.afrobarometer.org. Several of the key questions in my models were not asked in Zimbabwe, so I exclude Zimbabwe's respondents from this analysis. I am grateful to Michael Bratton of Michigan State University and Director of the Afrobarometer and Tetsuya Fujiwara, Data Manager of the Afrobarometer, for providing me with advance access to the Round 3 data on Nigeria.

restricting incomes of the rich and high-level corruption on the other hand. I use the Round 2 survey for Mali because it has a broader range of questions than the full Afrobarometer. Mali is hardly the most corrupt country – it is tied with 8 other countries for 88th place out of 160 nations in the 2005 TI rankings – but its raw score of 2.9 indicates that it still has a considerable share of malfeasance. I then focus on the 2005 (Round 3) data for Nigeria – tied with the Côte d'Ivoire and Equatorial Guinea in 153rd place in the 2005 TI rankings, establishing it as one of the most corrupt countries in the world.

Nigerians recognize that corruption is an exploitative relationship. Rich men with impeccable English often come to the marketplace believing that they can convince the less educated market women to lower their prices. The market women recognize that they are vulnerable and are not impressed by impeccable language. They turn aside when they see men who are well spoken: "You de use plenty grammar de cheat."[4]

The data from the Round 3 Afrobarometer indicate that Nigerians see a tight connection between how well the government handles corruption and whether they see more equitable treatment for all people than in the past: I estimate a simultaneous equation model for these two key components of the inequality trap. Measures of equality are among the most important determinants of whether people approve of the government's handling of corruption. Legal fairness is by far the most important factor shaping perceptions of equal treatment, though government handling of corruption is also important. So are democratic rights (free speech), which suggests that in Nigeria the inequality trap *is connected to democratic governance and institutional structures*. The tight ties between inequality and corruption come through loud and clear in Nigeria and any account of corruption that focuses primarily on institutional factors will miss the larger story.

As with transition countries, not all African countries are alike. In Africa, the "honesty leader" is Botswana, tied for 32nd place on the 2005 TI Corruption Perceptions Index with Qatar, Taiwan, and Uruguay with a raw score of 5.9 (slightly worse than Slovenia's 6.1). The next highest African countries are South Africa and Namibia, with scores of 4.5 and 4.3, respectively, above the mean for all 160 countries rated (4.07) and tied (in the case of Namibia) with Greece and Slovakia. While some African countries have lower levels of corruption than others, I shall first examine all countries in the same models, as I did for surveys throughout the world in Chapter 3 and in transition countries in Chapter 4. While cross-national data are not sufficiently available to do hierarchical linear models, I control for country-level effects (recognizing that countries are not all the same) by clustering the standard errors at the country level. I then turn to the least corrupt nation, Botswana, and find little support for the inequality trap when I analyze the Afrobarometer data for that country by itself.

---

[4] I owe this quote to Kems O. Adu-Gyan, Assistant Researcher, School of Business, Economics, and Law, Department of Business Administration, Goteborg University, private discussion at the Conference on "Measuring Diversity," Milan, Italy, January 27, 2006.

Botswana in several key respects resembles Hong Kong and Singapore: It has a strikingly high level of inequality (with a Gini coefficient of .63 from the United Nations Development Programme)[5] and very low out-group trust (14 percent believe that "most people can be trusted"; see Bratton, Mattes, and Gyimah-Boadi, 2005, 194). It is, to be sure, a democracy. In 2003, its scores on the political and civil rights indices of Freedom House are all twos, indicating a well-functioning, if imperfect, representative government. Yet Mali has identical scores from Freedom House (though Nigeria fares worse with scores of four on each measure). Yet, despite the high level of inequality and the low generalized trust, Botswana has a relatively honest government. When I estimate the full model for Round 2 just for Africa, very few of the measures for government handling corruption in the all-Africa model are significant for Botswana, especially those focusing on inequality.

Botswana, Hong Kong, and Singapore are exceptions to my argument about the inequality trap. How do I account for these instances of high inequality, low trust, but low corruption? Case studies of Botswana focus on its democratic government, but Singapore and Hong Kong are not democracies. Most accounts in these two Asian states focus on anti-corruption drives: Singapore's Corrupt Practices Investigation Bureau (CPIB), established in 1960, and Hong Kong's Independent Commission Against Corruption (ICAC), the Independent Commission on Corruption, established in 1974. Both anti-corruption agencies were endowed with strong and autonomous investigatory powers (Quah, 2001a; Lo, 2001). The inequality trap does not explain perceptions of corruption in these two city-states: Asian Barometer data for Hong Kong show that people's perceptions of corruption bear little relation to beliefs about inequality or about democracy and the salience of both inequality and corruption are low in Singapore – largely because both nations have become very wealthy and inequality has been declining, rather than increasing (as in much of Africa and the transition states).

If anti-corruption commissions are the key to reducing malfeasance in office, we need not worry about deeper structural problems such as high levels of inequality and less tractable issues such as raising out-group trust. What we need is elite political will, and while this may not be in abundant supply, surely it offers a more manageable solution to the problem of corruption than redressing what are likely long-standing grievances about economic and legal inequality.

Establishing an anti-corruption agency will not be sufficient to reduce malfeasance. Nigeria has established an Independent Corrupt Practices Commission and an Economic and Financial Crimes Commission. There is little evidence that either has reduced corruption and more than half of the respondents to the 2005 Nigeria Afrobarometer disapproved of the performance of the Independent Corrupt Practices Commission. Approval of the commission's performance is not simply a reflection of overall attitudes toward corruption. Instead,

---

[5] The Gini indices for Africa can be found at http://hdr.undp.org/reports/global/2005/pdf/ hdro5_HDI.pdf, 271–3, accessed December 2, 2006.

it reflects other conflicts in society, including trust in both other people and institutions and on economic fairness.

Many of the reasons for the success of anti-corruption efforts in Singapore and Hong Kong also apply to Botswana, especially the need to develop a robust economy to fend off external threats by opening markets and inviting foreign investment. Also, size matters. Each of the three nations found it easier to initiate anti-corruption campaigns because they have small populations. Singapore and Hong Kong are also city-states. Singapore is an island, as is much of Hong Kong. Finally, even though each of the three states ranks low on generalized trust, all have strong government policies designed to produce greater social solidarity across groups, thereby reducing the tendency of strong in-group trust to support corruption. I turn first to a discussion of corruption in Africa and then to how malfeasance has been largely eradicated in Singapore and Hong Kong.

Corruption, Inequality, and Low Trust in Africa

Africa is an ideal case study for the inequality trap thesis. The 37 black African countries rated in the 2005 TI Corruption Perceptions Index had the lowest mean score (2.79) and the smallest standard deviation (.88) of any region. The mean Gini index for 14 African nations for which there are data is 50.3, compared to 39.7 for non-African states; black African nations have a mean score of 7.96 on the Failed States uneven economic development index, compared to 6.56 for other countries. And trust is considerably lower in Africa, with a mean of 18.5 compared to 31.8 elsewhere.[6]

Many Africans see corruption everywhere in their society. They view it as troublesome; enriching the elite; and perpetuating economic, legal, and political inequality. Yet they also see it as unavoidable and ineradicable. The story of corruption as Africans express it and in the literature on corruption on the continent is very much that of the inequality trap. Few people see themselves enmeshed in an economic and moral quicksand more than the Nigerians.

Nigerians, like many people in high inequality/low trust societies, "view participation in politics as an investment, similar to putting money in the bank or buying stock in a firm" and "capturing an important political position is like winning the lottery: the new political office can be used to amass wealth for oneself and also reward one's supporters" (Mbaku, 1998b, 59). Nigeria's oil wealth should have made its citizens wealthy, but most of the income disappeared to the West "to establish comfortable retirement positions for the crooks who were busy cheating present and future Nigerians" or to providing "privileges . . . for a bloated, inefficient, and parasitic and corrupt bureaucracy" (Mbaku, 1998b, 69) – even as the country's per capita income fell to $240 US a year, making it one of the world's 20 poorest countries (Riley, 2000, 148).

---

[6] The African data come from Bratton, Mattes, and Gyimah-Boadi (2005, 194). Non-African data come from the imputed trust values reported in Chapter 4.

Similarly, in Kenya, income from sugar production was diverted to political leaders and their friends in the private sector. Over two-thirds of the civil service roster of Zaire (once again the Democratic Republic of the Congo) in the late 1970s was said to be fictitious, yet comprised almost half of the country's annual budget. Cameroon's President Ahmadou Ahidjo made the civil service, the military, labor unions, and universities his personal fiefdom, appointing and dismissing employees at will and enriching himself in the process (Mbaku, 1998b, 43, 61–2; Riley, 2000, 148).

Corruption in Africa, as elsewhere, has enriched the political elite, especially heads of state. Africans see corruption as tightly connected to inequality. Leaders such as Zaire's "kleptocrat" Mobutu Sese Seko amassed fortunes; Mobutu had mansions in Belgium, France, Morocco, Spain, and Switzerland (Riley, 2000, 149), while ordinary people saw their incomes plummet. African states had a score of 7.03 on the State Failure project's measure of sharp and severe economic decline compared to 4.86 for other countries. The Democratic Republic of the Congo and Mali had among the highest scores (above 8.0), while citizens of Botswana, with cleaner government (and especially South Africa and Mauritius) fared far better economically.

Mbaku (1998b, 27) points to the connection between corruption and inequality in Africa: "... corruption has allowed some groups to enrich themselves at the expense of the rest of the people, and, as a result, has been quite instrumental in exacerbating inequalities in the distribution of income and wealth." Williams (1987, 130) is even more emphatic: "In the conditions of underdevelopment, with their attendant shortages and paucity of resources, corruption tends mostly to accentuate and aggravate the political and economic inequalities which have characterized so may African states for so long."

Ordinary citizens see the link clearly. In Lagos, Nigeria (Packer, 2006, 69–70), people talk of the prevalence of corruption and the dependency of ordinary people on patrons that shapes all transactions, from the oil industry to the street merchant:

[A young itinerant trader said]: "Most of the people who lead us embezzle instead of using that money to create factories," he said. "Our parents' generation was O.K. But this generation is a wasted generation – unless God comes to the aid. Because we know there is money in Nigeria."

... almost no one works for himself. Everyone occupies a place in an economic hierarchy and owes fealty, as well as cash, to the person above him – known as an *oga*, or master – who, in turn, provides help or protection. Every group of workers – even at the stolen-goods market in the Ijora district – has a union that amounts to an extortion racket. The teen-ager hawking sunglasses in traffic receives the merchandise from a wholesaler, to whom he turns over ninety per cent of his earnings; if he tries to cheat or cut out, his guarantor – an authority figure such as a relative or a man from his home town, known to the vendor and the wholesaler alike – has to make up the loss, then hunt down his wayward charge. The patronage system helps the megacity absorb the continual influx of newcomers for whom the formal economy has no use. Wealth accrues not to the most imaginative or industrious but to those who rise up through the chain of patronage. It amounts to a predatory system of obligation, set down in no laws, enforced by implied threat.

Clarno and Falola (1998, 175) summarize the effects of this patron-client system: "Thus develops a system of two distinct classes working with and against each other in order to make the most of the situation. Though they support each other, it is an inherently unequal relationship that reinforces the division between classes." Much as the young man on the tram in Zagreb, Croatia, told me about power relations in transition countries, the rich justify their misdeeds as a legitimate perquisite of power (or *kom-yan*) while similar behavior by the poor is called "theft, cheating, and shameful sneaking around" or *zey-yan* (Olivier de Sardan, 1999, 42). The elite not only justify their own misdeeds, but often point to petty corruption as society's scourge. Nigerian General Sani Abacha, one of the more corrupt recent leaders, waged many campaigns against street-level corruption to deflect attention from his own misdeeds (Smith, 2006, 31).

This tight link between inequality and corruption leads to both pessimism and to low levels of trust outside of one's own circle. The sign as you enter Lagos simply says, "This is Lagos," and a sawmill worker said, "We understand this as 'Nobody will care for you, and you have to struggle to survive" (Packer, 2006, 64). Packer's (2006, 71) portrait of Lagos as a failed city with dispirited inhabitants echoes the gloom one sees in the subways in Russia, where people spend their days playing the slot machines because they have lost faith that hard work will bring economic success and that corruption or connections were the only way to get rich: "Folarin Gbadebo-Smith, the chairman of a district on Lagos Island [said]: 'The work ethic was...substituted by a lottery mentality. You were going to make it, not because you put in all this work but because you were lucky. You knew someone, or your ticket came in.'"

Patron-client relations reflect strong in-group ties. Those at the top of the economic pyramid have an obligation to support his clan, tribe, religious group, family, and his circle more generally. Africans don't identify with the larger society as readily as do people in other societies, especially in the West or in Asia. National boundaries are largely the creation of colonial powers, so loyalty to "the state" or the "society" of a country is weaker. The obligation of patrons to support their own kind further divides the society between in-groups and out-groups, who do not benefit from the largesse of a patron (Clarno and Falola, 1998, 175; Mbaku, 1998b, 65). As Smith (2006, 219) observes of Nigerians: "The focus on personal morality and loyalty to one's group, however – whether it is family, a church congregation, or an ethnic association – tends to deflect attention from the larger political structures that are most directly culpable in producing and reproducing social inequality."

Many Africans see themselves as trapped in a system of corruption that they acknowledge is wrong (Smith, 2006, 65), but that envelopes their lives. Smith (2006, 65, 217) argues:

Although Nigerians recognize and condemn, in the abstract, the system of patronage that dominates the allocation of government resources, in practice people feel locked in.... In a society where so many people suffer and struggle in order to survive, it is hard to begrudge people anything that offers help, hope, and solace.... Nigerians perceive the world of politics and the realm of the state as operating without morality.

Nigerians "tap into electrical lines, causing blackouts and fires; they pay off local gangs to provide security, which means that justice in the slums is vigilante justice" (Packer, 2006, 71). People see themselves as the victims of a corrupt system where everyone is forced into corrupt behavior in order to survive (Olivier de Sardan, 1999, 35). Your obligation to the *oga* reinforces strong in-group ties and a lack of concern for out-groups."

John Githongo, formerly head of Kenya's anti-corruption agency and now in exile at St. Antony's College at the University of Oxford after exposing graft at the highest levels, sees a direct link between corruption and inequality: "What's special about Africa's corruption is the starkness of the inequality.... That is unique – just how extreme the divide between those who have and those who don't is" (Cowell, 2006, A4). Furthermore, he links corruption to inequality *among ethnic groups* in his native Kenya (Githongo, 2006, 20–1, emphasis in original):

...the post-independence patrimonial state has disbursed resources to favour a ruling "minority." When the political traumas of the post-independence era are overlaid on these economic realities driven by patronage it creates particularly potent perceptions of inequality among ethnic groups... it's not the corruption in itself that people object to but the fact that it is perpetrated predominantly by an elite from one ethnic group to the exclusion of others, *especially theirs.*

Below, I provide strong empirical support for Githongo's argument. People in Africa (though Botswana is an exception) clearly link corruption and inequality to each other. In the survey for Mali – the only country where this question is posed so starkly – people who say that the President favors his own region in providing services are considerably more likely to say that corruption has been increasing.

As Russian mobsters take over control of legitimate businesses by brute force, Nigerian con artists engage in a wide range of scams (including many of those e-mail messages we get promising us riches if we send back our bank account details) under the rubric of "419" (four-one-nine), from the Nigerian criminal code on financial fraud. Scammers offer poor people's houses for sale and the poor warn potential buyers by painting signs: "This House Not for Sale: Beware of 419" on their outside walls (Packer, 2006, 72). As in Russia, there is little recourse. The police are not the purveyors of justice, but rather are complicit in illicit deals (Mbaku, 1998a, 258, 274–5). In the Afrobarometer, the police are considered to be the most corrupt public officials, with judges in third place behind customs officials (Bratton, Mattes, and Gyimah-Boadi, 2005, 233). The Economist Intelligence Unit legal fairness (imputed) measure indicates that African nations have a less fair legal system, with an average score of 2.0 on the five-point scale, compared to 3.06 for all other countries. In a 1992 survey in Sierra Leone 80 percent of the respondents believed that "there are two interpretations of the law in Sierra Leone – one for the rich and one for the poor" (Kpundeh, 1998, 129).[7] The partiality of the justice system makes ordinary people especially upset because the police are often very highly paid, so extortion by officers is not simply a matter of supplementing meager salaries with small bribes (Fombad, 2000, 245).

Nor is seeking redress through media exposure a likely means to end corruption. Fombad (2000, 248–9) argues that journalists who try to expose corruption face intimidation, torture, and jail. Newspaper stories about corrupt officials are often politically inspired, designed to score political points against public officials and most of all to sell newspapers (much as in Romania). The press is often less of a watchdog than a participant in the great game of corruption.

The inequality trap begins with a highly inequitable distribution of wealth throughout the continent, which is clearly a legacy of colonialism. The most "equal" countries, Tanzania and Mozambique, are slightly above the international average on the Gini index. Comparable levels of inequality are only found in Latin America. This inequality helps to solidify the strong in-group trust that has played such a powerful role in African culture. Attachment to your ethnic, religious, clan, tribal, or family group is not necessarily inimical to a larger, more generalized sense of trust (Uslaner, 2002, 26–32).

When people feel strongly bound *only* to their own group, believe that outsiders may be responsible for their economic plight, and that they will not be treated fairly throughout society's institutions, they will be more likely to mistrust out-groups. Group loyalty and the struggle for basic survival will overwhelm concerns about the rights and wrongs of corrupt behavior. Ordinary people confront petty thievery, not grand corruption, so their ethical dilemma is not as stark, especially if they believe that (1) their leaders, from the *oga* to the President, steal large amounts of money and get away with it; (2) the perpetrators of grand corruption are far less likely to face justice than they are; and (3) playing at the edge of moral acceptability is the only way to survive.

African corruption, some argue, ultimately rests upon a foundation of a grabbing state. On the other hand, Olivier de Sardan (1999, 42) argues that democratic governments in Africa are not barriers to corruption. Githongo (2006, 22) agrees, arguing that democratization "has not disrupted the corrupt networks established in the one-party era" and corrupt elites gather support from their own tribes or ethnic groups by dispensing patronage (cf. Mbaku, 1998, 274–5). Initially, there is some support for the claim that democratization leads to less corruption: The correlation between the Freedom House measure of political rights in 2003 and the 2005 TI Corruption Perceptions Index for 2005 is $-.678$ (N = 35), where high values on the Freedom House measure indicate lack of democratic rights. There is less evidence that *change in political rights*

---

[7] The sample only had 300 respondents, but the results seem realistic.

from 1973 to 2003 leads to less corruption; the correlation is only $-.319$ ($N =$ 30) and the change in corruption from 1996 to 2005 is barely related to changes in democratization ($r = .076$, $N = 13$), with the correlation not in the expected direction. So while there is support for the claim that institutions matter in the cross-sectional data, there is less evidence for the idea that *democratizing government* will lead to more honesty.

Sindzingre (2002, 453) makes an alternative argument about how the state promotes corruption: "The lack of state welfare schemes forces individuals into a perpetual quest for resources to protect themselves in case of adversity, which always looms on the horizon." This is a compelling argument and is consistent with the inequality trap argument. While there is no direct way to test the claim without better data on welfare policies, my analysis of Afrobarometer data strongly supports the claim that government performance on policies, especially welfare policies, shapes attitudes to both corruption and inequality.

Despite the uncertainty about institutional effects across countries, it may well be the case that *people's attitudes toward their institutions* tell us much about how they judge corruption in their societies. In the analyses of survey data below, I thus include measures of how satisfied people are with democracy, freedom of speech, trust in government and independent newspapers, trust in government institutions such as the courts and the police, how secure people believe that property rights are, and, following Sindzingre, how satisfied people are with social welfare – if not social welfare policies more specifically.

It would hardly be surprising to find that evaluations of institutional performance also shapes approval of how the government is handling corruption.[8] However, I expect that perceptions of inequality will have greater effects on evaluations of how well government is handling corruption than will attitudes toward institutions. I move now to the models for how well the government handles corruption and whether groups are treated equally in a society.

Testing the Inequality Trap in Africa

The Afrobarometer is a face-to-face survey based upon national probability samples in 15 African countries in 2002.[9] I use respondents from 14 nations in this analysis (see n. 2) initially and then move to separate analyses for Mali and Nigeria (Round 3 data for 2005). For the 14 countries I estimate ordered probit models of how well the government handles corruption and how frequently people are treated unequally. These estimations ideally should be estimated by simultaneous equation models since I posit that these two variables jointly shape

---

[8] Bratton, Mattes, and Gyimah-Boadi (2005, 232–3) argue that perceptions of corruption shape institutional trust and are often the strongest determinants of such confidence. This approach is similar to mine in Chapters 5 and 6, but here I focus on approval of government handling of corruption. I focus on trust in only specific institutions of justice.

[9] For the properties of the survey methodology, see http://www.afrobarometer.org/methods.html; the full list of countries is available at http://www.afrobarometer.org/countries.newmap.html, and a summary of results is available at http://www.afrobarometer.org/results.html.

each other. However, estimating such a model without controlling for variations within countries would lead to overestimating the significance of many, if not all, of the variables in the model. So I decided to use ordered probit analysis with robust standard errors, clustered across the 14 countries.[10] For Mali, I focus on whether people believe that corruption has been increasing since one-party rule and whether there is support for limiting the incomes of the wealthy. For Nigeria, I estimate a simultaneous equation model for how well the government is handling corruption and whether equal treatment for all is better now. Since this is a single-country survey, a two-stage least squares model does not risk overestimating significance levels.

For the ordered probit analyses, the "effects" are more complicated than for ordinary probit analyses. For a dichotomous probit, the effect is simply the change in probability of the dependent variable from the lowest to the highest level of a predictor. Such an interpretation makes little sense for ordered probit, since the dependent variable is not a simple dichotomy but a categorical (four- or five-category) variable. The effect in the tables is the *average* change in probability across the categories of the dependent variable.[11]

The models I formulate focus on variables most clearly connected to the inequality trap argument, how well the economy is performing more generally, and whether the government is delivering services to the people (rather than simply pocketing state revenue). I also include variables that test, as in transition countries, whether grand corruption has a greater impact on how well the government handles corruption than does petty corruption, as well as attitudes toward the police, the legal system, the press, democracy, property rights, and measures of trust.

I present the results of the 14 country estimations in Tables 7-1 and 7-2. As in previous chapters, I focus on the key variables of interest to the inequality trap argument, as well as those that reflect attitudes toward institutions, and leave discussion of other variables (especially demographics) to notes. The simple story of these two estimations is (1) government performance matters most for attitudes about corruption, but perceptions of equal treatment matter and rank very highly on statistical significance; (2) approval of how well the government handles corruption depends on perceptions of grand corruption and not petty corruption (as in transition countries); (3) perceptions of government performance also strongly shape attitudes toward how well the government handles corruption; and (4) perceptions of grand corruption, though not petty corruption in general, shape beliefs on how frequently people are treated unfairly.

---

[10] I also tried estimating fixed-effects models with dummy variables for the countries, but this still led to far higher significance levels than using robust standard errors with clustering.

[11] For a four-category variable, the effect is the average change in probability from category 1 to 2, 2 to 3, and 3 to 4. The sign reflects the same direction as the ordered probit coefficient The estimations were carried out using the prchange command in the spost routine for Stata 9 from J. Scott Long and Jeremy Freese at www.indiana.edu/~jslsoc/spost.htm. The prchange for ordered probit reports these average changes as absolute values.

TABLE 7-1. *Ordered Probit Analysis of How Well Government Handles Corruption: 2002 Afrobarometer*

Variable	Coefficient	Std. Error	MLE/SE	Effect
How frequently people are treated unequally	−.046***	.015	−3.00	−.028
Equal treatment for all: better now than under military	.042**	.024	1.73	.033
President is corrupt	−.184****	.030	−5.97	−.108
Teachers are corrupt	−.010	.028	−.37	−.006
Pay bribe to get place in school	.038*	.026	1.49	.030
Pay bribe to avoid problem with police	.005	.016	.32	.004
Pay bribe to get document or permit	.015	.032	.45	.009
Poverty/inequality country's most important problem	−.003	.028	−.10	−.002
Government manages economy well	.381****	.035	10.79	.216
Government manages service delivery better than past	.063***	.023	2.75	.050
Satisfied with democracy	.067***	.025	2.66	.053
Trust courts	.084***	.032	2.64	.050
Safer from crime and violence than under military	.101****	.028	3.65	.079
Property rights more secure than under military	.057**	.030	1.92	.045
Trust government newspapers	.062	.053	1.17	.085
Read newspapers frequently	.019	.017	1.10	.015
One's identity group treated unfairly	−.032**	.019	−1.69	−.019
Particularized trust	−.007	.058	−.13	.001
Age[+]	−.007	.008	−.85	−.018
Education	−.012	.024	−.51	−.019
Income	−.0004	.001	−.56	−.008
Gender	.033	.031	1.07	.006

Cut points not reported. Effects are average changes in probabilities across the five categories of trust in government. The effects represent the changes from each value to *the next higher value*. Standard errors are robust, clustered across the 14 countries in the sample.
[+]Effects calculated at +− one standard deviation.
*p < .10; **p < .05; ***p < .01; ****p < .0001
Estimated R^2 = .123; −2*Log Likelihood Ratio = 18019.13; N = 7709

Overall, 46.8 percent of the sample used for the estimation believe that government is handling corruption well or very well and 48.5 percent say that people are treated unequally either often or always. Both figures are greater than one might expect given the severity of corruption and inequality among African countries. Yet people see corruption and inequality as strongly interrelated.

How well the government handles corruption depends most strongly on government performance: A government that delivers the goods (specifically

TABLE 7-2. *Ordered Probit Analysis of How Frequently People Are Treated Unequally: 2002 Afrobarometer*

Variable	Coefficient	Std. Error	MLE/SE	Effect
Government handles corruption well	−.050**	.028	−1.82	−.030
President is corrupt	.147****	.024	5.99	.087
Police are corrupt	.029	.030	.97	.017
Teachers are corrupt	−.0002	.029	−.01	.0002
Pay bribe to get place in school	−.019	.047	−.40	−.015
Pay bribe to avoid problem with police	.016	.024	.65	.013
Pay bribe to get document or permit	.046**	.025	1.86	.037
Poverty/inequality country's most important problem	−.018	.032	−.53	−.010
Corruption country's most important problem	.052	.050	1.05	.010
Government manages economy well	−.082**	.037	−2.24	−.049
Government manages reducing income gap well	−.071**	.033	−2.15	−.042
Government provides food for all well	−.045	.037	−1.22	−.027
Schools should be free for all	.009	.011	.83	.007
Violent conflicts between groups in the country	.098****	.026	3.83	.078
Country's economic position very good	−.040*	.028	−1.42	.032
Own living condition very good	−.007	.019	−.37	−.006
One's identity group treated unfairly	.084***	.033	2.55	.050
Particularized trust	.125***	.041	3.06	.025
Trust traditional leaders	−.014	.021	−.66	.009
Age[+]	.001	.006	.19	.003
Education	−.021**	.012	−1.80	.034
Income	.001	.001	1.03	.011
Gender	.021	.022	.94	.004

Cut points not reported. Effects are average changes in probabilities across the five categories of trust in government. The effects represent the changes from each value to *the next higher value*. Standard errors are robust, clustered across the 14 countries in the sample.
[+]Effects calculated at +− one standard deviation.
*p < .10; **p < .05; ***p < .01; ****p < .0001
Estimated R^2 = .039; −2*Log Likelihood Ratio = 275510.51; N = 10,486

handling the economy) is perceived to be more honest and no other variable comes close to the effect of this one. For each increment in how well the government manages the economy, a respondent will have a .216-unit increase in her probability of approving handling of corruption. Approval of service delivery, as Sindzingre argues, also makes people more positive toward governmental honesty (an average of .05 increase). The significant variable with the third largest effect (8 percent) is whether people feel safer from crime and violence than under the military regime. Performance matters most of all.

If people believe that they are treated unequally, they will be less likely to approve of the government's handling of corruption. Both how frequently people are treated unequally and whether equal treatment is better now than under the military lead to significant increments in perceptions of government honesty. While the effects are not large, the significance of how frequently people are treated unequally is the fourth greatest in the model.[12] Unequal treatment does lead to greater dissatisfaction with government performance on curbing corruption. If better service delivery leads to less inequality, there is additional support for the inequality trap argument. If you believe that your identity group is treated unfairly, you will also be less likely to approve of government handling of corruption (though the effect is small). Particularized trust, as estimated by whether people identify more with their tribe or clan than with the country, is not significant. And whether people see poverty and inequality as the most important problem also does not shape attitudes toward corruption (perhaps because such a large share of the sample – over 72 percent – sees these problems as critical).

A key result from transition countries that underlies the inequality trap receives striking confirmation in the Afrobarometer data: It is grand corruption, not petty corruption, that shapes whether people think that the government is handling corruption well. The second biggest effect in the model (with an average change in probability of .108) is whether people think that the President is corrupt. Perceptions of low-level corruption (whether teachers are corrupt), demands for bribes for the police, or to get documents are insignificant. Paying a bribe to get into school is significant, but barely so (at $p < .10$). Petty corruption doesn't bother people as much as high-level corruption. Corruption at the very top matters most.

Attitudes toward institutions matter as well. People who are satisfied with democracy are, on average, 5 percent more likely (for each category) to approve of government handling of corruption. There are similar effects for trusting the courts and for believing that property rights are more secure. The other variables in the model – both demographics and attention to the media – are all insignificant.

People believe that strong institutions such as democracy, the courts, and secure property rights will lead to less corruption. But they also believe that malfeasance has a strong basis in inequality – in unfair treatment of groups and individuals and in misdeeds committed by the powerful rather than by ordinary people. Government performance seems the key (which is not surprising since the corruption question available asks about how well government handles malfeasance) – but even here there is a tie between economic performance and less inequality: The correlation (tau-c) between government management of the

---

[12] As determined by the MLE/SE (maximum likelihood estimate – or ordered probit coefficient divided by its standard error), which is analogous to a t-test in regression.

economy and whether equal treatment for all is better now is .327. Improved service delivery is also linked to more equal treatment (tau-c = .297), and trust in the police is at least modestly related to progress in equal treatment (tau-c = .190). So good government occurs when the state helps the most vulnerable and seems serious about reducing economic disparities and making people less dependent upon their *oga*.

Support for the inequality trap argument is even more powerful in the equation for how frequently people are treated unequally. By far the strongest predictor of unequal treatment is the belief that the President is corrupt (with an average effect of 8.7 percent). Believing that the government is handling corruption well is also significant, though only one measure of lower-level corruption (paying a bribe to get a document) increases inequality. Corrupt police or teachers and bribes to get into school or to avoid a problem with the police don't matter. Nor, perhaps surprisingly, does whether corruption is the country's most important problem – perhaps because only 10.5 percent of the sample said so. Yet social inequality seems to matter mightily. If you believe that there are violent conflicts between groups in the country, you will be 8 percent more likely across each category to say that people are treated unequally – and this variable ranks second in statistical significance in the model. Right behind is particularized trust – identification with your in-group rather than with the nation and belief that your identity group is treated unfairly. Government performance matters as well, though not everywhere. Management of the economy and of the income gap are significant, though not whether government provides food for all.[13] Perceptions of inequality thus reflect social tensions and government performance, but most of all reflect the belief that the President is corrupt. Almost three-quarters believe that some or all of the people in the office of the President are corrupt – and high-level corruption means grand theft, not petty larceny.

Corruption is widespread but not endemic in Africa. Botswana has a relatively clean government and there is little support for the inequality trap thesis there. I estimated the same ordered probit model for government handling of corruption for Botswana as I did for the full set of 14 countries in Table 7-1.[14] The model is striking for how few of the variables in this model are significant. The only exceptions, in order of their significance, are trust in the courts, the security of property rights, whether poverty and inequality are the most important problems, how well the government manages the economy, and particularized trust.

Overall, the model – except for poverty as a problem – approximates what one might expect for a developed democracy. The rule of law and government performance dominate the few significant predictors. For the unequal treatment

---

[13] Personal living condition, age, income, and gender are not significant, while the country's overall economic position was barely significant (at p < .10). Whether the poverty is the country's most important problem and whether schools should be free for all are also insignificant. More highly educated people are less likely to say that people are treated unequally – perhaps reflecting the higher status of people with education (though income is not significant).

[14] I do not present the estimates here. They are available upon request.

model, the only variables that are significant are unfair group treatment, particularized trust, how well the government is handling the economy, and whether people believe that schools should be free for all. All of these relate to economic and social tensions. None of the corruption variables predicts attitudes toward equal treatment significantly. Even though Botswana has a high degree of economic inequality, it has much lower corruption than other African countries. So it does not succumb to the inequality trap.

Botswanans are more concerned about progress on inequality than are people in any other country other than Nigeria in the 2002 Afrobarometer. Yet Botswanans are less likely to make a link between corruption and inequality than are people in most other countries. The simple correlation between perceptions of how well the government handles corruption and rising inequality is twice as high in Nigeria ($r = .340$) as it is in Botswana ($r = .177$).

Why does Botswana escape this trap? Botswana is a vibrant democracy with an active civil society (Holm, 2000, 290). But so is Mali, which does not escape the inequality trap (see below). Botswana has tremendous mineral wealth, but so does Nigeria. It also has a government committed to economic growth and foreign investment (Guest, 2003, 26; Riley, 2000, 153). Its economy has one of the world's highest growth rates, averaging between 8 and 10 percent a year (Holm, 2000, 295–6). It is landlocked, surrounded by Namibia, Zimbabwe, and South Africa – all of which were in the early years of Botswana's independence (1966) run by white racist regimes. So Botswana was rather vulnerable and its free-market policies that relied heavily upon foreign investment served to bolster its economic and institutional security.

As a country with a very small population, "less than the population of a single slum in Lagos" (Guest, 2003, 26), its economic growth was more manageable. Botswana has a clean government because it could not afford corruption. Foreign investors would not put their resources into a country where corruption ran rampant and Botswana would be vulnerable, because of its location (landlocked) and its size, without a strong economy. This story is remarkably similar to the one I shall tell below about Singapore and Hong Kong. (Economic) necessity may be the mother of (moral) subvention.

Corruption and Inequality in Mali and Nigeria

I turn now to an examination of the linkage between corruption and inequality in Mali in Round 2 of the Afrobarometer, and whether equal treatment for all is better now than under military rule in Round 3 (2005) for Nigeria.

I focus on Mali because the 2002 survey there included several questions not available in other countries in the Round 2 surveys, most notably limitations on incomes of the wealthy, the generalized trust question, trusting members of other tribes, perceptions of corrupt behavior among other people in the country, and beliefs about who should have access to or own resources such as education and public land. I focus on Nigeria in part for similar reasons – the 2005 survey included the generalized trust question as well as a much wider range of questions about petty corruption and questions on legal fairness. Most critically, Nigeria may be the classic case of the inequality trap – ranking as tied for the sixth most corrupt country in the world in the 2005 TI index as well as having very high levels of inequality and low levels of trust (a Gini of 50.5 and only 15 percent agreeing that "most people can be trusted").

I examine whether people see corruption increasing or decreasing since the period of one-party rule and whether the government should limit incomes of the rich among Malians. This permits comparisons with Romania, where I found support for a linkage between perceptions of rising inequality and disapproval of government handling of corruption and between perceived high levels of malfeasance and demands for limiting the incomes of the rich (see Chapter 5). People link corruption to inequality and in Romania (and other transition countries) they say that the only way to get rich is to be corrupt, so many people demand that the state limit the incomes of the (corrupt) rich. While there are no similar questions in Afrobarometer surveys, much of the literature on corruption in Africa points to a similar line of thought. Mali, with a relatively high level of corruption (2.9 on the 2005 TI index), considerable inequality (a Gini index of 50.5), as well as low generalized trust (.13), should be a good case to test this dynamic in Africa. In Mali, 60.6 percent believe that there has been an increase in corruption since the end of one-party rule following a 1991 coup, but surprisingly only 14 percent favor limiting the incomes of the rich.

Mali is a multiparty democracy with generally good relations among its ethnic groups, but it is one of the world's ten poorest countries with a per capita income of just $250 US a year. Democratic elections were held in 1992 although the 1997 elections were annulled by the courts; in 2002 General Amadou Toumani Toure, the former head of state during the 1991–2 transition following the coup, was elected in a multiparty election for a five-year term.[15] Almost two-thirds of Mali's land is either desert or semidesert, 10 percent of its population is nomadic, and 80 percent subsists on farming or fishing.[16]

Mali's poverty and great inequality suggest that there should be a strong connection between inequality and corruption – and between corruption and demands to limit wealth, even though only a small share of Malians favor restricting the incomes of the rich. And Malians do think about corruption, inequality, and limiting the incomes of the rich as the inequality trap would suggest – and in ways similar to Romanians. I present the ordered probit analyses for perceptions of increasing corruption and for supporting limiting incomes of the rich in Tables A7-1 and A7-2.

Issues of inequality and access to basic needs such as electricity are, together with beliefs about specific forms of corruption, the strongest determinants of perceptions of increasing corruption (see Table A7-1). The effect for more equal treatment (9 percent) is the second strongest in the model, following police corruption. Believing that government policies hurt most people (6 percent)

---

[15] http://www.state.gov/r/pa/ei/bgn/2828.htm, accessed December 31, 2006.
[16] https://www.cia.gov/cia/publications/factbook/geos/ml.html, accessed December 31, 2006.

and that electricity is difficult to get because it is too expensive (7 percent) are among the strongest determinants of corruption perceptions. Malians clearly make the link between malfeasance and inequality.

Perceptions about whether specific actors are corrupt lead to beliefs about rising malfeasance. The greatest impact is for police corruption (with an effect of .125), even more than believing that elected leaders or civil servants are corrupt (effects of .089 and .066). People who say that the President favors his own region in providing services are also more likely to say that corruption has been increasing – as are respondents who say that bribery is common among public officials (by average effects of about .05 for both). But there is no effect for businesspeople, teachers, customs officers, or for having to make a small bribe to get routine services. Malians, like Africans more generally as well as people in transition countries, seem concerned more by high-level, high-cost corruption than by petty dishonesty.

Even for variables reflecting institutional positions, there is evidence of an inequality trap. The police in many African nations earn far more than many ordinary people even before extortion – so constant harassment for "extra fees" may seem particularly offensive. Presidential favoritism also contributes to inequality by favoring some Malians over others. The strong effects on corruption perceptions for high-level malfeasance compared to petty bribery adds support to the inequality trap thesis.

So do two other variables with strong impacts. If you believe fellow citizens can get services without paying, you are acknowledging that some people have privileged access – and this leads to perceptions of increasing corruption. And if you can get cash through illicit sources, you either acknowledge your own favored position or admit that going outside normal channels is the only way to get by. Generalized trust doesn't matter, nor does trust in the courts. Generalized trust may not matter because it is so low in Mali – and the courts may seem less biased to average Malians than do other institutions.

Support for limiting the incomes of the wealthy (see Table A7-2) predominantly reflects perceptions of government performance in helping the poor as well as values for who should benefit from government policies. However, believing that bribery is frequent and that government is not handling corruption well are significant factors shaping demands to limit the incomes of the rich. No specific types of corruption – neither police, elected leaders, foreign businesspeople, nor teachers – have significant impacts on limiting incomes. Nor does petty bribery, trust in the courts, nor even tax evasion. However, when Malians get services without paying, they are violating norms of fairness and this leads to demands for redistribution (by an average effect of 7 percent, the second largest effect in the model).

Support for limiting incomes stems from other beliefs about economic policy and justice. People who say that education should be free for everyone and who believe that the community rather than individuals should own land are more likely to support redistribution (by averages of 7.5 and 5 percent, respectively). Believing that the government has reduced the income gap, that equal treatment has improved since miltary rule, and that individuals rather than government is responsible for the health of the economy all lead to less support for limiting incomes.

These effects are similar to the model for limiting incomes for Romania in Chapter 5 (see Table 5-1). In Romania, the most important factor shaping support for redistribution is the belief that people don't get sufficient support from the state. High-level corruption also makes people more sympathetic to limiting incomes. In Romania, wealth and the ability to afford "luxuries" such as a cellular telephone and a vacation away from home also shape support for limiting incomes – but they do not do so in Mali. Expectations for the next year or personal attacks do not lead to harsher judgments against others. But feeling safe makes people less likely to demand redistribution as does a sense of generalized trust – trust in members of other tribes. If you express faith in people unlike yourself, you will also be more willing to put faith in people with higher incomes. And if you feel safe walking alone, you may have a more positive view of human nature and find it easier to resist demands for retribution.

Malians link corruption and inequality, and those most concerned with corruption are also more likely to demand limiting the incomes of the rich. While most Malians oppose such mandatory redistribution, there are clear links, as my argument suggests.

The Inequality Trap in Nigeria

I turn now to the model for Nigeria. Corruption is "endemic in Nigeria," Dike (2005) argues. "Nigeria is a society where national priorities are turned upside down; hard work is not rewarded, but rogues are often glorified in Nigeria.... In Nigeria, you can hardly enter an office and get your 'file signed except you drop' some money. Even the security personnel at the door of every office will ask for (bribe) tip." Despite Nigeria's status as a major oil exporter and an official unemployment rate of only 2.9 percent, per capita GDP in 2005 was just $1400; 60 percent of the population lives below the poverty line.[17]

The first factor Dike (2005) cites as a cause of corruption is the "great inequality in distribution of wealth.... The brazen display of wealth by public officials, which they are unable to explain the source, points to how bad corruption has reached in the society. Many of these officials before being elected or appointed into offices had little or modest income."

Former President Sani Abacha reportedly stole as much as $1 billion from the country's treasury (Dike, 2005). Abacha's successor, Olusegun Obasanjo, promised a strong anti-corruption effort. Yet his administration has also fallen prey to dishonest dealings. In 1999, senators extorted approximately $6000 in exchange for votes for Evan Enwerem's nomination as Senate President. Four years later, ministerial nominee Mallam Nasir el-Rufai claimed that 54 senators demanded almost $400,000 to back his appointment. Despite President

[17] https://www.cia.gov/cia/publications/factbook/geos/ni.html, accessed January 1, 2007.

Obasanjo's promise to clean up the government, he has failed to order investigations into charges that state governors and the Inspector General of the Police have skimmed millions of dollars of public funds into their own pockets (Odunlami, 2004).

Nigeria has been marked by ethnic conflict – there was a civil war in the late 1960s when Christians in the East, the Ibos, tried to secede as an independent nation (Biafra). After that failed attempt, Nigeria has been wracked by sporadic, often very deadly, inter-ethnic and inter-religious violence spurred on at least in part by jealousy over economic status and sectarian conflicts. These conflicts have contributed to Nigeria's low out-group trust and strong in-group identification – as well as jealousy over group economic and political success.

I estimate a simultaneous equation model (using two-stage least squares) for how well the government is handling corruption and whether equal treatment for all is better than under military rule. The Round 3 Afrobarometer for Nigeria includes the generalized trust question – however, it was insignificant and led to a loss of cases. Instead, I use the measure of particularized trust that I used in the all-Africa model in Table 7-2 (whether a respondent identified more with her tribe than with the nation). The Round 3 data has a much wider battery of questions on petty corruption: whether people made bribes to obtain a public document, a school placement, a household service, medicine, or police protection. I constructed a bribe index by factor analysis of these questions. The survey also contained questions on how likely people believed the law would be enforced if they or high officials were charged with a serious crime. I constructed a measure of law enforcement bias from these two measures, ranging from seeing yourself as less likely to be prosecuted to equal likelihoods of prosecution or evading the law to believing that high officials would be less likely than yourself to face the wrath of the law.

The Round 3 survey for Nigeria asks the usual questions on how well the government is handling inequality and the economy. It also has a question on how well the government is handling the AIDS crisis. Since AIDS primarily affects poor people and its devastating effects can rob a family of its breadwinner and leave it even more vulnerable (McGeary, 2001; AVERT, 2006), dealing with AIDS fundamentally affects the level of economic inequality in Africa (as elsewhere). How a government chooses to respond to this health crisis tells us much about who benefits from government policies.

I present the model in Table 7-3. Nigerians see clear linkages between corruption and inequality. By far the strongest factor shaping views of how well the government is handling corruption is government performance on AIDS. At the bivariate level, 38 percent of Nigerians say that the government is handling corruption very badly (and 20 percent say that it handles the AIDS crisis very poorly); 82 percent who say that the government is handling AIDS badly also say that it is doing very poorly on corruption. Only 4.5 percent say that the government is handling the AIDS crisis badly and corruption well. The next two variables, by levels of significance, are how well the government handles the economy and whether equal treatment for all is better than under military

TABLE 7-3. *Simultaneous Equation Model for Government Handling Corruption and Changes in Inequality: Afrobarometer in Nigeria 2005*

Variable	Coefficient	Std. Error	t Ratio
Government handles corruption well			
Equal treatment for all better now	.201****	.033	6.00
President is corrupt	−.108****	.025	−4.34
Teachers are corrupt	.052	.025	2.07
Make bribes factor score	−.004	.021	−.02
Provide favors for services: right or wrong	.023	.042	.41
Law enforcement bias	.078	.027	2.80
Local government handles tax collection	.106****	.020	5.35
Government handles AIDS	.292****	.020	14.33
Government handles economy	.201****	.028	7.24
Government handles inequality	.105****	.030	3.47
Trust government media	.091****	.022	4.08
Political knowledge	.022**	.013	1.68
Constant	−.187	.145	−1.29
Equal treatment for all better now			
Government handles corruption well	.282****	.053	5.28
Unjust arrest less frequent now	.273****	.025	11.01
President is corrupt	−.044*	.031	−1.43
Teachers are corrupt	.040	.038	1.06
Health care workers are corrupt	−.038	.039	−.97
Trust police	.111****	.029	3.83
Government handles inequality	.096***	.037	2.64
Availability of goods better now	.051**	.022	2.25
National economy better next year	.079****	.019	4.19
Free speech more respected now	.145****	.023	6.21
Particularized trust	−.034*	.024	−1.42
No cash income	−.057***	.019	−3.08
Constant	.250*	.147	1.70

*p < .10; **p < .05; ***p < .01; ****p < .0001

N = 1681

RMSE (R^2) by equation: Government handles corruption: .378 (.753); equal treatment better: .336 (.912)

Endogenous variables in **bold**; endogenous dependent variables in ***bold italics***.

Exogenous variables: Gender, age, education, trust in the courts, trust other ethnic groups, discrimination against religion better now, police are corrupt, belief that people are obligated to pay taxes, listen to radio news often, discuss politics frequently.

rule. Right behind equal treatment is whether local government does a good job in collecting taxes – which is also likely to reflect attitudes toward inequality, since evading taxes is far more consequential (and perhaps frequent) among the wealthy. Another measure of inequality – whether the government is handling it well – also is a strongly significant predictor of approval of government efforts on corruption.

Nigerians who do not believe that the government is working hard enough to combat inequality overwhelmingly say that the state is corrupt. And they put the blame at the top – with the President (p < .0001) and not with teachers, and upon whether they are forced to make bribes, believing that providing favors for services is wrong. Surprisingly, law enforcement bias *has the wrong sign* – indicating that people who believe that high officials would be treated more leniently than they would are more likely to approve government performance on corruption.[18]

The equal treatment equation also supports the inequality trap argument. Two of the three variables with the strongest impacts on whether equal treatment for all is better now relate to the fairness of the legal system and to government handling of corruption. People who believe that there are fewer unjust arrests are far more likely to say that equal treatment for all is better now. Twenty-one percent believe that unjust arrests are now *more frequent* than under military governments and 19 percent say that inequality has gotten much worse. Half of the people who say that unjust arrests have increased a lot also say that inequality has gotten much worse. Of the 3 percent who say that there are far fewer unjust arrests, 28 percent say that equality has gotten much better (compared to an overall share of 4 percent). While there is little nostalgia for the military regime, Nigerians believe that things have not improved under democratic government.

The fairness of the legal system is the central factor shaping people's views of how equally people are treated. Trust in the police is also strongly related to perceptions of equal treatment (p < .0001). Also significant is whether the government is handling corruption well (p < .0001). When people believe that the police are a law unto themselves and can arrest anyone for any reason (including shaking them down for bribes), when people don't trust the police, and when they believe the political system is corrupt, they see unequal treatment. Again, petty corruption (from teachers and health care workers) doesn't matter, but higher-level malfeasance, in the office of the President, is significant (though only at p < .10).

Institutions matter as well. The second most important factor shaping equal treatment is whether free speech is more respected now. Also significant is government performance on the economy – whether people expect the economy to be better next year, whether more goods are available now, and whether people have no cash income. Identity with one's own tribe rather than with Nigerians more generally also leads people to say that equal treatment has worsened. Particularized trust is based upon – and leads to – envy of groups that may fare better than your own – and this mistrust of out-groups is a central part of the inequality trap.

---

[18] I thought that this unusual result might stem from multicollinearity, but checks indicated otherwise – and the relationship holds at the bivariate level. Also in the model and significant are whether people trust government media (the source of much information about corruption) and how knowledgeable they are (the more knowledgeable would be more likely to be aware of anti-corruption efforts). Both are significant.

Nigeria may be one of the strongest cases for the inequality trap among African nations – and there is clear evidence for my thesis here. The Nigerian evidence is even more dramatically supportive than the all-Africa models or those for Mali. The evidence for African nations is in many ways similar to that for transition countries, which have much lower levels of inequality and generally less corruption. There are, of course, exceptions, as the case of Botswana clearly shows. Botswana is relatively clean politically and even though it has low levels of trust and high inequality, it seems to escape the inequality trap.

The models for Africa do offer somewhat more support than I have found previously for institutionalist accounts. There is a strong bivariate relationship between political rights and corruption across African countries. And people throughout Africa judge the honesty of their governments and in some estimations how equally people are treated by the quality of their democratic institutions, especially freedom of the press and the quality of the legal system. This greater support for institutional effects than in previous chapters does not take away from the evidence for the inequality trap. In many African countries, weak institutions and high inequality contribute to the grabbing state. The survey evidence indicates that people link poor institutional quality to both economic and legal inequalities. It is not simply democracy that matters, but rather democratic institutions that work to reduce corruption and inequality together.

I now turn to two cases that are even more dramatic exceptions than Botswana and pose perhaps the most severe challenge to my argument about the inequality trap – and seem to suggest far more support for a distinctly institutionalist perspective: Singapore and Hong Kong.

Singapore and Hong Kong: The Great Exceptions

Singapore and Hong Kong are the most prominent exceptions to my argument linking high inequality and low trust to high levels of corruption. Singapore and Hong Kong rank among the most honest countries in the world, according to the TI Corruption Perceptions Index. Singapore's Gini index is at the mean of both the World Bank and the WIDER data sets, with a value about 39. Hong Kong has a less equal income distribution, with a score of 45 for the World Bank measure (in 1991) and of 48.5 in the more recent WIDER data. The two states rank relatively low on generalized trust – with 27 percent in Hong Kong and 28 percent in Singapore believing that "most people can be trusted" – about the same share as in Estonia but higher than almost any African nation.[19]

---

[19] These data come from the Aarhus Social Capital surveys underway at Aarhus University, Denmark, and were provided to me by Kim Sonderskov. Asian Barometer figures for 2004 give a somewhat higher share of trusters (34 percent) for Singapore (Inoguchi et al., 2004, 445) and an almost identical 29 percent for Hong Kong. The two African nations ranking higher are Namibia (34 percent) and Malawi (45 percent), as reported in Bratton, Mattes, and Gyimah-Boadi (2005, 194).

What makes Singapore and Hong Kong so clean? Certainly it is not Asian exceptionalism. Quah (2006, 177) tells of the long history of corruption in Mongolia, Thailand, and South Korea (see also You, 2005b), while Manion (2004, 29) discusses the historical roots of malfeasance in China and attributes the temporary rise in corruption in Hong Kong in the 1950s and 1960s to large-scale immigration from the mainland (see also Lo, 2001, 23). The reduction in corruption in Asia seems to be unique to Singapore and Hong Kong (Quah, 2006, 177).

For many years "corruption was common" in Hong Kong and "believed to have originated from traditional Chinese culture" (Lo, 2001, 21). In Singapore, Lee (2003) argues:

Gangs disrupted the lives of many people here, from big business to small shopkeepers.... The fledgling police force could do only so much since few wanted to be policemen.... Extortion, blackmail, kidnapings, murders, rapes, you name it, they did it in Singapore.... Murders took place with alarming regularity – in the streets, coffee shops, and in housing estates...we have changed dramatically, almost metamorphosed from a society caught in the grip of criminals...to the orderly and secure haven we have today.

Corruption was "a low risk, high reward activity" and the chief agents of enforcement, the police, were (as in many other countries) more part of the problem than of the solution (Quah, 2001b, 29–30).

In Hong Kong, corruption reflected strong in-group ties. Lee (1981, 358–9, 361–2) argues that

in the indigenous Chinese social setting particularism is a valued goal in itself, regardless of its possible function.... The emphasis on personal relations is strengthened by a long-standing characteristic of Chinese society – i.e., the dominance of social and moral norms over legal norms.... In the mind of most people...official status and wealth are very close.... [I]n traditional China people tended to accept certain "corrupt" practices as a normal way of life.

Corruption was deeply rooted in society in both Singapore and Hong Kong. How did Singapore and Hong Kong change from lawless societies to model city-states?

Most accounts focus on Singapore's Corrupt Practices Investigation Bureau (CPIB) and Hong Kong's Independent Commission on Corruption (ICAC). These anti-corruption agencies have been granted extraordinary powers of investigation and prosecution. Singapore's Prevention of Corruption Act, passed in 1960, gave the CPIB the power to arrest people and to investigate the bank records of officials and their families or agents – and required some-one found guilty to repay the amount of the bribe as well as any other penalty (Quah, 1995, 395). Lee (2003) credits Singapore Prime Minister Lee Kuan Yew, who took office in 1959 committed to ending crime and corruption: "His brass-knuckle, kick-butt approach was the only way to purge the scourge." In Hong Kong, ICAC has broad powers of investigation, search, and seizure, with a staff of 1200 (for a population of 6.5 million) and a police force of 35,000. ICAC has "draconian powers" and the Hong Kong law had a loose definition of corruption that permitted it to cast a very wide net. Further, "it is assumed that a person in possession of money which could not reasonably have been earned given his or her job, and which cannot reasonably be explained in court...commits an offense" (Lo, 2001, 24).

Singapore and Hong Kong battled corruption largely through political will and strong leadership (Lo, 2001, 27; Quah, 2006, 177). While much of the literature on corruption links clean government to democracy, Hong Kong and Singapore show that authoritarian states may be better situated to fight the demons of corruption (Root, 1996, 171). Neither Hong Kong or Singapore relies exclusively on the strong arm of the law. In both city-states, the anti-corruption agencies engage in extensive public education. In Hong Kong, posters all over town (especially in the subway) exhort people to report any suspected incidents of corruption. ICAC also conducts public education programs in the school system so that youngsters learn the importance of clean government (Manion, 2004, 47). The Singapore police also rely upon public support – community policing (Quah, 1998a, 118). In both city-states, a strong crackdown on corruption went hand in hand with public education – campaigns designed to win support for the government's efforts for greater honesty.

The anti-corruption agencies in Singapore and Hong Kong were dramatic success stories. Are they models for other countries? Could we reduce malfeasance by establishing similar agencies throughout the world?

It is not so simple. In Africa, among other places, there has been a long history of anti-corruption agencies that have failed. Sometimes the punishment of corrupt leaders is rather dramatic, as when Ghana's Flight Lieutenant Jerry Rawlings and Liberia's leader Samuel Doe ordered the execution of corrupt officials almost three decades ago. In Uganda, Kenya, Tanzania, Malawi, Zimbabwe, and Nigeria, anti-corruption agencies patterned after ICAC have been established but met with little success: "...the ICAC operates within a relatively well-regulated administrative culture, alongside a well-equipped police force" (Kpundeh, 2000, 134–5). The chief enforcers of the anti-corruption efforts, the police and the courts, are tainted by dishonesty themselves and there is no effective independent media that can hold authorities accountable (Manion, 2004, 31; Mbaku, 1998a, 274–5).

Return briefly to Nigeria. The 2005 Afrobarometer included a question on whether people trusted the country's anti-corruption agency (see Table 7-4). About half the survey respondents approved of the commission's performance and half did not. The ordered probit analysis of support for the commission shows that Nigerians base their approval mostly on whether they believe they will be getting the straight story about prosecutions. By far the most powerful determinant of support for the anti-corruption commission is whether people believe that they can trust independent newspapers (only 44.5 percent do). Of the small number who trust independent newspapers, two-thirds approve of the work of the anti-corruption commission – while two-thirds who don't have

TABLE 7-4. *Ordered Probit Analysis of Trust for Corruption Commission in Nigeria: 2005 Afrobarometer*

Variable	Coefficient	Std. Error	MLE/SE	Effect
Government handles corruption well	.138****	.032	4.28	.081
Make bribes factor score	.017	.031	.55	.016
Trust independent newspapers	1.012****	.037	27.66	.435
Trust ruling party	.199****	.036	5.64	.117
Approve President	−.037	.038	−.97	−.022
Trust other people	.110****	.032	3.42	.065
Equal treatment for all better now	.094****	.027	3.44	.073
Easy to get school place	.061***	.022	2.72	.047
National economy better next year	.047**	.023	2.05	.037

Cut points not reported. Effects are average changes in probabilities across the five categories of trust in government. The effects represent the changes from each value *to the next higher value*.
$^{*}p < .10$; $^{**}p < .05$; $^{***}p < .01$; $^{****}p < .0001$
Estimated $R^2 = .284$; $-2{}^*$Log Likelihood Ratio = 3373.78; N = 1752

faith in the press disapprove of the work of the agency. The effect is .435 – so that a one-unit increase in trusting the independent press will lead to an expected increase in approval of almost half a point *on average*. This is a powerful impact and can easily push someone from a negative view of the commission to a positive view by support for the press alone if one becomes more favorable to the media.

How well the government is handling corruption also matters, but it is far from the key factor shaping attitudes toward the commission. The ordered probit effect for approval of the government's handling of corruption (.081) is not even a fifth as large as that for trusting the independent media – and is less than for trust in the governing party (.117). Attitudes toward the commission seem largely reflective of whether people believe that the government will not interfere with the agency's mission. However, strong performance – a robust economy and making it easier to get a place in school – also builds confidence in corruption fighting. So does a sense of social solidarity: Generalized trust builds confidence in anti-corruption agencies – likely reflecting trusters' more optimistic view of human nature. And believing that equal treatment for all has gotten better also makes people believe that the government may be serious about a key consequence of inequality – corruption. Perhaps ironically – or perhaps not – demands for petty corruption (as represented by the bribes factor score) have no effect on approval of the anti-corruption commission. People don't expect anti-corruption agencies to deal with petty corruption. They understand that leaders such as Nigeria's Abacha – like those in transition countries – claim to be rooting out street-level dishonesty while continuing to line their own pockets (Smith, 2006, 31).

The roots of support for the anti-corruption commission in Nigeria tell us much about how Hong Kong and Singapore succeeded, though hardly the whole story. Both Hong Kong and Singapore have independent newspapers, but ICAC and CPIB have focused more on public education campaigns than on the press. But winning the hearts and minds of the public has been key to the success of these two agencies.

Perhaps the most important factor in fighting corruption, as in Botswana, has been the outside threat. Both Singapore and Hong Kong faced strong Communist movements after the Chinese revolution. These radical groups linked up with organized crime to create violent conflict (Lee, 2003) and instill feelings of solidarity with mainland China among the dominant ethnic Chinese populations in both city-states. The high level of economic inequality led to a radicalized labor movement, especially in Singapore, and local authorities (since Singapore was still ruled by Malaysia) feared a wider war in the region (Campos and Root, 1996, 30–1, 38).

In both Singapore and Hong Kong, the leaders fought the external threat by adopting a mix of free-market and state-centered economic policies designed to increase wealth and reduce inequality. They also focused on efforts designed to reduce identification with China and to build separate, more inclusive Singapore and Hong Kong identities. If people were wealthy, they would have little interest in Communism – and if inequality were falling, they would not be strong targets for radical groups. Singapore felt particularly vulnerable: Malaysia set it adrift in 1965 and the island's residents worried about external threats, especially as the war in Vietnam bolstered China's political and military might in Southeast Asia.[20] The conflict also threatened Hong Kong, but it was still under the wing of Great Britain, which had left Singapore and Malaysia in 1963.

Economic policies focused first on drawing international investors to the two city-states, to provide both an engine for economic growth and to give outside interests a stake in the independence of the two nations (Quah, 1997, 306). Hong Kong became "the world's closest approximation to a free market, private enterprise, capitalist, laissez-faire economy" (Lo, 2001, 22) and both city-states attracted large international companies. All of the 25 largest banks in the world have offices in Singapore and 24 have branches in Hong Kong. Half of the largest corporations have outlets in Hong Kong, 60 percent in Singapore (Quah, 1997, 305). The two city-states had among the highest growth rates of any country in the world from 1965 to 1989, achieving a higher growth rate than Japan (Quah, 1997, 304–5). And the share of the GDP from private investment was higher than for any high-performing Asian economy (Campos and Root, 1996, 9–27). The honesty of the two city-states' governments led to investment from the West and from Japan, the economic powerhouse of Asia and a bullwark against China.

Singapore and Hong Kong started out relatively poor. The real gross domestic product per capita (from the Penn World Tables) in 1960 for both countries was

---

[20] On the history of Singapore and its split from Malaysia, see http://www.aseanfocus.com/publications/history_singapore.html.

below average for the entire world in 1950, with Singapore at $482.54 and Hong Kong at $681.42, compared to an average of $690.55 for all countries. The two city-states did not catch up until approximately 1970 and then their economies took off. I present trajectories of the rise in real GDP for Singapore and Hong Kong in Figure A7-1 and the take-off point corresponds for Hong Kong with the establishment of ICAC. Singapore's economic rise strongly parallels that of Hong Kong, so it appears that the effect of the anti-corruption efforts there were somewhat delayed after the founding of the CPIB. There is a strong linear trend in the growth rates for both city-states: For Singapore, the regression coefficient for the variable year (from 1950 to 2000) is 708.8 ($r^2 = .886$) and for Hong Kong it is 763.3 ($r^2 = .917$), so that each year the two city-states had a predicted increase in their real GDP per capita of between $700 and $800. This is not simply a case of a worldwide trend. The regression coefficient for the full sample of 168 countries is only 188.3 ($r^2 = .244$). The rates of increase in GDP per capita for Hong Kong and Singapore were the third and fifth highest in the world.

Singapore and Hong Kong both still have relatively high levels of inequality, but the rates have been cut by almost 20 percent from 1965 to 1990 (though they increased by 40 percent in Hong Kong – from 37.3 to 52 – by 1996 according to the WIDER estimates). Other high-performing Asian economies only reduced their (lower levels of) inequality by 12 percent. Unemployment by 1990 was almost non-existent. Singapore has increased education spending by a factor of 90 in the effort to produce a social safety net (and to defuse political tensions) amidst a high level of inequality (Quah, 2001b, 291). While Hong Kong has favored a less active welfare state than Singapore, it has succeeded in sharply increasing the share of its income that goes to the middle class (Lo, 2001, 22; Campos and Root, 1996, 46).

In Table A7-3, I present some political and demographic comparisons based upon data sources I used in the aggregate models in Chapter 3. I compare the standings of Singapore and Hong Kong with all nations and especially with Sweden. I chose Sweden because it is the classic case of high trust, low inequality, and low corruption (Uslaner and Badescu, 2004). The data clearly point to the economic prowess of both city-states, which are almost on a par with Sweden and considerably better than the mean for all nations on the United Nations Development Programme measures. For the Penn World Tables indicators, the two city-states were already very strong by 1989 (with Hong Kong almost at Sweden's level of GDP per capita). By 2002, both had surpassed Sweden. And both city-states outrank Sweden on the openness of the economy, in 1989 and in 2000, both by Penn World Tables and Freedom in the World measures. All three countries have much higher risk ratings from the InterCountry Risk Group than average, as well as higher growth in GDP.

All three countries have relatively strong performance on hidden trade barriers and very little bureaucratic red tape. Hong Kong lags behind the others on the World Economic Forum's effective lawmaking – because the status of Hong Kong's legislature is under a cloud as China attempts to restrict the island's autonomy. Nevertheless, in the 2000 Gallup Millennium survey, the same share of people in Hong Kong said that the government was run by the will of the people (40 percent) as in Sweden – though Singapore residents were even more upbeat (61 percent). In all three countries, very few people called their government corrupt (only 1 percent in Singapore) and in all three business executives said that most firms were ethical, far more than among other countries. In both Singapore and Hong Kong, more executives said that businesses were involved in charitable works than even in Sweden (which, surprisingly, had a lower score than average).

The two city-states rank highly on most legal and property rights measures – not as strong as the Swedish "gold standard" but very much ahead of the rest of the pack – although Hong Kong rates even higher than Sweden on the impartiality of its courts. All three countries also score above average on ethnic tensions (from the ICRG), though not so dramatically as we might expect. And Hong Kong and Singapore lag behind Sweden and most other countries on democratic accountability – even as their citizens see government reflecting the will of the people. Even without democracy, Hong Kong and Singapore have flourished economically by opening their markets.

Both city-states have fostered a sense of greater social solidarity across ethnic groups. Hong Kong is marked by "a feeling of community and a sense of neighbourhood in the streets" (Quah, 1997, 316). Singapore is an immigrant society of multiple ethnicities, so it had to create a sense of "national identity." Its schools have a formal policy of bilingualism (Chinese and English) and the history of each of the major ethnic groups is taught to instill a sense of social cohesion – and to combat earlier violent ethnic conflicts (Quah, 1997, 314–15). Young Singaporeans interact with each other across ethnic lines, and 80 percent of Singaporeans say that they have friends in each of the major ethnic groups – Malay, Chinese, and Indians (Kong, 1998, 66–7; Quah, 1998b, 15). Education is central to building both a sense of identity and a commitment to opposing corruption (in Hong Kong as well).

What does all of this have to with corruption? It is difficult to sustain high levels of economic growth over a long period of time if your government is corrupt and if there are high levels of ethnic tensions. A country seeking external investment may find international businesses turning away if the leaders insist upon bribes. In a competitive international environment, corruption becomes a red flag for investors. Control over corruption – and over crime rates – becomes a *sine qua non* for rapid and sustained economic growth, especially for states that are small (as both Singapore and Hong Kong are), feel threatened by a nearby power, and are isolated (Singapore and Hong Kong are islands). Especially if the states are small, heavily populated, have few natural resources, and little if any agriculture, they will be dependent upon international trade. Singapore and Hong Kong, if they were to survive, had little choice but to push for rapid economic development and to fight both crime and corruption. To garner support for the anti-corruption drives, the governments had to create a wellspring of public support – and this meant that social tensions had to be reduced. In

Singapore, the efforts to create an inclusive "Singaporean identity" were combined with the message that people should treat others with respect and honesty.

Singapore has produced a society where people feel content with their state. In the Asian Barometer for 2004, only 16 percent of Singaporeans say that economic inequality in their society is a cause for worry – lower than in Japan and less than half as many as in Malaysia or China and almost a third as many as in Indonesia. Eighty-seven percent of Singaporeans say that their government is faring very or fairly well in combating corruption (only in Thailand is there a majority agreeing among Asian nations) and only 1 percent hold that corruption is widespread (compared to 18 percent in Thailand and over 40 percent in South Korea and the Philippines). Singaporeans are pleased (71 percent) with their government's efforts in combating unemployment, in supporting human rights (77 percent), in providing public services (87 percent), and especially in fighting crime (90 percent).[21] The high crime rate in Singapore is now a thing of the past with rates lower than most big cities in the world – and American states of approximately the same population (Lee, 2003; Quah, 1998a, 117).

I present a probit model for perceptions of corruption in the Hong Kong government in Table 7-5, using the Asian Barometer for the city-state. (The data for Singapore have not yet been released for independent analysis.) Fewer than 25 percent believe that all or most government officials are corrupt. Only 2.6 percent say that they or anyone they know has witnessed an act of corruption or bribery. Fifty-four percent say that people were more likely to be treated equally under British colonial rule.[22] There is overwhelming trust in key governmental institutions: 82 percent trust the courts and 69 percent have confidence in civil servants.

Neither equal treatment nor generalized trust is a significant determinant of perceptions of corruption in Hong Kong. Nor are beliefs about democratic governance: People who say that Hong Kong is democratic, who say that Hong Kong *ought to be* democratic, or that democracy is more important than economic development are no more likely to judge the island's government as honest than people who care little about institutional structure. There is also no evidence of any "jealousy" effect: People who are at the bottom of the economic, class, or educational ladder are no more likely to see malfeasance than those at the top. Nor do people who say that the Hong Kong government

---

[21] These figures come from Inoguchi et al. (2004), 473, 494–5, 504.

[22] The Asian Barometer is a set of surveys across 17 Asian nations (see http://www.asianbarometer. org/newenglish/introduction/). The Hong Kong survey in 2004 is a representative survey targeting "Hong Kong people aged 20 to 75 residing in permanent residential living quarters in built-up areas" who speak Chinese (Asian Barometer, 2004). The Hong Kong sample is 811. Questions on corruption and inequality were limited (compared to the surveys in other Asian countries) because these are less salient issues in Hong Kong. I am grateful to Kai-Ping Huang, Assistant Director, Asian Barometer, National Taiwan University, Taipei, Taiwan, for making the Hong Kong data available. The government corruption question is a four-category Likert scale. However, there were so few cases at both extremes that I collapsed the four categories into a dichotomy.

TABLE 7-5. *Probit Analysis of Perceived Government Corruption in Hong Kong: Asian Barometer 2004*

Variable	Coefficient	Std. Error	MLE/SE	Effect
People treated equally: Better than in past	.060	.117	.52	.039
Generalized trust	−.009	.191	−.05	−.002
Success/failure determined by fate	−.363***	.144	−2.51	−.246
Know anyone who has witnessed bribe	1.073***	.393	2.73	.306
Trust courts	−.609***	.194	−3.14	−.459
Trust civil servants	−.410***	.150	−2.72	−.282
How democratic is Hong Kong?	.068	.054	1.25	.123
Democracy would be good for Hong Kong	.007	.048	.14	.013
Democracy more important than development	−.082	.093	−.88	−.066
Government should own key enterprises	−.034	.159	−.021	−.022
Economic situation of Hong Kong good	−.252**	.137	−1.83	−.107
Closely follow news	−.066	.062	−1.07	−.059
Education	−.054	.047	−1.14	−.022
Income	−.037	.079	−.46	−.108
Social class (perceived)	−.085	.121	.71	−.070
Constant	3.250***	1.207	2.69	

*p < .10; **p < .05; ***p < .01; ****p < .0001
Estimated R^2 = .625; −2*Log Likelihood Ratio = 296.106; N = 383
Percent predicted correctly: 83.5 (model); 80.7 (null)

should own key enterprises – a surprising 73 percent in this haven of free-market capitalism – see government as more corrupt.[23]

What matters most is the belief that officials are trustworthy. If you have a lot of faith in the courts, you are 46 percent less likely to see government corruption than if you have little confidence in the justice system. If you trust civil servants a lot, you will be 28 percent less likely to see lots of malfeasance than if you have little faith in bureaucrats. And the handful of people who know someone who has witnessed a bribe are 31 percent more likely to see lots of corruption. Finally, people who strongly agree that wealth and poverty, success and failure are all determined by fate are 25 percent more likely to see widespread corruption than people who believe that your destiny is determined by your own

---

[23] I expected that people who more closely follow news in the newspapers or on television would be more likely to be aware of cases of corruption, but this does not hold. As expected, people who see Hong Kong's economic situation as good are 11 percent less likely to see corruption than those who say that it is very bad. I calculate the effect here excluding the 1 percent who say that the economy is very good.

efforts. Believing that your lot in life is controlled by fate is part of a pessimistic worldview in which people are merely tools, often of the same dark forces underlying corruption. Free will includes the capacity to resist corruption – so people who accept this worldview will see less malfeasance. The 61 percent of Hong Kong respondents who endorse this view of free will are a testimony to the city-state's capacity to change from a highly corrupt society to an over-whelmingly honest one.

By 2004, the people in Hong Kong have come to expect honesty in their government and clean, efficient jurists and bureaucrats – and who have faith in people's capacity to act for themselves. Hong Kong respondents care less for democracy than for prosperity and don't believe that it could be (or is) responsible for the success of anti-corruption policies. The Singapore story is likely very much the same – though the focus on a sense of national identity has loomed much larger there so generalized trust is more likely to be a significant determinant of perceiving corruption there. Inequality matters less for corrup-tion in Hong Kong and Singapore than elsewhere because it is less of a salient issue – and indeed by now there is widespread condemnation of corruption and almost no evidence that it affects people's daily lives. When there is little corruption, especially grand corruption, to worry about, there is little reason for people to be jealous of officials who are not, after all, enriching themselves.

Why Singapore and Hong Kong Are Not Easily Replicable

Even though Hong Kong and Singapore do not follow my story of the inequality trap, this does not mean that they offer a model for other countries seeking to combat corruption. Institutions clearly mattered in the two city-states. The anti-corruption commissions were the main vehicles for curbing malfeasance. Yet this does not provide an institutional blueprint that can readily be adopted as the way out of corruption. The experiences of Singapore and Hong Kong are not easily transferred to other high-corruption countries because:

- Many authoritarian leaders are more concerned with enriching themselves than their citizens. Countries with high levels of corruption generally have less to spend on social services, especially education. Singapore put a high premium on funding all social services to weaken the threat from Com-munists and their supporters in labor unions – and education, which is a major factor in producing generalized trust (and hence less corruption) was especially important.
- The relatively small populations and sizes of Hong Kong and Singapore – and their remote locations (as islands) – made control of corruption – and development of a thriving economy more attainable. While corruption lev-els are uncorrelated with population size (especially if we omit two outliers, India and China), once a country commits to taking action against malfea-sance, it is easier to *control and root out* corruption if there are fewer total miscreants.

- A strong commitment to social inclusion such as we see especially in Singapore helps overcome the particularized trust that we find in many countries with high levels of inequality – and high corruption. In both Singapore and Hong Kong, the drive to root out corruption by early socialization is closely tied with similar campaigns to instill a sense of inclusiveness within the society.
- The presence of an external threat was a key stimulus to the anti-corruption campaigns in both city-states. Perhaps more than anything else, the threat from both outside and within was a major force in initiating the anti-corruption campaigns.
- The anti-corruption agencies were part of grander development strategies. The campaign against dishonesty was both a drive to generate wealth and a movement to impart values of honesty and responsibility within the Hong Kong and Singaporean publics. As such, the citizens had direct stakes in the success of these programs. In many other cases, in Africa and elsewhere, anti-corruption campaigns are either disguised campaigns to purge political opponents, as some claim underlies anti-corruption campaigns in Nigeria and China (*The Economist*, 2007; Yardley 2007), or pure shams. The head of Afghanistan's anti-corruption campaign was arrested and jailed in Las Vegas in 1987 for selling heroin (Associated Press, 2007).
- Finally, living with an unequal distribution of wealth may not inhibit drives against corruption if (1) people see that inequality is declining, and (2) especially if people can clearly see their living standards rising. While inequality rose substantially after 1980 in Hong Kong, it fell dramatically from 1963 (before the anti-corruption campaign began) to 1980, according to WIDER estimates. Inequality in a wealthy land may be less consequential for corruption than an inequitable distribution of resources in a poor country. This is *not* to say that inequality doesn't matter and income is everything. The survey results in transition countries and in Africa provide clear support that perceptions of inequality are strongly linked with beliefs about the prevalence of corruption. Rather, inequality may be more strongly tied to corruption when people are most likely to feel envy – that is, when they have little themselves.

Singapore and Hong Kong are among the few countries that have escaped the scourge of corruption, which is generally widespread in both Asia and especially in Africa. Botswana stands out as the African exception. The reasons are in many respects similar to the story for Singapore and Hong Kong: Despite low trust and high inequality, Botswana experienced a period of sustained economic growth with declining inequality (Riley, 2000, 153). Between 1966 and 1990, income per capita rose at the fastest rate in the world (Guest, 2003, 26). It is a small country facing an external threat: It is not an island, but is landlocked between what used to be apartheid states that could easily have toppled its fragile government. So it sought foreign investment and, following Singapore and Hong Kong, had to ensure honesty in government and in private enterprises to get there. Yet Botswana is not quite Singapore: Its per capita income is still only $3000, far below the level of the rich city-states, and its level of inequality is still much higher – so it is not surprising that its battle against corruption is still a work in progress.

The data from the Afrobarometer, across a range of countries and specifically in Mali and Nigeria, provide strong support for the inequality trap argument. The deviant cases of Hong Kong and Singapore indicate that the fight against corruption needs strong institutions such as ICAC and CPIB, but anticorruption campaigns are not likely to succeed unless they rest upon a firm social and economic foundation – and especially upon the confidence of the public.

Institutions matter in Africa and especially in Singapore and Hong Kong. In many African countries, weak institutions are part of the inequality trap, not alternative ways to combat corruption. Africans see corruption and inequality not simply as problems stemming from bad leaders, but from weak democratic institutions. When people (in Africa or anywhere else) lament weak democratic institutions, it is unclear whether they distinguish between the political structures and the officeholders. People may quite reasonably fail to make this distinction, since they have seen a never-ending succession of high-ranking leaders stealing from the public purse and legal systems, and police that have long been key sources of corruption. In Singapore and Hong Kong, it took strong institutions to combat corruption, but these structures were part of broader economic and political strategies that largely eminated from an external threat. What ultimately made these policies successful was their almost universal acceptance throughout the societies of the two countries – something that has not occurred in other parts of the world (especially Africa). The story of Singapore and Hong Kong, as well as Botswana, is that just as we should not discount institutions, we should not presume that agencies can do the job without a supporting political and economic infrastructure.

8

Corruption Isn't Inevitable, But ...

Hark! Hark! Hark! Hark! Hark! Hark!
Victorious messenger riding comes, riding comes, riding comes....
In view of her coronation, Her Majesty has decreed that the prisoner Macheath
    forthwith be freed. (Hurray!)
Also of this moment he receives the rank of Knight of the Garter, a castle at
    Mucking on the Creek, Sussex, and an annual pension for life of 10,000
    pounds to the day of his death.
(Hurray!)
And to all the charming wedding couples here the Queen presents her royal
    felicitations....
Oh, I had no doubt...As the need is sorest, the answer comes soonest....
So now the story happily has ended, if only rights so easily were mended and
    our real world messenger descended.
        From "Finale: The Mounted Messenger," Berthold Brecht and Kurt Weill,
        The Threepenny Opera

While the inequality trap framework is also one of pessimism, it is not quite so hopeless. Some societies *do escape* high inequality, low trust, and high levels of corruption, most notably the Nordic countries (Sweden, Norway, and Finland).[1] Other countries, especially the United States, fall in the middle range of inequality and trust (both decreasing over time), but have modest levels of corruption. Within the United States, the level of corruption is not uniform. Some states have relatively clean government, others are more corrupt. In this chapter, I first show, using the 1995–7 wave (wave 3) of the World Values Survey, that there is little evidence of an inequality trap in the Nordic countries. I briefly examine possible reasons why these countries have escaped – or

---

[1] Denmark and Iceland are also Nordic countries. However, questions on corruption were not included in the 1995–7 World Values Survey in these countries. I dichotomize the corruption measure ("none" and "few" corrupt leaders versus "all" or "most") rather than using the full four-point scale because of very few responses for the "all" category.

overcome – this trap. Then I examine survey data from the United States showing only limited support for an inequality trap. An aggregate analysis of perceived corruption in the American states provides a different perspective: States with high levels of inequality, and especially racial inequality in poverty, as well as low generalized trust are more corrupt, just as my framework would expect.

Equal, Trusting, and Honest: The Nordics

The Nordic countries are the most trusting and the least corrupt in the world, with mostly high to above-average levels of economic equality. In the 2005 TI Corruption Perceptions Index, Finland ranks third, Sweden sixth, and Norway eighth (with Iceland in first place and Denmark in fourth). No other group of countries comes even close to these high rankings. The publics in these countries also perceive their societies as very honest. Finns and Norwegians rank first and second on the TI Global Corruption Barometer's question on petty corruption (followed by Denmark and Iceland in fourth and fifth place; Swedes were not surveyed). They also see very little grand corruption, with Finland and Norway ranking second and fourth (Denmark was third and Iceland seventh). In the 1995–7 World Values Survey, which I use to test the inequality trap thesis below, Norway and Finland ranked first and second of 51 countries in seeing their leaders as honest, while Sweden was seventh.

The Nordic countries are the most trusting countries in the world, with Norway and Sweden always battling for first and second place in surveys, with Finland not far behind (in seventh place in my trust measure).[2] The Nordic levels of trust are so high that some observers wonder whether they fit a larger pattern or are truly exceptional (Delhy and Newton, 2004). And they are also relatively equal: The World Bank data ranks Finland 12th out of 88, with Sweden only 32nd and Norway just 38th. The more recent WIDER estimates place Sweden and Norway 9th and 10th out of 75 nations, with Finland at 23rd. The Nordic countries are clear examples of nations that have escaped the inequality trap – and are "caught" in the "virtuous cycle" of relatively low inequality, high trust, and low corruption.

Where inequality and corruption are less bothersome, people will be less likely to make a connection between them. I examine the 1995–7 wave of the World Values Survey (WVS) and present a probit model for perceived corruption among a country's leaders. The WVS has no direct questions on inequality, but two measures are serviceable: how much poverty there is in the country and whether income differences are needed as incentives for effort. Beyond these measures, I also include in the model generalized trust; confidence in public institutions (the police, the parliament, the civil service); two measures of basic human character (whether competition brings out the worst in people and whether people prefer a strong sense of order or individual freedom); three measures of what Letki (2006) calls "civic morality" – the acceptability of

[2] Denmark ranks 3rd and Iceland 11th.

TABLE 8-1. *Probit Analysis of Perceived Corruption in Nordic Countries: 1995–7 World Values Survey*

Variable	Coefficient	Std. Error	MLE/SE	Effect
How much poverty in country	−.112	.091	−1.24	−.076
Need income differences as incentives for effort	.001	.024	.02	.002
Generalized trust	−.289****	.041	−6.90	−.094
Competition brings out worst in people	−.027	−.024	−1.14	−.078
Confidence in the police	−.193****	.012	−15.71	.197
Confidence in parliament	−.174****	.027	−6.50	.168
Confidence in civil service	−.238***	.097	−2.46	.225
Order versus individual freedom	−.083*	.053	−1.56	−.027
Cheating on taxes acceptable	−.016	.026	−.62	−.045
Buying stolen goods acceptable	.010	.023	.44	.030
Bribes acceptable	.073***	.028	2.60	.240
Age[+]	.010**	.005	2.16	.150
Education	−.028	.040	−.69	−.071
Income	−.028****	.005	−5.68	−.080
Constant	−1.842***	.606	−3.04	

[+]Effect for age calculated between 20 and 70.
Model estimated with robust standard errors clustered by country (Norway, Sweden, and Finland).
*p < .10; **p < .05; ***p < .01; ****p < .0001
Estimated R^2 = .390; −2*Log Likelihood Ratio = 2565.074; N = 2395
Percent predicted correctly: 73.8 (model); 72.1 (null)

cheating on taxes, buying stolen goods, and offering bribes; and demographics. I expect that people who worry about competition and who prefer order to freedom would be more likely to see more corruption. People who see cheating on taxes, buying stolen goods, and bribes as more acceptable would be more likely to see more corruption.[3] Older people, who might remember days when government was less honest, should see more corruption, while more educated and higher income people would see less malfeasance.

I present the probit model in Table 8-1. The proxy measures of inequality are not significant. By far the most important factors shaping perceptions of corruption are levels of confidence in institutions, especially the civil service and the police. People in the Nordic countries are most likely to see little corruption in public life if they believe that they are represented by public servants who actually serve the people. People with the highest level of confidence in the civil service are 25 percent less likely to see their leaders as corrupt; the effects of confidence in the police and the parliament are only slightly smaller (20 and 17 percent, respectively). Confidence in other people and in public institutions

---

[3] The counter-argument, that people who see these actions as unacceptable, would be more likely to say that the larger society is honest.

leads people to see their governments as clean. Seventy-two percent of Nordic respondents see their governments as honest, compared to 32 percent in other countries.

The establishment of a professional and honest civil service loomed large in the development of the Nordic welfare state in the late nineteenth century The uncorruptability of the civil service played a large role in resolving class conflicts in Sweden and in ensuring public support for a large role for the state in social insurance (Elvander, 1979; Flora, 1986; Rothstein and Uslaner, 2005, 57). Confidence in the bureaucrats who deliver essential services looms large in public evaluations of government honesty. The variable that has the strongest statistical significance is confidence in the police. The Nordic countries rank much higher than other nations on confidence in the police: 82 percent of Nordics, compared to 52 percent in other nations, express faith in law officers. All three Nordic countries rank at the top on the measure of legal fairness and they also rank 13th, 14th, and 16th in Freedom in the World's measure of impartial justice (out of 81 nations). Rothstein (2000, 491–2) cites confidence in the police as a key reason why Swedes have so much faith in their fellow citizens. Other values don't loom large in predicting corruption (discussed in n. 4).[4]

Trust is also central to perceived corruption. People who trust their fellow citizens are 9 percent less likely to see their leaders as corrupt. And here is much of the story of how the Nordic countries escape the inequality trap. The foundations of the modern welfare state in Nordic countries and high levels of social trust stem from a historical tradition of equality (Flora, 1986). As early as the thirteenth century, farmers in Sweden had representation in the parliament. Peasants owned their own land and were not subject to control by wealthy landowners (Rothstein and Uslaner, 2005, 57). The Nordic countries developed strong institutions as they formed a commitment to an egalitarian social order – and it is not clear which came first or if, indeed, they emerged together.

The Middle Case: The United States

The Nordic countries have high levels of trust and low corruption at least in part because they have no history of feudalism. Neither does the United States, which never developed the sharp class conflicts of many European nations (Sombart,

---

[4] Seeing competition as bad doesn't make people more likely to see their leaders as corrupt, while favoring order over freedom makes one just 3 percent more likely to see their leaders as corrupt. Only one of the three civic morality measures has a significant effect on corruption, in part because so few people see any of these acts as acceptable. Very few people anywhere say that bribes are acceptable, but in the Nordic countries, disapprobation is close to universal (about 90 percent). The few people who say that it might be acceptable also say that their leaders are corrupt. A 70-year-old is 15 percent more likely to see leaders as corrupt as a 20-year-old; someone at the top of the income scale is 8 percent less likely to do so, while education is not significant.

1976). The American war of independence was a rebellion against the highly stratified European class system, and the egalitarian ethos that has played such a large role in American society stemmed from this conflict (Wildavsky, 1989, 284). Two hundred years later 74 percent of Americans agreed that teaching that some types of people are better than others violates basic national values (McCloskey and Zaller, 1984, 66). When the Englishman Lord James Bryce (1916, 813) toured the United States at the end of the nineteenth century, he was struck by the centrality of egalitarian values in American society: "There is no rank in America, that is to say, no external and recognized stamp, marking one man as entitled to any social privileges, or to deference and respect from others." The egalitarian foundation of the American nation is different from the Nordic – and more widely understood – notion of equality. Central to the American identity is social equality and especially equality of opportunity – everyone has the same chance to succeed by their own efforts – rather than uniformity of results – a right to equitable distributions of income or wealth (Hartz, 1955).

America was the land of plenty, the foundation of generalized trust. *The Economist* (1987, 12) wrote: "Optimism, not necessity, has always been the mother of invention in America. To every problem – whether racial bigotry or putting a man on the moon – there has always been a solution, if only ingenuity and money were committed to it." The historian Henry Steele Commager (1950, 5) summed up the American sense of optimism: "Nothing in all history had succeeded like America, and every American knew it." Tocqueville (1945, 122–3), a French visitor to the New World, saw Americans as embodying generalized trust. They developed faith in people you don't know by pushing aside your own short-term interests for the common good, what Tocqueville called "self-interest rightly understood."

The first time the trust question was asked in a national survey (1960), almost 60 percent of Americans agreed that most people can be trusted (Almond and Verba, 1963). Since then, there has been almost a linear decline in the level of trust among the American public – and it closely tracks the rise in economic inequality (Uslaner, 2002, 6, 186–7). Trust has fallen to between 33 and 36 percent, where it has fluctuated since the mid-1990s. Economic inequality has increased by 25 percent from the mid-1960s to the early years of the twenty-first century.[5] The United States ranks 20th in trust among 94 nations and either 54th or 55th in the level of economic inequality (using the World Bank and the WIDER Gini indices, respectively). As inequality increased, the optimism that had marked American society for so many years gave way to a greater wariness for the future and lower levels of trust in people who might be different from yourself.

American history has not been an unmitigated story of low inequality and high trust. Huntington (1981) details the cycles of "creedal passion," of

---

[5] The inequality data come from the U.S. Bureau of the Census. The trust data largely come from the General Social Survey in the United States (see Uslaner, 2002, 6).

optimism and trust alternating with ethnocentrism, fundamentalism, and anti-immigrant and anti-foreigner sentiments. The nation that was founded on social equality was torn apart by immigration and the Industrial Revolution. In the late nineteenth and early twentieth centuries, labor and race relations were often marked by violence rather than cooperation. The immigrants who came to the United States fell prey to political machines, notably those led by George Washington Plunkitt (see Chapter 1) and Martin Lomasny (see Chapter 2). Journalists and historians made their reputations in exposing wrongdoing by politicians and businesses (Josephson, 1938; Steffens, 1931). The radical novelist Upton Sinclair won fame with his 1906 exposé of the dangerous meatpacking industry in Chicago and its protection by political leaders. His novel, *The Jungle*, propelled a political career culminating as the (unsuccessful) Democratic candidate for Governor of California in 1934.

This was a period of high inequality and both grand and petty corruption, especially in the big cities and in the South. Immigrants were dependent upon corrupt machine leaders for jobs and for social services – including getting people out of jail – that leaders used to keep new immigrants as loyal supporters (Merton, 1968, 131). In big cities and especially in the South – where African-Americans had few rights and many needs – political bosses enriched themselves while exploiting poor people. At the turn of the twentieth century, Gosnell (1968, 79–80) recounted a tale of how political leaders manipulated a larceny trial in Chicago, in the manner of Martin Lomasny:[6]

Altogether this defendant achieved nine continuances, two changes of venue, and three bond forfeitures. During the pendency of the case there appeared before Mr. Austin (the person robbed) in behalf of the defendant, whose guilt was unquestioned, two state senators, a member of the lower house (the defendant's attorney, who later was a Democratic candidate for judge of the Municipal Court), a chief clerk of the Appellate Court, two deputy clerks of the Municipal Court, the [party] club president and party committee chairman, and six others, citizens of more or less prominence, all of whom urged Mr. Austin to drop the case. In addition, Mr. Austin's principal witness, a youth of fifteen years, was threatened with kidnaping by gangsters, resulting in policemen being assigned to guard his home.

Wilson (1960, 55) wrote about Chicago six decades later: "Contacts between Negroes and police officers are more likely to be harsh or abusive (or to be felt to be harsh and abusive), and a mediator is more commonly in demand than among people who have less contact, or less discriminatory contact, with such forces."

Big cities and the South have long been fertile territory for corruption, since they have high levels of both poverty and economic inequality. As long as both persisted, so did the patron-client politics that are often the foundation of corruption.

---

[6] Gosnell was quoting Martin, 1936 (300).

There are no measures of corruption, inequality, or trust in the late nineteenth or early twentieth centuries. However, the stories of the roots of corruption give strong support to the idea of an inequality trap at the turn of the century. Key (1936, 407) argued many years ago: "Much of what we consider as corruption is simply the 'uninstitutionalized' influence of wealth in a political system" (quoted in Scott, 1972, 33). The turn of the twentieth century through the Great Depression was a turbulent – and often corrupt – period in American history.

Optimism returned as the United States economy boomed after World War II and especially in the 1960s. O'Neill (1986) called this era the "American High." As immigrants became financially successful, they were no longer dependent upon political bosses and the urban machines mostly withered away. Petty corruption became far less common, though hardly at the level of the Nordic countries. Trust, when first measured in the 1960s, was very high and the level of inequality was moderate. By the 1970s, inequality began to rise and trust fell.

Since economic inequality and trust are sticky, the United States is exceptional, if not unique, in the sharp increase in inequality and the decline of trust. Yet there is no major change in the corruption rating of the United States. In 1980–5, it ranked eighth out of 51 nations in the ICRG rankings. By 2005, the United States ranked 17th of 160 nations on the TI Corruption Perceptions Index, 14th on the TI Global Corruption Barometer on grand corruption, 11th on petty corruption, and 14th on the perceptions of corruption in the WVS. While it seems that corruption was fairly stable, the raw scores for 1980–5 and 2005 indicate that corruption may have increased. While comparing these raw scores is hazardous, there is some evidence of a retrenchment to greater corruption. Only 7 of the 19 Western countries had negative residuals when I regressed the 1980–5 scores against the 2005 TI index and the overall mean for residuals for Western countries was strongly positive (.402). Positive residuals indicate reduced corruption, negative ones increased malfeasance. The United States had the fourth largest *negative* residual.

Corruption has long been prevalent in some areas, especially the big cities in the Mid-Atlantic region and in the South. Other areas, most notably in the Midwest and the Prairie States, especially those with large Scandinavian-American populations, have historically had very clean politics. Even as the United States has become less corrupt in most areas, the patterns of corruption still show consistency over time (see below). The states with higher levels of corruption also have historically been those with the greatest amount of economic inequality (Uslaner and Brown, 2005; Uslaner, 2006b) – and in the South, in particular, of discrimination that has kept African-Americans poor and powerless.

Is there a connection among inequality, trust, and corruption in the United States? I examine this in two ways. First, I consider survey data from the 1987 General Social Survey (GSS), which asks whether people are essentially good or fundamentally corrupt. Then I turn to data on beliefs about "how many people in government" are crooked from the 2004 American National Election Study (ANES). These two questions let me test for two different ways of perceiving

TABLE 8-2. *Model of Whether People Are Good or Corrupt: 1987 General Social Survey in the United States*

Variable	Coefficient	Std. Error	t Ratio
Generalized trust	−.223***	.087	−2.58
World image: evil versus good	−.442****	.038	−11.68
Inequality exists for benefit of the rich	.041	.040	1.03
Working and middle classes in conflict	−.129**	.060	−2.13
Need wealthy family to get ahead	−.037	.049	−.76
Rank in social position	.063**	.035	1.79
Standard of living will improve	.072*	.046	1.58
Education	.001	.018	.06
Income	−.012	.018	−.71
Black	.135	.111	1.21
Confidence in business	.064	.092	.69
Confidence in federal government	−.160**	.068	−2.34
Confidence in judicial system	.035	.091	.39
Confidence in Congress	.102	.082	1.23
Religious fundamentalist	−.197***	.066	−2.96
Household Gini 1989	2.615	2.507	1.04
Constant	4.389***	1.196	3.67

Estimates are regression coefficients with standard errors clustered by country.
Number of countries: 40; number of observations: 1082
$R^2 = .295$; RMSE = 1.400
*p < .10; **p < .05; ***p < .01; ****p < .0001 (all tests one-tailed except for constants)

corruption – about human nature, on the one hand, and about political leaders on the other.

I estimate a model for whether people are good or corrupt in Table 8-2, with a state-level measure of economic inequality (household Gini index for 1989). Perceptions that people are corrupt should be higher in states with greater levels of economic inequality. The model includes three measures of perceptions of inequality: whether inequality exists for the benefit of the rich, whether the working and middle classes are in conflict, and whether one needs a wealthy family to get ahead, as well as measures of subjective and objective economic status. I also examine whether having confidence in business or public institutions leads to more favorable evaluations of society. Religious fundamentalists, who adhere to the notion that people are born in sin (the notion of "original sin"), should believe that people are essentially corrupt. African-Americans, who have long endured discrimination (and their ancestors' slavery), should also have negative feelings about others, while older people, who have lived through less contentious times, should rate others more positively. I also include two more general indicators of one's worldview: generalized trust and whether one sees the world as filled with evil or good.

Americans are in general favorably disposed toward their fellow citizens. Forty-two percent rate others at the top two positions on a seven-point scale, while only 9 percent give others either of the two lowest scores. The model provides little support for any effects of inequality on perceptions of human nature. The aggregate measure of income inequality is far from significant, as is the belief that inequality exists for the benefit of the rich or believing that you need a wealthy family to get ahead. Perceived class conflict, rank in social position (social class), and believing that your standard of living will not improve make people more likely to say that people are corrupt, but the impact of each variable is modest. Of the confidence measures, only confidence in the federal government reaches significance. In contrast to countries with higher levels of corruption, trust in the legal system does not spill over to judgments of other people.

What matters most are general worldviews. The strongest impact comes from the belief that the world is full of evil rather than good. Generalized trust also matters. Religious fundamentalists are far less likely to see human nature as good. Thirty-one percent of fundamentalists, compared to 46 percent of non-fundamentalists, rate their fellow citizens at the top two levels of the scale. Fifty-three percent of generalized trusters have positive views of others, compared to 30 percent of mistrusters.

The model provides very limited support for a connection between inequality and beliefs that people in general are corrupt. The household Gini index for 1989 is far from statistical significance.

Is there a stronger tie between inequality and believing that people in government are crooked? Most Americans accept the view, from the data in the 2004 ANES, that their public servants are honest. Only 38 percent say that most public officials are dishonest; 53 percent say just some are, but only 8 percent hold that hardly any are corrupt. I present the ordered probit model for how many people in government are crooked (with lower scores reflecting this position) in Table 8-3. I include two measures of perceived inequality (whether it is a big problem if everyone is not treated equally and how much change has there been in the income gap between rich and poor in recent years) as well as generalized trust, feeling thermometers (on which people rate groups from a very cold 0 to a very warm 100) for big business and for businesspeople, Congressional job approval, and whether people believe that elections make politicians pay attention. Also in the model, aside from demographics (age, income, education, Southern residence) is the question of whether the country's moral climate has fallen in the past four years. People with positive evaluations of public and private institutions and who believe that elections matter should be more positively disposed toward their leaders, while people who say that the country is in either moral or economic decline should be more willing to say that public officials are dishonest.

As with evaluations of fellow citizens, generalized trust has the strongest impact on perceptions of officials' honesty. However, the probit effects tell a somewhat different story. Trust matters (an average impact of .112), but changes in the income gap (effect = −.134), the moral climate in the country (−.152),

TABLE 8-3. *Ordered Probit of How Many People in Government Are Crooked: 2004 American National Election Study*

Variable	Coefficient	Std. Error	MLE/SE	Effect
Big problem if everyone not treated equally	−.052	.045	1.16	−.052
How much change in income gap	−.151**	.082	1.84	−.134
Generalized trust	.454****	.120	3.80	.112
Feeling thermometer: big business	.007**	.003	2.23	.180
Feeling thermometer: businesspeople	−.004	.004	−1.00	−.085
Congressional job approval	−.048	.038	−1.25	−.048
Elections make politicians pay attention	.172****	.048	3.59	.177
Moral climate in country fell since 2000	−.090***	.038	−2.41	−.152
African-American	−.161	.164	−.98	−.041
Age	.007**	.003	1.93	.114
Social class (working or middle)	.015	.030	.51	.026
Income	−.006	.009	−.63	−.032
Education	.076**	.039	1.97	.115
South	−.255**	.137	−1.86	−.065

Higher scores on "how many crooked" indicate few people are crooked.

Cut points not reported. Effects are average changes in probabilities across the five categories of trust in government. The effects represent the changes from each value *to the next higher value.*

*p < .10; **p < .05; ***p < .01; ****p < .0001

Estimated R^2 = .123; −2*Log Likelihood Ratio = 799.27; N = 505

whether elections make public officials pay attention (−.177), and the feeling thermometer about big business (.180) all matter more. In this model there is stronger support for the effect of inequality on corruption, although saying that it is a big problem if people are treated unequally is *not* significant.

People make a clear distinction between their feelings about big business (which shape perceptions of dishonesty) and of people in business (which are insignificant). Perhaps surprisingly, people who disapprove of Congress's performance are no more likely to say that public officials are dishonest. Yet people do believe that elections are important in holding officials accountable – and they link this rather strongly with their perceptions of public officials' integrity.[7]

For both models, fundamental values (generalized trust, morality, fundamentalism) play a much greater role in shaping perceptions of corruption than do beliefs about inequality. Inequality perceptions matter much more for evaluations of politicians than for ordinary people. This makes sense, since

---

[7] In the model, older people and those more highly educated were less likely to say that many people are crooked, while Southerners were more likely to agree with this statement. Income was insignificant. I did not estimate a hierarchical linear model because of the small size of the sample in the model.

people in public office will profit from corruption more than average folk. The difference in results might also reflect the time periods. Economic inequality increased by more than 10 percent from 1987 to 2004, so it may have become more salient.

Since both the corruption and the inequality questions are different, it is hazardous to compare the findings for the United States with those of other countries. Nevertheless, it is intriguing that the impact of inequality on corruption perceptions appears stronger in the United States than in either the Nordic countries or in Hong Kong, but weaker than in the transition countries or in Africa. To the extent that these findings are generalizable, they indicate that *inequality matters more when there are higher levels of corruption.*

Corruption in the American States: The Link to Inequality

Corruption varies widely among the American states – and within states. Some states have long been regarded as corrupt, perhaps most famously Louisiana. Its culture is a mixture of its French heritage intermixed with the more traditional Southern politics based upon racial exclusion. Louisiana politics has long been dominated by factions loyal to and opposed to the Long dynasty, as it is called. The founding fathers of this dynasty were Huey Long and his brother Earl. Huey was first elected Governor and then Senator and was planning a challenge to Franklin D. Roosevelt as the Democratic nominee for President in 1936 before he was assassinated a year earlier. Earl later served as Governor three times.

The Longs were both despots and legends, the subjects of numerous biographies and at least one famous work of fiction, *All the King's Men*, a Pulitzer Prize–winning novel by Robert Penn Warren about the rise and fall of Huey Long, who called himself "the Kingfish." In Long's Louisiana, everything was for sale – especially political influence. And brother Earl believed that this was a formula for winning the hearts and minds of voters. "Someday Louisiana is going to get 'good government.' And when they do, they ain't going to like it," he once said (quoted in Kolbert, 2006).

Louisiana's corrupt government did not end with the end of the Long dynasty (in the 1950s for the state house, in the 1970s in the Congress).[8] A recent four-term Governor, Edwin Edwards, was sentenced to 10 years in prison in 2001 for racketeering The capital city, New Orleans – especially its police department – is widely considered to be one of the most corrupt in the nation.[9] Former Senator John Breaux, while a member of the House, was once asked if his vote could be bought. He replied, "No, but it can be rented" (Edsall,

---

[8] The last member of the Long dynasty to serve in Congress was Speedy O. Long, who later lost his seat in a primary to his cousin Gillis Long, the liberal renegade in the family who was later succeeded by his widow Mary Catherine Small Long, who served from 1985 to 1987, the last member of the extended family in high office.

[9] See the report by Human Rights Watch at http://www.hrw.org/reports98/police/uspo92.htm, accessed January 19, 2007.

1983). Former Representative Billy Tauzin said (referring to the devastation of Hurricane Katrina), "Half of Louisiana is under water and the other half is under indictment" (New York *Daily News*, 2005).

Louisiana has one of the highest levels of inequality of any state. It ranks last on the Census Bureau household Gini index for 1989, and in Langer's (1999) annual series of Gini indices in the states from 1976 to 1995, Louisiana ranked last in the 50 states 11 times, 49th five times, 48th three times, and 47th once.[10] Louisiana's school system has the fewest number of computers per student in the country and the second highest share of adults who did not finish high school; it is also the only state not to pay for the defense of indigent people charged with crimes, leading to stays in jail of up to nine months before trial (New York *Daily News*, 2005). Louisiana ranked 35th out of 40 states on trust in the 1980s and 34th out of 44 in 1990.[11] Louisiana stands out as a classic example of the inequality trap.

On the other hand, the Prairie states are among the least corrupt in the nation. These states have large Nordic-American populations, ranging from 62 percent in North Dakota to the 30s in South Dakota and Minnesota and 19 percent in Wisconsin.[12] Social capital, including trust, follows ethnicity across national barriers (Rice and Feldman, 1997; Soroka, Helliwell, and Johnston, 2007). Putnam (2000, 294; see also Uslaner, 2008) has noted that social capital is higher in states with large shares of Nordic immigrants (Minnesota and the Dakotas). These four states have large shares of trusting citizens – especially North Dakota (ranking first in 1980 and second in 1990); all ranked in the top seven states in both decades (except for South Dakota, which did not have a sufficient sample size to estimate trust in the 1980s). The Dakotas and Wisconsin were among the most equal distributions of income in the 1989 Census Bureau data (though Minnesota only ranked 17th).[13]

These Midwest and Prairie states were the leaders in the movement for clean government that began in the late nineteenth century with the Populist party and culminated in the Progressive movement from the early twentieth century through the 1930s. These movements challenged the corruption of the two main parties. Throughout the Midwest (and later elsewhere), the Grange movement was a farmers' cooperative, which pooled resources and pressed for debt relief following the economic crisis after the Civil War. Similar organizations developed throughout the Prairie and Midwest states that also became political reform movements, such as the Nonpartisan League in North Dakota,

---

[10] The data are available at http://www.u.arizona.edu/omllanger/replication.htm, accessed January 19, 2007.

[11] For details on statewide estimation of trust, see Uslaner and Brown, 2005.

[12] The share of Nordic-Americans is based upon 2000 Census data reported at www.euroamericans.net.

[13] In the 1970s North Dakota and South Dakota ranked close to the bottom in inequality for the annual Langer data. By the 1990s, they had advanced to tied for 10th and 17th, respectively – still far above the Census Bureau estimates. Wisconsin ranked third by 1995 and Minnesota 17th.

the Farmer-Labor party in Minnesota, and most notably the Progressive Party in Wisconsin.

These parties all became key elements in fights against corruption and domination of farmers by large banks throughout the region. The Progressive Party was the most successful, becoming a national movement and running Robert LaFollette, who had served as Governor and then Senator from Wisconsin, for President in 1924. LaFollette won 17 percent of the national vote, with the largest shares in Wisconsin, North Dakota, Minnesota, Montana, and South Dakota. These states with a long tradition of political reform, high levels of trust, and relatively low inequality are, much like their Nordic ancestors, part of the virtuous, rather than vicious, cycle of the inequality trap.

How can I test this claim in the American states?[14] There are two major measures of government corruption: the indictment and conviction rates of political leaders and newspaper reporters' subjective estimates of corruption (Boylan and Long, 2001), which are closest to international estimates of corruption by Transparency International. The Boylan-Long measures for 47 states have Rhode Island and Louisiana as the most corrupt. Rhode Island has a traditional patronage-oriented Democratic machine that is dominant in state politics. Charges of corruption are common and former Providence mayor Buddy Cianci has served jail sentences for both assault (he was charged with attacking his wife's alleged lover with a lit cigarette, an ashtray, and a fireplace log) and racketeering, extortion, conspiracy, and witness tampering. He resigned following his first conviction but won reelection anyway. The Dakotas and Colorado rank as the most honest, with Minnesota seventh, and Wisconsin twelfth.

An alternative measure of corruption is the share of public officials indicted or convicted (Meier and Holbrook, 1992). The most corrupt states in 1995 were Florida and Virginia and the least corrupt were New Hampshire and Vermont. The two measures are *not* identical: Florida and Virginia rank 14th and 26th respectively on the Boylan-Long measure and the overall correlation between the two measures is just .259. The reporters' measure seems to be the better one, since it has greater face validity. Prosecution indicators may reflect the personal priorities of prosecutors (Boylan and Long, 2001, 3–4) – and it may simply be more difficult to gain an indictment and conviction in a heavily corrupt state. Thus, I rely upon the reporters' perception measure, which seems less troubled by endogeneity issues (such as whom to prosecute and whom to convict).

I estimate a model for perceived state corruption in Table 8-4. The predictors include two measures of inequality: a 1990 Gini index and the ratio of poverty between African-Americans and whites. The logic behind the Gini index is straightforward. The black/white poverty ratio is based upon the same logic as the Failed States indicator of uneven economic development: This measure not only includes economic distress, but it also incorporates the economic discrimination that is likely to give rise to particularized trust. Both of these indicators should lead to higher levels of corruption. I also include generalized

[14] Much of what follows is a variation on Uslaner, 2006b.

TABLE 8-4. *Model of Corruption Perceptions in the American States*

Independent Variable	Coefficient	Std. Error	t Ratio
Generalized trust	−2.495**	1.319	−1.89
Economic inequality 1990	11.849**	5.795	2.04
Black/white poverty ratio	.296***	.114	2.58
Per capita income 1990	−.0001***	.00005	−2.55
Traditional party organization	.443****	.054	8.18
Overall incarceration rate 1990	.001***	.0002	3.13
Constant	−1.303	2.796	−.47

Model estimated with robust standard errors.
$R^2 = .733$; Adjusted $R^2 = .678$; RMSE = .589; N = 30
***p < .01; **p < .05

trust and per capita income as in the models in Chapter 3. Also in the model are a measure of traditional party organization (Mayhew, 1986) and a measure of the overall incarceration rate for 1990. The incarceration rate is an indicator of the weakness of the rule of law in a state – corruption and street-level crime form a general syndrome (Azfar, 2005; and see Chapter 3).

Strong party states, which have what Mayhew (1986) called "traditional party organizations (TPOs)," place a heavy emphasis on organization and person-to-person get-out-the-vote drives; they are organized hierarchally and discourage citizen participation beyond knocking on doors and performing routine office jobs. Weaker party organizations give citizens a greater role in their affairs, including recruiting candidates. TPOs focus on winning elections, weaker organizations place greater emphasis on formulating policies and citizen activism. TPOs are fonts of patronage, which is the basis for both grand and petty corruption, so I expect states with such organizations to have higher scores on the perceived corruption measure. I use Mayhew's classification of party systems from weak to very powerful party organizations.

Inequality matters – a lot. Both simple inequality and especially the black/white poverty ratio are strong predictors of perceived corruption. So is the overall incarceration rate. States with a weak rule of law are more corrupt, as are states with lower levels of generalized trust. The most important factor is Mayhew's traditional party organization measure, which is hardly surprising. Parties that emphasize patronage, as did the machines led by George Washington Plunkitt and Martin Lomasny, are part and parcel of a more general syndrome of corruption.

Corruption in the United States does vary with both the level of trust and the extent of economic inequality. Where trust is low and inequality, especially racially based inequity, is high in the American states, corruption thrives – much as I showed in the cross-national model in Chapter 3. The states, many say, are a laboratory for comparative analysis and this model strongly confirms this claim.

The model tells an even more complex story. Mayhew's TPO index is more than a simple contemporaneous factor shaping current levels of corruption. Mayhew's measure reflects data from the 1960s and the 1970s and the corruption perceptions index represents a 1999 survey. By the end of the twentieth century, most American parties had become democratized as party bosses yielded their control over nominations to voters in primaries. Patronage had become less widespread as most municipal employees were selected by the merit system. The TPO measure is thus an indicator of the *historical* rather than the contemporary strength of state parties. Just as cross-national corruption is sticky, a party system's tradition reflects its current level of integrity.

Corruption in the American states has an even longer legacy than the 1960s. In Figure 8-1, I plot the reporter's corruption ratings against the statewide vote for LaFollette's Progressive Party candidacy in 1924. Since the Progressive Party focused primarily on clean government and structural reform, support for it is a reasonable proxy for public support in a state for anti-corruption initiatives. Of course, public preferences are hardly the same thing as actual performance and vote choice clearly reflects other factors (including evaluations of LaFollette himself, attachment to the traditional parties, and the Progressives' strong commitment to an activist role for government in the economy). The LaFollette vote nevertheless is the best available proxy for (lack of) corruption 70 years earlier.

While the fit with reporters' corruption perceptions is not overwhelming ($r^2 = .266$), (1) the bivariate correlation for the LaFollette vote is about as strong as any other variable in the model ($r = -.516$, compared to $-.533$ for generalized trust, $.497$ for the Gini index, and $.585$ for TPO), and (2) it does not enter the model because it is highly related to both trust and economic inequality ($r = -.533$ and $.487$) and moderately correlated with traditional party organizations ($r = -.362$).[15] The LaFollette vote is part of a more general syndrome of honest government, trust, and equality – even though it is measured almost three-quarters of a century ago. The Progressive vote in 1924 is strongly related to state-level estimates of trust in the 1980s and 1990s ($r = .696$ and $.564$) and especially to the share of a state's population of Nordic origin in the 1990s ($r = .749$). There is also a moderately strong relationship between the reporters' perception of corruption measure and the Nordic population in a state in the 1990s ($r = -.565$).

Missing from the model is a variable that seems central to the decline in corruption in the twentieth century – the displacement of patronage positions by civil service positions. Yet there is little support for the claim that states that were most proactive in enacting merit systems have less malfeasance in office than laggards. Ruhil and Camões (2003) have compiled data on the adoption

---

[15] The LaFollette campaign was a third-party effort. LaFollette had been a Republican but had split with the party (in 1936 he would endorse Democrat Franklin D. Roosevelt for President) and his fellow Progressives in Congress had helped to unseat a Republican Speaker of the House of Representatives in 1910.

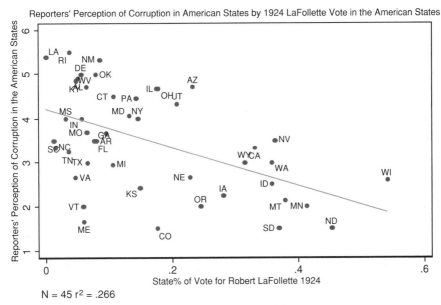

FIGURE 8-1. The Historical Roots of Corruption in the American States.

of merit systems in the states. Even though the Pendleton Act established a civil service system patterned after Great Britain's at the federal level in 1883, states were much slower in enacting these reforms. The civil service reforms dealt a blow to patronage, so early adopters would be the most likely to rate high on integrity at the turn of the century. Yet they weren't. The simple correlation between the year of adopting the merit system and the reporter's corruption measure is only −.014 – the correlation is even in the wrong direction!

The Historical Roots of Corruption in the United States

Corruption in the American states, as cross-nationally, is not only sticky, but it reflects long-standing social and economic patterns. In Table 8-5, I report models of both the 1924 LaFollette vote in the states, the proxy for earlier corruption, and reporters' corruption perceptions 75 years later. I use as predictors census data from the 1920s *and the 1880s* as predictors. The LaFollette vote is well predicted by the share of a state's workers who were in professional positions (and thus freed from the grips of the political machines) in the 1920 Census, as well as the population density of the state. States with high densities had large cities – and powerful political machines.

Even more impressive are the highly significant coefficients for the proportion of residents in each state with parents born in Scandinavia (Norway, Sweden, and Denmark) *from the 1880 census*. States with the highest share of parents born in Scandinavia were the most likely to cast ballots for LaFollette. Given the roots of the Progressive movement in the heavily Nordic Midwest and Prairie

TABLE 8-5. *Historical Models of the 1924 LaFollette Vote and Reporters' Corruption Perceptions*

Variable	LaFollette Vote 1924			Reporters' Corruption Perceptions 1999		
	Coefficient	Std. Error	t Ratio	Coefficient	Std. Error	t Ratio
Percent professional workers 1920	.035****	.009	4.04	−.266***	.106	−2.50
Population density 1920	−.0002****	.0000	−4.17	.004****	.0009	4.68
Proportion parents born Scandinavia 1880	1.596****	.446	3.58	−6.493**	3.430	−1.89
Average monthly teacher pay 1880	.003****	.001	3.69	–	–	–
Constant	−.132***	.034	−3.94	4.674****	.535	8.74
R²	.662			.392		
S.E.E.	.080			.922		
N	45			42		

Regressions are estimated with robust standard errors.

*p < .10; **p < .05; ***p < .01; ****p < .0001

states, this result is hardly surprising. Yet they do point to the cultural foundations of corruption – and to how lasting they are. Finally, the average monthly teacher pay in 1880 was also a significant predictor of the LaFollette vote. Education is the premier universalistic social welfare program (and the United States was the first country to provide free education to all young people). Average teacher pay is an indicator of a state's commitment to public education – and we see that a commitment to universalistic social welfare programs was associated with anti-corruption sentiment.

I use three of the four variables to predict reporters' perceptions of corruption in 1999. The professionalization of workers in 1920 significantly predicts less corruption almost 80 years later, as does (even more strongly) the population density in the same year. While average monthly teacher pay is not a factor in 1999,[16] the share of parents born in Scandinavia in 1880 is a significant predictor of corruption perceptions more than a century later, so that the state with the greatest Scandinavian heritage (South Dakota) would be predicted to have a score 1.18 less on the reporters' corruption scale (ranging from 1.5 to 5.5) than the state with the lowest share of Nordics in 1880 (North Carolina). This amounts to "making" Louisiana into Utah or Maryland – a substantial effect, especially given such a long time frame. While the predictive power of the reporters' corruption equation is not as strong as that for the LaFollette vote – hardly surprising given the time frames – the fit ($R^2 = .392$) is quite strong since the predictors are all from such a long time ago. The roots of corruption in the American states are long-standing, even more so than suggested by the TPO measure.

The cross-national ratings rate the United States relatively well for corruption. National surveys show that people base their perceptions of how corrupt ordinary people and even politicians are more by their moral worldviews than by perceptions of inequality – although there is a moderate connection between perceptions of inequality and believing that most political leaders are dishonest. Yet the country is diverse and in many states (and cities), corruption not only persists, it thrives. And these states are precisely the ones one might expect to lack integrity in public service from the inequality trap argument: high inequality, including disparities in income by race, and low trust.

The larger story is that the decline of corruption in the Nordic countries is not recent and has its roots in a more equitable distribution of wealth over a long period of time – and a commitment to providing universal social welfare. It was essential to have clean government. In the United States there is contemporary evidence for an inequality trap and the political machines that held immigrants captive to petty corruption and that enriched their leaders through grand corruption died out as the poor became middle class and no longer depended upon patronage for employment (see Chapter 9).

---

[16] It was significant in a regression not reported, but only because of collinearity. Its zero-order correlation with the reporters' corruption measure is only −.006, so I excluded it from the model rather than report what would clearly be an artifactual finding.

Corruption remains higher in the United States than in most other wealthy Western countries, while trust and inequality are higher. While inequality has been rising throughout much of the West, the United States started from a higher baseline. Corruption remains high in states with low trust and high levels of inequality, and there seems to be little hope for some regions to escape the inequality trap as punitive social welfare policies have become prevalent (Hacker, 2004; Soss, 2000).

While corruption is not falling in the United States, the overall level is lower than we might expect given the modest level of trust and the relatively high degree of inequality. I suggest two reasons why this may be the case. First, Americans are far less committed to reducing economic inequality than are Europeans (Osberg and Smeeding, 2005). They are less likely to acknowledge widespread disparities in wealth than are people in other nations, they believe that people can work their way up the economic ladder without government support, and, most critically, they do not link corruption to inequality. In the 1999 ISSP module on equality, Americans were among the least likely (3rd of 27 countries) to say that you must be corrupt to reach the top and to deny (also ranking 3rd) that income differences are too large (see Figure A8-1). Only 17.1 percent of Americans (compared to 36.6 percent elsewhere) say that you must be corrupt to reach the top and 66.2 percent say that income differences are too large, compared to 83.6 percent in other countries.

Americans also deny that you must come from a wealthy family to succeed (20.5 percent compared to 32.7 percent). They are also less likely to say that inequality exists because it benefits the rich (50.1 percent versus 69.4 percent). They are far less likely to say that government has a responsibility to reduce the income gap between rich and poor (35.3 percent compared to 70 percent) and far more likely to believe that people get rewarded for their efforts (64.7 percent versus 31.5 percent) and for their skills and efforts (73.7 percent versus 39.2 percent). Most critically, consistent with the two estimations above, Americans simply don't link corruption and inequality.[17] Even as inequality has increased, there is little of the envy that we see in many other parts of the world.

Second, the case of the United States – together with Hong Kong, Singapore, and Botswana – suggests that institutions may indeed matter. Rising living standards and greater equality went hand in hand with more honesty in government and business. The rising middle class was less likely to tolerate corruption (Banfield and Wilson, 1966, 123) and this provided a foundation for stronger institutions. Lower levels of corruption meant a court system that was more independent and less susceptible to political interference as well as a predominance of honest officials in elected offices. Americans strongly believe that they can hold their elected officials accountable – and they demonstrate this by regularly ousting most public officials accused of misconduct. Six of the 20 Republican incumbents defeated in the 2006 Congressional elections had

---

[17] The correlation between perceiving corruption as necessary to get to the top and income in the United States is only −.03 and for social class is −.08.

been accused of wrongdoing and the Republicans lost three additional seats where incumbents had resigned because they were accused of wrongdoing (even though the new candidates were unscarred).

These strengthened institutions were better situated to fight corruption – creating real sanctions for those who were dishonest. Even as inequality has increased in more recent years, there has been no widespread reversion to corruption. Strong institutions capable of combating corruption could not arise in a highly unequal society in which many people depended upon political machines for their livelihoods. Corruption persists in American states with high levels of inequality and low levels of trust. When strong institutions rest upon two fundamental foundations – public revulsion against corruption and the refusal to link it to economic inequality, as in much of the United States, Singapore, Hong Kong, and Botswana – they can play a key role in the fight against malfeasance in public life.

9

Conclusions

Therefore do all stand fast where you are standing.
And lift your voices in the choral anthem, devoted to the poorest of the poor.
For in real life the ending isn't quite so fine.
Victorious messenger does not come riding often.
And the reply to a kick in the pants is another kick in the pants.
So pursue but not too eagerly injustice.
> From "Finale: The Mounted Messenger," Berthold Brecht and Kurt Weill,
> *The Threepenny Opera*

The Threepenny Opera has a happy ending. The small-time criminal Macheath is freed from prison and given a lordship and a huge fortune. A thief living at the margins has been rewarded with the great riches ordinarily reserved for big-time plunderers. The lessons of this parable are that crime (and corruption) pays – and that you cannot eliminate small-time thievery or petty corruption. Yet the final song, "The Mounted Messenger," warns that this is just a story and in the real world, petty thieves neither become rich nor respectable. Macheath was supposed to be executed, as demanded by his antagonist (and father-in-law) Jonathan Peachum. While Peachum ultimately pleads (successfully) for a pardon for the prisoner for an uplifting end to the drama, he cautions: "Happy endings only really happen on stage, and people are saved from poverty only rarely."[1] The rich stay rich, the poor stay poor and messengers from the throne do not reward the latter with unexpected fortunes, much less social status.

Starting at the ground level and working one's way up to the top does not seem a fruitful way of combating malfeasance. We are thus thrown back to the inequality trap – and this means attacking the social roots of corruption. I offer some speculation about how one major American city, New York, may have reduced corruption, ending petty corruption, through the very sort of universal social welfare policy that marks the Nordic countries. Ironically, the institution

---

[1] See http://www.altoncollege.ac.uk/news.php?id=148, accessed January 18, 2007.

that probably did more to undo corruption than any other, the City University of New York (CUNY) with its free tuition, was established by city officials elected by a strong political machine mired in corruption. While my argument is speculative, it fits in well with the empirical findings I have presented here and elsewhere. I conclude with a discussion of what we know and what we don't about how corruption changes over time.

Broken Windows, Broken State?

The Threepenny Opera's real demons are the rich who exploit the poor and turn them to crime and petty corruption in order to survive. The story of *The Threepenny Opera* brings us back to a widely heralded proposed solution to both crime and corruption: Eliminate petty corruption and grand corruption will be sure to decrease as well.

Wilson and Kelling (1982) argue that disorder in the legal system can be traced, at least in part, to disorder on the street. Their "broken windows" thesis holds that failure to fix one broken window leads to another and the neighborhood quickly descends into a state of disrepair, sending a signal to potential predators: "Muggers and robbers, whether opportunistic or professional, believe they reduce their chances of being caught or even identified if they operate on streets where potential victims are already intimidated by prevailing conditions. If the neighborhood cannot keep a bothersome panhandler from annoying passers-by, the thief may reason, it is even less likely to call police to identify a potential mugger or to interfere if the mugging actually takes place" (Wilson and Kelling, 1982, 5). Just as you need to fix broken windows to reduce crime, you should clean up petty corruption first, and this will make it easier to tackle grand corruption.

The evidence I presented on pickpocketing as well as the survey data on petty corruption I considered in Chapters 3, 5, 6, and 7 suggests that cleaning up small-time criminals and ending "gift" payments will not suffice to curb grand corruption. Pickpocketing and other crimes are most common when grand corruption is greatest; petty corruption is largely restricted to countries with high levels of grand corruption (see Chapter 3). People in transition countries and in Africa seem most troubled by high-level corruption, with its big stakes and its perceived connection to inequality.

Cleaning up the streets, as many corrupt countries have done, largely diverts attention from grand corruption and its roots – high inequality and low trust. Ironically, by robbing people of their only source of income, routing out petty corruption might even increase inequality, though this is hardly a reason not to fight pickpocketing and other street crime. Reducing petty corruption – and fighting street crime – are worthy goals. Yet they are unlikely to "solve" the problem of malfeasance at the top.

The evidence on pickpocketing, as well as the sorry history of campaigns high-level officials start to clean up petty corruption, suggests that this strategy will not work. Pickpocketing is greatest when people see high levels of corruption at the top. Stealing wallets is far less critical, if at all, in making leaders more likely to rob the public purse. Cleaning up the street will not deter high-level corruption, as envisaged by advocates of the "broken windows" thesis.

Only 4 percent, on average, saw their countries marked by petty corruption but *not* grand corruption across the 62 countries in the TI Global Corruption Barometer and some of these responses seem almost random (such as the 10 to 20 percent of respondents in Luxembourg, Great Britain, Iceland, and the Netherlands who gave this response). In most Western countries (also Israel, Taiwan, Estonia, and the Czech Republic in the top 20 countries on this measure), 20 percent say that they see only grand corruption. However, except for Estonia and the Czech Republic, these are countries that have largely eliminated grand corruption as well (almost all have TI index scores above 8).

Trying to fix broken windows (street crime, petty corruption) is a worthy goal, but it is taking aim at the wrong target. Of course, arrest the pickpockets and fight people who try to extort money for routine services. But don't fool yourself into thinking that this is simply the first step in ending grand corruption. The gains from grand corruption are too great and it persists even where petty corruption has been eradicated or greatly reduced.

The End of a Machine?

The United States now ranks relatively highly on the TI Corruption Perceptions Index, in 20th place (out of 163 nations) in 2006. Yet for much of the nineteenth and early twentieth centuries, corruption was perceived as widespread in the United States, especially in big cities (Josephson, 1938; Steffens, 1931). Yet we know relatively little about how the decline of corruption in the United States – when it occurred and what led to it.

I offer some speculation about the decline of corruption in one American city – New York – and the waning of the political machine once led by George Washington Plunkitt. My argument focuses on rising living standards and especially educational attainment for immigrant groups that had long relied upon the corrupt machines for their livelihood. I suggest that the New York City machine may have inadvertently set the seeds for its own destruction by providing "too generous" benefits for the immigrants it served – thereby reducing inequality and the dependence of ordinary people upon elites for their livelihood.

Merton (1968, 131) and Scott (1968, 1150) detail how political machines, especially in urban America but also in the South (Cornwell, 1964, 29), were essential in both maintaining power for the wealthy – and whites in the South. At the same time, they helped provide basic services for the poor – Irish, Italian, and Jewish immigrants in large American cities such as New York and African-Americans in the South. These machines provided both "honest" and "dishonest" graft. Dishonest graft involved very rich no-bid contracts, pay-offs for government favors, and the selling of justice – and judicial positions – for rather large sums of money (Caro, 1975, 712; Sayre and Kaufman, 1960, 539). Caro (1975, 712) writes: "it almost seemed as if being on the [police] force was synonymous was being on the take – and in which sacred justice was sold in the very temples of justice." Civil service reforms had largely passed New York City by; when city officials were required to follow the law on merit selection, they manipulated the tests and the results to reward their loyal followers (Caro, 1975, 71).

Lowi (1964, 175–6) tells of the testimony of a leader (or "boss") of New York City's Democratic Party, Richard Croker, before a special committee of the New York legislature at the turn of the twentieth century:

> Mr. Moss: So we have it . . . that you, participating in the selection of judges before election, participate in the emolument that comes . . . at the end of their judicial proceeding, namely, judicial sales.
> Mr. Croker: Yes, sir.
> Mr. Moss: And it goes into your pocket?
> Mr. Croker: I get – that is part of my profit.
> Mr. Moss: Then you are working for your own pocket, are you not?
> Mr. Croker: At the time, same as you.

Just as critical to the machine was the provision of jobs and services to the poor, who would then demonstrate their political loyalty to the party (usually the Democratic Party) that provided such "honest graft." Scott (1968, 1150) argues that the machine depended upon a large immigrant population that was both poor and unfamiliar with the political system and a small middle class that might become more politically active and pose a threat to the reigning political order.

Cornwell (1964, 30) describes how the machines functioned:

Above all, [immigrants] needed the means of physical existence: jobs, loans, rent money, contributions of food or fuel to tide them over, and the like. Secondly, they needed a buffer against an unfamiliar state and its legal minions: help when they or their off-spring got in trouble with the police, help in dealing with inspectors, in seeking pushcart licenses, and in other relations with the public bureaucracy.

In New York City, "Offices were filled with so many clerks and secretaries that supervisors couldn't possibly provide work for all of them" (Caro, 1975, 71).

Political bosses provided these services in return for the electoral loyalty of the immigrants. They were not above some "subtle" manipulation to insure that their clientele remained dependable. Ivins (1970, 20) noted: ". . . the voting [in primaries] is usually done at the liquor store, cigar store, livery-stable, or other place where the contestant favored by the leader can best control the house, its exits and entrances, and can most easily and speedily gather his votes together." In 1884, 72 percent of the political meetings in New York City were held either in saloons or right next door (Ivins, 1970, 21). The machines were devoted to the political incorporation of immigrants such as the Irish, *but not to their economic or social advancement* – which would have made them less dependent upon the political organizations (Erie, 1988, ch. 7).

Over the course of the twentieth century, machine power waned in most American cities (Chicago seems to be a notable exception). Challenges to political bosses were nothing new in New York City: Reform mayors were elected following scandals in the city in 1901, 1913, and most notably in 1933, when Fiorello LaGuardia was elected for the first of three four-year terms. LaGuardia ran what might have been the most honest administration in the city's history (Caro, 1975, 712). When LaGuardia retired in 1945, the machine was back: "The party was on again. New York was again a city in which *SCANDAL* and *GRAFT* and *FRAUD* blared bold and black out of the headlines stacked on newsstands" (Caro, 1975, 712; italics and capitals in original).

In the 1950s a nascent Reform movement began challenging the Democratic party establishment, winning victories here and there, mostly in Manhattan. By 1961, Reformers had won a series of victories for city, state, and federal offices. Mayor Robert Wagner, Jr., had fallen out of favor with the machine and became a born-again Reformer in his quest for reelection. Former First Lady Eleanor Roosevelt endorsed Wagner and the mayor startled many observers by winning the Democratic primary and reelection. The 1961 election marked the end of the career of the last head of Plunkitt's Tammany Hall organization and its leader, Carmine deSapio (who in 1969 was convicted of conspiracy and bribery). The machine was no longer the dominant force in city politics, although it did resurface in 1973 to elect another mayor (Abe Beame).

Even though it was out of power in the mayor's office following the elections of 1901, 1913, and especially under LaGuardia (for 12 years), the machine controlled virtually all of the lower-level offices in the city until the 1960s. Reform mayors had no political base of their own, since all but Wagner ran on Fusion tickets of disaffected Democrats, Republicans (who were a minuscule force in city politics), and assorted third parties – through the mayoralty of John V. Lindsay in 1965–73. The civil rights and peace movements of the 1950s and 1960s mobilized many New Yorkers into activity in the Reform wing of the Democratic party. Over time, the Reform movement shifted from a small group of upper-middle-class Protestants and Jews based in lower and midtown Manhattan into a powerful political force in city politics.

While Reformers only controlled Manhattan and parts of Brooklyn, the regular organizations that dominated the other boroughs were a shell of their former self: In 1933, there were 1000 political clubs in the city; by 1972, there were only 262. Patronage jobs did not vanish. Even Lindsay had more than 25,000 jobs to dispense at the end of his term in 1973 (Shefter, 1985, 99). The regular organizations still offered lower-level jobs in the mid-1980s; however, the hiring became entwined in a larger corruption scandal. Courts held that the machine's distribution of jobs discriminated against minorities and was terminated (Mollenkopf, 1992, 123–4). The regular organization had shifted its focus from mobilizing voters through civic jobs to a "new patronage" focused on the higher stakes of "honest graft" – awarding contracts for community organization programs (Mollenkopf, 1992, 80, 227, n. 24). New York had not been taken over by liberal activists, but the machine no longer dominated city politics. Only a tiny share of the city's electorate at any time was dependent upon political bosses for their livelihoods.

Corruption hardly vanished. The 1964 World's Fair was a veritable bonanza for politically connected construction and insurance firms, with city contracts totaling at least $60 million (Caro, 1975, 1087–91). In the 1980s, one county leader channeled expensive city contracts to nonexistent firms he owned and another took kickbacks on a different city business deal (Mollenkopf, 1992, 123). It is still hard to read local publications such as the *New York Times* or even *The New Yorker* with any regularity and not see reports of major scandals in city government, even under the mayoralty of Michael Bloomberg, a billionaire who hardly needs any gains he might accrue from political life (Mead, 2005).

Nevertheless, it is likely – though impossible to verify – that grand corruption is considerably less than when machines were dominant. It is indisputable that petty corruption has largely vanished.

Why? People in the city became less dependent upon the machine for their sustenance. Even before the organization atrophied, the middle class had grown – they were the base for reform politics in the city – and the poor had become less dependent upon political leaders for their livelihood. Much of this is attributable to the social welfare policies enacted in Franklin D. Roosevelt's New Deal in the 1930s. Of at least equal importance was the spurt in educational levels among city residents and across the nation (Cornwell, 1964, 34; Lowi, 1964, 194). Education is perhaps the strongest route to upward mobility – and to a more equitable distribution of wealth in a society (Rothstein and Uslaner, 2005, 47–51). Goldin (1998, 362, 364) shows that high school attendance rates in the Northeast peaked in the 1940s. Graduation rates surged in the 1950s, but had been growing at a fast – and almost linear – rate since the 1920s. The success of reform politics in New York occurred just as the graduation rate was spiking.

As more people became educated – and especially went to college – their economic mobility rose and they were no longer dependent upon political machines. At the end of World War II, the U.S. Congress passed the G. I. Bill of Rights, which provided scholarships to colleges and universities for veterans of the war and greatly expanded the share of young people who attended university (Mettler, 2005).

However, free – not just subsidized – education was available to New York City residents long before the G. I. Bill. CUNY, founded in 1847, provided free education for all city residents who were admitted (though modest tuition charges were instituted when New York City went bankrupt in 1976). CUNY boasts of its world-famous faculty (with one of the highest number of Nobel Prize winners in the world).[2] It was clearly a means of advancement for the ethnic minorities in the city from the 1930s onward as enrollments rose

---

[2] On the history of CUNY, see http://portal.cuny.edu/portal/site/cuny/?epi_menuItemID= 840a1e9cd3eccca64bef4d5178304e08&epi_menuID=a00e05b73704d3407d840d5541a08a0c &epi_baseMenuID=a00e05b73704d3407d840d5541a08a0c, accessed January 20, 2007.

dramatically. Immigrants poured into New York City from Europe from the late nineteenth century through the first third of the twentieth century. They lived in tenements, worked hard, and were often dependent upon the machine for their livelihood. The free education at CUNY meant that their children's university education would not be a burden on them. Thousands took advantage of this as the City College became a magnet for many students who could not get into Harvard because of ethnic and religious discrimination. Two new branch campuses, Brooklyn College and Queens College, were founded in 1930 and 1937, respectively.

The political machine that expanded CUNY's role and enhanced its status as a "social benefit" for the immigrant communities could not have realized that it may have been preparing the seeds of its own downfall. As more people became educated, not only did they have greater opportunities for social mobility. They also became more trusting: Education is one of the strongest determinants of generalized trust. The gains to trust from education come primarily through university education (Uslaner, 2002, 98–100). Scott (1968, 1150) argued that the political machine flourished when "the sense of community was especially weak, and when the social fragmentation made particularistic ties virtually the only feasible means of corruption." More educated people are more likely to trust others – and trust leads to less corruption. The activists in the Reform movement were political idealists who "were far more likely than machine politicians to be well-educated, to be employed in the professions, and to have acquired the cosmopolitan demeanor and views of the social stratum they had entered" (Shefter, 1985, 45).

The machine thought it was providing a material benefit – a university education – to its clientele. The plan worked well as long as only a handful of people – mostly the elite – went to the university. When in the mid- to late-twentieth century more and more people graduated from high school and attended university and inequality in the United States began to decline (Pikety and Saez, 2003), the machine's lifespan was doomed. Not only were the children of immigrants who received degrees from CUNY no longer dependent upon the machine for jobs, but many were surely among the law school graduates who put Tammany leaders such as DeSapio in jail.

As the children of immigrants received university educations, there were fewer immigrants for political leaders to court. In 1920, almost 40 percent of the American population was born abroad, including 64 percent in New York (Cornwell, 1964, 29). Prior to World War I, more than 8 million people a decade were immigrating to the United States – a figure that dropped to less than 1.5 million from 1915 to 1930 and dropped to "a mere trickle" after that (Cornwell, 1964, 34). By the time immigration picked up again in the latter part of the twentieth century, the machine had already atrophied and the new poor relied more on governmental programs for support than on political leaders.

New York City political leaders in the mid-nineteenth century clearly envisaged free tuition as a benefit for a tiny elite, the well endowed who desired a college degree. There were few immigrants in the city in 1847 and the demand for admission to the City College was limited.[3] They certainly could not see free tuition as a threat to their own political survival – not even in the early twentieth century, when most immigrants depended upon city largesse for their survival. Yet the growth in government programs designed to combat the effects of the Depression, the economic boom during World War II, and especially the demand for higher education by the children of immigrants laid the foundation for a new era of greater economic equality, more political activism, and less corruption.

Poverty Reduction and Economic Equality as an Anti-Corruption Tool

The big question remains: How might we reduce corruption? To answer this, we would need time series data on corruption, inequality, trust, legal fairness, and institutional quality (among other variables) for a large number of countries. There is a paucity of data to examine the determinants of *change in corruption*. There are only data for 42 countries on corruption levels in 1980–5 and there are only complete data for 18 countries (Argentina, Australia, Belgium, Canada, Denmark, Finland, Hungary, Ireland, Italy, Japan, Mexico, the Netherlands, South Korea, Spain, Sweden, the United Kingdom, the United States, and West Germany) on corruption, inequality, and trust measured in both the 1980s and early twenty-first century. This is hardly sufficient to do any multivariate analysis. The bivariate correlations strongly support the inequality trap thesis, especially if I exclude the one transition country (Hungary): The average (absolute) correlation between the corruption indices, trust, and the Ginis is .700. But the sample excludes most countries with high levels of corruption and thus cannot answer the key question of how we might break out of the inequality trap.

We lack data on legal fairness over time. While there are good data on strangling regulation over time from the World Bank – and there is considerable evidence that countries can escape from bad policies – the r^2 between the 1996 and 2005 indices of regulation is "just".655 (N = 182). The biggest gains in regulatory policy have come in the transition countries – with 12 of the 26 most "improved" countries being transition countries – and ones with high levels of corruption. However, less strangling regulation from 1996 to 2005 does not lead to a decline in corruption. Across 151 countries, the r^2 is only .078 – and it is actually weaker for countries where economic regulation has improved. There is a somewhat stronger link in transition countries ($r^2 = .206, N = 33$).

Bad policy can lead to higher levels of corruption, but changes in policy do not seem sufficient – especially in transition countries with rising inequality – to overcome the dilemma of dishonesty in public life. Even in transition countries, even large changes in regulatory policy have modest effects on corruption overall. Yet there are some countries where changes in regulatory policy do

---

[3] I have no firm data on this. City College and City University officials maintain no historical records (before the 1970s) on enrollment figures. (Personal communications, March 2007.)

track improvements in corruption, even if modest: Armenia, Bulgaria, Lithuania, Serbia, Turkmenistan, and Tajikistan seem to have benefitted from policy changes – even if most other countries in the world have not. All of these countries have a long way to go in combating dishonesty, especially as inequality has been rising and people see the legal system as unfair. Yet there is some evidence that policy changes do matter.

Not many states succeed in moving from high to low corruption. In the shorter time frame of 1996 to 2005, the World Bank corruption measures (covering more countries) shows an even stronger level of stability than the 1980–5 to 2005 comparison in Chapter 2. Across 151 countries rated in both years by the World Bank, the r^2 is .827. While there is movement in individual country scores, almost all of the largest changes reflect movement within the clusters of honest and corrupt countries. Few countries move from negative scores (highly corrupt) to positive values – a pattern that is replicated in the smaller sample of countries in the Transparency International samples in both years.

With relatively little movement over time and with a paucity of longitudinal data, statistical analysis is unlikely to be the best tool to uncover whether there is a way out of the inequality trap. The way to see how some countries have succeeded is to focus on case studies – but such research is in its infancy. The stories of Hong Kong and Singapore are the best known because they seem to have come the farthest. Yet these cases seem to be more exceptions than the rule and they both faced external threats. Yet the escape from high levels of dishonesty in public life also came about because Hong Kong and Singapore linked anti-corruption campaigns to economic growth and a commitment to raising living standards for all.

You (2005b, 117–39) suggests that this pattern may be critical elsewhere. South Korea and Taiwan both promoted land reform after World War II, but the Philippines resisted pressures to do so. Land reform was coupled with a vast increase in the enrollment in elementary schools and in universities – rises of 800 to 1000 percent, which in turn led to greater economic growth and a more equitable distribution of income – and ultimately to less corruption. However, there was a reversion to greater inequality in South Korea (largely due to the influence of large conglomerates called *chaebols*) and a corresponding rise in corruption. Taiwan followed a path closer to that of Hong Kong and Singapore – but with an even greater commitment to an equitable distribution of income. Both South Korea and Taiwan were threatened by China – and these external pressures made it easier – and more imperative – to develop corruption-free markets that would fight Communism from within. Without such external pressures, the Philippines never promoted either economic transformations or anti-corruption campaigns (You, 2005b, 118–41).

Inequality is clearly not the whole story of why corruption is so persistent. There are clearly exceptions to my argument even beyond Hong Kong and Singapore. Spain moved from a moderately uncorrupt position to much cleaner government from 1996 to 2004 on both the TI and World Bank measures, even as inequality rose slightly. Its neighbor Portugal showed little change in either corruption or inequality during the same period. Both countries had democratic transitions in the early 1970s from authoritarian regimes. Portugal's democratization led to a strong spurt toward greater honesty in government from 1980 to 2004, but there was little change for Spain – which already had a relatively low level of corruption. Both countries have moderate levels of inequality (Ginis around .35) that have not changed much over time. Nor have their economies taken off as in Hong Kong, Singapore, Taiwan, and South Korea.

While Spain and Portugal seem to be exceptions to my argument, each faced an internal threat from Communist parties and radical labor unions that threatened their early transitions to democracy – and in this sense, the pressures toward a corruption-free market economy were similar to those in Hong Kong, Singapore, Taiwan, and South Korea. In each of these cases, support for the left (as in transition countries) reflected political and social tensions arising from inequality and poverty. Threats from Communism seem to play a role in leading some countries to more honest government. However, with Marxist ideology out of favor throughout most of the world, the threat from leftists is unlikely to be a guide to curbing corruption in the twenty-first century.

The aggregate analysis suggests that inequality and especially uneven economic development can lead to low levels of out-group trust and then to high levels of malfeasance. The survey evidence from transition countries and much of Africa suggest that people see corruption and inequality as inextricably linked. Even if elites do not see this connection – as in Estonia – rising inequality will cement the link in people's minds. People's perceptions of corruption are rarely so out of sync with "reality" – and without an engaged and supportive public, anti-corruption campaigns as in Hong Kong and Singapore will be difficult to sustain. Corruption thrives when elites control the economic fate of ordinary citizens – and where people believe that they have no alternative in getting by. The sort of corruption that engulfs ordinary citizens – petty corruption – is not as morally troubling as the grand thievery of the rich and powerful.

Institutions are essential to combating both corruption and the inequality that underlies much of malfeasance. In Singapore, Hong Kong, Botswana, Taiwan, South Korea, and New York City, the drives to reduce corruption either were linked directly to economic growth and greater equality or came as the result of policies that fostered both growth and a more equitable distribution of resources. The social welfare policies that play a key role in fighting inequality are not cheap and in each case there was a critical role for the state. The most egalitarian, most trusting, and least corrupt societies are the Nordic nations, where universalistic social welfare policies originated. There is thus little support for the claim that the route to ending corruption is through a reduction in the role of government, as Alesina and Angeletos argue (2004, abstract): "Bigger governments raise the possibilities for corruption; more corruption may in turn raise the support for redistributive policies that intend to correct the inequality and injustice generated by corruption." I found little support for a connection between the size of government and corruption (Chapter 3). As the measure of strangling regulation indicates, greater opportunities for grabbing hands leads to higher levels of malfeasance. Strangling regulations are not the same as a strong state – many of the countries with the most expansive public sector (such as the Nordic nations and other Western countries) rank very well on the World Bank regulation measure.

Universalistic policies in Sweden came about, most analysts argue, because of a strong state and an independent and fair civil service. Civil servants designed and implemented these policies (Heclo, 1974, 40–2). What made these policies work – and what led to their acceptance by the Swedish public – was that they were administered *fairly* by honest civil servants (Knudsen and Rothstein, 1994; Rothstein, 1998, 141). This argument brings us full circle to the argument that you can't get strong policies to fight inequality just by hiring lots of well-qualified – or even well-paid – civil servants (see Chapter 3). Higher pay for civil servants doesn't lead to less corruption, nor does efficient government. To combat inequality, you need *clean* government (see Chapter 3; Rothstein and Uslaner, 2005, 57–8). *Yet, to reduce corruption, you need to start with battling inequality* (see Chapter 2). This is the heart of the inequality trap.

It is not so easy to break out of this trap by creating new institutions exogenously. Path dependency speaks to why it is so difficult to break out of any equilibrium, be it good, bad, or middling. Not only are there strong incentives to follow the policies of the past, but political leaders may have erected strong institutional barriers to changing course so that they can commit their predecessors to policies (Pierson, 2004, 42–4).

Arguments based upon path dependence differ from my thesis in at least two key ways. First, most discussions of path dependence suggest that change is possible. Change can occur either by "blunt" events such as an earthquake in the physical world or a major exogenous shock to a political system or gradually and imperceptibly (Pierson, 2003; Rothstein, 1998, 29). On such accounts, a major event such as the collapse of Communism could have led to reductions in corruption in the transition countries. It did not (see Chapter 4). The two most prominent shock events were the anti-corruption campaigns in Hong Kong and Singapore, which (1) did not involve democratic transitions, and (2) were hardly exogenous, but well planned and designed by leaders who realized that they needed the support of their citizens.

There may be evidence of "slow-moving" effects, as Pierson (2003) argues. Democracy may not matter in the short run. Testing for the "immediate" effects of democracy after "only" twenty years, as I did in Chapter 4 for transition countries, may be unfair. Democracy may need much longer to take root and to have strong effects on corruption. I have argued elsewhere (Uslaner, 2002, 227) that long-standing democracies have more trusting citizenries – but that it takes 46 years of democracy to move a country from well below the mean in trust to above it. The level of continuous years of democracy is also strongly related to corruption (r = .848, N = 39), but even more powerfully related to the level of GDP per capita (r = .908). The problem with "big slow movements" over long periods of time is that lots of things happen over time and it is usually extremely difficult to disentangle one effect from the other.

Second, path dependence arguments almost always start with an initial choice of an outcome or a policy. When we are trying to explain changes in programs or transformations of institutions, this is perfectly appropriate. It is far more difficult to trace the historical roots of corruption. Even when we focus on the adoption of specific policy choices, it is not clear that the initial choice of a program should be considered to be an exogenous event. Sweden was a pioneer in enacting universalistic social welfare policies. The social basis for a universalistic social welfare policy goes back centuries. Swedish peasants, like their brethren in Norway, never endured the brutalities of feudalism (Trägårdh, 2001, 141–2; cf. Rothstein and Uslaner, 2005, 57):

Because the Swedish peasantry largely escaped feudalism and even retained its rights to be represented as a separate estate in the *Riksdag* [parliament], it could play a role unparalleled elsewhere.... the Swedish political culture came to be cast in a mold very different from that of other Western democracies.... it was a process of universalizing the egalitarianism of the peasant community...

Denmark, by contrast, did have a feudal past with a highly unequal distribution of income. In the late eighteenth and early nineteenth centuries, extensive land reforms and the establishment of universal primary education came about in a peaceful revolution. The development of farmers' cooperatives, the expansion of trade, strong economic growth, and rapid industrialization led to a more egalitarian distribution of income within a relatively short period of time (Paldam, 1991, 70–1).

The enactment of universalistic policies in Nordic countries was based upon a long-standing set of beliefs in an egalitarian social order. Civil servants in such societies had fewer incentives to act dishonestly: They would be immediately suspect if they became rich – but the egalitarian social order gave them little reason to envy others in the society – and thus to provide justifications for acting corruptly. The commitment to an egalitarian society persists today, although there has been some erosion of social solidarity in recent decades (Rothstein, 1998, 192–5).

Many of the countries with the highest levels of corruption also have been former colonies (since the twentieth century). The mean TI Corruption Perceptions Index for former colonies is 3.86; for other countries, it is 6.65 ($r^2 = .319$, $N = 89$). Former colonies also have higher levels of inequality ($r^2 = .553$, $N = 50$ for the 2000 WIDER measure, excluding former and present Communist nations) and uneven economic development ($r^2 = .369$, $N = 62$, also excluding nations with a history of Communism). So the levels of corruption and inequality in many former colonies may not be traceable to "policy choices" they made as much as by choices made for them.

I am not arguing that the path along the inequality trap is always – or even generally – shaped centuries in the past. The Swedish (and perhaps other Nordic) cases may be exceptions. Nor am I arguing that whatever equilibrium a country lands in (top, middle, bottom) is like quicksand. Surely one can trace Swedish history back long enough to find evidence of corruption. In the United States, changes in corruption are likely to be far more recent.

The history of government honesty and dishonesty may not be a different story than the current equilibrium in the inequality trap. We have a far better idea of why countries rank where they do now than how they got there. Some stories go back centuries (as in Sweden, Norway, and many former colonies). Others' histories are not so long, while a handful of cases (Botswana, Hong Kong, and Singapore) provide us with enough information to tell compelling stories – that we know are atypical.

Path dependence may be better able to explain how countries such as the United States and Hong Kong stay free of corruption even as one might expect them to slide backwards. Inequality in the United States was high in the early twentieth century and began to decline in the 1940s before rising again in the 1980s (Pikety and Saez, 2003). A more equitable distribution of income in the 1940s laid the foundation for the decline of patronage-based politics in some cities, notably New York, and to the ultimate elimination of much of petty corruption. In Hong Kong the anti-corruption drive was linked to a program of social welfare legislation that led to a sharp reduction in inequality, but after corruption had been curbed, inequality rose – although corruption remained low (see Chapter 7). Countries with lots of grand corruption also have a great deal of petty corruption (as seen by their publics). Once petty corruption had largely been eviscerated, it became more difficult to "reestablish" widespread grand corruption, even as inequality was increasing. Here is a perhaps modest lesson in optimism: Once reduced, corruption may not "return" to its previous levels. But the reduction in corruption is a Herculean task in itself.

Conclusion

The key to reducing corruption seems to involve making people less dependent upon it. Of course, the demise of the machine had its most notable impact on petty corruption. Petty corruption, however, was not an end in itself. It served to keep in power leaders who robbed the public purse and made themselves and their conspirators wealthy. This is why in so many contexts ordinary people resent elites and believe that they got rich only because they are corrupt. In so many cases, they are correct, and corruption not only depends upon inequality, but exacerbates it. Once people find a way to succeed in life without depending upon corrupt leaders, they are more likely to turn their backs on malfeasance in public life.

The key mechanism to make people less dependent upon corrupt leaders is a universal social welfare regime – and especially one based upon education for all. My speculation about New York City focuses on making university education available to all citizens, something that is also firmly established in Sweden. Denmark marked the end of feudalism by adopting universal education. Botswanan officials confronted a highly inegalitarian educational system after independence from Great Britain; in 1997, the government introduced universal education and now 90 percent of Botswanan children are enrolled in elementary school, education now consumes over 9 percent of the state budget, and "[t]he goal of universal free education (up to junior secondary level) has been more or less achieved."[4] Singapore, Hong Kong, and South Korea all provide free education to all children and this has been a key component in their economic growth.[5]

It will not be easy. Countries that have low levels of inequality, high levels of trust, and honest governments will be much more likely to adopt policies that reduce inequality. People pay their taxes without hesitation because they believe that their money will actually go to the programs they see as important in maintaining – or producing – a more equitable distribution of resources (Rothstein and Uslaner, 2005). In states with high levels of inequality, low trust, and elevated rates of corruption, people won't pay their taxes to fund the programs that would alleviate poverty, the health and education systems are rife with demands for "extra gift" payments, and employees may be tempted to steal books or medicines from the schools or hospitals. As I have argued in Chapter 2, clean government seems to be a key determinant of government policies that might reduce inequalities, especially universal education. This is the essence of the inequality trap – and even if we know what path to take, we may not know how to get there.

People who do see a clear link between corruption and inequality blanche at the solution of universal education. When I have broached this solution in talks in China and Bangladesh – countries where there is much concern for both corruption and inequality – audiences ranging from undergraduate students to members of Parliament have grimaced. We cannot afford such programs, they say. When I counter that they cannot afford *not* to have universal education – for reasons of economic growth as well as combating corruption – they just sigh and seem resigned to their fate.

Rothstein (2007) argues that the adoption of universal education in Sweden in the mid-nineteenth century was central to the long-term decline in corruption. We don't have sufficient evidence to cement the claim, but the circumstantial evidence has begun to add up. Yet there are exceptions. Communist states and their successors as transition nations may face rising inequality. However, they have historically had greater levels of equality as well as universal education. Universal social welfare programs – and even inequality – are not sufficient to ensure a path toward honest government.

Did universal education and equality fail to curb corruption under Communism because of weak institutions? Of course, Communism, with its persistent

---

[4] See http://ubh.tripod.com/bw/bhp6.htm; see also http://www.nationsencyclopedia.com/Africa/Botswana-EDUCATION.html and http://education.stateuniversity.com/pages/185/Botswana-CONSTITUTIONAL-LEGAL-FOUNDATIONS.html, accessed July 16, 2007.

[5] See http://www.moe.gov.sg/speeches/2004/sp20040526_print.htm, http://www.yearbook.gov.hk/2004/en/07_04.htm, and especially Manzo (2007).

shortages and its privileges for the leaders, was rife with corruption. But malfeasance has not gone away with the adoption of democratic constitutions and neither Singapore nor Hong Kong can be called effective democracies. A more likely explanation for *when universal social welfare programs and equality work* to overcome corruption might be based upon economic growth and people's expectations for the future. People in Communist countries were poor and they had little expectation that they could better their life chances. After transition, there was a spurt in optimism that quickly faded as inequality rose and corruption proved persistent – and social welfare benefits often demanded fees. To be sure, many "universal" services were not "free" under Communism since many, perhaps most, people had to make "gift" payments to receive these services, including good grades at school and admission to universities.

In every other case I have considered, universal education was not only a key to more equality, but also to economic growth more generally – and to upward mobility for people who became educated. This growth, both societal and personal, freed ordinary people from the grips of corrupt patrons and gave them the hope for the future that underlies generalized trust (Uslaner, 2002, chs. 2, 4).

Perhaps it takes, in Rothstein's (2007) felicitous phrase, a "big bang" to curb corruption – a major shift in government priorities that reflects rising social tensions *together with* the emergence of bold leaders and new institutional designs, all at the same time. This seems to be the story of how the Danes ended feudalism and how people in Hong Kong, Singapore, and Botswana were rallied to join their leaders in the fight against malfeasance. Such a perspective offers both hope – we know it can be done – but also more than a bit of despair, since "big bangs" cannot be easily engineered by social reformers.

Reprise

The decline of the political machine in New York seems to tell a story that is at variance with my larger argument: Petty corruption was eliminated while grand corruption persists, even if less widespread. Wouldn't an assault on petty corruption accomplish the same goal – and doesn't this count against my claim that ordinary people, including pickpockets, take their cues from their corrupt leaders? No, for two reasons. First, it seems that the amount of high-level malfeasance in New York City declined substantially by the late twentieth century.

Second, the key issue is how petty corruption largely disappeared. There was no frontal attack on gift payments or patronage. Rather "clients" became less dependent upon their "patrons" *as the power of the machine atrophied.* Cutting the umbilical cord that ties ordinary people to their leaders is the first step in reducing corruption. A more prosperous citizenry rebelled against the dominant political class. The revolt succeeded because the leaders no longer controlled access to livelihoods. Reduced petty corruption goes hand in hand with lower levels of grand corruption (see Chapter 1). Most attempts to rid societies of petty corruption are either foils to protect grand corruption or are based upon a giddily optimistic expectation that pushing away street vendors is the first step toward eliminating kleptocracies.

Strong institutions clearly matter, but they do not emerge from constitutional conventions and often not even from anti-corruption commissions. The citizens of many transition countries believed in an institutional magic wand, where constitutional engineers would turn their societies into democratic Cinderellas, all dressed up for the ball and ready to take their place among the rich nations of Europe. The transition countries are almost all in the European Union now, but their citizens realize that democracy is not a cure-all. The market created lots of inequality and increased social tensions. Elected leaders can pilfer the public purse just as the Communist dictators did. Strong institutions depend upon strong societies and public policies that work to reduce social tensions.

The battle against corruption ultimately rests upon public support. Even a determined leader such as Singapore's Lee Kwan Yew could not engineer a reduction in corruption by police work and a powerful court system alone (Quah, 2004, 4). In a world of inequality and low trust, the agencies of justice – the police and the courts – are likely to be among the most corrupt. Unequal justice and seeing the corrupt become rich leads people to be cynical – of other people, especially people unlike themselves – and of institutions as well.

Of course, we should put the bad guys in jail and try to eliminate petty corruption and street crime. These measures are not *the solutions* to the problem of malfeasance in public and private life (cf. Merton, 1968, 135). Democracy makes it more difficult for miscreants to hide their bad deeds because public officials no longer have a monopoly on information (Warren, 2004, 331–2). Voters sometimes punish corrupt politicians – as in the 2006 elections in the United States (see Chapter 8) and sometimes don't (as in Italy, see Chapter 2).[6] Sometimes the public is so dependent upon patrons that turning them out could be very costly. And sometimes authoritarian states find it easier to mobilize the public to fight corruption (as in Singapore and Hong Kong).

Effective government depends upon low levels of both poverty and ethnic tensions, both of which are (directly or indirectly) related to corruption (see Chapter 3). And we need clean government to lay the foundation for the equity that indirectly leads back to clean government. The persistence of corruption over time and the close linkages people make with inequality where both malfeasance and inequity are high suggest that stronger medicine is necessary.

---

[6] Of course, not all public officials accused of – or even convicted of – corruption have been defeated. In 2006, Representative William Jefferson joined a long list of (New Orleans) Louisiana officials who have been charged with wrongdoing (in his case, bribery, with $90,000 found in his home freezer) but won another term anyway.

Appendix

TABLE A1-1. *Transparency International Corruption Perceptions Index 2005 and Corruption Perceptions Global Corruption Barometer 2004: Correlations*

Global Corruption Barometer Variables	TI Corruption Perceptions Index	Bribed Last Year Global Barometer	Corruption Affects Own Life Global Barometer
Grand corruption a problem	−.809	.430	.731
Petty corruption a problem	−.862	.512	.767
Corruption affects business environment	−.584	.359	.661
Corruption affects political life	−.512	.294	.572
Business corrupt	−.666	.388	.547
Political parties corrupt	−.622	.325	.633
Parliament corrupt	−.716	.388	.702
Military corrupt	−.610	.389	.600
Tax system corrupt	−.797	.495	.733
Customs officials corrupt	−.892	.670	.740
Education system corrupt	−.799	.475	.793
Legal system corrupt	−.858	.553	.739
Medical system corrupt	−.774	.454	.673
Police corrupt	−.847	.618	.767
Registry corrupt	−.852	.504	.715
Utilities corrupt	−.658	.341	.763
Media corrupt	−.165	.032	.302
NGOs corrupt	−.477	.164	.540
Religion corrupt	−.078	.172	.305

N = 61

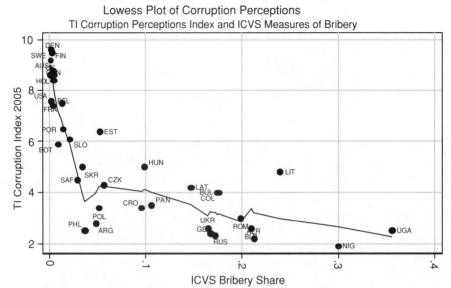

FIGURE A1-1.

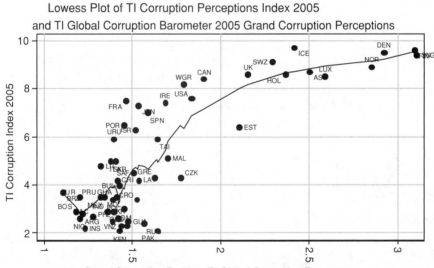

FIGURE A1-2.

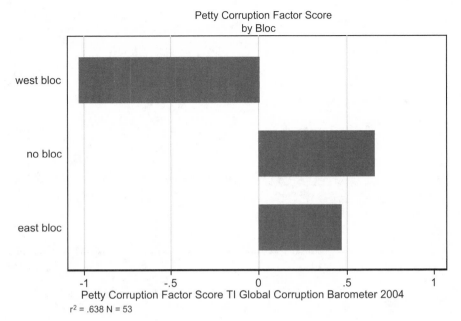

FIGURE A1-3.

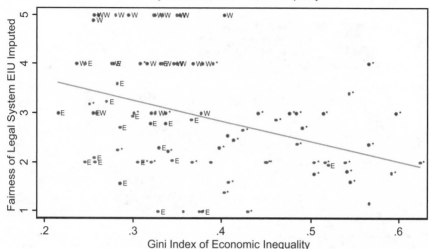

Fairness of Legal System EIU Imputed
by Gini Index of Economic Inequality

r² = .131 N = 88 r² = .279 N = 65 without Former and Present Communist Nations

W = Western bloc E = former and present Communist countries * In neither bloc

FIGURE A2-1.

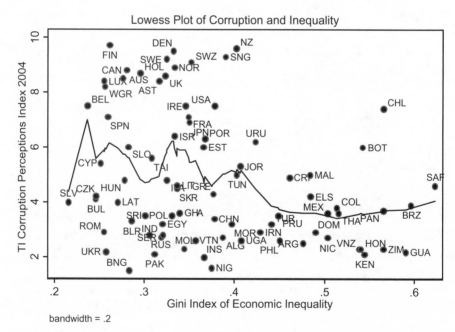

bandwidth = .2

FIGURE A2-2.

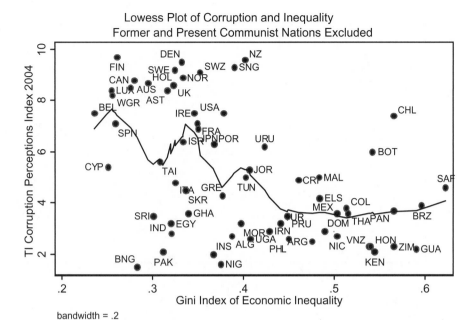

FIGURE A2-3.

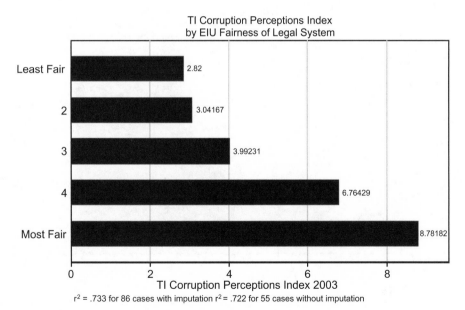

FIGURE A2-4.

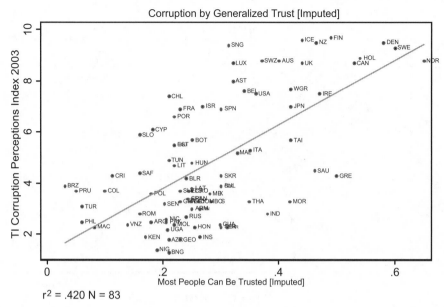

FIGURE A2-5.

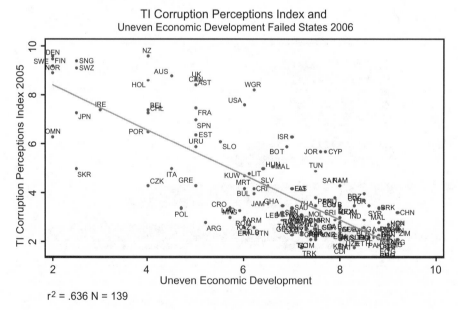

FIGURE A2-6.

TABLE A3-1. *Factor Analysis of Government Effectiveness Measures:* World *Economic Forum Executive Opinion Survey 2004*

Variable	Loading	Communality
Judicial independence	.919	.908
Efficiency of legal system	.976	.971
Efficiency of legislative system	.913	.852
Wastefulness of government spending	.876	.801
Favoritism of government decision-making	.942	.901
Transparency of government decision-making	.934	.883

TABLE A3-2. *Correlations of Corruption, Effective Government, and Failed State Indicators (2006)**

Indicator	Corruption TI 2005	Corruption TI 2005 Full Sample	Effective Government
Overall Failed States index	−.867	−.869	−.672
Uneven economic development among groups	−.801	−.797	−.620
Mounting demographic pressures	−.798	−.786	−.585
Massive movement of refugees	−.617	−.554	−.404
Legacy of vengeance: seeking group grievance	−.699	−.675	−.527
Sharp or severe economic decline	−.728	−.751	−.669
Criminalization/delegitimization of state	−.863	−.874	−.670
Progressive deterioriation of public services	−.859	−.861	−.650
Widespread violation of human rights	−.783	−.797	−.577
Security apparatus as "state within a state"	−.777	−.792	−.620
Rise of factionalized elites	−.755	−.760	−.580
Intervention of other states/external actors	−.733	−.735	−.617
N	87	139	80

*Failed state indicators from http://www.fundforpeace.org/programs/fsi/fsindicators.php, accessed May 15, 2006.

TABLE A3-3. *Model of Perceived Corruption: Gallup International Millennium Survey 2000*

Variable	Coefficient	Std. Error	t Ratio
Country governed by the will of the people	−.217****	.028	−7.88
All are equal under the law	.070****	.009	7.61
Government does good job handling crime	.084****	.009	9.48
Standard of living matters most in life	.037***	.014	2.57
Discrimination on political beliefs common	.035****	.007	5.13
Age	−.006**	.003	−1.68
Attended college/university	−.018	.018	−.99
Gini (You average index) transition countries	.006***	.002	2.77
Gini (You average index) other countries	.004****	.001	3.65
Constant	.093	.070	1.34

Estimates are regression coefficients with standard errors clustered by country
Number of countries: 52; Number of observations: 33,935
$R^2 = .225$; RMSE = 1.000
*p < .10; **p < .05; ***p < .01; ****p < .0001 (all tests one-tailed except for constants)

TABLE A3-4. *Models of Grand and Petty Corruption a Problem: Transparency International Global Corruption Barometer 2004*

| | Grand Corruption | | | | | | Petty Corruption | | | | | |
| | East Bloc | | No Bloc | | West Bloc | | East Bloc | | No Bloc | | West Bloc | |
Variable	Coefficient	t	Coefficient	t	Coefficient	t	Coefficient	t	Coefficient	t	Coefficient	t
Affects own life	.037**	2.19	.071****	−5.65	.208****	−6.00	.077****	4.93	.076****	6.08	.184****	5.65
Offered bribe	.047**	−1.69	.001	.03	.049	.87	.044	1.21	.002	.07	.128**	1.92
Poverty problem	.240****	5.02	.317****	4.10	.241****	4.82	.200****	5.83	.303****	4.26	.165****	3.68
Human rights big problem	.188****	9.32	.235****	6.46	.252****	5.75	.261****	10.2	.245****	6.03	.298****	6.59
Family income	−.002	.01	−.005	.01	−.016	.014	.014**	1.69	−.014	−1.33	−.015	−1.00
Education	−.019*	−1.47	−.001	.01	.033	1.09	−.015*	−1.31	.029	1.67	.103	3.08
Age	−.031**	−1.93	−.003	−.33	−.033*	−1.64	−.028	−1.27	.003	.29	−.018	−.72
Gender	.016	1.07	.013	−.56	.014	.06	−.003	−.15	.013	.01	−.007	−.27
Employed	.013	1.77	−.005	.01	−.007	−.04	.008	.65	−.009	−1.00	−.020	−1.05
Muslim	−.058	.07	−.149***	−2.19	.111	.83	−.120	−1.08	.084	1.37	.062	.43
Catholic	−.071**	.04	−.047*	−1.34	.071	.67	−.027	−.49	.005	.11	.012	.10
Jewish	−.299****	−4.92	−.147***	−3.14	−.173**	−1.68	−.469****	−7.20	−.072	−.84	−.019	−.18
You average Gini	.008****	5.02	−.001	.00	−.032	−2.47	.007**	2.19	−.005	−1.51	−.012	−1.08
Constant	.752****	.158	.870****	9.75	2.260****	5.28	9.604****	4.30	1.090****	7.06	1.840****	5.15

* p < .10; ** p < .05; *** p < .01; **** p < .0001 (all tests one-tailed except for constants)
Estimates are regression coefficients with standard errors clustered by country

Summary of Diagnostics for TI Global Corruption Barometer Models

| | Grand Corruption | | | Petty Corruption | | |
	East Bloc	No Bloc	West Bloc	East Bloc	No Bloc	West Bloc
N	7208	11629	10717	7331	11716	10742
R^2	.164	.263	.337	.187	.253	.276
RMSE	.635	.607	.765	.705	.660	.804
Countries	12	16	19	12	16	19

TABLE A3-5. *Model of Corruption Affects Own Life: Transparency International Global Corruption Barometer 2004*

Variable	Coefficient	Std. Error	t Ratio
Offered bribe in last 12 months	.248****	.046	5.43
Poverty big problem	.125****	.027	4.70
Human rights big problem	.110****	.023	4.78
Medical system corrupt	.088****	.019	4.64
Education system corrupt	.100****	.016	6.08
Legal system corrupt	.056****	.017	3.35
Business corrupt	.036**	.018	2.01
Employed	−.023**	.012	−1.93
East bloc country	−.247	.153	−1.61
Gini (UNDP)	.010*	.007	1.46
Legal fairness	−.136***	.055	−2.47
Constant	1.989****	.438	4.54

Estimates are regression coefficients with standard errors clustered by country.
Number of countries: 52; Number of observations: 33,935
$R^2 = .225$; RMSE = 1.000
*p < .10; **p < .05; ***p < .01; ****p < .0001 (all tests one-tailed except for constants)

TABLE A3-6. *Aggregate Model of Corruption Affects Own Life: Transparency International Global Corruption Barometer 2004*

Variable	Coefficient	Standard Error	t Ratio
Average Gini (You data)	.011**	.006	1.82
Trust (imputed)	−.981**	.469	−2.09
Regulation of business (World Bank)	−.173*	.106	−1.64
Informal sector (Executive Opinion Survey)	.097*	.068	1.43
Constant	1.947*****	.399	4.88

N = 51; $R^2 = .635$; RMSE = .348
*p < .10; **p < .05; ***p < .01; ****p < .0001 (all tests one-tailed except for constants)

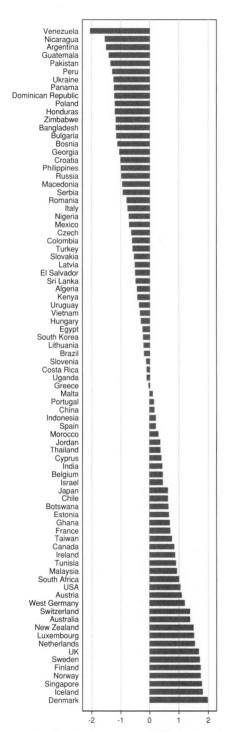

FIGURE A3-1. Government Effectiveness Factor Scores (World Economic Forum Executive Opinion Survey 2004)

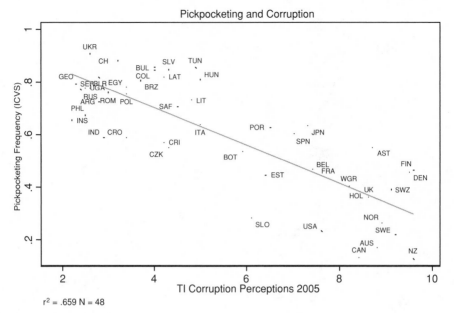

FIGURE A3-2.

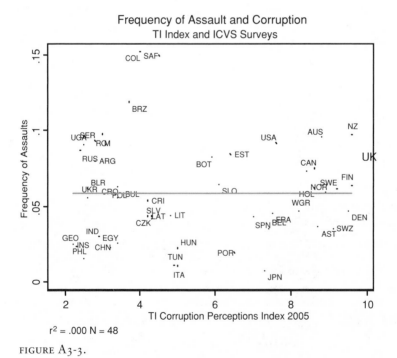

FIGURE A3-3.

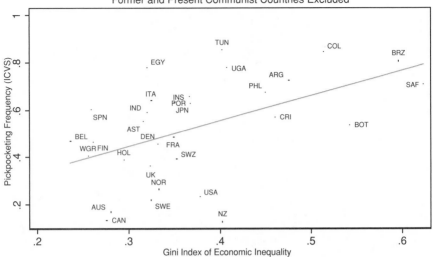

FIGURE A3-4.

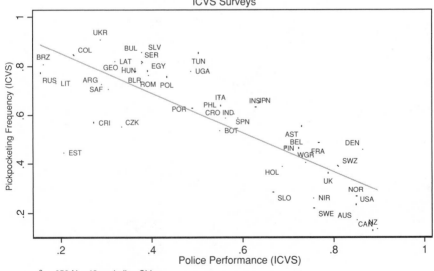

FIGURE A3-5.

TABLE A4-1. *Determinants of State Failure and Public Service Deterioration in Transition Countries*

Variable	State Failure			Public Service Deterioration		
	Coefficient	Standard Error	t Ratio	Coefficient	Standard Error	t Ratio
Corruption (TI 2005)	−7.019****	1.589	−4.42	−.418***	.130	−3.22
Change in inequality (WIDER)	17.683**	7.578	2.33	1.473**	.620	2.38
Democratization (Freedom House 2003)	−7.151**	3.068	−2.33	−.777***	.251	−3.09
Constant	66.884	11.775	5.68	4.973****	.964	5.16
R²	.900			.896		
S.E.E.	5.866			.480		

N = 21
*p < .10; **p < .05; ***p < .01; ****p < .0001

TABLE A4-2. *Determinants of Service Interruption in Transition: Aggregate Models from BEEPS 2005 (Robust Standard Errors)*

Variable	Low Water Supply			Lack of Phone Service			Power Outages		
	b	S.E.	t Ratio	b	S.E.	t Ratio	b	S.E.	t Ratio
Change in Gini index (WIDER) 1989–99	5.84****	1.371	4.25	1.520***	.619	2.45	15.220**	7.211	2.11
Confident legal system enforce contracts and property rights	3.026**	1.79	1.69	.476	.824	.58	19.893**	8.459	2.35
TI Corruption Perceptions Index 2004	−1.577****	.357	−4.20	−.484***	.199	−2.43	−5.998***	2.029	−2.96
Constant	−13.368**	6.308	−2.12	−1.497	3.054	−.49	−72.787**	30.177	−2.41
R^2		.684			.424			.535	
RMSE		2.030			.981			10.526	

*p < .10; **p < .05; ***p < .01; ****p < .0001
N = 21

TABLE A4-3. *Determinants of Shares of Business Sales on Credit in Transition BEEPS 2005 Aggregate Model (With Robust Standard Errors)*

Variable	Coefficient	Std. Error	t Ratio
Change in Gini index (WIDER) 1989–99	−18.551***	8.897	−2.53
Corruption Perceptions Index (TI)	6.695****	1.504	4.45
Chamber of Commerce membership	28.374****	8.897	3.19
Constant	37.423**	13.206	2.83

RMSE = 6.16; R^2 = .866; N = 21

*p < .10; **p < .05; ***p < .01; ****p < .0001

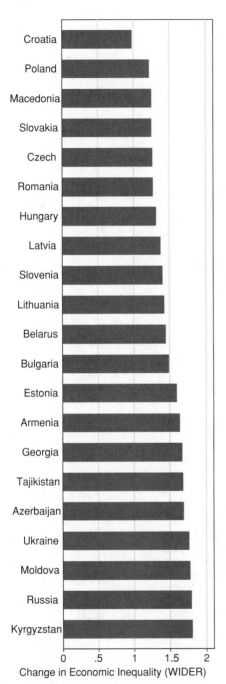

FIGURE A4-I. Changes in Economic Inequality (WIDER Measures) from 1989 to 1999: Transition Countries.

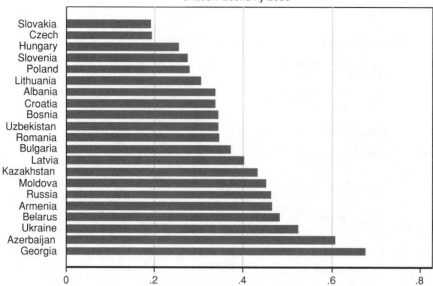

FIGURE A4-2.

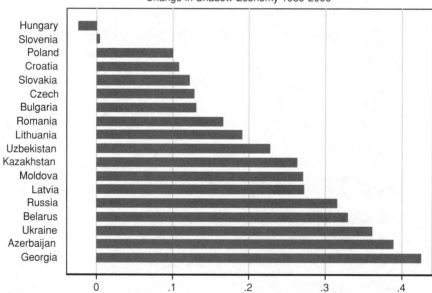

FIGURE A4-3.

TI Corruption Perceptions Index 2004 Transition Countries

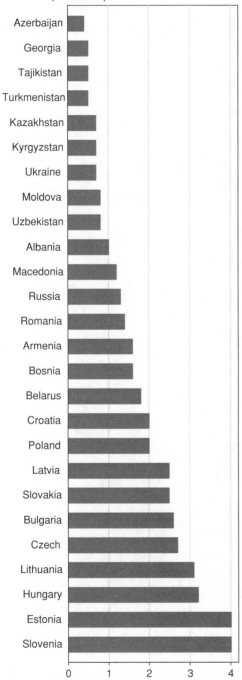

FIGURE A4-4.

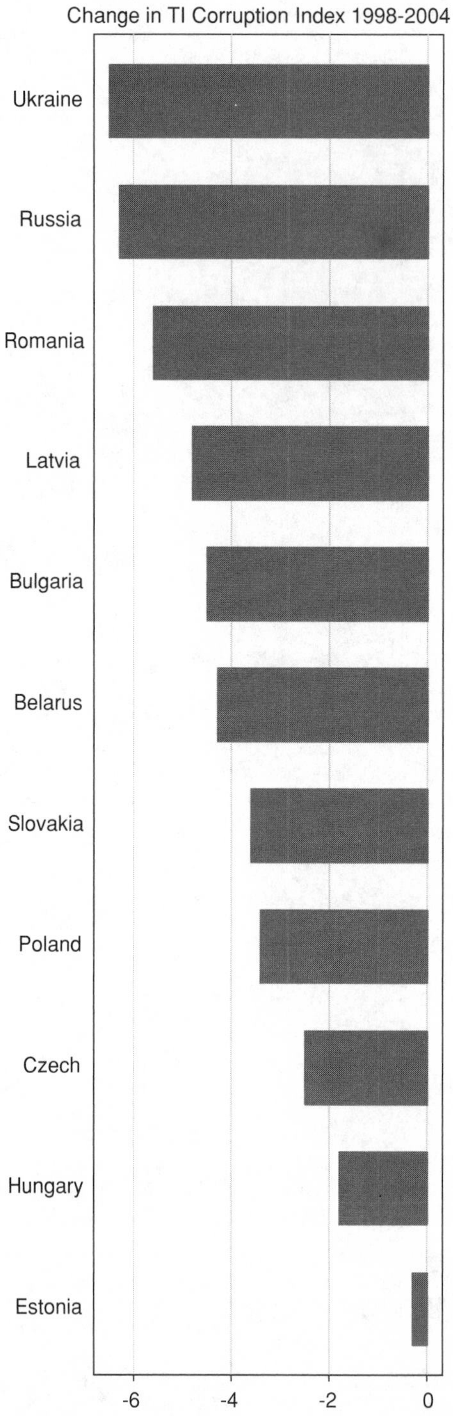

Change in TI Corruption Index 1998-2004
Ukraine
Russia
Romania
Latvia
Bulgaria
Belarus
Slovakia
Poland
Czech
Hungary
Estonia
-6
-4
-2
0

FIGURE A4-5.

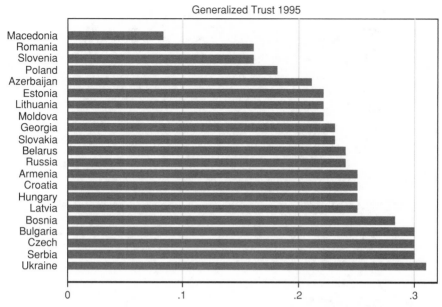

FIGURE A4-6.

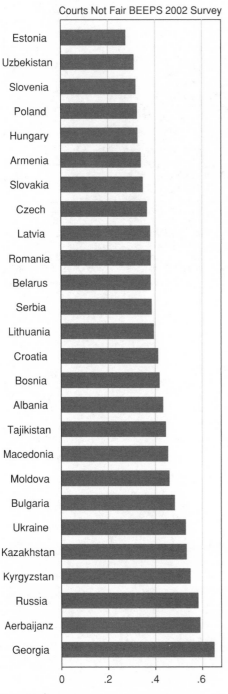

Courts Not Fair BEEPS 2002 Survey

FIGURE A4-7.

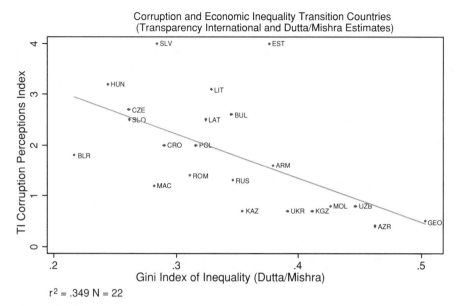

FIGURE A4-8.

FIGURE A4-9.

Appendix

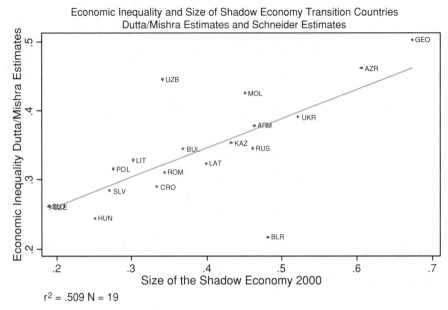

FIGURE A4-10.

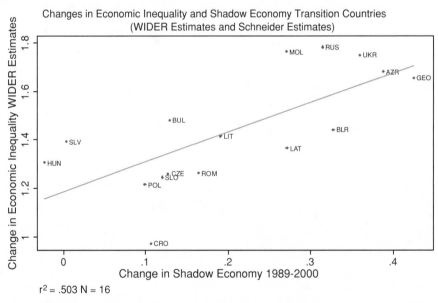

FIGURE A4-11.

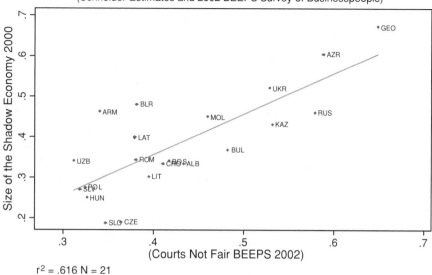

Size of Shadow Economy and Belief Courts Not Fair Transition Countries
(Schneider Estimates and 2002 BEEPS Survey of Businesspeople)

$r^2 = .616$ N = 21

FIGURE A4-12.

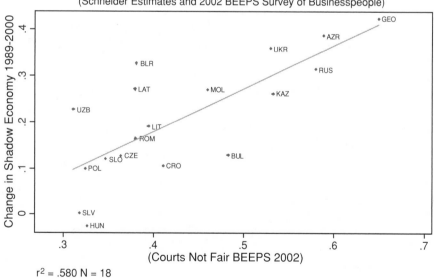

Change in Shadow Economy and Belief Courts Not Fair Transition Countries
(Schneider Estimates and 2002 BEEPS Survey of Businesspeople)

$r^2 = .580$ N = 18

FIGURE A4-13.

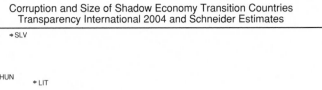

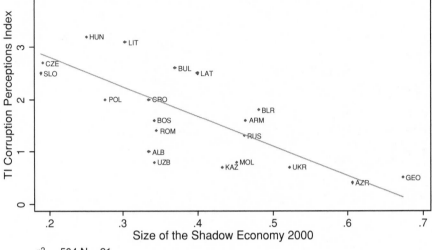

$r^2 = .504$ N = 21

FIGURE A4-14.

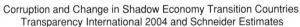

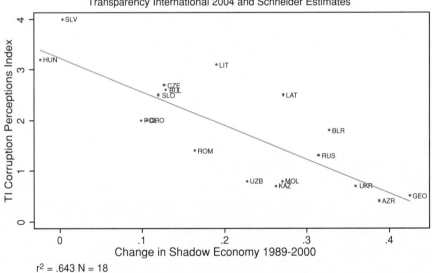

$r^2 = .643$ N = 18

FIGURE A4-15.

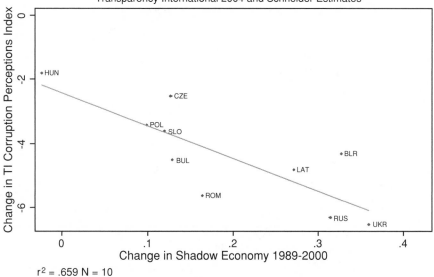

FIGURE A4-16.

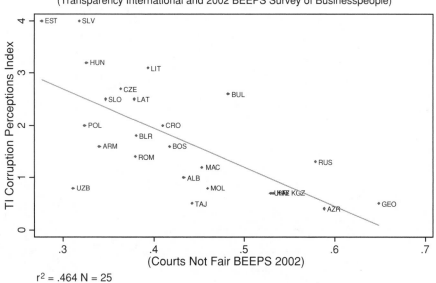

FIGURE A4-17.

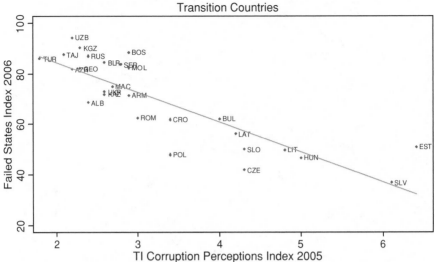

Failed States Index and TI Corruption Perceptions Index 2005
Transition Countries

r² = .722 N = 27 r² with Wider Change in Economic Inequality = .429 N = 21

FIGURE A4-18.

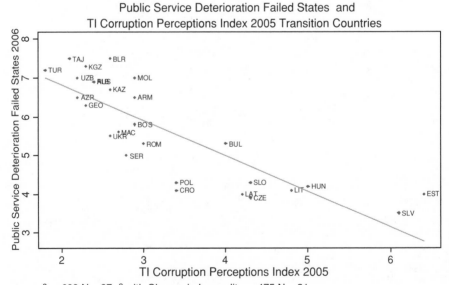

Public Service Deterioration Failed States and
TI Corruption Perceptions Index 2005 Transition Countries

r² = .693 N = 27 r² with Change in Inequality = .475 N = 21

FIGURE A4-19.

TABLE A5-1. *Rankings on Transition Indicators for Romania*

Measure	Value	Transition Rank	# Ranked	Overall Rank	# Ranked
TI Corruption Index 2004	1.4	13	26	88/90	146
TI Corruption Index 2005	3	11	27	85/87	160
Change in Corruption TI 1998–2004	−1.6	8	11	28/32	85
Change in Corruption 1996–2004 World Bank	−.11	11	26	84/86	151
Trust	.16	19/20	21	82	94
Shadow economy share*	.34	10	21	47/48	90
Change in share of shadow economy 1989–2000*	.164	8	18	–	–
Gini index (WIDER) 1999*	.299	5	16	29	60
Gini index (Dutta/Mishra)*	.311	8	22	–	–
Change in Gini index (WIDER) 1989–99*	1.261	6	21	6	44
Change in Gini index (Rosser/Rosser/Ahmed)*	.048	7	16	–	–
Courts not fair (BEEPS 2002)*	.38	10	26	–	–
Rule of law (nations in transition) 2004*	4.38	10	27	–	–
Democratization (nations in transition) 2004*	3.25	10	27	–	–
GDP per capita Penn World Tables 2000	5023	17	23	77	136
GDP growth 1975–2003 UNDP	−.8	6	14	69	76
UN Human Development Index (1990)	.772	12	18	46/47	82
Uneven economic development (Failed States)*	6	6/8	27	33/39	146
Failed States Index*	62.6	11	27	102	146
Internal conflicts (ICRG)	10.5	14	20	32/56	154
Ethnic tensions (ICRG)	3.5	13/14	20	87/97	141

*Low values indicate better performance.

Rankings based upon number of transition countries rated. Multiple rankings indicate countries tied.

– Data not available or only transition countries ranked.

TABLE A5-2. *Perceptions of Romanians on Inequality, Corruption, Government Performance, Democracy, the Market, Fellow Citizens, Their Government, Connections, and Gift Payments*

Attitude	Percent Agreeing
Inequality has increased	91.6
Satisfied with the way democracy works	33.5
Satisfied with the way the market works	13.4
Most people can be trusted	34.1
Trust government	24.5
Is the current government fighting corruption	17.9
Corruption decreased in current government	8.1
Satisfied with government efforts to reduce corruption	10.1
Satisfied with government performance in fighting corruption	23.3
Government measures to fight corruption good	37.7
Satisfied with police fighting corruption	26.9
Satisfied with courts fighting corruption	21.9
Satisfied with media fighting corruption	64.4
Most members of parliament are corrupt	85.0
Most government ministers are corrupt	79.0
Most businesspeople are corrupt	75.0
Most politicians are corrupt	74.0
Most politicians are corrupt	69.0
Most members of local council are corrupt	58.0
Most teachers are corrupt	57.0
Most government functionaries are corrupt	56.0
Most professors are corrupt	36.0
Most journalists are corrupt	26.0
Satisfied with government performance on the quality of life	25.0
Satisfied with government performance on public safety	14.0
Satisfied with government performance on privatization	19.0
Have connections for medical treatment	35.1
Trust President	38.5
Trust Parliament	15.1
Trust city hall	43.9
Trust justice system	22.0
Trust police	36.7
Trust army	66.3
Trust political parties	9.9
Have connections for finding job	11.1
Have connections to rely on in the business world	6.6
Have connections for problem at city hall	20.7
Have connections to help get loan from bank	10.0
Have connections for problem with county government	5.4
Have connections to deal with courts/lawyers	11.6
Have connections to deal with police	15.6
Have connections to rely on in foreign country	11.2
Made "extra" payments to doctor	25.0
Made "extra" payments to bank in getting loan	.7
Made "extra" payments to police	1.4
Made "extra" payments to courts	3.2
Made "extra" payments to city officials	2.5
Made "extra" payments to county officials	.3

TABLE A5-3. *Likelihood that Romanians Would Pay an* Atentie *(Gift/Bribe) for Public Service: World Bank Corruption Diagnostic Survey 2000*

Public Service	Paying "Gift"	Paying "Gift" Voluntarily
Hospital stay	66	37
Emergency	62	29
Dentist	56	39
Medical specialist	52	33
Gas installation/repair	40	31
Power connection or repair	33	28
General practitioner	32	17
Building permit	29	19
Driving license	27	17
Vocational school	27	8
Elementary school	25	9
Real estate registration	22	16
Telephone connection/repair	22	16
Courts	22	16
High school	21	10
Loan application	19	8
Water connection/repair	18	15
University	17	9
Employment office	16	9
Passport	15	12
Unemployment benefits	11	7
Identity card	8	4
Police (crime victims only)	4	3

Source: Anderson et al. (2001, 13)

TABLE A5-4. *Simultaneous Equation Model of Optimism for the Future and Perceptions of Government Handling Corruption Well from Aggregated Surveys*

Variable	Coefficient	Std. Error	t Ratio
Optimism for the future			
Government success in controlling corruption	1.848****	.327	5.65
GDP growth rate (Penn World Tables)	2.838***	.890	3.19
Constant	39.894****	6.218	6.42
RMSE = 14.411; R^2 = .591; N = 17			
Government success in controlling corruption			
Optimism for the future	1.036****	.206	5.04
Informal market (Heritage Foundation)	−23.952***	8.401	−2.85
Constant	30.822	19.826	1.55
RMSE = 9.145; R^2 = .702; N = 17			

*p < .10; **p < .05; ***p < .01; ****p < .0001

Endogenous variables in **bold**; endogenous dependent variables in ***bold italics***.

Exogenous variables: Trust in justice, quality of life next year.

Growth rate in gross domestic product for the year taken from Penn World Tables from 1996–2000 and from http://www.dfat.gov.au/geo/fs/roum.pdf for 2001–3. Informal market estimate and wage and price controls taken from Heritage Foundation, http://www.heritage.org/research/features/index/downloads/PastScores.xls.

TABLE A5-5. *Satisfaction with Democracy in Romania: Ordered Probit*

Independent Variable	Coefficient	Std. Error	t Ratio
Quality of life next year	.086**	.047	1.85
State of national economy in three years	.246****	.045	5.49
Life satisfaction	.187****	.054	3.44
Wealth (can afford consumer goods)	−.022	.012	−1.75
Performance of government on quality of life	.249***	.104	2.44
Performance of government in enhancing public safety	.364***	.124	2.94
Performance of government in reducing corruption	.238****	.049	4.89
Romania needs a strong leader	−.112***	.043	−2.62
State should control media and political parties	−.043**	.025	−1.75
Supporter of PSD (former Communist party)	.140****	.028	4.90
Age	−.003*	.002	−1.44
Made "extra" payments when visiting doctor	−.108*	−.080	−1.35
Made "extra" payments to court	−.324*	.200	−1.62
Made "extra" payments to city officials	−.030	.225	−.13
Made "extra" payments to county officials	1.804	.797	1.36
Made "extra" payments to police	−.189	.259	−.73
Made "extra" payments to bank	−.021	.399	−.53
Have any connections to rely upon+	.069**	.034	2.07
Have connections to rely upon for medical treatment+	.102	.070	1.46
Have any connections to rely upon in court/lawyer+	.116	.100	1.16
Have any connections to rely upon at city hall+	.116	.078	1.46
Have any connections to rely upon dealing with county+	.091	.131	.69
Have any connections to rely upon for police problem+	.181**	.078	2.06
Have any connections to rely upon for bank loan+	.198**	.103	1.93
Have any connections to rely upon for finding job+	.157*	.102	1.54
Have any connections to rely upon in business world+	.013	.121	.11
Have any connections to rely upon in foreign country	−.249**	.099	−2.51

*p < .10; **p < .05; ***p < .01; ****p < .0001
−2*Log Likelihood Ratio = 2560.94; N = 1082
Coefficients for variables other than "connections" are for "any connections." Cut points omitted.
+ Two-tailed test of significance (all other tests one-tailed).

TABLE A5-6. *Satisfaction with Market Economy in Romania: Ordered Probit*

Independent Variable	Coefficient	Standard Error	t Ratio
Quality of life next year	.125***	.045	2.79
Satisfaction with income	.085**	.051	1.68
Life satisfaction	.108**	.058	1.87
Wealth (can afford consumer goods)	−.020	.013	−1.56
Performance of government on quality of life	.424***	.103	4.10
Performance of government in enhancing public safety	.188*	.124	1.52
Performance of government in reducing corruption	.254****	.048	5.33
Most businesspeople are corrupt	−.086**	.04	−2.13
Trust in private firms	.178****	.036	5.01
Age	.001	.002	.69
Made "extra" payments when visiting doctor	−.069	.078	−.89
Made "extra" payments to court	.068	.177	.39
Made "extra" payments to city officials	.249	.206	1.21
Made "extra" payments to county officials	.134	.804	.17
Made "extra" payments to police	−.226	.277	−.82
Made "extra" payments to bank	−.090	.399	−.23
Have any connections to rely upon	−.044*	.034	−1.30
Have connections to rely upon for medical treatment	.006	.071	.09
Have any connections to rely upon in court/lawyer	−.106	.102	−1.03
Have any connections to rely upon at city hall	−.051	.081	−.63
Have any connections to rely upon dealing with county	−.151	.139	−1.08
Have any connections to rely upon for police problem	−.047	.088	−.05
Have any connections to rely upon for bank loan	−.129	.105	−1.22
Have any connections to rely upon for finding job	−.132	.102	−1.29
Have any connections to rely upon in business world	.185	.805	.23
Have any connections to rely upon in foreign country	−.351***	.102	−3.45

*p < .10; **p < .05; ***p < .01; ****p < .0001
−2*Log Likelihood Ratio = 2462.92; N = 1086
Coefficients for variables other than "connections" are for "any connections." Cut points omitted.

TABLE A5-7. *Trust in Government Scale in Romania: Regression Analysis*

Independent Variable	Coefficient	Std. Error	t Ratio
Generalized trust	.213****	.048	4.41
Direction of country right or wrong	.237***	.051	4.65
Inequality change	−.097**	.035	2.78
Wealth (can afford consumer goods)	.000	.007	.02
Performance of government on quality of life	.103*	.065	1.58
Performance of government in enhancing public safety	.588****	.080	7.37
Performance of government in reducing corruption	.231****	.032	7.14
Supporter of PSD (reformed Communist party now in power)	.237****	.019	12.73
State should control media and political parties	−.031**	.017	−1.89
Live in Bucharest (capital)	−.284****	.069	−4.14
Frequency attendance at religious services	.027*	.018	1.50
Frequency of contact with officials	.049***	.019	2.57
Made "extra" payments when visiting doctor	.025	.055	.45
Made "extra" payments to court	−.049	.136	−.36
Made "extra" payments to city officials	.245	.144	1.70
Made "extra" payments to county officials	−.174	.364	−.48
Made "extra" payments to police	−.051	.176	−.29
Made "extra" payments to bank	.053	.239	.22
Have any connections to rely upon	−.00003	.176	−.29
Have connections to rely upon for medical treatment	−.002	.048	−.04
Have any connections to rely upon in court/lawyer	.046	.068	.69
Have any connections to rely upon at city hall	.053	.057	.92
Have any connections to rely upon dealing with county	.005	.094	.05
Have any connections to rely upon for police problem	.027	.060	.45
Have any connections to rely upon for bank loan	.008	.073	.12
Have any connections to rely upon for finding job	−.119**	.067	−1.79
Have any connections to rely upon in business world	−.046	.082	−.56
Have any connections to rely upon in foreign country	−.158**	.068	−2.30

*p < .10; **p < .05; ***p < .01; ****p < .0001
R^2 = .481; RMSE = .708; N = 1052
Coefficients for variables other than "connections" are for "any connections."

TABLE A6-1. *Rankings on Transition Indicators for Estonia and Slovakia*

Measure	Estonia			Slovakia			# Ranked Transition	# Ranked Total
	Value	Transition Rank	Total Rank	Value	Transition Rank	Total Rank		
TI Corruption Index 2004	4.0	1	31/33	2.5	6	57/58	27	146
TI Corruption Index 2005	6.4	1	27	4.3	5	47/50	27	160
Change in Corruption TI 1998–2004	−1.7	4	33/35	−1.4	2	20/23	11	85
Change in Corruption 1996–2004 World Bank	.79	2	6	−.09	14	83	26	151
Trust	.22	12/13	62/68	.23	15/16	58/61	21	94
Shadow economy share*	–	–	–	.189	1	83	21	151
Change in share of shadow economy 1989–2000*	–	–	–	.12	5	–	18	–
Gini index (WIDER) 1999*	.401	12	36	.249	1	1	16	60
Gini index (Dutta/Mishra)*	.376	15	–	.262	4	–	22	–
Change in Gini index (WIDER) 1989–1999*	1.585	13	33	1.245	4	28/29	21	44
Change in Gini index (Rosser/Rosser/Ahmed)*	.127	14	–	0	1	–	16	–
Courts not fair (BEEPS 2002)*	.276	1	–	.347	7	–	26	–
Rule of law (nations in transition) 2004*	2.13	3	–	2.63	5/6	–	27	–
Democratization (nations in transition) 2004*	1.94	6	–	1.81	3/4	–	27	–
GDP per capita Penn World Tables 2000	10873	5	40	12619	3	36	23	136
GDP growth 1975–2003 UNDP	.4	3	54/56	.5	2	53	14	76
UN Human Development Index (1990)	.812	6	37	.831	3	31	18	82
Uneven economic development (Failed States)*	5	3	20/27	6.5	13	47/48	27	146
Failed States Index*	51	7	111	49.9	6	112	27	146
Internal conflicts (ICRG)	11.5	1/4	4/17	11	5/8	4/17	20	154
Ethnic tensions (ICRG)	2.5	19	118/125	3.5	13/14	87/97	20	141

*Low values indicate better performance.

Rankings based upon number of transition countries rated. Multiple rankings indicate countries tied.

– Data not available or only transition countries ranked.

TABLE A6-2. *Perceptions of the Consequences of Corruption: World Bank Corruption Diagnostic Surveys of the Romanian and Slovakian Publics and Elites Proportion Naming Each Consequence as First or Second Most Important*

| Consequence | Romania | | Slovakia | | |
	Public	Entrepreneurs	Public	Entrepreneurs	Officials
Increase inequality	.53	.37	.37	.31	.43
Lowers income	.53	.41	.20	.22	.25
Infringes on human rights	.17	.07	.17	.20	.35
Contributes to dishonesty	.11	.14	.15	.32	.36
Leads to increased crime	.12	.09	.15	.28	.32
Contributes to moral decline	.15	.23	.38	.20	.32
Hurts transition	.05	.09	.25	.22	.25
Lose confidence in one's own abilities	NA	NA	.27	.31	.27
Hurts private enterprise	.04	.18	.09	.21	.20
Leads to loss of foreign investment	.12	.26	.29	.38	.27
Endangers security of state	.18	.14	.20	.10	.31

TABLE A6-3. *Probit Analysis of Perceptions of How Corruption Increases Economic Inequality: World Bank Corruption Diagnostic Survey of the Slovakian Public*

Variable	Coefficient	Std. Error	MLE/SE	Effect
Corruption causes crime	−1.273****	.111	−11.47	−.376
Corruption causes human rights violations	−1.469****	.182	−8.08	−.356
Corruption hurts development of private sector	−.484***	.163	−2.96	−.133
Corruption hurts transition	−1.124****	.206	−5.45	−.279
Must bribe courts because courts not fair	−.040	.041	−.99	−.046
Bribe part of everyday life	−.009	.047	−.20	−.008
Social class	.017	.038	.43	.033
Constant	.427*	.253	1.68	

*p < .10; **p < .05; ***p < .01; ****p < .0001
Estimated R^2 = .520; −2*Log Likelihood Ratio = 912.178; N = 903
Percent predicted correctly: 75.4 (model); 62.1 (null)

TABLE A6-4. *Probit Analysis of Perceptions of How Corruption Increases Economic Inequality: World Bank Corruption Diagnostic Survey of the Romanian Entrepreneurs*

Variable	Coefficient	Std. Error	MLE/SE	Effect
Corruption is abuse of position	.264*	.163	1.62	.080
Corruption leads investors to lose confidence in Romania	−.562***	.190	−2.96	−.165
Corruption leads to moral decline in society	−.969****	.206	−4.71	−.275
Corruption slows development of private sector	−1.210****	.243	−4.97	−.320
Competitors don't pay fair share of taxes	.096**	.047	2.03	.117
Low pay major cause of corruption	.286**	.161	1.77	.088
Government has greatest responsibility for fighting corruption	.982***	.397	2.48	.307
Political instability hinders my company	.188**	.110	1.71	.212
Member business association	−.347**	.187	−1.85	−.103
Constant	−1.120*	.468	−2.39	

*p < .10; **p < .05; ***p < .01; ****p < .0001
Estimated R^2 = .422; −2*Log Likelihood Ratio = 331.66; N = 309
Percent predicted correctly: 71.2 (model); 63.8 (null)

TABLE A6-5. *Probit Analysis of Perceptions of How Corruption Increases Economic Inequality: World Bank Corruption Diagnostic Survey of Slovakian Entrepreneurs*

Variable	Coefficient	Std. Error	MLE/SE	Effect
Corruption is abuse of position	−.464	.222	−2.09	−.099
Corruption causes human rights violations	−2.088****	.599	−3.49	−.261
Corruption hurts transition	−1.098****	.322	−3.41	−.195
Corruption hurts development of private sector	−.792***	.281	−2.82	−.148
Corruption caused by ordinary citizens	.485**	.275	1.76	.111
Deputies really want to solve corruption	−.204*	.144	−1.42	−.127
Gift payments obstacle to business development	.917****	.231	3.98	.210
Income change in business from 1998 to 1999	−.007***	.003	−2.36	−.392
Constant	−1.120*	.468	−2.39	

*p < .10; **p < .05; ***p < .01; ****p < .0001
Estimated R^2 = .723; −2*Log Likelihood Ratio = 186.241; N = 244
Percent predicted correctly: 81.2 (model); 78.3 (null)

TABLE A6-6. *Probit Analysis of Perceptions of How Corruption Increases Economic Inequality: World Bank Corruption Diagnostic Survey of Slovakian Officials*

Variable	Coefficient	Std. Error	MLE/SE	Effect
Corruption is abuse of position	.298**	.176	−1.69	−.088
Corruption causes human rights violations	−1.202****	.275	−4.38	−.286
Corruption causes increase in crime	−1.235****	.208	−5.94	−.318
Corruption endangers security of state	−1.075***	.334	−3.22	−.282
Corruption hurts transition	−1.047****	.242	−4.33	−.286
Corruption leads foreign investors to lose confidence	−.742****	.203	−3.67	−.213
Corruption caused by weak legal system	−.200	.270	−.74	−.058
Corruption increased over past three years	.010	.089	.11	.012
Is there corruption in education system	.053	.113	.05	.031
Education	−.354**	.158	−2.23	−.211
Constant	2.154**	.702	3.07	

*p < .10; **p < .05; ***p < .01; ****p < .0001
Estimated R² = .444; −2*Log Likelihood Ratio = 285.154; N = 271
Percent predicted correctly: 72.7 (model); 57.2 (null)

TABLE A6-7. *Ordered Probit Analysis of Trust in Government: World Bank Corruption Diagnostic Survey of Slovakian Entrepreneurs*

Variable	Coefficient	Std. Error	MLE/SE	Effect
Corruption causes inequality	.070	.201	.035	.010
Corruption increased in past three years	−.236**	.114	−2.07	−.065
Parliament is corrupt	−.282***	.084	−3.27	−.157
Bureaucracy obstacle to business development	−.227**	.098	−2.32	−.117
Clientelism obstacle to business development	−.010	.088	−.01	−.006
Infrastructure obstacle to business development	−.147**	.075	−1.96	−.085
Quality of services traffic police	.188***	.077	2.44	.103
Quality of services energy	.161**	.089	1.82	.094

Cut points not reported. Effects are average changes in probabilities across the five categories of trust in government. The effects represent the changes from each value to *the next higher value.*
*p < .10; **p < .05; ***p < .01; ****p < .0001
Estimated R² = .105; −2*Log Likelihood Ratio = 487.604; N = 202

TABLE A6-8. *Ordered Probit Analysis of Trust in Government: World Bank Corruption Diagnostic Survey of Slovakian Officials*

Variable	Coefficient	Std. Error	MLE/SE	Effect
Corruption causes inequality	.226	.195	1.16	.033
Corruption increased in past three years	−.271***	.100	−2.70	−.151
Corruption caused by weak court	−.039	.305	−.13	−.006
Ministries are corrupt	−.238**	.138	−1.72	−.068
Education system is corrupt	−.022	.126	−.17	−.006
Traffic courts are corrupt	−.032	.128	−.25	−.009
Health system is corrupt	−.172*	.131	−1.32	−.045
Central administration takes bribes for influencing decisions	−.266**	.137	−1.94	−.139
Embezzlement in central administration	−.252**	.137	−1.83	−.068
Offered small gift in past two years	−.054	−.120	−.45	−.067
Gift payments for services common	−.333*	.232	−1.44	−.050
Central administration: poor quality	−.013	.195	−1.16	−.008
Social class	−.045	.110	−.41	−.026

Cut points not reported. Effects are average changes in probabilities across the five categories of trust in government. The effects represent the changes from each value to *the next higher value.*
$^*p < .10; ^{**}p < .05; ^{***}p < .01; ^{****}p < .0001$
Estimated $R^2 = .151$; −2*Log Likelihood Ratio = 313.386; N = 141

TABLE A7-1. *Ordered Probit Analysis of Corruption Increasing Since Period of One-Party Rule: 2002 Afrobarometer in Mali*

Variable	Coefficient	Std. Error	MLE/SE	Effect
Equal treatment for all: better now than under military	−.120***	.039	−3.10	−.091
Government policies hurt or help most people	−.084**	.037	−2.24	−.063
President favors own region in providing services	.080**	.045	1.76	.045
Electricity difficult to get because of high cost	.393****	.097	4.05	.074
Elected leaders corrupt	.162***	.055	2.96	.089
Police corrupt	.230***	.079	2.91	.125
Civil servants corrupt	.120**	.061	1.97	.066
Businesspeople corrupt	.066	.073	.91	.037
Teachers corrupt	−.023	.043	−.55	−.013
Customs officers corrupt	−.109	.084	−1.30	−.063
Bribery is rare among public officials	−.086**	.047	−1.82	−.048
Need to bribe to get services entitled to	−.044	.049	−.89	−.025
Can get cash through illicit sources	.301***	.094	3.22	.056
How often Malians get services without paying	.095**	.037	2.02	.054
Trust courts	.036	.039	.92	.020
Generalized trust	.024	.133	.18	.005

Cut points not reported. Effects are average changes in probabilities across the five categories of trust in government. The effects represent the changes from each value to *the next higher value.*
*p < .10; **p < .05; ***p < .01; ****p < .0001
Estimated R² = .100; −2*Log Likelihood Ratio = 1512.49; N = 618

TABLE A7-2. *Ordered Probit Analysis of Limiting Incomes of the Wealthy: 2002 Afrobarometer in Mali*

Variable	Coefficient	Std. Error	MLE/SE	Effect
Government manages reducing income gap well	−.077**	.037	−2.06	−.035
Equal treatment for all: better now than under military	−.047*	.033	−1.43	−.029
Important education provided free for everyone	.162***	.052	3.14	.075
Individuals/community should own land	.077***	.032	2.42	.047
Government/people responsible for economy	.081****	.024	3.39	.049
Bribery is rare among public officials	−.069**	.041	−1.70	.032
Need to bribe to get services entitled to	−.044	.042	−1.05	−.020
Government handles corruption well	−.090**	.038	−2.34	−.042
Teachers are corrupt	−.013	.037	−.35	−.006
Elected leaders corrupt	.020	.049	.42	.009
Police corrupt	.064	.055	.98	.029
Civil servants corrupt	.027	.053	.50	.012
Foreign businesspeople corrupt	−.119	.056	−2.10	−.035
How often do Malians evade taxes	−.060	.054	−1.11	−.028
How often Malians get services without paying	.151***	.056	2.68	.069
Trust courts	.011	.035	.32	.005
Trust members of other tribes	−.105***	.036	2.91	−.049
How safe walking alone	−.066**	.030	−2.19	−.041
Self, family member, or friend attacked in year	.068	.082	.84	.010
How satisfied with life expectations next year	−.027	.036	−.76	−.017

Cut points not reported. Effects are average changes in probabilities across the five categories of trust in government. The effects represent the changes from each value to *the next higher value*.
*p < .10; **p < .05; ***p < .01; ****p < .0001
Estimated R² = .050; −2*Log Likelihood Ratio = 2153.83; N = 842

TABLE A7-3. *Selected Institutional and Demographic Comparisons: Sweden, Singapore, and Hong Kong*

Indicator	Mean	Sweden	Singapore	Hong Kong
UNDP Human Development 1975	.600	.864	.761	.725
UNDP Human Development 1995	.680	.958	.882	.861
GDP per capita 1989 (PennWorld Tables)	6022.92	17717.14	13730.89	17389.74
GDP per capita 2000 (PennWorld Tables)	9520.86	24628.44	28643.59	27892.50
Openness of economy 1989 (PennWorld Tables)	69.09	57.01	291.63	182.67
Openness of economy 2000 (PennWorld Tables)	87.36	91.15	–	309.58
Overall risk rating (ICRG)	70.35	87.8	87.8	83.5
Democratic accountability (ICRG)	4.02	6.0	2.0	2.5
Real GDP growth (ICRG)	8.67	8.5	9.0	9.0
Ethnic tensions (ICRG)	4.02	5.0	6.0	5.0
Judicial independence (freetheworld.com)	6.27	8.68	7.35	7.68
Legal/property rights (freetheworld.com)	5.84	9.02	8.53	7.23
Impartial courts (freetheworld.com)	5.90	8.35	7.68	8.85
Tariffs (freetheworld.com)	7.20	9.25	9.94	9.93
Country is corrupt (Gallup Millennium 2000)	.39	.11	.01	.07
Country run by will of the people (Gallup Millennium 2000)	.35	.40	.61	.40
Hidden trade barriers (World Economic Forum)	4.53	6.3	6.3	5.8
Bureaucratic red tape (World Economic Forum)	2.73	2.4	2.3	2.3
Effective lawmaking (World Economic Forum)	3.43	5.0	6.0	3.6
Ethical firms (World Economic Forum)	4.35	6.1	5.9	5.1
Charitable involvement (World Economic Forum)	4.53	3.9	5.4	5.5

Measures come from the United Nations Human Development Program, the Penn World Tables, Free the World (http:www.freetheworld.com), the Gallup Millennium Survey (2000), the World Economic Forum's Executive Opinion Survey (2004); and the InterCountry Risk Group (2005). See Chapter 3 for the specific citations.

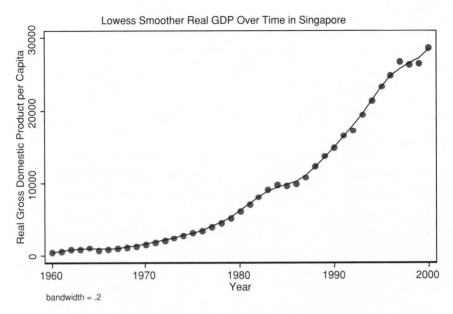

bandwidth = .2

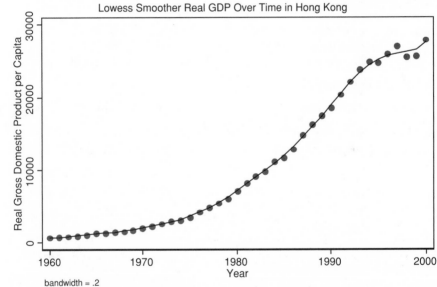

bandwidth = .2

Data from Penn World Tables.

FIGURE A7-1. Lowess Plots for Real GDP Per Capita Over Time: Singapore and Hong Kong.

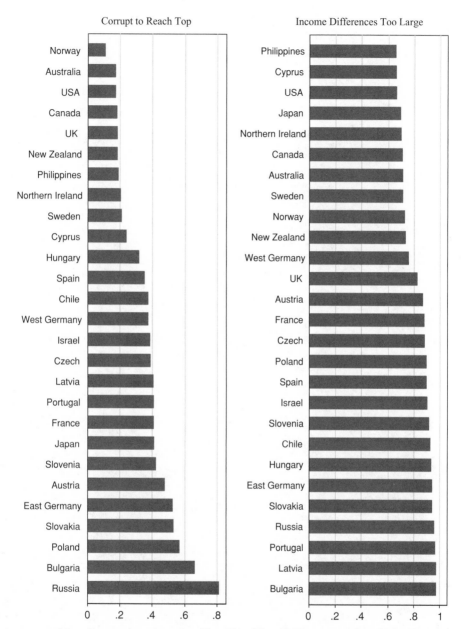

FIGURE A8-1. Proportions Agreeing That You Must Be Corrupt to Reach the Top and Income Differences Are Too Large, 1999 ISSP.

References

Abramo, Claudio Weber. 2005. "How Far Go Perceptions?" Brasilia: Transparencia-Brasil, at http://www.transparencia.org.br/docs/HowFar.pdf, accessed October 31, 2006.

Adevarul. 2003. "Feeling the Smell of the Money, Rolls-Royce Phantom Enters to East Europe through Romania," November 19: 2.

Adsera, Alicia, Carles Boix, and Mark Payne. 2000. "Are You Being Served? Political Accountability and Quality of Government." Washington: Inter-American Development Bank Research Department Working Paper No. 438.

Ahmed, Ehsan, J. Barkley Rosser, Jr., and Marina V. Rosser. 2004. "Income Inequality, Corruption, and the Non-Observed Economy: A Global Perspective," at http://cob.jmu.edu/rosserjb/NOE.Inequality.Global.doc, accessed January 5, 2005.

Alesina, Alberto, and George-Marios Angeletos. 2004. "Corruption, Inequality, and Fairness," at http://post.economics.harvard.edu/faculty/alesina/papers/corruptionAug04.pdf, accessed January 5, 2004.

Alesina, Alberto, Arnaud Devleeschauwer, William Easterly, Sergio Kurlat, and Romain Wacziarg. 2003. "Fractionalization," *Journal of Economic Growth*, 8: 155–94.

Almond, Gabriel, and Sidney Verba. 1963. *The Civic Culture*. Princeton: Princeton University Press.

Anderson, Christopher, Andre Blais, Shaun Bowler, Todd Donovan, and Ola Listhaug. 2005. *Losers' Consent: Elections and Democratic Legitimacy*. New York: Oxford University Press.

Anderson, James. 2000. *Corruption in Slovakia: Results of Diagnostic Surveys.* Washington: World Bank, at http://siteresources.worldbank.org/INTWBIGOVANTCOR/Resources/slovrep44.pdf.

Anderson, James, Bogdan Cosmaciuc, Phyllis Dininio, Bert Spector, and Pablo Zoido-Lobaton. 2001. *Diagnostic Surveys of Corruption in Romania*. Washington, DC: World Bank, at http://www1.worldbank.org/publicsector/anticorrupt/RomEnglish.pdf.

Andvig, Jens Chr. n.d. "Corruption: A Review of Contemporary Research." Oslo: Norwegian Institute of International Affairs.

Asian Barometer. 2004. *"Sampling Procedures of East Asia Barometer Project."* Tapei: National Taiwan University.

Associated Press. 2007. "Afghan Anticorruption Chief Sold Heroin in Las Vegas in '87," *New York Times*, Washington edition (March 10): A6.

AVERT. 2006. "HIV and AIDS in Africa," at http://www.avert.org/aafrica.htm, accessed December 31, 2006.

Azfar, Omar. 2005. "Corruption and Crime." In Transparency International, *Global Corruption Report*. Berlin: Transparency International.

Azfar, Omar, and Tugrul Gurgur. 2005. "Government Effectiveness, Crime Rates and Crime Reporting," IRIS Center and Department of Economics, University of Maryland–College Park, at papers.ssrn.com/sol3/Jeljour_results.cfm?Network= no&SortOrder=ab_approval_date&form_name=journalB, accessed January 18, 2007.

Badescu, Gabriel. 1999. "Miza Politica a încrederii" ("The Political Consequences of Trust"), *Sociologie româneasca*, 2: 97–122.

_____. 2003. "Social Trust and Democratization in the Post-Communist Societies." In Gabriel Badescu and Eric M. Uslaner, eds., *Social Capital and the Transition to Democracy*. London: Routledge.

Badescu, Gabriel, Paul Sum, and Eric M. Uslaner. 2004. "Civil Society Development and Democratic Values in Romania and Moldova," *Eastern European Politics and Society*, 18: 316–41.

Badescu, Gabriel, and Eric M. Uslaner, eds. 2003. *Social Capital and the Democratic Transition*. London: Routledge.

Banfield, Edward. 1958. *The Moral Basis of a Backward Society*. New York: Free Press.

Banfield, Edward C., and James Q. Wilson. 1966. *City Politics*. New York: Vintage.

Bellver, Ana, and Daniel Kaufmann. 2005. "'Transparenting Transparency' Initial Empirics and Policy Applications." Washington, DC: World Bank, at http://www.worldbank.org/wbi/governance/pdf/Transparenting_Transparency171005.pdf.

Bendor, Jonathan, and Piotr Swistak. 1997. "The Evolutionary Stability of Cooperation," *American Political Science Review*, 91: 290–307.

Bennett, John, and Saul Estrin. 2005. "Corruptibility, Transparency, and (De-) Centralization of the Bureaucracy," at http://www.york.ac.uk/depts/econ/seminars/papers/bennett_paper.pdf.

Bertelsmann Stiftung, ed. 2006. *Bertelsmann Transformation Index 2006*. Gütersloh, Germany: Bertelsmann Siftung Verlag.

Boix, Carles, and Daniel N. Posner. 1998. "Social Capital: Explaining Its Origins and Effects on Government Performance," *British Journal of Political Science*, 28: 686–93.

Boylan, Richard T., and Cheryl X. Long. 2001. "A Survey of State House Reporters' Perception of Public Corruption." Unpublished manuscript, Department of Economics, Washington University in St. Louis.

Bratton, Michael, Robert Mattes, and E. Gyimah-Boadi. 2005. *Public Opinion, Democracy, and Market Reform in Africa*. Cambridge: Cambridge University Press.

Brehm, John, and Wendy Rahn. 1997. "Individual Level Evidence for the Causes and Consequences of Social Capital," *American Journal of Political Science*, 41: 888–1023.

Brubaker, Rogers, Margit Feischmidt, Jon Fox, and Liana Grancea. 2006. *Nationalist Politics and Everyday Ethnicity in a Transylvania Town*. Princeton, NJ: Princeton University Press.

Brunetti, Aymo, and Beatrice Weder. 2003. "A Free Press Is Bad News for Corruption," *Journal of Public Economics*, 87: 1801–24.

Bryce, James. 1916. *The American Commonwealth*. Vol. 2. Rev. ed. New York: Macmillan.

Campos, Jose Edgardo, and Hilton L. Root. 1996. *The Key to the Asian Miracle: Making Shared Growth Credible*. Washington, DC: Brookings Institution.

Caro, Robert A. 1975. *The Power Broker: Robert Moses and the Fall of New York*. New York: Vintage Books.

Chang, Eric C. C., and Miriam A. Golden. 2004. "Does Corruption Pay? The Survival of Politicians Charged with Malfeasance in the Postwar Italian Chamber of Deputies." Presented at the Meeting on Political Accountability, Waseda University, Japan, October, at http://www.msu.edu/~echang/Research/wasedapaper.pdf.

Citrin, Jack. 1974. "Comment: The Political Relevance of Trust in Government," *American Political Science Review*, 68 (September): 973–88.

Clarno, Andrew, and Toyin Falola. 1998. "Patriarchy, Patronage, and Power: Corruption in Nigeria." In John Mukum Mbaku, ed., *Corruption and the Crisis of Institutional Reforms in Africa*. Lewiston, New York: Edward Mellen Press.

Commager, Henry Steele. 1950. *The American Mind*. New Haven: Yale University Press.

Commission of the European Communities. 2006. *Monitoring Report on the State of Preparedness for EU Membership of Bulgaria and Romania*, available at http://ec.europa.eu/enlargement/pdf/key_documents/2006/sept/report_bg_ro_2006_en.pdf

Constable, Pamela. 1999. "India's Democracy in Uncertain Health," *The Washington Post* (April 21): A17, A19.

Cornwell, Elmer E., Jr. 1964. "Bosses, Machines, and Ethnic Groups," *Annals of the American Academy of Political and Social Sciences*, 353: 27–39.

Coulloudon, Virginie. 2002. "Russia's Distorted Anticorruption Campaign." In Stephen Kotkin and Andras Sajo, eds., *Political Corruption in Transition: A Skeptic's Handbook*. Budapest: CEU Press.

Cowell, Alan. 2006. "An Exile Sees Graft as a Piece of Kenya's Social Puzzle," *New York Times* (March 18): A4.

Culic, Irina, Istvan Horvath, and Cristina Rat. 2000. "Ethnobarometer." In Lucian Nastasa and Levente Salat, eds., *Interethnic Relations in Post-Communist Romania*. Cluj-Napoca, Romania: Ethnocultural Diversity Resource Center.

Dahl, Robert A. 1971. *Polyarchy: Participation and Opposition*. New Haven, CT: Yale University Press.

Deininger, Klaus, and Lyn Squire. 1996. "A New Data Set: Measuring Economic Income Inequality," *World Bank Economic Review*, 10: 565–92.

Delhy, Jan, and Kenneth Newton. 2004. "Social Trust: Global Pattern or Nordic Exceptionalism?" Berlin: Wissenschatszentrum Berlin Fur Sozialforschung Discussion Paper.

della Porta, Dontella, and Alberto Vannucci. 1999. *Corrupt Exchanges: Actors, Resources, and Mechanisms of Political Corruption*. New York: Aldine de Gruyter.

deMello, Luiz, and Matias Barenstein. 2002. "Fiscal Decentralization and Governance: A Cross-Country Analysis." In George T. Abed and Sanjeev Gupta, eds., *Corruption and Economic Performance*. Washington, DC: International Monetary Fund.

DiFrancesco, Wayne, and Zvi Gitelman. 1984. "Soviet Political Culture and 'Covert Participation' in Policy Implementation," *American Political Science Review*, 78: 603–21.

Dike, Victor E. 2005. "Corruption in Nigeria: A New Paradigm for Effective Control," *Africa Economic Analysis* (December 21), at http://www.africaeconomicanalysis. org/articles/gen/corruptiondikehtm.html, accessed January 1, 2007.

DiTella, Rafael, and Robert MacCulloch. 2003. "Why Doesn't Capitalism Flow to Poor Countries?" Unpublished paper, Harvard Business School.

Djankov, Simeon, Ira Lieberman, Joyita Mukherjee, and Tatiana Nenova. 2003. "Going Informal: Benefits and Costs." In Boyan Belev, ed., *The Informal Economy in the EU Accession Countries*. Sofia, Bulgaria: Center for the Study of Democracy.

Downs, Anthony. 1957. *An Economic Theory of Democracy*. New York: Harper and Row.

Dreher, Axel, and Friedrich Schneider. 2006. "Corruption and the Shadow Economy: An Empirical Analysis." Presented at the Annual Meeting of the Public Choice Society, New Orleans, March/April.

Dugger, Celia W. 2005. "Where a Cuddle with Your Baby Requires a Bribe," *New York Times*, Washington edition (August 30): A1, A8.

Dutta, Indiral, and Ajit Mishra. 2005. "Inequality, Corruption and Competition in the Presence of Market Imperfections." Unpublished manuscript, UNU-WIDER, Helsinki, Finland.

The Economist. 1987. "Whatever Happened?" (September 12): 11–12.

———. 2007. "A Blacklist to Bolster Democracy" (February 17): 50.

Edsall, Thomas B. 1983. "Democrats' Lesson: To the Loyal Belong the Spoils," *The Washington Post* (January 14): A7.

Elvander, Nils. 1979. *Scandinavian Social Democracy: Its Strength and Weakness*. Stockholm: Almqvist and Wiksell International.

Erie, Steven P. 1988. *Rainbow's End: Irish-Americans and the Dilemmas of Machine Politics, 1840–95*. Berkeley: University of California Press.

Esposito, John L., and John O. Voll. 1996. *Islam and Democracy*. Oxford: Oxford University Press.

European Commission Employment and Social Affairs. 2003. *Social Protection in the 13 Candidate Countries: A Comparative Analysis*, Luxembourg: European Commission Directorate-General for Employment and Social Affairs Unit E.2, available at http://europa.eu.int/comm/employment_social/publications/2004/ke5103649_en.pdf.

Fajnzylber, Pablo, Daniel Lederman, and Norman Loayza. 2002. "Inequality and Violent Crime," *Journal of Law and Economics*, 45 (April): 1–40.

Fan, Maureen. 2006. "Chinese Rights Activist Stands Trial After Police Detain Defense Team," *The Washington Post* (August 19): A10.

Fearon, Jeams D. 1998. "Commitment Problems and the Spread of Ethnic Conflict." In David A. Lake and Donald Rothchild, eds., *The International Spread of Ethnic Conflict*. Princeton, NJ: Princeton University Press.

Finn, Peter. 2006. "For Russians, Car Wreck Is a Case Study in Privilege," *The Washington Post* (February 13): A1, A18.

Fisman, Raymond, and Roberta Gatti. 2000. "Decentralization and Corruption: Evidence Across Countries." Washington, DC: The World Bank.

Flap, Henk, and Beate Völker. 2003. "Communist Societies, the Velvet Revolution, and Weak Ties: The Case of East Germany." In Gabriel Badescu and Eric M. Uslaner, eds., *Social Capital and the Transition to Democracy*. London: Routledge.

Flora, Peter, ed. 1986. "Growth to Limits." *The Western European Welfare States Since World War II*, v. 1. Berlin: de Gruyter.

Fombad, Charles M. 2000. "Endemic Corruption in Cameroon: Insights on Consequences and Control." In Kempe Ronald Hope, Sr., and Bornwell C. Chikulo, eds., *Corruption and Development in Africa*. New York: St. Martin's Press.

Fox, Jonathan. 2006. "World Separation of Religion and State into the 21st Century," *Comparative Political Studies*, 39: 537–69.

Friedman, Eric, Simon Johnson, Daniel Kaufmann, and Pablo Zoido-Lobaton. 2000. "Dodging the Grabbing Hand: The Determinants of Unofficial Activity in 69 Countries," *Journal of Public Economics*, 76 (2000): 459–93.

Galtung, Fredrik. 2005. "Measuring the Immeasurable: Boundaries and Functions of (Macro) Corruption Indices." In Frederik Galtung and Charles Sampford, eds., *Measuring Corruption*. London: Ashgate.

Gambetta, Diego. 1993. *The Sicilian Mafia: The Business of Private Protection*. Cambridge: Harvard University Press.

———. 2002. "Corruption: An Analytical Map." In Stephen Kotkin and Andras Sajo, eds., *Political Corruption in Transition: A Skeptic's Handbook*. Budapest: CEU Press.

Gibson, James L. 2001. "Social Networks, Civil Society, and the Prospects for Consolidating Russia's Democratic Transition," *American Journal of Political Science*, 45: 51–69.

Gilens, Martin. 1999. *Why Americans Hate Welfare*. Chicago: University of Chicago Press.

Githongo, John. 2006. "Inequality, Ethnicity, and the Fight Against Corruption in Africa: A Kenyan Perspective," *Economic Affairs*, 26: 19–23.

Glaeser, Edward L., Rafael LaPorta, Florencio Lopez-de-Silanes, and Andrei Shleifer. 2004. "Do Institutions Cause Growth?," National Bureau of Economic Research Working Paper 10568, at http://papers.nber.org/papers/w10568.pdf.

Glaeser, Edward L., Jose Scheinkman, and Andrei Shleifer. 2003. "The Injustice of Inequality," *Journal of Monetary Economics*, 50: 199–222.

Golden, Miriam A., and Eric C. C. Chang. 2001. "Competitive Corruption: Factional Conflict and Political Malfeasance in Postwar Italian Christian Democracy," *World Politics*, 53 (July): 588–622.

Goldin, Claudia. 1998. "America's Graduation from High School: The Evolution and Spread of Secondary Schooling in the Twentieth Century," *Journal of Economic History*, 58: 345–74.

Goodwin, Jason. 2000. *On Foot to the Golden Horn*. New York: Henry Holt.

Gosnell, Harold. 1968. *Machine Politics: Chicago Model*, second ed. Chicago: University of Chicago Press. Originally published in 1937.

Greenberg, Ilan. 2004. "The Not-So-Velvet Revolution," *New York Times Magazine* (May 30): 36–9.

Guest, Robert. 2003. *The Shackled Continent: Power, Corruption, and African Lives*. Washington, DC: Smithsonian Books.

Gupta, Sanjeev, Hamid R. Davoodi, and Rosa Alonso-Terme. 2002. "Does Corruption Affect Income Inequality and Poverty?" In George T. Abed and Sanjeev Gupta, eds., *Corruption and Economic Performance*. Washington, DC: International Monetary Fund.

Gupta, Sanjeev, Hamid R. Davoodi, and Erwin R. Tiongson. 2002. "Corruption and the Provision of Health Care and Education Services." In George T. Abed and Sanjeev Gupta, eds., *Corruption and Economic Performance*. Washington, DC: International Monetary Fund.

Gupta, Sanjeev, Luiz deMello, and Raju Sharan. 2002. "Corruption and Military Spending." In George T. Abed and Sanjeev Gupta, eds., *Corruption and Economic Performance*. Washington, DC: International Monetary Fund.

Gyarfasova, Olga. 2002. "A Survey of the Economic Elite's Opinions on Topical Issues Concerning the Slovak Economy." Bratislava: Institute for Public Affairs.

Gyimah-Brempong, Kwabena. 2002. "Corruption, Economic Growth, and Income Inequality in Africa," *Economics of Governance*, 3: 183–209.

Hacker, Jacob S. 2004. "Privatizing Risk without Privatizing the Welfare State: The Hidden Politics of Social Policy Entrenchment in the United States," *American Political Science Review*, 98: 243–60.

Hanousek, Jan, and Filip Palda. 2006. "Quality of Government Services and the Civic Duty to Pay Taxes in the Czech and Slovak Republics, and Other Transition Countries." In Nicholas Hayoz and Simon Hug, eds., *Trust, Institutions, and State Capacities: A Comparative Study*. Bern: Peter Lang AG, available at http://home.cerge-ei.cz/hanousek/quality4b.pdf.

Hartz, Louis. 1955. *The Liberal Tradition in America*. New York: Harcourt, Brace, and World. http://www.bsos.umd.edu/gvpt/uslaner/uslanerstgallen.pdf

Hayoz, Nicolas. 2003. "Arms'-Length Relationships, Political Trust, and Transformation in Eastern and Central Europe," *Finance and Common Good*, 13/14: 35–48.

Heclo, Hugh. 1974. *Modern Social Policies in Britain and Sweden*. New Haven, CT: Yale University Press.

Hedstrom, Peter. 2005. *Dissecting the Social: On the Principals of Analytical Sociology*. Cambridge: Cambridge University Press.

Heidenheimer, Arnold. 2002. "Perspectives on the Perception of Corruption." In Arnold Heidenheimer and Michael Johnston, eds. *Political Corruption*, third ed. New Brunswick, NJ: Transaction.

Hellman, Joel S., Geraint Jones, and Daniel Kaufmann. 2003. "Seize the State, Seize the Day: State Capture, Corruption, and Influence in Transition," *Journal of Comparative Economics*, 31: 751–73.

Holm, John D. 2000. "Curbing Corruption through Democratic Accountability: Lessons from Botswana." In Kempe Ronald Hope, Sr., and Bornwell C. Chikulo, eds., *Corruption and Development in Africa*. New York: St. Martin's Press.

Holmes, Leslie. 2006. *Rotten States?* Durham, NC: Duke University Press.

Hopkin, Jonathan. 2002. "Review Article: States, Markets and Corruption: A Review of Some Recent Literature," *Review of International Political Economy*, 9: 574–90.

Hosking, Geoffrey. 2004. "Forms of Social Solidarity in Russia and the Soviet Union." In Ivana Markova, ed., *Trust and Democratic Transition in Post-Communist Europe*. Oxford: Oxford University Press.

Howard, MarcMorje. 2002. *The Weakness of Civil Society in Post-Communist Europe*. New York: Cambridge University Press.

Hunt, Jennifer. 2004. "Trust and Bribery: The Role of the Quid Pro Quo and the Link with Crime." National Bureau of Economic Research Working Paper 10510.

———. 2006. "How Corruption Hits People When They Are Down," William Davidson Institute Working Paper No. 836, available at http://ssrn.com/abstract = 924632.

Huntington, Samuel P. 1981. *American Politics: The Promise of Disharmony*. Cambridge, MA: Belknap Press of Harvard University Press.

———. 2002. "Modernization and Corruption." In Arnold Heidenheimer and Michael Johnston, eds. *Political Corruption*, third ed. New Brunswick, NJ: Transaction.

Hutchcroft, Paul D. 2002. "The Politics of Privilege: Rents and Corruption in Asia." In Arnold Heidenheimer and Michael Johnston, eds. *Political Corruption*, third ed. New Brunswick, NJ: Transaction.

Indem. 2006. "Corruption Process in Russia: Level, Structure, Trends," at http://www.indem.ru/en/publicat/2005diag_engV.htm, accessed July 21, 2006.

Inglehart, Ronald. 1999. "Trust, Well-Being and Democracy." In Mark Warren, ed., *Democracy and Trust*. Cambridge: Cambridge University Press.

Inoguchi, Takashi, Akihiko Tanaka, Shigeto Sonoda, and Timur Dadabaev. 2004. *Human Beliefs in Striding Asia*. Tokyo: Akashi Shoten.

Ivins, William Mills. 1970. *Machine Politics and Money in Elections in New York City*. New York: Arno Press and the *New York Times*. Originally published in 1887.

Jarvis, Christopher. 2000. "The Rise and Fall of Albania's Pyramid Schemes," *Finance and Development* (International Monetary Fund), 37: 46–9.

Johnston, Michael. 2005. *Syndromes of Corruption: Wealth, Power, and Democracy*. New York: Cambridge University Press.

Josephson, Matthew. 1938. *The Politicos*. New York: Harcourt, Brace, and World.

Jowitt, Kenneth. 1974. "An Organizational Approach to the Study of Political Culture in Marxist-Leninist Systems," *American Political Science Review*, 68: 1171–91.

Kahn, Joseph. 2004. "China's 'Haves' Stir the 'Have-Nots' to Violence," *New York Times*, Washington edition (December 31): A1, A16.

————. 2005. "Legal Gadfly Bites Hard, and Beijing Slaps Him," *New York Times*, Washington edition (December 13): A1, A16.

Kaplan, Cynthia S. 1995. "Political Culture in Estonia: The Impact of Two Traditions on Political Development." In Vladimir Tismananeau, ed., *Political Culture and Civil Society in Russia and the New States of Eurasia*. Armonk, NY: M. E. Sharpe.

Karklins, Rasma. 2005. *The System Made Me Do It: Corruption in Post-Communist Societies*. Armonk, NY: M. E. Sharpe.

Kaufmann, Daniel, and Art Kraay. 2007. "On Measuring Governance: Framing Issues for Debate." *Draft Issues paper prepared for the Roundtable on Measuring Governance Hosted by the World Bank Institute and Development Economics*, The World Bank, on January 11, 2007, at http://siteresources.worldbank.org/INTWBIGOVANTCOR/Resources/1740479-1149112210081/2604389-1167941884942/On_Measuring_Governance.pdf.

Kaufmann, Daniel, Art Kraay, and Massimo Mastruzzi. 2005. "Governance Matters IV: Governance Indicators for 1996–2004." Washington, DC: World Bank, at http://www.worldbank.org/wbi/governance/pubs/govmatters4.html.

————. 2007a. "The Worldwide Governance Indicators Project: Answering the Critics." Washington, DC: World Bank, at http://siteresources.worldbank.org/INTWBIGOVANTCOR/Resources/1740479-1149112210081/2604389-1167941884942/Answering_Critics.pdf.

————. 2007b. "Growth and Governance: A Reply," *Journal of Politics*, 69: 555–62.

Kaufmann, Daniel, Judit Montoriol-Garriga, and Francesca Recanatini. 2005. "How Does Bribery Affect Public Service Delivery? Micro-evidence from Service Users and Public Officials in Peru," Washington, DC: World Bank, at http://www.worldbank.org/wbi/governance/pdf/Peru_services_Nov21.pdf.

Key, V. O. Jr. 1936. *The Techniques of Political Graft in the United States*. Chicago: University of Chicago Libraries.

Kinder, Donald R., and D. Roderick Kiewiet. 1979. "Economic Discontent and Political Behavior: The Role of Personal Grievances and Collective Economic Judgments in Congressional Voting," *American Journal of Political Science*, 23: 495–527.

King, David C., Richard J. Zeckhauser, and Mark T. Kim. 2001. "Explaining the Management Performance of U.S. States." Unpublished manuscript, John F. Kennedy School of Government, Harvard University.

King, Ronald F., with Irina Kantor, Andrei Geheorghita, and the Students of "System and Structures of Central and Eastern Europe" (Fall 2001), Faculty of Political and Administrative Sciences, Babes-Bolyai University, Cluj-Napoca, Romania. 2003. "The Rationalities of Corruption: A Focus Group Study with Middle-Sized Business Firms," *Journal of Romanian Society and Politics*, 3: 132–64.

Klitgaard, Robert. 1988. *Controlling Corruption*. Berkley: University of California Press.

Kluegel, James R., and David S. Mason. 2000a. "Market Justice in Transition." In David S. Mason and James L. Kluegel, eds., *Marketing Democracy*. Lanham, MD: Rowman and Littlefield.

_____. 2000b. "Political System Legitimacy: Representative? Fair?" In David S. Mason and James L. Kluegel, eds., *Marketing Democracy*. Lanham, MD: Rowman and Littlefield.

Knack, Stephen. 2002. "Social Capital and the Quality of Government: Evidence from the States," *American Journal of Political Science* 46 (October): 772–87.

Knack, Stephen, and Philip Keefer. 1997. "Does Social Capital Have an Economic Payoff? A Cross-Country Investigation," *Quarterly Journal of Economics*, 112: 1251–88.

Knudsen, Tim, and Bo Rothstein. 1994. "State Building in Scandinavia," *Comparative Politics*, 26: 203–20.

Kolarska-Bobinska, Lena. 2002. "The Impact of Corruption on Legitimacy of Authority in New Democracies." In Stephen Kotkin and Andras Sajo, eds., *Political Corruption in Transition: A Skeptic's Handbook*. Budapest: CEU Press.

Kolbert, Elizabeth. 2006. "The Big Sleazy: How Huey Long Took Louisiana," *The New Yorker* (June 12), at http://www.newyorker.com/printables/critics/060612crbo_books, accessed January 19, 2007.

Kolsto, Pal. 2002. "Conclusion." In Pal Kolsto, ed., *National Integration and Violent Conflict in Post-Soviet Societies*. Lanham, MD: Rowman and Littlefield.

Kong, Chiew Seen. 1998. "National Identity, Ethnicity, and National Issues." In Jon S. T. Quah, ed., *In Search of Singapore's National Values*. Singapore: Times Academic Press.

Kornai, Janos. 2000. "Hidden in an Envelope: Gratitude Payments to Medical Doctors in Hungary," at http://www.colbud.hu/honesty-trust/kornai/pub01.pdf.

Kpundeh, Sahr John. 1998. "Limiting Administrative Corruption in Sierra Leone." In John Mukum Mbaku, ed., *Corruption and the Crisis of Institutional Reforms in Africa*. Lewiston, NY: Edward Mellen Press.

_____. 2000. "Corruption and Corruption Control." In E. Gyimah-Boadi, ed., *Democratic Reform in Africa*. Boulder, CO: Lynne Rienner.

Kramer, Andrew. 2004. "He Doesn't Make Coffee, but He Controls 'Starbucks' in Russia," *New York Times*, Washington edition (October 12): C1, C4.

_____. 2006. "From Russia with Dread: American Faces a Truly Hostile Takeover Attempt at His Factory," *New York Times*, Washington edition (May 16): C1, C4.

Kramer, John M. 1977. "Political Corruption in the U.S.S.R.," *Western Political Quarterly*, 30: 213–24.

Kunicova, Jana. 2005. "Political Corruption: Another Peril of Presidentialism," at http://www.hss.caltech.edu/~jana/perilous%20presidentialism%20sep05.pdf.

Kunicova, Jan, and Susan Rose-Ackerman. 2005. "Electoral Rules and Constitutional Structures as Constraints on Corruption," *British Journal of Political Science*, 35: 573–606.

Kurer, Oskar. 2003. "Corruption: An Alternative Approach to Its Definition and Measurement," *Political Studies*, 53: 222–39.

Lambsdorff, Johann Graf. 1999. "Corruption in Empirical Research – A Review," Transparency International Working Paper, at http://www.transparency.de/working-papers.html/lambsdorff_eresearch.html, accessed March 23, 2001.

_____. 2002a. "What Nurtures Corrupt Deals? On the Role of Confidence and Transaction Costs." In Dontella della Porta and Susan Rose-Ackerman, eds., *Corrupt Exchanges*. Baden Baden, Germany: Nomos Verlag.

_____. 2002b. "How Confidence Facilitates Illegal Transactions," *American Journal of Economics and Sociology*, 61: 829–54.

_____. 2005a. "Consequences and Causes of Corruption: What Do We Know from a Cross-Section of Countries?" University of Passau, Discussion Paper V-34-05.

_____. 2005b. "The Methodology of the 2005 Corruption Perceptions Index." Transparency International and the University of Passau (Germany), at http://ww1.transparency.org/cpi/2005/dnld/methodology.pdf.

Lane, Robert E. 1959. *Political Life*. New York: Free Press.

Langer, Laura. 1999. "Measuring Income Distribution Across Space and Time in the American States," *Social Science Quarterly*, 80: 55–67.

LaPorta, Rafael, Florencio Lopez-de-Silanes, and Andrei Schleifer. In press. "What Works in Securities Laws?" *Journal of Finance*, available at http://www.afajof.org/afa/forthcoming/laporta.pdf, accessed March 2, 2006.

LaPorta, Rafael, Florencio Lopez-de-Silanes, Christian Pop-Eleches, and Andrei Schleifer. 2003. "Judicial Checks and Balances." NBER Working Paper WP9775.

LaPorta, Rafael, Florencio Lopez-de-Silanes, Andrei Schleifer, and Robert W. Vishney. 1999. "The Quality of Government," *Journal of Law, Economics, and Organization*, 15: 222–79.

Lassen, David Dreyer. 2003. "Ethnic Divisions, Trust, and the Size of the Informal Sector," at http:www.econ.ku.dk/ddl/files/ethnic%20nov03.pdf, accessed January 5, 2005.

Lauristin, Marju, and Peeter Vihalemm. 1997. "Recent Historical Developments in Estonia: Three Stages of Transition (1987–1997)." In Marju Lauristin and Peeter Vihalemm, eds., *Return to the Western World: Cultural and Political Perspectives on the Estonian Post-Communist Transition*. Tartu, Estonia: Tartu University Press.

Ledeneva, Alena. 1998. *Russia's Economy of Favours*. Cambridge: Cambridge University Press.

_____. 2004. "The Genealogy of *Krugovaya Poruka*: Forced Trust as a Feature of Russian Political Culture." In Ivana Markova, ed., *Trust and Democratic Transition in Post-Communist Europe*. Oxford: Oxford University Press.

_____. 2005. "Leadership and Corruption in Russia, 2000–2004." Working Paper 54, Centre for the Study of Economic and Social Change in Europe, University College, London.

Lederman, Daniel, Norman Loayza, and Ana Maria Menendez. 2000. "Violent Crime: Does Social Capital Matter?" Washington, DC: World Bank.

Lederman, Daniel, Norman V. Loayza, and Rodrigo R. Soares. 2005. "Accountability and Corruption: Political Institutions Matter," *Economics and Politics*, 17: 1–35.

Lee, Philip. 2003. "Had LKY Not Been Tough Then," *Straits Times* (Singapore), September 20: 27.

Lee, Rance P. L. 1981. "The Folklore of Corruption in Hong Kong," *Asian Survey*, 21: 355–68.

Leite, Carlos, and Jens Weidmann. 1999. "Does Mother Nature Corrupt? Natural Resources, Corruption, and Economic Growth?" Washington, DC: International Monetary Fund Working Paper WP/99/85.

Letki, Natalia. 2006. "Investigating the Roots of Civic Morality: Trust, Social Capital, and Institutional Performance," *Political Behavior*, 28: 305–26.

Levi, Margaret. 1998. "A State of Trust." In Margaret Levi and Valerie Braithwaite, eds., *Trust and Governance*. New York: Russell Sage Foundation.

Leys, Colin. 2002. "What Is the Problem about Corruption?" In Arnold Heidenheimer and Michael Johnston, eds. *Political Corruption*, third ed. New Brunswick, NJ: Transaction.

Lindsay, Drew. 1998. "*After a Lengthy Court Fight, There's Still No Sign of a Consensus on How to Improve Urban Schools*," at http://www.edweek.org/sreports/qc98/states/nj-n2.htm, accessed May 19, 2001.

Linz, Juan J. 1990. "The Pitfalls of Presidentialism," *Journal of Democracy*, 1: 51–69.

Lipset, Seymour Martin, and William Schneider. 1983. *The Confidence Gap: Business, Labor, and Government in the Public Mind*. New York: Free Press.

Lo, Jack M. K. 2001. "Controlling Corruption in Hong Kong: From Colony to Special Administrative Region," *Journal of Contingencies and Crisis Management*, 9: 21–8.

Lowi, Theodore J. 1964. *At the Pleasure of the Mayor*. New York: Free Press of Glencoe.

Macauley, Stewart. 1963. "Non-Contractual Relations in Business: A Preliminary Study," *American Sociological Review*, 28: 55–67.

Manion, Melanie. 2004. *Corruption by Design*. Cambridge: Harvard University Press.

Manzo, Kathleen Kennedy. 2007. "Worldwide Education Achievable, Study Says," *Education Week* (January 19), 16, at http://amacad.org/pdfs/EducatingAllChildren.pdf, accessed July 16, 2007.

Marketplace. 2005. "Ridin' on the New Delhi Gravy Train," Public Radio International (November 30): Transcribed by the author (Eric M. Uslaner) from a recording made from WAMU radio, Washington, DC.

Martin, E. M. 1936. *The Role of the Bar in Electing the Bench in Chicago*. Chicago: University of Chicago Press.

Martin, John P. 2003. "Ex-Paterson Mayor Gets 37-Month Term: His Apparent Lack of Remorse in Corruption Case Stuns Courtroom," *Star-Ledger* (April 29), at http://www.nj.com/news/ledger/index.ssf?/corruption/stories/030429sl_barnes.html.

Mateju, Petr. 1997. "Beliefs About Distributive Justice and Social Change: Czech Republic 1991–5," *Socialni Trendy/Social Trends*, Prague, Czech Republic.

Mauro, Paolo. 1995. "Corruption and Growth," *Quarterly Journal of Economics*, 110: 681–712.

———— 1997. "Why Worry About Corruption?" Washington, DC: International Monetary Fund.

_____ 1998a. "Corruption: Causes, Consequences, and Agenda for Further Research," *Finance and Development* (International Monetary Fund), March: 11–14.

_____. 1998b. "Corruption and the Composition of Government Expenditure," *Journal of Public Economics*, 69: 263–79.

_____. 2002. "The Effects of Corruption on Growth and Public Expenditure." In Arnold Heidenheimer and Michael Johnston, eds. *Political Corruption*, third ed. New Brunswick, NJ: Transaction.

_____. 2004. "The Persistence of Corruption and Slow Economic Growth," IMF Staff Papers, 51, 1. Washington, DC: International Monetary Fund.

Mayhew, David R. 1986. *Divided We Govern*. New Haven, CT: Yale University Press.

_____. 1991. *Placing Parties in American Politics*. Princeton, NJ: Princeton University Press.

Mbaku, John Mukum. 1998a. "Corruption and the Crisis of Institutional Reforms in Africa." In John Mukum Mbaku, ed., *Corruption and the Crisis of Institutional Reforms in Africa*. Lewiston, NY: Edward Mellen Press.

_____. 1998b. "Corruption as an Important Post-Independence Institution in Africa." In John Mukum Mbaku, ed., *Corruption and the Crisis of Institutional Reforms in Africa*. Lewiston, NY: Edward Mellen Press.

McCloskey, Herbert, and John Zaller. 1984. *The American Ethos: Public Attitudes toward Capitalism and Democracy*. Cambridge, MA: Harvard University Press.

McGeary, Johanna. 2001. "Death Stalks a Continent," *Time* (November 12), at http://www.time.com/time/magazine/printout/0,8816,999190,00.html, accessed December 31, 2006.

McMillan, John, and Pablo Zoido. 2004. "How to Subvert Democracy: Montesinos in Peru," *Journal of Economic Perspectives*, 18: 69–92.

Mead, Rebecca. 2005. "New York Journal: Mr. Brooklyn: Marty Markowitz – the Man, the Plan, the Arena," *The New Yorker* (April 25), at http://www.newyorker.com/fact/content/articles/050425fa_fact, accessed January 29, 2007.

Meier, Kenneth J., and Thomas M. Holbrook. 1992. "'I Seen My Opportunities and I Took 'Em': Political Corruption in the United States." *Journal of Politics*, 54 (February): 135–55.

Merton, Robert K. 1968. *Social Theory and Social Structure*, enlarged ed. Glencoe: Free Press.

Mettler, Suzanne. 2005. *Soldiers to Citizens: The G. I. Bill and the Making of the Greatest Generation*. New York: Oxford University Press.

Mikhalev, Vladimir. 2005. "Inequality and Transformation of Social Structures in Transitional Economies," Helsinki: United Nations University World Institute for Development Economics Research for Action 52.

Miller, William L., Ase B. Grodeland, and Tatayana Y. Koshechikina. 2001. *A Culture of Corruption: Coping with Government in Post-Communist Europe*. Budapest: CEU Press.

Miller, William L., Tatayana Y. Koshechikina, and Ase B. Grodeland. 2004. "Diffuse Trust or Diffuse Analysis?: The Specificity of Political Distrust in Post-Communist Europe." In Ivana Markova, ed., *Trust and Democratic Transition in Post-Communist Europe*. Oxford: Oxford University Press.

Ministry of Justice of the Republic of Estonia, Department of Criminal Policy. 2005. "Corruption in Estonia 2004: A Study of Three Target Groups." *Studies in Criminal Policy*, 2. Tallinn, Estonia.

Mollenkopf, John H. 1992. *A Phoenix in the Ashes*. Princeton, NJ: Princeton University Press.

Mueller, John. 2001. *Democracy, Capitalism, and Ralph's Pretty Good Grocery*. Princeton, NJ: Princeton University Press.

Mungiu-Pippidi, Alina. 1997. "Crime and Corruption after Communism: Breaking Free at Last: Tales of Corruption from the Postcommunist Balkans," *East European Constitutional Review*, 6, at http://www.law.nyu.edu/eecr/vol6num4/feature/breakingfree.html, accessed September 28, 2006.

―――. 2003. "Corruption or State Failure?" In Boyan Belev, ed., *The Informal Economy in the EU Accession Countries*. Sofia, Bulgaria: Center for the Study of Democracy.

Murphy, Kim. 2006. "Forging Ahead in Moscow," *Los Angeles Times* (July 10), at http://www.latimes.com/news/nationworld/la-fg-fakes19jul10,0,5893954.story?coll-la-home-headlines.

Myers, Steven Lee. 2006a. "A New Cycle of Bribes and Purges," *New York Times*, Washington edition (June 11): C5.

―――. 2006b. "Rife as Onion Domes, Moscow's Casinos Face Closing," *New York Times*, Washington edition (November 2): A3.

New York *Daily News*. 2005. "The Ugly Truth: Why We Couldn't Save the People of New Orleans" (September 5), at http://www.nydailynews.com/front/story/343324p-292991c.html.

New York Times. 2005. "Metro Briefing } New Jersey: Paterson: Former School Official Is Arrested" (September 22), at http://query.nytimes.com/gst/fullpage.html?res=9C02E5DA1730F931A1575AC0A9639C8B63.

Newton, Kenneth. 1997. "Social Capital and Democracy," *American Behavioral Scientist*, 40: 575–86.

Norgaard, Ole, and Lars Johannsen with Mette Skak and Rene Hauge Sorensen. 1996. *The Baltic States after Independence*. Cheltenham, UK: Edward Elgar.

Norwood, Christopher. 1974. *About Paterson*. New York: Harper Colophon.

Odunlami, Tayo. 2004. "Nigeria: Corruption Notebook," at http://www.globalintegrity.org/2004/country.aspx?cc=ng&act=notebook, accessed January 1, 2007.

Office of Research. 1999. "On the Take: Central and East European Attitudes Toward Corruption." Washington, DC: U.S. Department of State.

Olivier de Sardan, J. P. 1999. "A Moral Economy of Corruption in Africa?" *Journal of Modern African Studies*, 37: 25–52.

O'Neill, William L. 1986. *American High: The Years of Confidence, 1945–1986*. New York: Free Press.

Orkeny, Antal. 2000. "Trends in Perceptions of Social Inequality in Hungary, 1991–1996." In David S. Mason and James L. Kluegel, eds., *Marketing Democracy*. Lanham, MD: Rowman and Littlefield.

Orkeny, Antal, and Maria Szejelyi. 2000. "Views on Social Inequality and the Role of the State: Posttransformation Trends in Eastern and Central Europe," *Social Justice Research*, 13: 188–218.

Orwell, George. 1946. *Animal Farm*. New York: Signet Classics.

Osberg, Lars, and Timothy Smeeding. 2005. "Social Values for Equality and Preferences for State Intervention in the USA and Europe." Unpublished paper, Center for Policy Research, Maxwell School, Syracuse University.

Owsiak, Stanislaw. 2003. "The Ethics of Tax Collection," *Finance and Common Good*, 13/14: 65–77.

Packer, George. 2006. "The Megacity: Decoding the Chaos of Lagos," *The New Yorker* (November 13): 63–75.

Paldam, Martin. 1991. "The Development of the Rich Welfare State of Denmark." In Magnus Blomstrom and Patricio Meller, eds., *Diverging Paths: Comparing a Century of Scandinavian and Latin American Development*. Baltimore: Johns Hopkins University Press.

———. 2002. "The Cross-Country Pattern of Corruption: Economics, Culture and the Seesaw Dynamics," *European Journal of Political Economy*, 18: 215–40.

Panagiotou, R. A. 2001. "Estonia's Success: Prescription or Legacy?" *Communist and Post-Communist Studies*, 34: 261–77.

Persson, Torsten, Guido Talbellini, and Francesco Trebbi. 2000. *"Electoral Rules and Corruption."* Unpublished manuscript, Institute for Economic Studies, Stockholm University, Stockholm, Sweden.

Pierson, Paul. 2001. "Increasing Returns, Path Dependence, and the Study of Politics," *American Political Science Review*, 94: 251–68.

———. 2003. "Big, Slow-Moving, and . . . Invisible: Macro-Social Processes in the Study of Comparative Politics." In James Mahoney and Dietrich Rueschemeyer, eds., *Comparative Historical Analysis*. Cambridge: Cambridge University Press.

———. 2004. *Politics in Time: History, Institutions, and Social Analysis*. Princeton, NJ: Princeton University Press.

Pikety, Thomas, and Emmanuel Saez. 2003. "Income Inequality in the United States, 1913–1998," *Quarterly Journal of Economics*, 143: 1–39.

Polgreen, Lydia. 2005. "As Nigeria Tries to Fight Graft, a New Sordid Tale," *New York Times*, Washington edition (November 29): A1, A12.

Popov, Nikolai. 2006. *"To Give and Take,"* available at http://www.indem.ru/en/publicat/Popov/Give&Take.htm.

Putnam, Robert D. 1993. *Making Democracy Work: Civic Traditions in Modern Italy*. Princeton, NJ: Princeton University Press.

———. 2000. *Bowling Alone*. New York: Simon and Schuster.

Quah, Jon S. T. 1995. "Controlling Corruption in City-States: A Comparative Study of Hong Kong and Singapore," *Crime, Law, and Social Change*, 22: 391–414.

———. 1998a. "Singapore's Model of Development: Is It Transferable?" In Henry S. Rowen, ed. *Behind East Asian Growth*. London: Routledge.

———. 1998b. "National Values and Nation-Building: Defining the Problem." In Jon S. T. Quah, ed., *In Search of Singapore's National Values*. Singapore: Times Academic Press.

———. 2001a. "Combating Corruption in Singapore: What Can Be Learned?" *Journal of Contingencies and Crisis Management*, 9: 29–35.

———. 2001b. "Singapore: Meritocratic City-State." In John Funston, ed., *Government and Politics in Southeast Asia*. Singapore: Institute of Southeast Asia Studies.

———. 2004. "Best Practices for Curbing Corruption in Asia," *The Governance Brief*, 11–2004, Governance and Regional Cooperation Division, Regional and Sustainable Development Department, Singapore.

———. 2006. "Curbing Asian Corruption: An Impossible Dream?" *Current History*, 150 (April): 176–9.

Quah, Stella. 1997. "Values and Development in Asia: A Historical Illustration of the Role of the State," *International Sociology*, 10: 295–328.

Raiser, Martin, Andrew Rousso, and Franklin Steves. 2004. "Measuring Trust in Transition: Preliminary Findings from 26 Transition Economies." In Janos Kornai, Bo Rothstein, and Susan Rose-Ackerman, eds., *Creating Social Trust in Post-Socialist Transition*. New York: Palgrave Macmillan.

Raun, Toivu U. 2001. *Estonia and the Estonians*. Updated second edition. Stanford, CA: Hoover Institution Press.

Rawls, John A. 1971. *A Theory of Justice*, Cambridge: Harvard University Press.

The Record. 2001. "Fava's Big Challenge: Wanted: A New Type of Passaic County Sheriff," editorial, at http://www.bergen.com/editorials/fava200103292.htm, accessed May 19, 2001.

Rice, Tom W., and Jan Feldman. 1997. "Civic Culture and Democracy from Europe to America," *Journal of Politics*, 59: 1143–72.

Riley, Stephen P. 2000. "Western Policies and African Realities: The New Anti-Corruption Agenda." In Kempe Ronald Hope, Sr., and Bornwell C. Chikulo, eds., *Corruption and Development in Africa*. New York: St. Martin's Press.

Riordan, William. 1948. *Plunkitt of Tammany Hall*. New York: Alfred A. Knopf.

Rohter, Larry. 2006. "Brazil's President Roars Back to Win Vote," *New York Times*, Washington edition (October 30): A6.

Root, Hilton L. 1996. *Small Countries, Big Lessons: Governance and the Rise of East Asia*. Hong Kong: Oxford University Press.

Rose-Ackerman, Susan. 1978. *Corruption: A Study in Political Economy*. New York: Academic Press.

_____. 1999. *Corruption and Government: Causes, Consequences, and Reform*. New York: Cambridge University Press.

_____. 2004. "The Challenge of Poor Governance and Corruption." Copenhagen Consensus Challenge Paper, at http://www.copenhagenconsensus.com/files/filer/cc/papers/governance_and_corruption_300404_%280.7mb_version%29.pdf.

Rosenberg, Morris. 1956. "Misanthropy and Political Ideology," *American Sociological Review*, 21: 690–5.

Rosser, J. Barkley, Marina V. Rosser, and Ehsan Ahmed. 2000. "Income Inequality and the Informal Economy in Transition Countries," *Journal of Comparative Economics*, 28: 156–71.

Rothstein, Bo. 1998. *Just Institutions Matter*. Cambridge: Cambridge University Press.

_____. 2000. "Trust, Social Dilemmas, and Collective Memories: On the Rise and Decline of the Swedish Model," *Journal of Theoretical Politics*, 12: 477–99.

_____. 2007. *"Anti-Corruption – A Big Bang Theory."* Presented at the Conference on Corruption and Democracy, Centre for the Study of Democratic Institutions, University of British Columbia, Vancouver, British Columbia, June 8–9.

Rothstein, Bo, and Dietlind Stolle. 2002. "How Political Institutions Create and Destroy Social Capital: An Institutional Theory of Generalized Trust." Paper prepared for delivery at the Annual Meeting of the American Political Science Association, Boston, August–September.

Rothstein, Bo, and Jan Teorell. 2005. "What Is Quality of Government? A Theory of Impartial Institutions." Presented at the Annual Meeting of the American Political

Science Association, Washington, DC, September, available at http://www.pol.gu.se/file/Person/Rothstein/APSA-QoG-Rothstein%26Teorell.pdf.

Rothstein, Bo, and Eric M. Uslaner. 2005. "All for All: Equality, Corruption, and Social Trust," *World Politics*, 58: 41–72.

Ruhil, Anirudh V. S., and Pedro J. Camões. 2003. "What Lies Beneath: The Political Roots of State Merit Systems," *Journal of Public Administration Research and Theory*, 13: 27–42.

Rutland, Peter. 2005. "Why Is Russia Still an Authoritarian State? (Or What Would Tocqueville Say?)." Presented at the Annual Meeting of the American Political Science Association, Washngton, September.

Sachs, Jeffrey D., and Andrew M. Warner. 1997. "Natural Resource Abundance and Economic Growth," Harvard University Center for International Development, available at http://www2.cid.harvard.edu/Warner's%20Files/Natresf5.pdf.

Sampson, Steven. 2005. "Integrity Warriors: Global Morality and the Anticorruption Movement in the Balkans." In Chris Shore and Dieter Hall (eds.), *Corruption: Anthropological Perspectives*. London: Routledge. Pages from manuscript.

Sayre, Wallace S., and Herbert Kaufman. 1960. *Governing New York City*. New York: Russell Sage Foundation.

Schmemann, Serge. 2003. "In Going Legit, Some Russian Tycoons Resort to Honesty," *New York Times* (January 12), at http://www.nytimes.com/2003/01/12/weekinreview/12SCHM.html, accessed January 14, 2003.

Schneider, Friedrich. 2003. "Shadow Economies Around the World: What Do We Know?" University of Linz, Linz, Austria.

Schoenfeld, Eugen. 1978. "Image of Man: The Effect of Religion on Trust," *Review of Religious Research*, 20: 61–7.

Scott, James C. 1968. "Corruption, Machine Politics, and Political Change," *American Political Science Review*, 63: 1142–58.

———. 1972. *Comparative Political Corruption*. Englewood Cliffs, NJ: Prentice-Hall.

Seligman, Adam B. 1997. *The Problem of Trust*. Princeton, NJ: Princeton University Press.

Semjonov, Aleksei. 2002. "Estonia: Nation-Building and Integration – Political and Legal Aspects." In Pal Kolsto, ed., *National Integration and Violent Conflict in Post-Soviet Societies*. Lanham, MD: Rowman and Littlefield.

Shefter, Martin. 1985. *Political Crisis/Fiscal Crisis*. New York: Basic Books.

Sindzingre, Alice. 2002. "A Comparative Analysis of African and East Asian Corruption." In Arnold Heidenheimer and Michael Johnston, eds. *Political Corruption*, third ed. New Brunswick, NJ: Transaction.

Singer, Matthew M. 2005. "Competition and Corruption: When Do Elections Induce Parties to Look the Other Way?" Presented at the Annual Meeting of the American Political Science Association, Washngton, September.

Sitkin, Sim B., and Nancy L. Roth. 1993. "Explaining the Limited Effectiveness of Legalistic 'Remedies' for Trust/Distrust," *Organization Science*, 4: 367–92.

Smith, Daniel Jordan. 2006. *A Culture of Corruption: Everyday Deception and Popular Discontent in Nigeria*. Princeton, NJ: Princeton University Press.

Soares, Rodrigo R. 2004. "Crime Reporting as a Measure of Institutional Development," *Economic Development and Cultural Change*, 52 (July): 851–71.

Soloman, Deborah. 2005. "A Refugee Among Refugees: Questions for Andrei Codresucu," *New York Times* (September 11): 19.

Sombart, Werner. 1976. *Why Is There No Socialism in the United States?* White Plains, NY: M. E. Sharpe. Originally published in 1906.

Soroka, Stuart N., John F. Helliwell, and Richard Johnston. 2007. "Modeling and Measuring Trust." In Fiona Kay and Richard Johnston, eds., *Diversity, Social Capital, and the Welfare State.* Vancouver: University of British Columbia Press.

Soss, Joe. 2000. *Unwanted Claims: The Politics of Participation in the U.S. Welfare System.* Ann Arbor: University of Michigan Press.

Stan, Lavinia. 2003. "Fighting the Demons of the Recent Past: Prospects for Romanian Reconstruction and Development." Presented at the Conference on Southeastern Europe: Moving Forward, January 24–26, Carleton University, Ottawa, Ontario, available at http://www.carleton.ca/ces/papers/january03/stan03.pdf.

Stanley, Alessandra. 2001. "Rome Journal: Official Favors: Oil That Makes Italy Go Round," *New York Times*, Washington edition (April 20): A4.

Steffens, Lincoln. 1931. *The Autobiography of Lincoln Steffens.* New York: Literary Guild.

Stephenson, Svetlana. 2000. "Public Beliefs in the Causes of Wealth and Poverty and Legitimization of Inequalities in Russia and Estonia," *Social Justice Research*, 13: 83–100.

Stephenson, Svetlana, and Ludmila Khakhulina. 2000. "Russia: Changing Perceptions of Social Justice." In David S. Mason and James L. Kluegel, eds., *Marketing Democracy.* Lanham, MD: Rowman and Littlefield.

Stodghill, Ron. 2006. "Oil, Cash, and Corruption: How Influence Flowed Through Political Pipelines," *New York Times*, Washington edition (November 5): BU1, BU8–9.

Stoyanov, Alexander, Maragarita Pavlikianova, Andrej Nontchev, and Galja Krasteva. 2000. "Bulgaria: Political and Economic Crisis; Democratic Consolidation." In David S. Mason and James L. Kluegel, eds., *Marketing Democracy.* Lanham, MD: Rowman and Littlefield.

Svenjar, Jan. 2002. "Transition Economies: Performance and Challenges," *Journal of Economic Perspectives*, 16: 3–28.

Sztompka, Piotr. 1999. *Trust: A Sociological Theory.* Cambridge: Cambridge University Press.

Tang, Wenfang. 2005. *Public Opinion and Political Change in China.* Stanford, CA: Stanford University Press.

Tanzi, Vito. 1998. "Corruption Around the World: Causes, Consequences, Scope and Cures." *IMF Staff Papers*, 45: 559–94.

———. 2002. "Corruption Around the World: Causes, Consequences, Scope, and Cures." In George T. Abed and Sanjeev Gupta, eds., *Corruption and Economic Performance.* Washington, DC: International Monetary Fund.

Tavernise, Sabrina. 2003. "Russia Is Mostly Unmoved by the Troubles of Its Tycoons," *New York Times*, Washington edition, (November 3): A3.

Tavits, Margit. 2005. "Causes of Corruption: Testing Competing Hypotheses." Presented at the Joint Sessions of Workshops, European Consortium for Political Research, Nicosia, Cyprus, April, at http://www.nuffield.ox.ac.uk/Politics/papers/2005/Tavits%20Nuffield%20WP.pdf.

Tayler, Jeffrey. 2005. *Angry Wind.* Boston: Houghton Mifflin.

Thomas, Vinod, Yan Wang, and Xibo Fan. 2001. "Measuring Education: Gini Coefficients of Education." Policy Research Working Paper 2525, Office of the Vice President and Economic Policy and Poverty Reduction Division. Washington, DC: World Bank.

Tierney, John. 2006. "New Europe's Boomtown," *New York Times* (September 5), at http://select.nytimes.com/search/restricted/article?res=F30A13FF3D550C768CDDA 00894DE404482.

TNS EMOR. 2004. "Corruption Study in Estonia: Technical Report." Tallin, Estonia.

Tocqueville, Alexis de. 1945. *Democracy in America*, 2 vols. Translated by Henry Reeve. New York: Alfred A. Knopf. Originally published in 1840. Citations to vol. 1 are to the Vintage Books reprint, ed. Phillips Bradley.

Torgler, Benno. 2003. "Tax Morale in Central and Eastern European Countries." Presented at the Conference on Tax Evasion, Trust, and State Capabilities, St. Gallen, Switzerland, October 17–19.

Trägårdh, Lars. 2001. "Welfare State Nationalism: Sweden and the Specter of 'Europe'." In Lene Hansen and Ole Wæver, eds., *European Integration and National Identity: The Challenge of the Nordic States*. London: Routledge.

Treisman, Daniel. 1999. "Decentralization and Corruption: Why Are Federal States Perceived to Be More Corrupt?" Presented at the Annual Meeting of the American Political Science Association, September, Atlanta.

———. 2000. "The Causes of Corruption: A Cross-National Study," *Journal of Public Economics*, 76: 399–457.

Triandis, Harry C. 1995. *Individualism and Collectivism*. Boulder, CO: Westview.

Tyler, Tom R. 1990. *Why People Obey the Law*. New Haven, CT: Yale University Press.

Uslaner, Eric M. 1993. *The Decline of Comity in Congress*. Ann Arbor: University of Michigan Press.

———. 2001. "Volunteering and Social Capital: How Trust and Religion Shape Civic Participation in the United States." In Paul Dekker and Eric M. Uslaner, eds., *Social Capital and Participation in Everyday Life*. London: Routledge.

———. 2002. *The Moral Foundations of Trust*. New York: Cambridge University Press.

———. 2003. "Trust and Civic Engagement in East and West." In Gabriel Badescu and Eric M. Uslaner, eds., *Social Capital and the Transition to Democracy*. London: Routledge.

———. 2004a. "Trust and Corruption." In Johann Graf Lambsdorff, Markus Taube, and Matthias Schramm, eds., *Corruption and the New Institutional Economics*. London: Routledge.

———. 2004b. "Coping and Social Capital: The Informal Sector and the Democratic Transition." Presented at the Conference on "Unlocking Human Potential: Linking the Formal and Informal Sectors," Helsinki, Finland, September 17–18, 2004.

———. 2006a. "Tax Evasion, Trust, and the Strong Arm of the Law." In Nicholas Hayoz and Simon Hug, eds., *Trust, Institutions, and State Capacities: A Comparative Study*. Bern: Peter Lang AG, available at http://www.bsos.umd.edu/gvpt/uslaner/ uslanerstgallen.pdf.

———. 2006b. "The Civil State: Trust, Polarization, and the Quality of State Government." In Jeffrey Cohen, ed., *Public Opinion in State Politics*. Stanford, CA: Stanford University Press, available at http://www.bsos.umd.edu/gvpt/uslaner/ uslanercivilstate.pdf.

———. 2008. "Where You Stand Depends upon Where Your Grandparents Sat: The Inheritability of Generalized Trust," *Public Opinion Quarterly*, 72.

———. In press. "Trust as a Moral Value," in Dario Castiglione, Jan W. van Deth, and Guglielmo Wolleb, eds., *Handbook of Social Capital*. Oxford: Oxford University Press.

Uslaner, Eric M., and Gabriel Badescu. 2004. "Honesty, Trust, and Legal Norms in the Transition to Democracy: Why Bo Rothstein Is Better Able to Explain Sweden than Romania." In Janos Kornai, Susan Rose-Ackerman, and Bo Rothstein, eds., *Creating Social Trust: Problems of Post-Socialist Transition*. New York: Palgrave.

Uslaner, Eric M., and Mitchell Brown. 2005. "Inequality, Trust, and Civic Engagement," *American Politics Research*, 31: 868–94.

Varese, Frederico. 1997. "The Transition to the Market and Corruption in Post-Socialist Russia," *Political Studies*, 45: 579–96.

———. 2001. The Russian Mafia: Private Protection in a New Market Economy. Oxford: Oxford University Press.

Vasecka, Michal. 1999. *Civil Society and Governance in Slovakia*. Bratislava: Institute for Public Affairs. Pages refer to manuscript.

Verba, Sidney, Kay Lehman Schlozman, and Henry Brady. 1995. *Voice and Equality: Civic Voluntarism in American Politics*. Cambridge: Harvard University Press.

Verdery, Katherine. 1993. "Nationalism and National Sentiment in Post-socialist Romania," *Slavic Review*, 52: 179–203.

———. 1995. "'Caritas' and the Reconceptualization of Money in Romania," *Anthropology Today*, 11: 3–7.

Verwiebe, Roland, and Bernd Wegener. 2000. "Social Inequality and the Perceived Income Gap," *Social Justice Research*, 13: 123–49.

Vetik, Raivo. 2002. "The Cultural and Social Makeup of Estonia." In Pal Kolsto, ed., *National Integration and Violent Conflict in Post-Soviet Societies*. Lanham, MD: Rowman and Littlefield.

Vick, Karl. 2005. "Change May Elude Kyrgyzstan," *The Washington Post* (April 3): A26, A27.

Vlachova, Klara. 2000. "Economic Justice in the Czech Republic, 1991–5." In David S. Mason and James L. Kluegel, eds., *Marketing Democracy*. Lanham, MD: Rowman and Littlefield.

Wax, Emily. 2006. "'We're a Thirsty Land of Empty Promises'," *The Washington Post* (February 20): A11.

Warren, Mark E. 2004. "What Does Corruption Mean in a Democracy?" *American Journal of Political Science*, 48: 328–43.

———. 2006. "Political Corruption as Duplicitous Exclusion," *PS: Political Science and Politics*, 39: 803–7.

Weder, Beatrice. 1999. *Model, Myth, or Miracle? Reassessing the Role of Governments in the East Asia Experience*. Tokyo: United Nations University Press.

Wildavsky, Aaron. 1989. "A World of Difference – The Public Philosophies and Political Behaviors of Rival American Cultures." In Anthony King, ed., *The New American Political System*, 2d version. Washington, DC: AEI Press.

Williams, Robert. 1987. *Political Corruption in Africa*. Aldershot, UK: Gower Publishing.

Wilson, James Q. 1960. *Negro Politics: The Search for Leadership*. New York: Free Press.

Wilson, James Q., and George L. Kelling. 1982. "The Police and Neighborhood Safety: Broken Windows," *Atlantic Monthly* (March): 29–38, at http://www.manhattan-institute.org/pdf/_atlantic_monthly-broken_windows.pdf#search=%22%22Wilson%22%20%22Broken%20Windows%22%22 (page numbers refer to Web edition).

Wittgenstein, Ludwig. 1953. *Philosophical Investigations*. Translated by G. E. M. Anscombe. New York: Macmillan.

Xin, Xiaohohui, and Thomas K. Rudel. 2004. "The Context for Political Corruption: A Cross-National Analysis," *Social Science Quarterly*, 85 (June): 294–308.

Yardley, Jim. 2007. "Chinese Premier Emphasizes Energy, Pollution, and the Poor," *New York Times*, Washington edition (March 5): A8.

You, Jong-sung. 2005a. "Corruption and Inequality as Correlates of Social Trust: Fairness Matters More Importantly Than Similarity." Unpublished manuscript, Harvard University.

———. 2005b. *A Comparative Study of Income Inequality, Corruption, and Social Trust: How Inequality and Corruption Reinforce Each Other and Erode Social Trust*. Unpublished draft of Ph.D. dissertation, John F. Kennedy School of Government, Harvard University, http://ksghome.harvard.edu/~youjong/dissertation%20contents.htm, accessed on November 15, 2005.

———. 2006. "Corruption as Injustice." Presented at the Annual Meeting of the Midwest Political Science Association, Chicago, IL, April.

You, Jong-sung, and Sanjeev Khagram. 2005. "A Comparative Study of Inequality and Corruption," *American Sociological Review*, 70 (February): 136–57.

Zmerli, Sonya, José Ramón Montero, and Ken Newton. 2003. "Trust in People, Confidence in Political Institutions, and Satisfaction with Democracy." Unpublished manuscript, University of Mannheim.

Index

Note: Page numbers in italics indicate figures and tables.